THE ANXIETY OF THE JURIST

The Edinburgh/Glasgow Law and Society Series
Series Editors: Professor Emilios A. Christodoulidis and Dr Sharon Cowan

Titles in the Series

'Integration through Law' Revisited
The Making of the European Polity
Edited by Daniel Augenstein

The Public in Law
Representations of the Political in Legal Discourse
Edited by Claudio Michelon, Gregor Clunie, Christopher McCorkindale and Haris Psarras

The Many Constitutions of Europe
Edited by Kaarlo Tuori and Suvi Sankari

Law as Institutional Normative Order
Edited by Maksymilian Del Mar and Zenon Bańkowski

Law and Agonistic Politics
Edited by Andrew Schaap

Public Law and Politics
The Scope and Limits of Constitutionalism
Edited by Emilios Christodoulidis and Stephen Tierney

Transformations of Policing
Edited by Alistair Henry and David J. Smith

The Universal and the Particular in Legal Reasoning
Edited by Zenon Bańkowski and James MacLean

Law and the Politics of Reconciliation
Edited by Scott Veitch

The Anxiety of the Jurist

Legality, Exchange and Judgement

Edited by

MAKSYMILIAN DEL MAR

Queen Mary University of London, UK

CLAUDIO MICHELON

University of Edinburgh, UK

Routledge
Taylor & Francis Group
LONDON AND NEW YORK

First published 2013 by Ashgate Publishing

Published 2016 by Routledge
2 Park Square, Milton Park, Abingdon, Oxfordshire OX14 4RN
711 Third Avenue, New York, NY 10017, USA

First issued in paperback 2016

Routledge is an imprint of the Taylor & Francis Group, an informa business

British Library Cataloguing in Publication Data
A catalogue record for this book is available from the British Library

The Library of Congress has cataloged the printed edition as follows:
The anxiety of the jurist : legality, exchange and judgement / edited by Maksymilian Del Mar and Claudio Michelon.
pages cm. -- (Edinburgh / Glasgow law and society series)
Includes bibliographical references and index.
ISBN 978-1-4094-4902-7 (hardback)
1. Lawyers. 2. Sociological jurisprudence. 3.
Judgments. I. Bańkowski, Zenon, honouree. II. Michelon, Claudio, editor of compilation.
III. Del Mar, Maksymilian, 1979- editor of compilation.

K117.A69 2013
340'.1--dc23

2013009600

ISBN 13: 978-1-138-27971-1 (pbk)
ISBN 13: 978-1-4094-4902-7 (hbk)

Contents

List of Contributors *vii*

1 Introduction 1
Maksymilian Del Mar and Claudio Michelon

PART 1: THE JURIST AT WORK

2 The Jurist's Conscience: Reflections around Radbruch 13
Roger Cotterrell

3 Citizenship and Social Class Revisited: Liberal Reason, Sociology and Publics 27
John Holmwood

4 Thinking in Images in Legal Theory 43
Maksymilian Del Mar

5 History in the Service of Life: Law's Authority and Dealing with the Past 69
Adam Czarnota

PART 2: LEGALITY

6 But to Live Inside the Law, You Must Be Honest 83
Claudio Michelon

7 Living Under Dead Ideas: Law as the Will of the People 101
Fernando Atria

8 Iconoclasm Revisited: Zenon Bańkowski, Law, Love and *Antigone* 141
Emilios Christodoulidis

9 Fulfilling the Law by Breaking It? Formalism within Legality 155
Francisco Saffie

PART 3: EXCHANGE

10 The Ethical Character of Market Institutions 173
Russell Keat

11 The Law of Contract and the Limits of the Welfare State 195
David Campbell

12 What's Love Got to Do with Development? 225
Oche Onazi

PART 4: JUDGEMENT

13 Analogy and Parable in Legal Reasoning 241
John Bell

14 'Holding the Middle', or 'Dancing on the Edge…'? 257
James MacLean

15 A Logical Journey: The Anxiety of the Leśniewski Quantifiers 277
Burkhard Schafer

PART 5: LOOKING BACK/LOOKING FORWARD

16 The Long Goodbye: A … Life In and Out of the Law 299
Zenon Bańkowski

17 Afterword 321
Neil Walker

Bibliography of the Works of Zenon Bańkowski 325

Index *333*

List of Contributors

Fernando Atria is Professor of Law at the Faculty of Law, University Adalfo Ibanez, Chile.

Zenon Bańkowski is Emeritus Professor of Legal Theory, School of Law, University of Edinburgh.

John Bell is Professor of Law at the School of Law, University of Cambridge.

David Campbell is Professor of Law, Lancaster University Law School.

Emilios Christodoulidis is Professor of Legal Theory at the School of Law, University of Glasgow.

Roger Cotterrell is Anniversary Professor of Legal Theory, Department of Law, Queen Mary University of London.

Adam Czarnota is Associate Professor of Law at the Faculty of Law, University of New South Wales, Australia, and Professor of Law at the Faculty of Law, University of Białystok, Poland.

Maksymilian Del Mar is Senior Lecturer in Law and Philosophy, Department of Law, Queen Mary University of London.

John Holmwood is Professor of Sociology at the Faculty of Social Sciences, University of Nottingham.

Russell Keat is Honorary Fellow and Professor Emeritus at the School of Social and Political Science, University of Edinburgh.

James MacLean is Lecturer at the School of Law, University of Southampton.

Claudio Michelon is Senior Lecturer in Law and Legal Theory at the School of Law, University of Edinburgh.

Oche Onazi is Lecturer in Law, University of Dundee.

Francisco Saffie is a PhD candidate at the School of Law, University of Edinburgh.

Burkhard Schafer is Professor of Computational Legal Theory at the School of Law, University of Edinburgh.

Neil Walker is Regius Professor of Public Law, and the Law of Nature and Nations at the School of Law, University of Edinburgh.

In honour of Zenon Bańkowski

Chapter 1
Introduction

Maksymilian Del Mar and Claudio Michelon

Jurists

To Anglo-Saxon ears, the term 'jurist' sounds antiquated. Certainly, it is recognized as an important historical category. It is acknowledged, for example, that in Ancient Rome, jurists had a vital advisory role, providing magistrates, and thus also the parties involved, with a legal language and form for resolving their disputes (see, for example, Schiavone 2012). It is also known that later, in medieval Europe, jurists – or *juristae* – were said to share 'the same legal culture, based on the same texts', that is, the *Corpus Iuris Civilis*, 'expounded in the universal language of the educated people, Latin', and were said to engage in the same task: namely to interpret local law based on their knowledge of, and with the techniques of, Roman law (Stein 1985: 244). Later still, it is said, in the sixteenth century, and influenced by humanism, jurists came to pay more attention to law's unity and arguably rationality, especially by reference to its coherence, thereby taking on a more recognizably academic function, though also laying the groundwork for the codification movement in the eighteenth and subsequent centuries (see Stein 1985: 248–9 and 252). There is, then, widespread recognition that we have had jurists, and that they have performed vital roles in the life of the law. In contemporary times, however, the term 'jurist' does not seem to identify anyone – we have scholars, legal practitioners (barristers, solicitors, in-house counsel and so on), and judges – but not jurists. Furthermore, if anyone did claim to be a jurist, they might well be accused of unnecessary pomposity – something akin to claiming to be a 'Renaissance man'.

And yet, perhaps precisely because it seems so strange to contemporary ears, reviving the notion of a 'jurist', especially in our days of fragmented scholarship, might be a timely excavation. Were this to occur, we would need an initial definition. Here is one attempt, looking back and identifying commonalities across the ages: jurists are persons learned in law, with the abilities and desire to contribute to – to care for – the good of law; for example, its overall coherence and delivery of justice. Theirs is a relatively independent station, one that is not subservient to a particular ideology and thus somewhat removed from the political spotlight, and yet by no means one that is disengaged politically. While interested in particulars, jurists are not involved directly in dispute resolution – they do not serve adjudicatory or representative functions. Their canvas is broad – the whole of law as a public good, a resource for the common weal – but their paintbrushes are at times minute and the work is detailed, with no nook or cranny being overlooked. Their methods and resources, too, are catholic: they are willing and able to combine conceptual, historical and empirical methods, and are open to insights from every stream of scholarship and popular culture. They have one ear to the needs of the institution and its officials, and one to the public. And they work together, in communities, building on past achievements, but not shy to make improvements. In contemporary language, jurists fall into a position somewhere between lawyers, scholars and public intellectuals: arguably, a forgotten somewhere, and regrettably so.

Historically, such a portrait is no doubt idealized. As an exemplar, it may well be too demanding – but no less refreshing for modern times. For it to be helpful, we shall need to put more flesh on the bones: what other characteristics, for example – indeed, what virtues – might a jurist be said to possess? In particular, does a jurist have a temperament, and if so, how might this temperament be of special service to the good of law?

Anxiety

A few years ago, when the editors of this book were taking part in one of the Centre for Law and Society seminars at the School of Law in Edinburgh, one of the participants produced an objection to a particular claim by showing how the acceptance of that claim would generate social anxiety. Zenon Bańkowski immediately interjected, asking: 'What is wrong with anxiety?' The ensuing discussion on the subject of anxiety's pros and cons ended inconclusively.

It is possible to point to a number of cultural leaps that have been produced (at least in part) by a drive to reduce or eliminate anxiety. A common story about the pre-Socratic beginning of Western philosophy sees it as a reaction to the anxiety of a world of contingency and stability, as an attempt to find something stable lurking underneath ever-changing appearances (Guthrie 1950: 23). As the story goes, this is the drive behind Anaxagoras, Anaximander, Thales and that particular philosophical trope.[1] In that narrative, the anxiety caused by the world's contingency and stability, would be the first motor of philosophy.[2]

1 An alternative ancient philosophical trope reacts to that uncertainty either by surrendering to it or else by celebrating it, while trying to soothe the anxiety caused by instability in other ways, as did Heraclitus, and later, and more radically, the Pyrrhonic sceptics.

2 We recognize, of course, that there are many other narratives relating to the origins of philosophy. For example, and still in the context of Ancient Greek philosophy, Nightingale (2004) locates the origins of the philosophical impulse in a pilgrimage abroad to witness, and ultimately report on, foreign and strange spectacles. In this view, the origins of philosophy are sparked by curiosity about, as well as the ethics of responding to, otherness. One could add that, in this view, such encounters and one's response to them, are training for practical wisdom, or phronesis.

Limiting, or even eradicating, anxiety is often placed at the core of the justification of law. In fact, attempts at providing such justification are frequently predicated on the dangers of uncertainty, unpredictability, instability and, in the extreme, anarchy. Lawyers regularly see the minimization of uncertainty as part of the legitimation of their institutionalized practice. Many grudgingly admit that uncertainty might be unavoidable and even sometimes useful, as when a vague concept might be placed strategically in legal sources to leave some scope for legal discretion (however weakly or strongly discretion might be conceived). But by and large law is seen to be there to respond to this great anxiety about instability and uncertainty.

The views of these lawyers and those of pre-Socratic philosophers are not too far from each other. Moreover, in responding to anxiety negatively, by trying to eliminate it, their attitude mirrors most people's attitudes when oppressed by anxiety. Anxiety implores resolution. So, on first blush, it would seem that one is in good company in surmising that anxiety is something negative – something that needs to be tackled and overcome.

Yet the very fact that the development of both philosophy and law might have been partly caused by anxiety should give us pause for thought. Perhaps anxiety has had a bad press, after all. The fact that anxiety and the drive to eliminate it are co-original might explain the tendency to focus on its negative aspect. Closer inspection, then, might assist us in seeing anxiety in a more positive light: as a driving force for change, and as a powerful energy against stagnation. It is true that sometimes anxiety might be numbing, but the absence of it is always so.

The Anxious Jurist

Zenon Bańkowski, to whose work the contributions in this volume pay homage, has spent most of his career trying to come to terms with the stability of law, with its tendency to normalize what is contingent, to simplify what is complex, and to make invisible what would otherwise be manifest. In performing those roles, law is not necessarily doing a bad thing, as normalization, simplification, and even concealment, might be productive, at least in certain contexts (or so the Bańkowski of *Living Lawfully* (2001) seems to believe). From that, however, one cannot (and should not) conclude that the performance of those roles is either *always* advantageous or *intrinsically* connected to law. From the claim that law performs its many functions by facilitating this normalization, simplification and concealment it does not follow that law would be better realized the more it normalizes, simplifies and conceals. Those coping strategies often connected to law need to allow for the irruption of contingency and complexity. The complete elimination of the anxiety caused by those destabilizing events would also eliminate law's capacity to evolve, learn and adapt. That is not to say, of course, that legal systems would not be able to change. Changes in the formal sense would still be possible through the application of the relevant rules of change, but those modifications would always come from outside law.

Bańkowski's intellectual project is one of denouncing the excesses of law's attempt to eliminate anxiety, and keeping in check the tendency to expand its normalizing role beyond an appropriate limit. But anxiety plays a double role in Bańkowski's work. It is, as we have just seen, *what* he investigates, but it is also present as a driving *energy* of his thinking. Everyone who knows Bańkowski also knows his anxiety about his own work. His attempt to understand normalization has moved from a more radical rejection of law's role in concealing the truth (in *Images of Law* – 1976) to the more nuanced approach that tries to understand law's normalization as in some way productive, which we find in his later work (in *Living Lawfully* and in the 'Beyond Text in Legal Education' project, for example). This is a shift arguably marked by an anxiety that his previous work had not recognized the values of law's normalization, and at the same time it is a shift that constitutes the taming of anxiety (that non-normalizing force within law). Anxiety, then, is both the spirit and substance of Bańkowski's work.

The depth and complexity of the ways in which Bańkowski approaches these problems, as well as the continuities and discontinuities between these Bańkowskis, cannot be done justice in this short introduction, but all are explored in the contributions to this volume. In their own distinctive ways, then, all the contributors included here paint a portrait of Bańkowski as an anxious jurist in that double sense: of the jurist who is anxious, and of the jurist concerned with anxiety as a value.

Contributions to This Volume

The contributions to this volume discuss many related aspects of Bańkowski's engagement with the problems around law's normalization (and thus also the revitalizing force of anxiety). They range from political critique to methodological issues, and from the role of human rights in development to the role of parables and analogy in legal reasoning. The breadth of contributions is in itself a testament to the richness of Bańkowski's scholarship, as well as to the applicability of his core ideas to a wide range of issues.

Earlier versions of the chapters in this volume were presented at the workshop organized by the editors in Edinburgh, in August 2011, under the auspices of the Edinburgh School of Law. The workshop was intended to commemorate Bańkowski's career as he approached retirement, and brought together many (but certainly not all) of the scholars who were deeply influenced by his ideas and by his generous attitude in his teaching. Some are former colleagues, some are former students, and some are both, all sharing the sense of having been affected intellectually and personally by their contact with Bańkowski.

The contributions in this book relate in complex ways to one another, and are grouped together in four parts sandwiched between this introduction and, in the fifth and final part, Bańkowski's valedictory lecture (delivered in Edinburgh in June 2011), Neil Walker's afterword and a bibliography of Bańkowski's work.

Part I: The Jurist at Work

The focus of the first part of the book is on the role and methods of the jurist. The first contribution, Chapter 2 by Roger Cotterrell, engages directly with the role of jurists. That role, he argues, is of safeguarding and promoting law's general well-being. Under a role so conceived, jurists are not wedded to any particular discipline (philosophy, sociology, theology and so on), nor to any particular aspect of legal practice. Instead, they are committed to the worth of law, including its clarity, coherence, fairness, consistency, reputation, accessibility, enforcement and effectiveness. Cotterrell recognizes that any further understanding of the juristic role requires attention to historical context, and he thus examines the work of two jurists: Gustav Radbruch (1878–1949) and Ronald Dworkin (1931–2013). Both Radbruch and Dworkin were committed to understanding law as a value-laden cultural phenomenon (where those values are seen to be subject to ongoing evolution), and to engaging with specific legal issues in both time and place. They differed radically, however, in their styles: where Radbruch was hesitant and uncertain, Dworkin was confident and ambitious. In his mix of general and particular analysis of jurists, Cotterrell's piece provides the ideal opening salvo for a collection focused on the anxiety of the jurist.

As noted above, to live the life of a jurist is to be engaged, to be morally concerned and politically astute. Arguably, this kind of life must be difficult – it must be, precisely, anxious. Some of the difficulties of living that life are identified and discussed in Chapter 3 by John Holmwood, who, drawing on the history of sociology (his own discipline), calls for a renewed engagement with social inequalities. Holmwood observes that whereas sociology was born in passionate dissatisfaction with 'liberal public reason and its embrace of the market and associated theory of the possessive individual', it has more recently lost that sense of anxiety and urgency, acquiescing to the normalization of social inequality. Bringing to bear the work of John Dewey on the idea of the public, and George Herbert Mead's idea of the social self, Holmwood reinvigorates not only the sociological project, but also the transdisciplinary, or even non-disciplinary, responsibility for social justice. In doing so, he articulates a vital dimension of the task, and the ceaseless burden, of an anxious jurist.

Chapter 4, by Maksymilian Del Mar, investigates another dimension of the juristic role: its mode of expression and means of thought. More specifically, the chapter explores the role of images in (legal) philosophical thought. Del Mar argues that philosophers frequently neglect how often they use, and how much they rely on, images – one need think only of Plato's cave, Hegel's owl, Locke's tabula rasa, Wittgenstein's language games and Quine's web of belief, to remind oneself how pervasive are such images. They immediately bring to mind certain ideas and arguments, but also philosophical temperaments. After considering the role of images in philosophical methodology, Del Mar then develops an account of Bańkowski's imaginary – that is, the stock of images that appear in his work – and the roles that those various images play. Bańkowski's imaginary is full of anxiety: for example, it consists of unresponsive ATM machines, hungry tigers, and messages broadcast in a language that nobody understands. Even at its most abstract, Bańkowski's work is replete with such images, all of which play a vital role in his portrayal of the moral fragility of law and the legal life.

The final chapter in this part – Chapter 5 by Adam Czarnota – continues the theme of moral responsibility, posing the question: what approach ought we to take to the past, particularly when that past involves such atrocities as the Holocaust, genocide, war crimes, colonization and the slave trade, to mention just a few? How, in other words, can we have a history that manages a 'delicate balance between remembering and forgetting' – a history in the service of life? The issue is of profound importance for jurists, who need to examine and evaluate the role of law and legal institutions in dealing with the past. Czarnota argues that there is a moral obligation to face the problems of the past with as much openness as possible. As he puts it, 'a difficult past can be suppressed for a while, but then will return and create more problems'. Such open dealing of the past is done for the sake of both the present and the future. Crucially, such open dealing needs to have a public character as well as some authority. Law has these characteristics – it has, in other words, 'peculiar institutional authority' – and this is what renders it the most appropriate forum for dealing with the difficult past. However, the kind of legal mechanism that ought to be adopted is not a retributive one, but rather a constitutional one – that is, a process of 'reshaping ourselves and our societies'.

Part II: Legality

The second part is dedicated to exploring different aspects of Bańkowski's conception of legality. Claudio Michelon's contribution in Chapter 6 attempts to explain the ethical framework that would make it possible for lawyers develop an ability to respect legality by sometimes deciding the reverse of what law seems to require. This ability to 'fulfil the law by breaking it' is at the centre of *Living Lawfully*'s conception of legality as being able to occupy the 'middle area' between the many oppositions it should hold in tension (universal/particular, aspiration/duty and so on). This framework, according to Michelon, is to be found in an understanding of the virtue of *practical wisdom*, whose operation requires the development of skills that resist reduction to methodology or procedure. That solution, in turn, generates new problems, among which is the question as to whether (and, if so, how) those skills can be said to be different in practically wise lawyers and practically wise individuals.

In Chapter 7, Fernando Atria investigates how (and whether) law can be said to speak with one voice, as the voice of the people. Atria's argument tries to steer the way between, on the one hand, a reading of 'the people' that is prey to thick conceptions of the people (cultural, historical and so on) and, on the other, the minimalist liberal project of moving away from any thick conception of the people. Atria argues that the 'will of the people' needs to be construed as a post-institutional concept – that is, a concept that anticipates the arrival of humanity in a world where alienation is overcome. This anticipatory nature is the key to understanding how legal and political concepts operate, and crucial to showing how their justificatory capacity is not predicated on their closeness but, on the contrary, on their radically incomplete signification.

In Chapter 8, Emilios Christodoulidis engages directly with the continuities and discontinuities between Bańkowski's early radical critique of legality (presented canonically in *Images of Law*) and his later attempt to re-conceive legality as allowing for a creative tension between law and love, the universal and the particular, and many of the other oppositions that permeate *Living Lawfully*. Christodoulidis then asks whether the register of law and legality might allow for the negotiation of all those tensions. He does so by reflecting on the character of Antigone and, in particular, on Bańkowski's understanding of her attitude. To do so, he draws on what Alain Badiou identified as Antigone's 'fidelity to the event', a fidelity that sets itself in opposition to the *situation* – that is, to the straitjacket that locks the participants into a particular perspective (with the accompanying sets of reasons and conceptual structures). Within the context of the dynamics between the *situation's normalization* and the always precarious possibility of an *irruption of truth*, Christodoulidis reflects on whether the tension theorized by Bańkowski between all those oppositions can be accommodated within legality.

Bańkowski's reconstruction and defence of legality is also examined in Chapter 9, by Francisco Saffie, who attempts to demonstrate that there is an important gap in *Living Lawfully*'s argument: the absence of a theory of political and legal institutions. Saffie argues that this gap forces Bańkowski's argument to rely excessively on the personal ethical engagement of the individual who is trying to live lawfully and, as a consequence, his argument ultimately favours formalism, despite Bańkowski's declared intention of striking a balance between formalism and contingency in his concept of legality. For Saffie, the way to preserve that balance is to fill the gap by introducing political institutions which would allow to the agent to 'love lawfully'.

Part III: Exchange

One of the tropes of Bańkowski's critique of the abstractions generated by law is the relationship between law and the market. The contributions in Part III attempt to tackle and develop aspects of that critique. This part opens with Russell Keat's attack in Chapter 10 on the common tendency found in theorists at both ends of the political spectrum (such as Friedrich Hayek and Karl Polanyi) to insulate markets from ethical considerations. Keat's strategy is to show how different kinds of market economy may 'favour', though in different terms, work that has ethically relevant features. 'Liberal' and 'Co-ordinated' market economies are both *market* economies, but their institutions are structured in such a way as to foster different sorts of relations between producers, and that difference is, as Keat demonstrates, ethically relevant.

In Chapter 11, David Campbell discusses a very topical left-wing approach to contract theory, namely one that espouses Amartya Sen's capabilities approach (see, for example, Deakin and Supiot 2009) and claims to be able to justify both contractual interventionism and the freedom of contract. Campbell is sceptical about the latter claim and argues that freedom of contract cannot be given appropriate weight (and is thus misrepresented) if grounded on the capabilities approach. The freedom of contract – that crucial cornerstone of contract theory – thus becomes an inconvenient element of contract theory, something that the capabilities approach needs to account for, but is not enthusiastic about.

Oche Onazi's contribution in Chapter 12 uses Bańkowski's critique of law's abstraction to discuss some of the entrenched assumptions about the relationship between law and development. Onazi is particularly worried about the shortcomings of the widespread model that sees in human rights an appropriate framework to convey ethical claims relating to development initiatives. The mediation between the ethical and the development initiatives of human rights conceals at least as much as it reveals, as it fails to convey the ethical demands stemming from many forms of human suffering that resist categorization in terms of human rights. Onazi argues that Bańkowski's work is an appropriate antidote for the complacency that comes from relying heavily on human rights law, as the latter's critique of the limits of law evidences the need for openness to suffering and vulnerability that cannot be codified in the abstract structures of human rights law.

Part IV: Judgement

The fourth part of the book engages with the theory of legal reasoning, and in particular with the anxious responsibility of reaching a judgement in a particular case. The first of the chapters in this part, Chapter 13 by John Bell, examines the role of analogy and parable in legal reasoning. Traditionally, both of these aspects of legal reasoning have posed difficulties for theorists of legal reasoning. On the one hand, theorists have recognized that they play a role in legal reasoning (though with more recognition of analogy than parable); while, on the other hand, they have tended to confine that role to a heuristic, something that may aid reasoning, but is not itself of justificatory import. Bell challenges this view, arguing that 'both parable and analogy are capable of offering justifications for new rules', even if the justifications they offer may not be as complete as that provided by the application of precedent. Analogy identifies a relevant similarity between a past case and an instance case, and – as is demanded by fairness – therefore justifies a similar outcome in the two cases. A parable is 'a story within which a hypothetical case is used to challenge the formulation of a rule and to suggest a direction in which the solution to an instant case may be found within the law'. In that sense, parable too makes it reasonable to move from one particular to another, though without the use of a generalization (whether a rule or a principle). Thanks to Bell, the anxious jurist facing the reality of judgement now has two more justificatory resources at his or her fingertips.

For his part, in Chapter 14, James MacLean eschews the language and imagery of both the universal and the particular. Instead, he locates legal decision-making 'in the middle'. Drawing on process philosophy – as present in the work of Alfred North Whitehead, Henri Bergson and Gilles Deleuze – MacLean paints a picture of legal reasoning as an 'open, processual understanding of becoming'; as something that is 'never already made but always in the making'. The task is a familiar one to readers of Bańkowski's work: how to combat law's tendency to self-closure, to a static and stagnant state of blind normalization. MacLean's argument is that if we understand the true locus of authentic deliberation to be in the dynamic and broken middle, then we shall also help decision-makers to open themselves up to what is unexpected, novel and diverse – which is precisely what they need to do if they are to maintain law's capacity to respond to injustice, suffering and harm. It is by remaining in the anxious middle that we can protect the value of law.

The final chapter in this part, Chapter 15, is by Burkhard Schafer. Like MacLean, Schafer seeks to capture the quality of legal reasoning when it is understood as a precarious process of 'change-in-interaction' – that is, of a constant process of rearrangement as a result of an encounter, for example, with the concepts, histories and modes of problem-solving of another legal system. This understanding of legal reasoning is particularly pertinent to the dynamic multi-jurisdictional environment that characterizes the European Union. With characteristic gusto and creativity, Schafer's chapter articulates the kind of logic that is relevant to legal reasoning in such an environment. Schafer draws on three kinds of logic as examples: paraconsistent logic; formal description of ontology evolution; and the formal logic of Stanisław Leśniewski. Unlike classical logic, these logics are 'capable of not just handling contradiction, but allowing contradictions and tensions to challenge us and thus become creative forces'. Schafer draws out neatly the connection between logic of this kind and anxiety: when understood in the context of an encounter, anxiety becomes a creative force – that is, 'the constant need to redefine oneself in the face of the "irritants" that one incorporates from the outside'. The anxious jurist now has an anxious logic.

Conclusion

We offer these contributions as a portrait of the anxious jurist: his or her role and methods, and his or her engagement with the problems of legality, exchange and judgement. This book does not offer a portrait of Bańkowski, but it is inspired by him, both as a scholar and a person. We hope that, taken collectively, these chapters go some modest way to revealing the virtues of juristic anxiety, including how badly, and how ceaselessly, law needs those virtues.

Bibliography

Deakin, S.F. and Supiot, A. 2009. *Capacitas: Contract Law and the Institutional Preconditions of a Market Economy*. Oxford: Hart.

Guthrie, W.K.C. 1950. *The Greek Philosophers from Thales to Aristotle*. London: Routledge.

Nightingale, A.W. 2004. *Spectacles of Truth in Classical Greek Philosophy: Theoria in Its Cultural Context*. Cambridge: Cambridge University Press.

Schiavone, A. 2012. *The Invention of Law in the West*, Trans. J. Carden and A. Shugaar. Cambridge, MA: Belknap Press.

Stein, P. 1985. 'Judge and Jurist in the Civil Law: A Historical Interpretation'. *Louisiana Law Review* 46: 241–57.

PART 1
The Jurist at Work

Chapter 2
The Jurist's Conscience: Reflections around Radbruch

Roger Cotterrell*

Who Guards the Idea of Law?

The term 'jurist' has not been much analysed in recent literature about law and its practice. Its meaning is vague and varies with different national legal traditions. In common law systems it often suggests a role somewhat higher in intellectual status than does the term 'lawyer'. Jurists tend to be thought of as *scholars* of law, which entails more than merely being legally well informed or skilled. Not every lawyer is necessarily a jurist. Many practising Anglophone lawyers would not call themselves jurists and might even be embarrassed or puzzled by the title. But theorists of law, whose work is often considered to be of much less everyday significance than that of legal practitioners, are sometimes called jurists.

What's in a name? The term 'jurist' can be given many different kinds of significance. This chapter harnesses it for a particular purpose and uses it to identify a particular role in relation to law – one that is hard to define with precision but is nevertheless important. To see this role as the specifically 'juristic' one – the special responsibility of the jurist – is a starting point for clarifying it and giving it a prominence it lacks at present. The role is that of maintaining *the idea of law* as a special kind of practice and enabling that idea to flourish. One might say that the jurist's role, on this understanding, is to safeguard and promote law's general *well-being*. This cannot be a simple matter, because conceptions of this well-being will vary greatly. This chapter attempts to unpack it as far as possible, while recognizing that different jurists will understand it in different ways. This also entails distinguishing this role from other roles touching on law with which it could be confused.

* This essay was developed from a paper presented at the Edinburgh conference held to mark Zenon Bańkowski's retirement. I am grateful to all who contributed to discussion on that occasion. Zenon's friends, colleagues and students, who have long admired the ethical commitment of his writing about law, will readily understand a main source of inspiration for the essay's title. His work certainly is much concerned with the conscience of jurists faced with the need to define their professional role. This essay attempts to develop a conceptual framework for such a role. I am grateful to Stanley L. Paulson for many insightful comments on a version of this text, and to Sean Coyle, Maks Del Mar, Nicky Priaulx and Jirí Pribán for further discussion.

One such role – strange as it might seem to distinguish it immediately – is that of the legal philosopher. Writers on law do not necessarily treat 'jurisprudence', typically seen in the common-law world as what jurists profess, as being identical with legal philosophy. Julius Stone (1968: 8) wrote: 'Most of the problems of jurisprudence ... are in substance different from those of philosophy ... any writer who pretends to bring ... [jurisprudence's] full range within any particular philosophical tradition is deceiving at least himself.' The jurist, in this view, is not primarily a professional philosopher, or even a philosopher of law; and not a sociologist of law either. The idea at the base of Stone's claim is that the jurist's responsibility is to *law* as such, as a broad, diverse field of practice and experience; not to any intellectual discipline (philosophy, sociology, theology and so on) for which law may be one object of study among others.

The jurist's work is certainly allied with that of other legal professionals such as practising lawyers and judges. But, to use Stone's (ibid.: 16) term, it is a form of lawyers' 'extraversion', a turning out beyond everyday practice to a wider, more broadly informed view of the nature of law. So the jurist's ultimate responsibility might be considered to be to law generally, and not to any particular aspect of its practice. Judges, for example, may be, but are not necessarily, jurists. The jurist's scholarship is not bounded by the demands of deciding particular cases or interpreting the application of law to specific disputes. It is not bound to confine itself within (though to be realistic it must take into account) the bounds of precedent, parliamentary sovereignty or existing legal or constitutional structures. Nor is it bounded by the requirements of legally advising or representing specific clients (individuals, groups, organizations, governments, administrative agencies) as do practising lawyers.

The jurist's focus could be said to be on law as a practical idea in general, or as embodied in the legal system (or type of legal system) that the jurist serves. The focus is on the worth of law, its *meaningfulness* as a social institution. To this extent, a juristic perspective goes beyond the everyday practice of law in courts or lawyers' offices, but is one of *committed*, not disinterested, analysis or observation of law; it is concerned with *all aspects* of law's well-being: for example, its clarity, coherence, fairness, consistency, reputation, accessibility, enforcement and effectiveness. That suggests a theoretical sensibility, but not necessarily adherence to any wide-ranging theoretical system. Rather, if the concern is with law in general, the jurist will need some general framework of thought, a way of envisaging or modelling law as a phenomenon, at least provisionally in relation to the time and place – that is, in the particular political and historical context in which he or she works.

Modern legislators and administrators may seek to use legislation to codify, simplify, systematize, consolidate or clarify law; or to reform procedures to make the administration of justice through law work better. But often they make or use law purely as a tool of government and governance, and policy is the exclusive focus of attention. Thus legislative or administrative responsibility is not necessarily focused on the integrity of law as a social institution. Again, practising lawyers have a responsibility to the legal system in which they work, but their role is also to serve the interests of their clients in relation to law. How the balance is struck – between allegiance on the one hand, to the general well-being of law, and on the other, to client interests – can be studied empirically but may be hard to theorize outside the context of particular cases or types of practice.

Equally, legal journalists may be committed to law reform and exposing legal scandals, but their job is also to get a good story and satisfy the expectations of those who employ or commission them to write. Again, not all legal scholars are jurists according to the conception followed here: academic lawyers, legal theorists and social scientists may or may not have a commitment to law, to its worth and well-being. Their primary commitment may be to scholarship *rather than* to law, and a distinction can be drawn between those whose scholarship is intended to improve or sustain law and those whose intellectual aim is to unmask or debunk it,[1] or just to find out about it.

Thus the idea of law seen in terms of a concern for and commitment to its general well-being is hard to view as an exclusive focus for any specific category of professionals, unless this idea can be set at the centre of the jurist's work. If this is done, 'jurist' becomes not merely an honorific title. It can be the label to attach to a specific role that entails *serving law*, in all its complexity, contradictions and ambiguities, in a comprehensive and exclusive way. The jurist's role, in this view, sits between broad philosophical or social scientific visions of law, on the one hand, and the specificities of legal practice and reform on the other – distinct from yet linked to both, in a shifting, variable relationship. The remainder of this chapter explores what this postulated juristic commitment to law might entail.

Juristic Role: Radbruch and Dworkin

It is surely unrealistic to think of juristic responsibility as if it were the same in, say, a police state, a theocracy or a liberal democracy, an unstable polity or a stable one, or a society whose history has been one of violence and disorder compared with one that has long benefited from relative internal peace. The jurist's responsibility exists in specific historical contexts, usually in relation to a particular legal system or type of legal system, and with a concern for the kinds of legal practice that exist or are possible in that system or type. And it will be a multifaceted responsibility, reflecting law's multifaceted character. But how to clarify that responsibility when law itself can be seen from so many points of view, with so many tasks assigned to it, and such diverse expectations attached to it? And how to do so when those tasks and expectations vary with historical and political context?

1 A classic case is that of the Soviet legal theorist Evgeny Pashukanis (1978), a learned and profound scholar of law, who, following Marx's teaching, saw his role as being to pave the way for law's demise. In the Anglo-American world, some critical legal studies writing can similarly be seen as legal scholarship beyond the jurist's role as this chapter presents it.

The work of the German legal scholar, Gustav Radbruch, in the first half of the twentieth century, informed by the political turmoil of the Weimar period and the Nazi experience, and still largely neglected in the Anglophone world, offers useful pointers in trying to answer such questions. Radbruch does not demarcate the jurist's special role explicitly in the way this chapter aims to do, but his work seems none the less to exemplify that role. It also suggests how to solve a dilemma in conceptualizing it: on the one hand, to specify what is distinctive about the role; and on the other, to allow for great variability in the way it can be played. In what follows, some of his key ideas about law and its well-being are used as a starting point for developing this chapter's themes.

Radbruch is significant here for three reasons. First, he emphasizes consistently the role of jurists as being one of moral responsibility for the well-being of law. Second, he presents the jurist's view of the idea of law as necessarily highly malleable or fluid in important respects, adapted to context and varying as that context changes. Third, he doubts the utility for the jurist of any seemingly timeless philosophical 'system' whose abstractions exist independently of empirical inquiries about social variation. The jurist, it might be said, has to be not a 'hedgehog' but a 'fox': not committed single-mindedly to one value orientation, such as the pragmatic pursuit of chosen social 'purposes' of law, or the elaboration of a philosophy of 'justice', or the preservation of established 'order' at all costs. Instead, the jurist's commitment is to a permanent but shifting relationship between ideas of justice, order and purpose implicated in law.

Erik Wolf, discussing the 'practical bent' of Radbruch's jurisprudence, sees him as sympathetic to sociology – as understood in the German context in which he worked in the first half of the twentieth century (Wolf 1958: 11). For Radbruch, jurists cannot be uncommitted sociological observers of law; but they should recognize that, for the most part, justice and other legal values do not have timeless content but must find their meaning in specific socio-historical contexts. More precisely, the space for realistic debate around those values would be set by this context, by what Radbruch calls 'the nature of the objective situation' (*Natur der Sache*) (Radbruch 1950: 53–5, 172–4; Wolf 1958: 11).

Important parallels can be noted between Radbruch's juristic outlook and that of Ronald Dworkin. For example, first, both insist that law is a *value-laden cultural phenomenon.* It expresses fundamental values, rooted in the political community. It is the jurist's responsibility to bring these to light and to work out their interrelation in the ongoing business of plotting law's practical development over time, and keeping legal/judicial practice in step with what Dworkin (1986) thinks of as law's 'integrity' or what Radbruch (1950: 73) calls the 'idea of law' – law as doctrine expressing a distinctive combination of values.

Second, Radbruch sought a jurisprudence to engage with specific *legal issues in time and place.* He tried to do this by making the relationships between what he saw as the fundamental values of law variable in his thinking, and asking how these relationships might alter with circumstances and how the content of the values themselves could change in different conditions. Dworkin also tried explicitly to make his jurisprudence of principle a practical tool of commentary on changing law. He applied it as a public intellectual, criticizing, for example, decisions of the United States Supreme Court that he saw as 'unprincipled' and thus undermining the integrity of American law.[2]

Third, for both writers, the juristic role seems to assume an *ongoing evolution of law's values*. For Dworkin, this evolution occurs in the continual re-interpretation of law: the effort (especially by judges) to see the legal system in terms of the 'soundest' theory they can develop, which will allow the 'best' reading of legal doctrine and the most 'attractive' integration of legal standards in their application to specific cases or issues. Law as an integrated system of principle is built 'from the inside', so to speak, in the ongoing interpretation and application of its precepts. Potentially, as the common lawyers once insisted, law 'works itself pure'.[3] That is, 'integrity' characterizes the relation between the value elements expressed in legal doctrine at any given time.

For Radbruch, too, what seems important is a shifting reconciliation of legal values in time and place. Nevertheless, ultimately this is very different from Dworkin's idea of a systematic integration of values. Often the relationship between legal values as Radbruch portrays them is one of irreconcilable *tension*, sometimes *conflict*; the issue is often how to *compromise* them against each other; the terms of the compromise changing over time. And it seems that sociology as well as philosophy can serve the jurist in understanding how this compromise may be achieved and under what conditions. For Radbruch, there is a need in any legal system to balance values of order, justice and purpose in law, and this balance may well vary in different contexts. This suggests a comparative dimension of the concept of law: between different legal systems, and between historical phases of law's existence (Wilhelmine, Weimar, Nazi, and post-war Germany, in Radbruch's case).

Juristic Style: Radbruch and His Critics

Law's 'well-being' is, therefore, a variable notion, and not definable in any timeless fashion.[4] There is the sharpest possible contrast between Radbruch's hesitant, uncertain, often provisional outlook (sometimes seen by critics as inconstancy) and Dworkin's confident ultimate intellectual commitment to a fully integrated, comprehensive, philosophical system of values, elaborated with increasing ambition and scope in his work (Dworkin 2011b). Dworkin recently stated that the role of moral and political philosophers is 'to try to construct self-conscious articulate systems of value and principle out of widely shared but disparate moral

2 Recently, for example, among many publications, Dworkin 2008; Dworkin 2011a.

3 See *Omychund* v *Barker* (1744) 1 Atk 21, at 33; Dworkin, 1986: 400.

4 And perhaps its analytical structure as 'law' can be left as a primarily technical matter for legal scholars of all kinds (including jurists) to debate.

inclinations, reactions, ambitions and traditions' (ibid.: 109). Thus, when law is seen, as he finally saw it, as 'a subdivision of political morality' it takes its place as one region in 'a large and complex philosophical theory' that 'proposes a way to live' (ibid.: 1, 405), a total philosophical system focused on a rational elaboration and integration of ultimate values.

This is very far removed from Radbruch's juristic outlook. Accepting contradictions and compromise reflecting actual legal life, rather than building a system of thought to explain 'a way to live', Radbruch's jurist is wracked by self-questioning: 'we are to believe in the profession of our life and yet ... in some deepest layer of our being, again and again to doubt it' (Radbruch 1950: 139). Indeed, the relativistic (or existential) aspect of his outlook (ibid.: 55–9; Friedmann 1960: 198–9) may be what is most important about his thought, distinguishing its exploratory, interrogatory style and accounting for a remarkable polarization in evaluations of his work. This is important because it may illustrate differences between juristic and some legal philosophical outlooks.

Some scholars, especially those of continental European origin writing in (or translated into) English, highlight the respect in which Radbruch was held as a jurist (Friedmann 1960: 192, 209). One praises the 'wisdom which permeates the whole of his work ... a thoroughness of erudition, a sincerity of tolerance ... a total absence of the slightest intellectual arrogance' (Chroust 1944: 23). Wolf (1958: 8–9) lauds 'his attitude of open-mindedness ... his constant readiness to listen to others and to consider other viewpoints as valid', his wish to keep apart 'from that type of legal philosophy which had hardened into a "professional discipline"'; 'his disdain for polemical discussions'; and his 'rejection of the demand for a closed legal philosophical system'.

These are statements about *a way of carrying out jurisprudence*, not about the substance of a theory. They indicate ways of thinking that might be devalued, even treated as indicators of intellectual weakness, from a certain philosophical standpoint. Thus Radbruch's willingness to rethink his pre-war views after 1945 in the light of the Nazi experience has, for H.L.A. Hart, 'the special poignancy of a recantation' (the assumption being that he had disowned his earlier legal theory) but his 'passionate demand' (rather than intellectual argument?) addressed to the German conscience was linked, so Hart claims, with 'an extraordinary naivety'. Radbruch, in fact, had 'only half digested the spiritual message of liberalism' (Hart 1983: 72, 74, 75).

Yet his juristic experience had, in important respects, been *far wider* than that of many of his critics. He had served honourably in government and been active as a liberal scholar and social democrat during the Weimar Republic. After expulsion from his teaching position by the Nazis, he had lived through the Hitler era in Germany to welcome the post-World War II rebuilding of his country and to assist at its foundation. Perhaps a more nuanced judgement on his thought is possible,[5]

5 Cf. A.P. d'Entrèves writing to Lon Fuller: 'I share your feelings about Hart's "strokes of the oar." I confess that in both hearing and reading his strictures on Radbruch

one that envisages the jurist 'in the thick of events', trying to hold to the idea of law while being acutely aware of the contexts of its application, rather than the philosopher elaborating concepts that might claim a validity independent of changing conditions. But if jurists are not philosophical system-builders or seekers after abstract truth it is necessary to ask what kind of practical framework of thought is appropriate to their task.

The jurist needs a flexible way of thinking about law, but one that does not lose sight of viable criteria of law's worth and measures of its well-being, relative to time and place: that is, criteria and measures that can embrace, in some way, everything that is valued in law by those who live under it and appeal to it. Radbruch provides, up to a point, a model for such a way of thinking. I take him as presupposing that, because the jurist's focus is on 'law', no single 'external' system of thought (economic/utilitarian, theological, sociological, moral or political) can be allowed to dominate it. The jurist is left to work out an independent destiny for the idea of law and the realization of that idea in particular contexts.

Juristic Focus: Law's Variable Geometry

The idea of law can be thought of juristically as a 'triangle' of three central values – a triangle that can be stretched into different shapes depending on context; we might say that law as a structure of values has a *variable geometry*. Thus, for Radbruch, the idea of law is a balance of the values of (i) *justice*, (ii) *order* (or security or certainty), and (iii) (suitability for) *purpose* (*Zweckmäßigkeit*), or expediency or utility. Justice is fundamental, the 'specific idea' of law (Radbruch 1950: 75, 90) as equal treatment of equals, and different treatment of different cases. But this cannot be sufficient: the 'purpose' of law (purpose being a value that is given content in socio-historical time and place) determines who and what are to be considered equal and different; how justice is to be measured and realized (ibid.: 90–91). Order, the third value of law, is, in one sense, even more fundamental. Without order, ideas of justice and purpose become meaningless. Even where the judge cannot do justice through law there is an obligation to serve the value of order, which demands certainty in legal doctrine and predictability in legal decisions. Doing justice and pursuing aims through law presuppose law's stability. To that extent, providing order is the first task of law (ibid.: 108).

The variable geometry of law may well explain Radbruch's so-called 'recantation' – his apparent change of outlook on the conditions of law's well-being after the experience of Nazism. It is probable that he thought, in Weimar times, that *order* was ultimately the non-negotiable value. Without it – in a Hobbesian

... I could not help feeling sorry for the incurable smugness of our English friends' (quoted in Lacey 2010: 22). On Radbruch's political views and activities, especially in the Weimar period, see the excellent discussion in Herrera 2003: 147–71.

state of disorder – there could be no society and no law. Weimar's irresponsible anti-constitutional politics, its prejudiced judiciaries failing to apply the letter of the law consistently and its gangs of street thugs dispensing everyday non-legal 'justice' and pursuing their political 'purpose', might well have suggested that a realistic jurist *in such a context* must privilege order, even though (Radbruch insists) the central value of the idea of law is always justice. But his emphasis on the need for consistent, predictable application of legal doctrine pre-dates the Weimar period (Paulson 2006: 34–6).

He is very explicit: 'It is more important that the strife of legal views be ended than that it be determined justly and expediently' (Radbruch 1950: 108). What law in this image (reflecting a dread of social collapse) stands against, as law's opposite (its total denial), is *chaos* and *anarchy*. Yet there is no 'absolute precedence' of 'legal certainty ... fulfilled by any positive law, over the demands of justice and expediency, which it may ... have left unfulfilled' (ibid.: 118).

Later, a different opposite of law (perhaps wholly unforeseen as a modern European phenomenon) seemed to be revealed to Radbruch by Nazism: law's opposite or total denial now becomes *barbarism* resulting from *total unconcern for fair treatment*; the complete abolition of justice as a value. The emphasis in Radbruch's outlook certainly shifts – the geometry of the triangle has changed: its centre of gravity has moved from the 'order' point towards the 'justice' point – but surely neither his method nor his frame of reference changes. The value-triangle still represents the idea of law, its values held in tension; but the balance between them alters with circumstances and the wise jurist in extreme crisis times must, it seems, focus especially on what might destroy the whole triangle. The complete disappearance of one point of the triangle would mean that the idea of law could no longer be sustained.

Those who defend Radbruch against charges of inconstancy (especially the charge that he discarded a pre-war legal positivist position in favour of a natural law position after 1945) tend to stress a continuity in his thought that is capable of embracing revision and reinterpretation in the light of experience (Wolf 1958; Friedmann 1960; Paulson 1994, 1995, 2006). He argued after 1945 that where 'there is not even an attempt at justice' in positive law, so that 'equality, the core of justice, is deliberately betrayed', a statute may lack 'completely the very nature of law' (Radbruch 2006: 7). His argument about Nazi law can be treated as identifying an end-state: one in which the extremely variable *conditions of justice* (a value always fundamental to law as an idea) have been shown, in particular historical circumstances, to have reached their limit of existence. So, what seems to be, from one viewpoint, philosophical inconstancy appears, from another, as the jurist's constant effort to preserve a flexible but ultimately non-negotiable idea of law in changing political conditions.

An approach such as this cannot specify what is law's well-being. It merely sets parameters and guidelines – a framework of thought within which jurists are to work. But the guidance is firm (order and justice are the values that jurists must always serve) even if it is strictly limited. Only at the extremes (the collapse of order, or the disappearance of all semblance of justice)[6] does it seem to call on the jurist's conscience to protest the destruction of the idea of law. In 'normal' times everything, it seems, is left to personal judgement on the optimal balance of order and justice in law.

The Idea of Law in Its Cultural Setting

Is it not possible to say anything in general terms about what might be 'good' or 'wise' juristic judgement in such matters? Radbruch contributes here in his discussion of the third point in the triangle of law's values – law's orientation to 'purpose' (*Zweckmäßigkeit*). He sees order (as legal certainty) and justice (as equal treatment of equal cases) as being permanent, constant (if formal) legal values (Radbruch 1950: 108–9), so they are surely within the jurist's province to analyse and apply. But law's 'purpose' is given *culturally*, by the prevailing ideas of the times; that is, law is guided in different socio-historical contexts by different conceptions of 'the good'. These give rise to different views of the individual's relation to state and society, or different allegiances or orientations of life – for example, to individual freedom, to the good of state and nation, or to the building of human culture more widely (ibid.: 90–95).

Thus, purpose refers to *objectives set for the idea of law by socio-historical conditions*; and purpose sets criteria for justice as a value served by law. It affects the social meaning of this value. So, it would appear that the jurist's concerns cannot be limited to purely technical reconciliations of order and justice (as in the idea of the rule of law combining legal certainty and equality before law). The jurist has to look beyond law's technical efficiency to its existence as an idea embodying cultural expectations. Order and justice are, at one level, fundamental (technical) values that must always animate law's practices and procedures. At another they are expressions of law's significance relative to time and place. A continuum seems to link the technical and social aspects of order and justice. What Radbruch does not make clear, however, is how far jurists can be expected to contribute to the social realization of these values; in other words, how far they may venture into the terrain of social theory, or moral and political philosophy.

Radbruch's thought can, it seems, take us no further, but it is not necessary to stop with him. In dealing with order and justice as technical legal matters the jurist is clearly on firm ground. As often portrayed in positivist legal thought, these are purely matters of efficiency in the working of a system of rules, and the rule of law as the reconciliation of these technical values can appear not necessarily as a social (or moral) good but as merely the condition of a working rule system (Raz 2009: 210–29). At another level, however, the realization of order and justice as *social* values is demanded from law (Cotterrell 1995: 154–5, 316–17).

6 Or, we might speculate, the *total* dominance in law of policy-driven pragmatism, expediency or instrumentalism – but Radbruch does not appear to address this issue.

Individuals no doubt interpret these values differently in different socio-historical contexts. One might ask, for example, how much order is possible, and what will order be taken to mean – in a peaceful or stable state, in a chaotic or corrupt state, in a tyrannous state, or in conditions of war? What will justice as equality or fairness relate to – in a society of classes, castes or ranks, a slave society, or a liberal democracy? How far will people privilege order over justice (as they understand these values) or the reverse; with how much of one or the other will they be satisfied? The relative importance of these values may vary greatly with time and place.

What this points to is the need to think juristically in non-dogmatic (relativistic) ways (see Radbruch 1950: 55–9) – emphasizing *flexible frameworks* of thought about law's well-being. Radbruch's 'idea of law' is one such framework – instructive in implying a variable geometry of legal values. Others, in more recent times, are John Finnis's (1980: 276–81) idea of a 'focal meaning' of law, and Nigel Simmonds' (2007: 52) idea of 'archetypes' of the legal 'to which actual instances of law merely approximate to various degrees'. Above all, one might refer to Lon Fuller. For Fuller, it is only at the direst extreme that law's existence becomes an all-or-nothing matter (when law does or does not conform to *minimum* demands of a 'morality of duty'). Far more practically important (because applicable to all legal systems) is his claim that social order can be *more or less* 'legal', that legality is a matter of degree, and the task of the jurist is to *build* legality as a moral value structure (Fuller 1969: 122–3).

Just as Radbruch was sometimes criticized for vagueness or indeterminacy, so Fuller is criticized for not being able to specify *exactly* what legal excellence means, or how conflicting attributes of legality are to be reconciled, or when law begins or ceases to exist. These are demands for a *system of thought* to explain law comprehensively as a phenomenon. But the addressees of these demands here are writers (such as Fuller or Radbruch) who are not interested primarily in such systems and think of their legal theory as aiding a *juristic craft*, not as offering timeless or conclusive answers but merely a framework for practical, time-bound ones.[7] Thus, *juristic craft and philosophical system seem to be almost antithetical ideas*. Karl Llewellyn, far from being a system-builder, insisted that 'and-not' (rigid conceptualization) is 'bad jurisprudence' and eventually put the idea of juristic craft at the heart of his socio-legal theory (Llewellyn and Hoebel 1941: 297–309; Llewellyn 1962: 83; Twining 1973: 199–200, 505–12, 516). Juristic wisdom is merely this craft practised at the highest possible level.

Here, then, is surely the most constructive way to think of 'purpose' in law from a juristic perspective: not in terms of a theory of law's purpose, as though law had a single purpose to be discovered, or as if a systematic elaboration of such a purpose were possible. A juristic view of purpose in law is surely no more than constant empirical concern in the jurist's work for its specific socio-historical context, in

7 For Fuller's 'affirmations of the middle-range' in theory and his unequivocal juristic rejection of 'complete' philosophical systems, see Winston 2001: 61–3, 305–13.

so far as that context informs the content of citizens' aspirations and expectations for order and justice. Attention to purpose involves not a philosophical effort to expound social values rigorously but a *sociological* attempt to identify currents of ideology present in the jurist's socio-historical environment, so that the idea of law can be advanced in *that* context, in relation to *those* aspirations and expectations. It demands sensitivity to the ways that values of order and justice are understood and experienced in a given society at a particular time.

Why take into account juristically these popular aspirations and expectations? The answer is that jurists, if they are to promote law's worth and well-being, will work to show its social significance. So they will be led to shape and present law as far as possible as a unifying force (Cotterrell 2003: 8–11) socially and politically in their society – a social institution that potentially benefits all. The idea of law must, in this view, confront social diversity and conflict without attempting to reason it away or merely replicate it. Law itself must be made to appear *juristically* as a unity[8] in which social diversity is accepted, ordered, stabilized and balanced. Law as an idea 'here and now' must relate not just to a myriad of individual interests; it must appear as a convincing framework for social life, serving *the whole* of society. If it cannot be so portrayed, cynicism about it spreads; and becomes a threat to the well-being which the jurist seeks for it (Tamanaha 2006).

Conclusion

Someone has to speak for the idea of law as a flexible, but distinctive and unifying, value structure – as something like the variable geometric structure that Radbruch's juristic thought evokes. If *no one* speaks forcefully and influentially for law in this sense, but people generally seek only to make use of it for their political or personal ends, history shows a range of risks, ultimately including that of constitutional collapse, as in the Weimar Republic. Even in the contemporary USA some related dangers have been noted. Dworkin has written of the American present as 'a period of special political danger', in which US citizens 'are no longer partners in self-government; our politics are rather a form of war' (Dworkin 2006: 1). Even at the highest judicial levels, a view of law that seems to deny any possibility of a consensus around it has sometimes been expressed.[9] The idea of

8 That is, a single, coherent, practical regulatory framework appropriate to the time and place. Ongoing juristic efforts to portray law's regulatory unity are identical with efforts to portray its authority as being conclusively settled. This search for regulatory unity is to be distinguished clearly from any philosophical deduction of a 'unity of value' (Dworkin, 2011b: 1) in which different ultimate values are finally harmonized.

9 See Toobin (2007: 237), quoting US Supreme Court Chief Justice William Rehnquist in private conversation with an unnamed colleague in 2004: 'Don't worry about the analysis and the principles in the case. Just make sure the result is a good one this time

law as something distinct from government or from the pursuit of specific interests – something of general juristic importance – needs its advocates, it seems.

One solution (Dworkin's) is to seek deep, unifying principles which reasonable people might be persuaded to acknowledge despite differences in ideologies and world views, and to reason politico-legal ideas from them.[10] But why should it be assumed that there are deep principles on which people could be persuaded to agree? What if there are only different outlooks and ideologies? What if 'irrationality' (in the sense Max Weber meant, in characterizing some habitual and emotional action) or *different* rationalities confront philosophical reason (Weber 1978: 25; Brubaker 1984: 50–51)?

The jurist's task is surely not to try to rationalize conflict away, but to identify where it lies and how law can respond to it; the question here is how to preserve law as a universal good in the face of moral and political disagreement, or simply in the face of popular lack of interest in questions about ultimate values. In short, the juristic issue is how the idea of law can survive in the socio-historic conditions it faces. So the jurist's concerns are sociological as much as philosophical; but neither philosophy nor sociology can *remove* these concerns; they remain the responsibility of the jurist.

To harness the term 'jurist' and give it a special meaning, as this chapter has done, is a device for identifying and assigning this responsibility. The idea of the juristic role as discussed here refers to an ideal type in Weber's sense: that is, it provides a kind of model that might approximate, to some degree and in some way, the role that many (but certainly not all) who are called jurists actually play. What is presented here is a thought experiment. It asks: what would follow if there was such an accepted specialized role of guardianship of the idea of law and its well-being? What issues would then present themselves? How then would juristic work be judged? Some who could be called jurists might deny any concern for law as a value structure, seeing their focus as being only on its intellectual structure, practical effectiveness, logical soundness, or policy relevance. But their concern with law's well-being might still be expressed in terms of values of order and justice, and sensitivity to context, as this chapter has done.

Nevertheless, the elaboration here of an approach to these legal values is intended to suggest that the role of the jurist as guardian of the idea of law should be more than a professional guardianship of law's intellectual techniques. It should also embrace law's responsibilities for promoting social order and social justice. Thus the juristic role proposed here is not only a Weberian pure type, a conceptual model to interpret aspects of reality. It is also an ideal in the more usual normative sense. The claim is that this role is important; an ideal that ought to be pursued.

---

around – because those principles you announce will be ignored in the next case.' See, more generally, West 2005.

10 Dworkin (2006: 9) seems to admit that this is not necessarily a juristic response to the issues, noting that in this context, 'my main interest is in political principle, not law'.

When juristic responsibility becomes confused with the professional priorities and paradigms that dominate other kinds of engagement with law, its special focus is lost. That does not mean that the role of jurist must be monopolized in practice by any particular professional group. Philosophers, sociologists, judges, legislators, academic lawyers and client-focused practitioners of law sometimes slip, more or less readily, in and out of the juristic role. Jurists are certainly not debarred from filling other roles in relation to law; and others don the cap of the jurist in parts of their work. Even if the role is seen as distinct, the professional allegiances of those who fill it need not be.

But it is surely necessary to identify a distinctive professional commitment to guardianship of the idea of law, perhaps especially when the moral aspects of many public roles are widely seen as requiring clear definition. The juristic role exists alongside many other kinds of intellectual and practical engagement with law. Often it has been obscured by those other kinds. Yet if the idea of law is valued in itself, the jurist's role in the sense discussed here could be the most fundamental engagement of all.

Bibliography

Brubaker, R. 1984. *The Limits of Rationality: An Essay on the Social and Moral Thought of Max Weber.* London: Allen & Unwin.

Chroust, A.-H. 1944. 'The Philosophy of Law of Gustav Radbruch'. *Philosophical Review*, 53: 23–45.

Cotterrell, R. 1995. *Law's Community: Legal Theory in Sociological Perspective.* Oxford: Clarendon Press.

Cotterrell, R. 2003. *The Politics of Jurisprudence: A Critical Introduction to Legal Philosophy*, 2nd edn. Oxford: Oxford University Press.

Dworkin, R. 1986. *Law's Empire*. Oxford: Hart. Reprinted 1998.

Dworkin, R. 2006. *Is Democracy Possible Here? Principles for a New Political Debate*. Princeton, NJ: Princeton University Press.

Dworkin, R. 2008. *The Supreme Court Phalanx: The Court's New Right-Wing Bloc*. New York: New York Review of Books.

Dworkin, R. 2011a. 'The Court's Embarrassingly Bad Decisions'. *New York Review of Books*, 26 May, 40–41.

Dworkin, R. 2011b. *Justice for Hedgehogs*. Cambridge, MA: Harvard University Press.

Finnis, J. 1980. *Natural Law and Natural Rights*. Oxford: Clarendon Press.

Friedmann, W. 1960. 'Gustav Radbruch'. *Vanderbilt Law Review*, 14: 191–209.

Fuller, L.L. 1969. *The Morality of Law*, revised edn. New Haven, CT: Yale University Press.

Hart, H.L.A. 1983. *Essays in Jurisprudence and Philosophy*. Oxford: Clarendon Press.

Herrera, C.M. 2003. *Droit et gauche: Pour une identification.* Saint-Nicolas, Québec: Les Presses de l'Université Laval.

Lacey, N. 2010. 'Out of the Witches' Cauldron: Reinterpreting the Context and Reassessing the Significance of the Hart–Fuller Debate'. In P. Cane (ed.), *The Hart–Fuller Debate in the Twenty-First Century*. Oxford: Oxford University Press, 1–42.

Llewellyn, K.N. 1962. *Jurisprudence: Realism in Theory and Practice.* New Brunswick, NJ: Transaction Publishers. Reprinted 2008.

Llewellyn, K.N. and Hoebel, E.A. 1941. *The Cheyenne Way: Conflict and Case Law in Primitive Jurisprudence.* Norman, OK: University of Oklahoma Press.

Pashukanis, E.B. 1978. *Law and Marxism: A General Theory*, trans. B. Einhorn. London: Ink Links.

Paulson, S.L. 1994. 'Lon L. Fuller, Gustav Radbruch, and the 'Positivist' Thesis'. *Law and Philosophy*, 13, 313–59.

Paulson, S.L. 1995. 'Radbruch on Unjust Laws: Competing Earlier and Later Views?' *Oxford Journal of Legal Studies*, 15, 489–500.

Paulson, S.L. 2006. 'On the Background and Significance of Gustav Radbruch's Post-War Papers'. *Oxford Journal of Legal Studies*, 26, 17–40.

Radbruch, G. 1950. 'Legal Philosophy'. In *The Legal Philosophies of Lask, Radbruch and Dabin*, trans. K. Wilk. Cambridge, MA: Harvard University Press, 43–224.

Radbruch, G. 2006 [1946]. 'Statutory Lawlessness and Supra-Statutory Law', trans. B.L. Paulson and S.L. Paulson. *Oxford Journal of Legal Studies*, 26: 1–11.

Raz, J. 2009. *The Authority of Law: Essays on Law and Morality.* 2nd edn. Oxford: Oxford University Press.

Simmonds, N.E. 2007. *Law as a Moral Idea.* Oxford: Oxford University Press.

Stone, J. 1968. *Legal System and Lawyers' Reasonings.* Sydney: Maitland Publications.

Tamanaha, B.Z. 2006. *Law as a Means to an End: Threat to the Rule of Law.* Cambridge: Cambridge University Press.

Toobin. J. 2007. *The Nine: Inside the Secret World of the Supreme Court.* New York: Doubleday.

Twining, W. 1973. *Karl Llewellyn and the Realist Movement.* London: Weidenfeld & Nicolson.

Weber, M. 1978. *Economy and Society: An Outline of Interpretive Sociology*, trans. E. Fischoff *et al.* Berkeley, CA: University of California Press.

West, R.L. 2005. 'The Lawless Adjudicator'. *Cardozo Law Review*, 26: 2253–61.

Winston, K.I. 2001. *The Principles of Social Order: Selected Essays of Lon L. Fuller.* Revd edn. Oxford: Hart.

Wolf, E. 1958. Revolution or Evolution in Gustav Radbruch's Legal Philosophy. *Natural Law Forum*, 3: 1–23.

Chapter 3
Citizenship and Social Class Revisited: Liberal Reason, Sociology and Publics

John Holmwood

This chapter addresses T.H. Marshall's essay on citizenship and social class in the light of a subsequent attack on social rights of citizenship under the increasing dominance of neo-liberal political reason, and its adoption by Conservative and New Labour governments in the UK. The essay was written at a time when the growth of social rights and the amelioration of social inequalities seemed to be an unproblematic extension of political rights and the growth of the welfare state. This was also aligned with the professional ethos of sociology and social policy as disciplines. However, with the increased emphasis on replacing state-provided services by the market, including, now, the introduction of the market into the delivery of higher education, Marshall's prognosis that social rights would transform the market appears to be reversed. This poses serious questions for the constitution of sociology as a discipline (and for its future in a context where public 'impact' is imperative to secure funding, and the impact agenda is itself a product of a neo-liberal 'knowledge regime'). In this chapter I suggest that sociology needs to renew itself through a re-examination of its relation to the public. In doing so, I shall draw upon John Dewey's idea of the public and George Herbert Mead's idea of the social self to outline their significance for a sociological critique of liberal public reason and a renewed engagement with social inequalities relevant to legal scholarship. I shall suggest that this may provide the key to unlock Marshall's concept of citizenship from its rather problematic association with a dated moment in the development of social democratic welfare provision. At the same time, it can provide sociology with a new 'jurisdiction'.

The chapter also reflects many discussions with Zenon Bańkowski, and some disagreements, but always friendly and engaged. I was a colleague of Bańkowski's for about 20 years at the University of Edinburgh. I was in the Department of Sociology and a member of the Social and Political Theory seminar that brought together staff and postgraduates from politics, sociology, law and the humanities for fortnightly meetings for a good many of those years (it ran from about 1985 through to 2003). Our discussions ranged across many issues, but a constant theme was the relation between explanatory social science and normative argument. In particular, problems of inequality and social justice were paramount, especially in a context where the discourse of class was losing public salience. Essentially, the seminar took place through a period of the emergence and consolidation of neo-liberal public reason. In consequence, the nature and moral meaning of markets was a preoccupation of our discussions, as was the fate of social democracy. In a period where social rights of citizenship were being dissolved in favour of the standard liberal freedoms, and where the sovereignty of the individual subject was rendered as consumer sovereignty, the meaning of freedoms expressed collectively was a central topic of discussion.

Ironically, from the 1970s onwards, T.H. Marshall's (1950) classic account of the social rights of citizenship had been subjected to emergent Marxist criticism as being a functionalist argument, where social rights served the reproduction of capitalism and did not challenge its essential structures of power (Gough 1979). Citizenship and social class were mutually compatible, it was argued, and in the phrase of the time, 'democracy was the best shell for capitalism' (Jessop 1978). By the mid-1980s, it seemed that the advocates of market capitalism disagreed, and social rights of citizenship were being challenged as incompatible with liberal freedoms and market efficiencies. I recall discussing Norman Barry's critique of welfare at the seminar, and his very telling statement:

> Some socialists and all consistent Marxists have to regard the typical welfare institutions as in a very real sense harmful because they are structured on a pre-existing capitalist order. Their thriving would be inimical to the future aim of abolishing the capitalist order ... Indeed, in theoretical Marxism, since the state is defined in essentialist terms as a coercive force to protect class interests, any welfare role that social theorists might attribute to it must be illusory. Almost all overt socialists saw welfare as a form of social control. (1990: 41)

And then Barry delivers his *coup de grace*: 'as indeed it was' (ibid.).This chapter, then, is a continuation of a conversation begun in Edinburgh, and an expression of thoughts first released under Bańkowski's gentle probing. My own sense of the relation among the disciplines represented at the seminar was that law and politics appeared to operate in counterpoint, whereas sociology seemed to introduce a discordant and jarring note. This, I have come to believe, derives from the fact that sociology has a special relation to the problem of inequality, deriving from the circumstances in which it arose as a discipline. Broadly, this was at the turn of the nineteenth/twentieth centuries with the emergence of corporate capitalism, and what Sidney Fine (1956) called the idea of the 'general' welfare state and the critique of classical political economy to provide a role for the state in social reform. In this context, I suggest, a sociological project first emerged around a critique of liberal public reason, and its embrace of the market and associated theory of the possessive individual. Here, sociology was associated with the possibility of reform and its expression through the recognition of social interdependence – an interdependence that became ever more evident as the reality of the modern capitalist corporation outstripped the ideological representation of capitalist organization in terms of market competition and entrepreneurial effort.

In contrast to sociology, it seemed to me that the disciplines of law and politics had developed much more straightforwardly as expressions of liberal public reason. In part this alignment is reflected in that favoured trio of subjects for Britain's governing class, namely politics, philosophy and economics (preferably read at Balliol), and the alignment of legal philosophy and liberalism within them. Of course, there are heterodox voices within those disciplines (not least Bańkowski's). However significant the 'critical legal studies' movement has been in challenging this liberal orthodoxy, it has done so largely from a tradition of continental philosophy and Frankfurt School theory, in particular. In this context, Marxist accounts of capitalism functioned as a surrogate for sociological engagement with contemporary social relations and institutions. Acceptance of what I shall suggest are essentially 'unreal' Marxist categories functioned to signify the 'real' and to enable a critique of sociology for its insufficiently critical stance, as evidenced in the wider Marxist critique of Marshall and the limits of the welfare state.

What I regard as a quite different sociological sensibility can be demonstrated in key contributions from Emile Durkheim and G.H. Mead, through to Karl Polanyi and T.H. Marshall (among others; though it is significant that I include neither Max Weber nor Karl Marx – nor the traditions associated with them – in this list. I shall return later to this deliberate omission).[1] Yet, my defence of a distinctive sociological sensibility and the urging of its significance was precisely that – *defensive*. It was conducted in a context where I felt that sociology had also lost its way. In this chapter, then, I shall argue that the critique of liberal public reason has become attenuated within sociology, especially in the contemporary period. I also want to suggest that this forms a crisis within sociology that is associated with a wider normalization of social inequality. In other words, we currently face a troubling question: what is the role of sociology if, in T.H. Marshall's (1950) words, in the 'war between citizenship and social class', the latter is perceived to have won? And what is the consequence for citizenship of the normalization of inequality? The seminar coincided, more or less, with a widening of inequalities from its lowest range in the early 1980s to now, when inequalities have returned to the levels last seen in the USA and UK at the turn of the nineteenth/twentieth centuries, a moment I regard as foundational for the development of sociology.

---

1 Of course, there are sociologists who have embraced methodological individualism, or who have been ardent proponents of capitalist political economy – Herbert Spencer and William Sumner come to mind as significant figures historically. However, this view may be regarded as the heterodox position in sociology. Equally, sociology itself was also strongly influenced by Marxism during the 1970s and after, at the same time as critical legal studies came to prominence.

Sociology's Jurisdiction

In arguing for a particular sociological sensibility associated with social reform, I am suggesting that sociology has a special relation to democratic developments that have challenged structured social inequality. However, it is more usual, to identify T.H. Marshall with a tradition of 'political arithmetic'; that is, of social knowledge serving the purposes of government (see Halsey 1994). Indeed, this characterization of Marshall is not that distant from the wider characterization of the problem of sociology employed within critical theory, from Max Horkheimer to Jürgen Habermas, namely that sociology was a discipline at the service of administered capitalism. However, this is at odds with the democratic impulse of Marshall's work, evident in his seminal work, 'Citizenship and Social Class'. If correct, it would serve to bind sociological knowledge to interests of government, something that has become fashionable in the light of Foucauldian accounts of governmentality, or Bauman's (1987) argument about the 'legislatory' tendency of sociological theory. However, as I shall suggest, while Marshall does not provide an explicit sociological grounding of his idea of social citizenship, its status as an 'alternative road' to the 'classless' society (Marshall 1950 [1938]) is an important part of his argument and one that belies the representation of him as part of a tradition of political arithmetic. This latter idea is also important, and I shall return to it in the context of addressing an alternative view in sociology (derived from Weber and Marx), namely, that *capitalism is necessarily a class society* and that its forms of citizenship are in the service of class.

To disentangle some of these arguments, I turn to the American pragmatist philosopher, John Dewey, and, in particular, his idea of the 'public and its problems' (the title of a book written by him in 1927). His ideas are fertile because they have a strong affinity with sociology, not least because of his influence on Mead and the latter's idea of the social self. I want to suggest that Dewey and Mead also have a strong conception of the mutual relations between sociology, the social self and social reform, and that they articulate these relations in terms of what, following Savage's (2010) terminology, I call a 'founding jurisdiction' of sociology. It is precisely the conception of the 'social self' that I argue marks both a distinctive sociological sensibility and a challenge to the liberal self that is constitutive of the dominant approaches in other disciplines, such as economics, politics and philosophy (including legal philosophy).[2]

Dewey's concept of the social self is of the individual who forms associations and is, in turn, formed by them (and cannot be conceived of as acting outside them). The social self is necessarily antagonist to the liberal self, conceived as a rational calculating subject abstracted from social relationships. Whereas the latter

2 It should also be evident that the critique of liberal public reason associated with the pragmatic (and sociological) idea of the social self and the relations among social selves as 'publics' goes some considerable way to providing the dialogical account of public philosophy attentive to civic struggles that is sought by Tully (2008).

is expressed in market exchanges, the social self is expressed in social reform. As Mead puts it,

> in social reform, or the application of intelligence to the control of social conditions, we must make a like assumption, and this assumption takes the form of belief in the essentially social character of human impulse and endeavor. We cannot make persons social by legislative enactment, but we can allow the essentially social nature of their actions to come to expression under conditions which favor this. (1899: 370)

The application of intelligence in the service of reform is strongly attached to the pragmatist emphasis on problem-solving, an association that leads Horkheimer (1947) and later writers to suggest that its concerns are piecemeal and accepting of the status quo. However, it is clear that the idea of problem-solving is understood as 'world-creating'. Thus Mead writes that, 'it is not surprising that in our reflective experience the world should present itself as an object of knowledge, for it is there primarily as the locus of a problem; and, when the problem is solved, if it is solved, it will be a different world from that which preceded the appearance of the problem' (1938 [1900]: 63). This is also extended to the idea of the self, which, for pragmatists does not have a fixed form. 'The growth of the self', Mead argues, 'arises out of a partial disintegration, – the appearance of the different interests in the forum of reflection, the reconstruction of the social worlds, and the consequent appearance of the new self that answers to the new object' (1964 [1913]: 149).

For Margaret Archer, Mead's social self is 'over-socialised', and therefore 'conformist' in character, where the actor's internal conversation is between 'the I and the we', as Archer puts it, rather than 'the I and the me'. 'His "I"', she suggests, 'does not speak *for itself,* but for another "We", that of a different community' (2003: 79). However, it is quite evident from the previous quotations that the 'social self' is not defined by stasis, but only arises as a consequence of necessary engagement with problems in a world of other selves. In this way, the 'I' that speaks for another 'we', speaks for a 'new community' as the product of a transformed social world and transformed self, alike.

The idea of the social self, then, brings reform into being, but, for Mead, it also brings sociology into being and does so together with its function to serve the public (or publics). In this way, Dewey and Mead are arguing for a conception of social science that serves the public, independently of any use of that knowledge by the state. It is of fundamental significance that neither Dewey nor Mead associates the public with the state. Dewey, for example, argues that the public is a category independent of the state and prior to it. The key to the definition of a public is contained in the idea of action in the world having effects and consequences that are ramified and impact on others who are not the initiators of the action. Essentially, all action is associative action, but a public is 'brought into being' in consequence of being indirectly and seriously affected by the actions of others.

Part of Dewey's analysis of the problem of modern democracy is concerned with the imbalance in the development of associations and the proliferation of problems in areas where publics cannot properly defend themselves. Given that a 'public' is defined by the consequences of action on individuals, it is necessarily the case that it is initially formed as a 'passive' entity; that is, as a group to which things happen. The main issue is how their interest in self-defence is to be developed.

This is the point at which Dewey shifts gear to argue that the wider idea of a public achieves a level of generality that requires organization and personnel to express it, namely the idea of a state as a congeries of public authorities. Thus, Dewey proposes that, 'the lasting, extensive and serious consequences of associated activity bring into existence a public. In itself it is unorganized and formless. By means of officials and their special powers it becomes a state. A public articulated and operating through representative officers is the state; there is no state without a government, but also there is none without the public' (1927: 67).

Dewey by no means suggests that these developments mean that a state necessarily will act in the public interest – power can be accrued, authority exercised despotically, and, indeed, the personnel of government can act on their own private or other special interests. The fundamental point, however, is that the state takes its meaning from the idea of a public and its interests, and that this is conceived as a dynamic thing. This means that, for Dewey, not only associations external to the state, but the state itself, and its modes of organization, are subject to change and revision in the light of other changes in the development of associative life. In other words, though the state exists in relation to the problems of associative social life that create a public, its forms and modes of organization may come to constitute a problem for the expression of that public, though, paradoxically, that is its *raison d'être*.

Whereas a conventional view of the functions of government is the representation of publics, with experts playing a mediating role in informing government decisions, Dewey is concerned with the self-organization of publics and the role of expertise in that process. Knowledge, for Dewey, should serve publics, not government. In other words, it is directly opposed to a 'legislator' idea of knowledge and its uses. The idea of a 'public' (or 'publics') contains a strong idea of democracy associated with participation and dialogue, but does not deny that there will be functionally differentiated publics, whose articulation will be at issue. Thus Dewey writes of democracy that, 'from the standpoint of the individual, it consists in having a responsible share according to capacity in forming and directing the activities of the groups to which one belongs and in participating according to need in the values which the groups sustain. From the standpoint of the groups, it demands liberation of the potentialities of members of a group in harmony with the interests and goods which are in common. Since every individual is a member of many groups this specification cannot be fulfilled except when different groups interact flexibly and fully in connections with other groups' (1927: 147).

Equally, the idea of the 'public' does not depend on an ideal form that acts as a regulatory idea for critique. As Mead puts it, 'a conception of a different world comes to us always as the result of some specific problem which involves readjustment of the world as it is, not to meet a detailed ideal of a perfect universe, but to obviate the present difficulty; and the test of the effort lies in the possibility of this readjustment fitting into the world as it is' (Mead 1899).

This argument establishes a critique of 'utopian' ideas of reform, and advocates instead the reform and reconstruction of existing institutions. Utopian reform, in contrast, is based on a fixed idea of the future, not on a readjustment of the world as it is; that is, *the world as it is within a sociological discernment of the developments that reform could bring into being.* Of course, the direct antagonist of Mead's argument is utopian socialism, including so-called Marxist scientific socialism, for which sociology is now presented as the 'true' scientific successor. However, the target – especially in Dewey – is also the liberal utopia of the self-regulating market. The representation of liberal reason as a (pathological) market utopia, then, is central to the tradition of sociological argument I am outlining here.

Dewey's account of publics was conceived, in part, as a riposte to Walter Lippmann (1925) and his idea that, in a democracy, the 'public' is a 'phantom category' (that is, something that functioned only in theories of democracy and had little real substance). For Lippmann, the 'eclipse of the public' was a necessary consequence of the complexity of modern societies that increasingly required organized expertise of various kinds. In consequence, 'expert opinion' would replace 'public opinion', and democracy would necessarily be attenuated (expert opinion, then, for Lippmann would function as a form of political arithmetic, a mode of calculation made available to elites and not to inform wider publics). Lippmann anticipated that expert opinion would operate in conjunction with the state and economic corporations in a manner that anticipated what, subsequently, has come to be understood as the 'Fordist' system of economic governance, in which social scientific knowledge became heavily implicated (Steinmetz 2005). However, Dewey also noted that the 'eclipse of the public' is prefigured in the very idea of the market economy in which decisions by (consumer) sovereign individuals are perceived to be efficiently aggregated through impersonal market exchanges. This is held to be in contrast to their inefficient aggregation by collective political decision-making through the agency of the state (Barry 1990). In other words, the idea of a political realm in which the public expresses its democratic will is severely compromised by the liberal distrust of 'group', or collective, actions and the idea that it is only the market that properly expressed the general interest. From the point of view of liberal individualism, then, modern capitalism has produced an appropriate eclipse of the public, in the sense of rendering the idea of the public nugatory. However, according to Dewey, this doctrine emerged just as the idea of an 'individual' free of associations was being rendered untenable by the very developments of corporate capitalism with which it was linked. Thus Dewey says that, '"the individual", about which the new philosophy centred itself, was in process of complete submergence in fact at the very time in which he was being elevated on high in theory' (1927: 96).[3] Given that publics express the nature of the individual's social self, the liberal antagonism to publics is, in truth, both anti-social and damaging to the individual. In this way, the liberal idea of the market is not only utopian, but it expresses a pathology, in much the same way as is argued by Durkheim (see Dawson 2012).

I hope it is clear that if we place Marshall's arguments about social citizenship in the context of the social self and the public, we would get a more robust – or perhaps more explicit – critique of public policy based on the utopia of market exchange and the liberal individual. We would also get an argument about reform that displaces the state from its implicit role at the centre of consideration. The state is replaced by the idea of the 'public', though that does not discount the importance of the agency of the state as one possible expression of the public. To spell it out a little further – though I hesitate to do so – we might see that the idea of the 'public' provides a specification of what might be entailed by the idea of a 'Big Society', but does so by showing that its enemy is primarily the market (or, more precisely, the 'utopia' of the market and its role in the formulation of public policy), which is why the present government's policies towards the promotion of the 'Big Society' are self-defeating.

So, what went wrong? And why was sociology displaced from its role in relation to publics to a role in relation to government?

Sociology and the Welfare State

For much of the period since Dewey was writing (that is, post-World War II), the social sciences operated relatively unselfconsciously under an understanding that was broadly aligned with Lippmann, rather than Dewey. This perhaps did not matter too much, in the sense that this period also coincided with the rise of the welfare state and the latter was frequently seen as a response to public demands. In this context, the state might be seen as the expression of the public interest, and so the latter could be embodied in a developing professional ethos for sociology and perceptions of its growth in line with the growth of the welfare state. This, I suggest, is much the way that Marshall's own contribution was understood as 'political arithmetic'. Its corollary was that the nature of sociology (and other social sciences) as a public good was relatively unproblematic and need not be addressed directly. Indeed, in so far as the welfare state can be regarded as emerging to ameliorate the social problems of a market society, then a sociological project that was itself associated with the growth of the welfare

3 Livingston (1994, 2001) identifies the rise of the corporate economy as the moment of pragmatism. For Dewey, the idea of 'individualism' was peculiarly well suited to the promotion of the class-based associations of business activities and brought into being the corporate economy that is patently at odds with that individualism.

state might also be understood as being organized in relation to a 'normalized' critique of liberal public reason (though, of course, Dewey would have demurred at this 'normalization' of the idea of the public).

However, in the 1970s and after, this normalized version of sociology's 'jurisdiction' began to break down with the emergence of critiques of welfare state capitalism. Indeed, as I have suggested, Marshall's arguments concerning social rights of citizenship and the possibility of reform were themselves argued to be little more than ideological justifications for the reproduction of capitalism. In the language of sociological critiques of the 1970s and 1980s, since the welfare state was perceived as being functional for capitalism, it therefore lacked the positive substance that Marshall had sought to attribute to social rights of citizenship.

These criticisms were also aligned with critiques of professional organization, whose growth Marshall (1950 [1939]) had also identified as being associated with the growth of citizenship, in so far as citizenship rights require separate occupations designed to sustain them; see also Parsons (1939, 1959) for a different version of the argument. These criticisms extended to the professionalization of sociology itself (Gouldner 1970; Larson 1977; Collins 1990; Steinmetz 2005). While the criticisms were frequently intended to serve a greater democratization, the concurrent resurgence of neo-liberal public reason and its increasing influence over governments keen to reduce the scale of the welfare state and to de-regulate their economies meant that critique was easily absorbed by the neo-liberal project. Sociological critiques of welfare capitalism defined the problem as being that welfare was a system of social control; neo-liberals agreed and, of course, they that inherited the prize. This has left sociology (and arguments against inequality) adrift.

This is so in two respects. First, social scientific knowledge is organized increasingly in instrumental terms as a 'co-production' (Jasanoff 2004) of the academy, government and private agencies with little independent normative grounding, other than its putative significance for national social and economic goals. This is an updated version of political arithmetic, but it is now a general arithmetic of useful knowledge available to any beneficiary. Social science is no longer to be simply the servant of government but of anyone who will pay the piper, or on whose behalf the piper pays. This is the understanding intrinsic to the current 'impact' agenda that dominates the academy in the UK (Holmwood 2011a). Second, in so far as critical sociologies have emerged since the 1970s to challenge professional orthodoxies, they are victims of what Burawoy (2005: 20) has called a 'scissors movement' in their relation to the wider public, where public opinion has moved in the opposite direction from sociological opinion. Declarations 'for public sociology', then, potentially face a public that is itself not 'for sociology'. In this context, sociological argument has a declining capacity to influence public debate and, indeed, is readily represented as both a special interest and as a politicized form of knowledge within that debate, a fate that also befalls other forms of critique, including those within liberal studies.

The Decline of Class?

This is an impasse where sociology takes its meaning as being *for the public* and yet appears *estranged from the public* it seeks to serve. I now want to address this impasse via the fate of the sociological analysis of class inequality. Some will be familiar with the recent debate in British sociology over the putative 'death of class' (Lee and Turner 1996). The debate needs to be understood in the light of the re-emergence of Marxist and Weberian forms of class analysis in the period after Marshall was writing (and frequently in criticism of his works). This analysis was frequently designed to show the resilience of class in the face of the welfare programmes associated with what Marshall perceived as the expansion of social citizenship. It seemed that social citizenship could not be represented as the path to a classless society (though it should be noted that, for Marshall, the classless society was not to be construed as a society without inequality).

However, what might be represented as the increased significance of class in the subjective consciousness of sociologists was matched by its decline in the consciousness of the wider population. The ultimate failure of class analysis is that the language of class no longer has much salience in public discourse, at least not in the form that sociologists propose. At best, 'class' is used in popular understanding as a means of locating family experience in terms of the relation of the past to the present; for example, as a description of how things have improved (for 'people like us'), or as part of a narrative of identification with other family members, especially those of earlier generations ('where we have come from'). It is no longer the forward-looking discourse of social justice, or of necessary action to ameliorate inequality.

It is all very well for sociologists to offer the argument that subjective ideas about inequality are mediated by ideological legitimations, or other intervening factors such as gender or ethnicity, and that class as an 'objective reality' remains (Sayer 2005). The issue would still arise of how to understand and explain everyday ideas of inequality and social justice, their relation to the supposedly objective understandings of sociologists, and how different ideas of social justice might become effective in social change. Indeed, connecting the ideas of social commentators and publics through effective dialogue is a necessary task of public philosophy 'in a new key', as argued by Tully (2008). In this context, any sociological distinction between the 'objective' and the 'subjective' must function as the alienation of that dialogue.

I shall now introduce a slightly different terminology. My wider interest concerns the 'moral economy' of inequality. The idea of a 'moral economy' was coined by E.P. Thompson (1971) to capture the everyday understanding of inequality, prices and mutual (if asymmetrical) obligations that sustained economic relations in eighteenth-century England prior to the emergence of the capitalist system of extended exchange relations. Thompson did not address what lay beyond capitalist *political economy* (or liberal public reason), though his own Marxism implied a radical transformation of society. However, if my arguments so far are correct, the sociological tradition I am elaborating identifies Marxism as a form of utopianism based on a fixed idea of the future. In contrast, the idea of reform and the social self postulates the possibility of capitalism itself as being capable of producing a different *moral economy*. It is this idea that has been lost in contemporary sociology. But, notice that the emergence of such a moral economy would necessarily displace the language of class in public discourse and, seemingly, this is what sociologists find, though as I have also argued that they are somewhat bewildered about its meaning.

This is because class analysis is tied to a theory of class society that makes it impossible to conceive of reforms except as the reproduction of the defining relationships of capitalism. For example, the idea of a modern society was for many sociologists prior to the 1970s an idea that incorporated the idea of a capitalist economy, but did not reduce society to such an economy. In this way, society necessarily had a substance beyond the principles deemed to organize the economy, and the latter were understood as being subsumed (or embedded) within them.[4] The fact that neo-liberal public reason reduces society to the market economy and conceives public policies on that reduction does not constitute an understanding of the reality of social relations, but rather the active production of anomie in the space previously occupied by reform.

According to the theory of class society, and to use a resonant phrase coined by Charles Perrow (1984), in a different context, production and distribution in a capitalist system are perceived as simply being too 'tightly coupled' to allow reforms. Reforms in the area of 'distribution', for example, cannot take place without the transformation of relations of production, and those relations of production are also tightly coupled. Each part is mutually dependent on other parts, and change to one part cannot be undertaken without a simultaneous change to other parts. From the perspective of 'tight coupling', fundamental transformation is the only answer to the problem of reform.

In different ways and with different motivation, I suggest, the theory of class society and political economy (whether classic liberal or neoliberal) alike present capitalism as a tightly-coupled system. In each, the argument arises as an intellectual obstacle to reform. However, if the capitalist system is not tightly coupled, then reform is possible (indeed, it has been seen to take place). The paradox is that 'loosely coupled systems' are reliant on ideological justifications to sustain the mutual reproduction of their parts. Thus the view that the only true alternative is a form of radical transformation for which the sociological conditions are no longer regarded as plausibly occurring, has the consequence of reinforcing the liberal version of tight coupling as a form of ideological justification – 'there is

4 Polanyi, for example, writes that, 'the end of market society means in no way the end of markets. These continue, in various fashions, to ensure the freedom of the consumer, to indicate the shifting of demand, to influence producers' income, and to serve as an instrument of accountancy, while ceasing altogether to be an organ of economic self-regulation' (1957 [1944]: 252).

no alternative' – that secures the mutual reproduction of the parts in their currently problematic forms.

I suggest that the promise of sociology in its 'founding jurisdiction' is precisely that it challenged the idea of capitalism as a 'tightly coupled' system. However, this 'promise' of sociology is now undermined by the re-emergence within sociology of the idea that capitalism is indeed tightly-coupled. This is manifested in a number of ways. For example, as I have suggested, it is a feature both of arguments from the 1970s onwards, that welfare reforms were functional for capitalism (Habermas 1976; Gough 1979), and of many recent arguments about the nature of globalization and the new constraints it places on social reform by reducing the capacity of national welfare states (for discussion, see Hirst and Thompson 1996). Yet reforms have taken place, even if sociologists have given up the development of a positive language in which to express them. Those reforms contribute to the 'lived experience' of publics, and thus help to form their everyday understanding of inequalities and their reproduction. In this way, it is unlikely that their understandings would match those of sociological accounts which argue that class-based understandings are paramount and remain unaltered by reforms designed to ameliorate them.

A second, related problem is that, at critical junctures in the process of capitalist development, there are moments of 'counter-reform' that rely on a new iteration of liberal public reason. In this way, the very 'idea' of 'capitalism', I suggest, can itself become a form of critique, in much the same sense that has come to be attributed to critique in sociology. As Polanyi (1957 [1944]) observed, capitalism and the idea of the self-regulating market are 'anti-social' when viewed from a sociological perspective. However, from the perspective of the market, the 'social' is the source of obstacles to the operation of effective market relations that embody individual autonomy and freedom. In this way, liberal public reason can present the 'social' as the embodiment of various kinds of 'monopolistic' appropriation, with the market as their dissolution.

In the absence of a critique of the market as being both utopian and pathological, the market holds a default role as the basis of a critique of social institutions. Actual social practices may deviate from those represented within market models, but that enables the 'abstracted' – utopian – model of market relations to be represented as the basis of public policy to restore the rationality believed to be expressed within it. It is precisely this feature that explains the recurrence of the claim that the market is a 'spontaneous' phenomenon and yet, at the same time, has to be 'planned'.[5] Governments presently 'plan' the marketization of public

5 There are similarities with Polanyi (1957 [1944]), too. The latter argues that, 'while laissez-faire economy was the product of deliberate state action, subsequent restrictions on laissez-faire started in a spontaneous way' (1944: 141). Dewey, for his part, comments that, 'actual economic conditions were thoroughly artificial, in the sense in which the theory condemned the artificial' (1927: 96).

functions, including, in England, the marketization of the public university (see Holmwood 2011b, for a discussion).

In fact, this analysis helps to make sense of the politics of our present time. The legacy of the 1980s in sociology and politics is a dualism of 'state' and 'market' as the organizing dualism of public discourse. This creates a rhetoric of the 'public' and its 'interests', which is the antithesis of that outlined by Dewey. For example, the public is variously invoked as having an interest in the reduction of the fiscal deficit, an interest in greater choice, and an interest in the efficient delivery of services. In this way, the public is identified as an aggregate of private individuals, and the government is tasked with representing its interests. The public interest, conceived in this way, is set against a tendency of groups to exert a form of collective power to maintain services for their own, private benefit. In this way, 'producers' of services are set against 'consumers', and the way to prevent their 'monopolistic' appropriation is via a mechanism that serves consumer interests directly, that of the market. In fact, this problem of 'collectivities' is extended to the government itself, which, apparently, must represent the public against its own tendency to appropriate decision-making.

Thus, on its website, the Cabinet Office states, 'The Big Society is about helping people to come together to improve their own lives. It's about putting more power in people's hands – a massive transfer of power from Whitehall to local communities.'[6] One of the weaknesses of this rhetoric is that the transfer is to communities in which markets also operate. At best, it represents the self-organizing community as the solution to 'market failure.'[7] However, the market is also represented as putting more power in people's hands, and so the policies that promote the 'big society' are simultaneously engaged with the promotion of the market. What is missing is any understanding that the market is itself 'anti-social', bringing about the 'disorganization' of the community whose empowerment is being sought. The 'big society' is counter to the 'big state', but there is no equivalent analysis of the role of the market. However, once we recognize the significance of the Deweyan idea of the 'public', we can understand that the weakness of the state/market dualism is that both the state and the market stand in a potentially antagonist relation to the 'public'.

Indeed, nowhere is this more evident than in the 'Occupy' movement. For many, the movement is puzzling precisely because it seems to make no conventional demands in terms of specific claims on government to enact policies and so on. Yet, in another respect, it stands as the symbolic antithesis of the 'market', as a claim for dialogue and for spaces in which it can be enacted. The market, as the aggregation of the choices of self-oriented individuals is the antithesis of the idea of a public of 'other-oriented' social selves engaged in the resolution of their

6 See http://www.cabinetoffice.gov.uk/big-society. Accessed 30 November 2012.

7 It has to be assumed that there is a market failure or, from the logic of the position, there would be nothing for the 'big society' to do, yet there is no indication of what market failure might consist.

problems through dialogue. Indeed, as governments across Europe respond to the deficits created by the bailing out of the financial system by austerity measures introduced by technocratic and unelected governments, or governments claiming that there is no alternative, we are potentially witnessing a profoundly anti-democratic moment, whose character is revealed once the idea of the public as the foundation for democracy is fully embraced. Democracy, it seems, is no longer the best shell for (financialized) capitalism.

Conclusion

The sociological task of critique is distinctive (and difficult) precisely because it must be advanced by substantive sociological argument, rather than by reference to an alternative principle. In other words, reforms are always specific to problems and their solution, and cannot be derived from the operation of a principle externally applied to those circumstances, whether that is the utopia of the market, or of some other 'ideal' alternative to capitalist society.

It is my contention that this critique needs to be renewed for each new phase of capitalist development, but that, at present, we have entered a phase when sociological argument has itself seemed to become aligned to liberal reason. Sociology's jurisdiction remains defined by the problem of inequality, but to be equal to the task imposed on us, we need to undertake an exercise of reconstruction of our core categories of capitalism and class *and* an exercise of recuperation. The recuperation we need is the re-engagement with sociology's founding jurisdiction of social self, social reform and the public, addressed to problems of our own age. It is a recuperation that would serve legal studies more substantially than countering one utopia with another.

Bibliography

Archer, M.S. 2003. *Structure, Agency and the Internal Conversation.* Cambridge: Cambridge University Press.

Barry, N. 1990. *Welfare*. Milton Keynes: Open University Press.

Bauman, Z. 1987. *Legislators and Interpreters.* Cambridge: Polity Press.

Burawoy, M. 2005. 'For Public Sociology'. *American Sociological Review*, 70(1): 2–28.

Collins, R. 1990. 'Market Closure and the Conflict Theory of Professions'. In M. Burrage and R. Torstendahl (eds), *Professions in Theory and History*. London: Macmillan, 24–43.

Dawson, M. 2012. 'Against the Big Society: A Durkheimian Socialist Critique'. *Critical Social Policy*. Available at: http://csp.sagepub.com/content/early/2012/02/22/0261018312439364; accessed 30 November 2012.

Dewey, J. 1927. *The Public and Its Problems.* Athens, OH: Swallow Press.

Fine, S. 1956. *Laissez-Faire and the General-Welfare State: A Study of Conflict in American Thought 1865–1901.* Ann Arbor, MI: University of Michigan Press.

Gough, I. 1979. *The Political Economy of the Welfare State.* London: Macmillan.

Gouldner, A.W. 1970. *The Coming Crisis of Western Sociology.* London: Heineman.

Habermas. J. 1976. *Legitimation Crisis*. London: Heineman.

Halsey, A.H. 1994. 'Sociology as Political Arithmetic'. *British Journal of Sociology*, 45(3): 427–44.

Hirst, P.Q. and Thompson, G. 1996. *Globalization in Question: The International Economy and Possibilities of Governance.* Cambridge: Polity Press.

Holmwood, J. 2011a. 'The Impact of "Impact" on UK Social Science'. *Methodological Innovations Online*, 6(1): 13–17. Available at: http://www.pbs.plym.ac.uk/mi/pdf/09-06-11/5.%20Viewpoint%20-%20Holmwood%20 13-17%20(proofed).pdf; accessed 30 November 2012.

Holmwood, J. (ed.). 2011b. *A Manifesto for the Public University.* London: Bloomsbury Academic.

Horkheimer, M. 1947. *Eclipse of Reason*. New York: Oxford University Press.

Jasanoff, S. 2004. 'Ordering Knowledge, Ordering Society'. In S. Jasanoff (ed.), *States of Knowledge: The Co-Production of Science and Social Order*. London: Routledge, 13–45.

Jessop, B. 1978. 'Capitalism and Democracy: The Best Possible Political Shell?' In G. Littlejohn et al. (eds), *Power and the State*. London: Croom Helm, 10–51.

Larson, M.S. 1977. *The Rise of the Professions: A Sociological Analysis.* Berkeley, CA: University of California Press.

Lee, D.J. and Turner, B.S. (eds) 1996. *Conflicts about Class: Debating Inequality in Late Industrialism*. London: Longman.

Lippmann, W. 1925. *The Phantom Public.* London: Macmillan.

Livingston, J. 1994. *Pragmatism and the Political Economy of Cultural Revolution, 1850–1940.* Chapel Hill, NC: University of North Carolina Press.

Livingston, J. 2001. *Pragmatism, Feminism and Democracy: Rethinking the Politics of American History.* New York: Routledge.

Marshall, T.H. 1950 [1938]. 'The Nature of Class Conflict'. In T.H. Marshall, *Citizenship and Social Class: And Other Essays*. Cambridge: Cambridge University Press, 114–27.

Marshall, T.H. 1950 [1939] 'The Recent History of Professionalism in Relation to Social Structure and Social Policy'. In *Citizenship and Social Class: And Other Essays*. Cambridge: Cambridge University Press, 128–54.

Marshall, T.H. 1950. 'Citizenship and Social Class'. In *Citizenship and Social Class; And Other Essays*. Cambridge: Cambridge University Press, 1–86.

Mead, G.H. 1899. 'The Working Hypothesis in Social Reform'. *American Journal of Sociology*, 5: 367–71.

Mead, G.H. 1938 [1900]. *The Philosophy of the Act.* Chicago: University of Chicago Press.

Mead, G.H. 1964 [1913]. 'The Social Self'. In A.J. Reck (ed.), *Selected Writings: George Herbert Mead.* Chicago: University of Chicago Press, 142–9.
Parsons, T. 1939. 'The Professions and Social Structure'. *Social Forces*, 17(4): 457–67.
Parsons, T. 1959. 'Some Problems Confronting Sociology as a Profession'. *American Sociological Review*, 24(4): 547–58.
Perrow, C. 1984. *Normal Accidents: Living with High Risk Technologies.* New York: Basic Books.
Polanyi, K. 1957 [1944]. *The Great Transformation: The Political and Economic Origins of Our Time*. Boston, MA: Beacon Press.
Savage, M. 2010. *Identities and Social Change in Britain since 1940: The Politics of Method.* Oxford: Oxford University Press.
Sayer, A. 2005. *The Moral Significance of Class.* Cambridge: Cambridge University Press.
Steinmetz, G. 2005. 'Scientific Authority and the Transition to Post-Fordism: The Plausibility of Positivism in U.S. Sociology since 1945'. In G. Steinmetz (ed.), *The Politics of Method in the Human Science: Positivism and its Epistemological Others*. Durham, NC: Duke University Press, 275–325.
Thompson, E.P. 1971. The Moral Economy of the English Crowd in the Eighteenth Century. *Past and Present*, 50: 76–136.
Tully, J. 2008. *Public Philosophy in a New Key*, 2 Vols. Cambridge: Cambridge University Press.

Chapter 4
Thinking in Images in Legal Theory

Maksymilian Del Mar*

Introduction

The use of images in philosophy is at once both familiar and all too often ignored. Any student of philosophy will recall learning about Plato's cave, Hegel's owl, Locke's *tabula rasa*, and, more recently, Wittgenstein's language games. Indeed, such images are often effective ways of remembering some of the key contributions of those philosophers. One might say, more strongly, that a good part of the legacy of these philosophers is precisely the images they introduced into the thinking of subsequent generations. And yet, few of us have read philosophical works with an eye to the role of images in them. Arguably, even fewer of us are aware of the role(s) that images play in our own philosophizing, or in thinking generally.

This chapter attempts to pay a little more attention to images and their role(s) in philosophy. It does so in two steps. First, in Part I, the chapter looks to two authors who have considered the role(s) of images in philosophy: Michèle Le Doeuff and Marguerite La Caze. Both authors have approached the task of reading philosophy by focusing on the images that appear – and indeed reappear – in philosophical texts. Le Doeuff's canvas is broad, harking back to the Ancient Greeks, while La Caze's is more contemporary, focusing on analytical philosophy. There are other differences too: Le Doeuff thinks that images both enable philosophical thought and, at the same time, undermine it. Images embody in some way the tussle of doubt and faith upon which thought depends. La Caze is less paradoxical, and focuses on the way that images are 'embedded' in philosophy – that is, she identifies a variety of constructive functions that images play in philosophy. This chapter embraces both approaches: it looks at how images play various constructive functions in the making of philosophy, but also at how those images can be read to undermine the very constructive roles they play in any one text. Part I offers an account of what work images do in philosophizing and in philosophical texts. Part II then uses this account of images to examine some of the contributions Zenon Bańkowski has made to the philosophy of law.

* An earlier version of this chapter was delivered at the conference held on the occasion of Zenon Bańkowski's retirement, 'The Anxious Jurist: Themes from the Work of Zenon Bańkowski', at the School of Law, University of Edinburgh, 22–23 August 2011. I am grateful to the participants for their comments and questions.

Together with Neil MacCormick, Zenon Bańkowski was my supervisor for my doctorate in Edinburgh. This chapter, and this volume as a whole, is an opportunity to engage with his work, but also to thank him. He and I have collaborated on projects, in part while I was still a doctoral student. More often than not, our philosophical agreements and disagreements have revolved around an image or a set of images. It is in recognition of the role that images have played in our discussions that I offer the modest examination below.

Images of Thought

One of the first philosophers to discuss the importance of images in philosophical thought was Michèle Le Doeuff. In her *The Philosophical Imaginary* (1989), Le Doeuff sets out to write a history of philosophy in which images take central stage; it is thus expressly a history that does not centralize 'concepts, procedures or systems' (Le Doeuff 1989: 2). As she notes, there is a tension between, on the one hand, (some, perhaps most?) philosophers' own self-description of their enterprise as one that 'declares its status as philosophy through a break with myth, fable, the poetic, the domain of the image', and, on the other, the fact that when one looks more closely at the texts themselves they are replete with images – with, in Le Doeuff's words, 'statues that breathe the scent of roses … foundations, dwellings, doors and windows, sand, navigators, various musical instruments, clocks, horses, donkeys and even a lion … scenes of sea and storm, forests and trees' (Le Doeuff 1989: 1). There is, indeed, a 'whole pictorial world' (ibid.) to be mined in the history of philosophy – one that is all the more interesting in that it is so often disowned or simply ignored by philosophers themselves.[1]

Le Doeuff reports that there was one hypothesis related to the role of images in philosophical thought – one out of many identified at the outset of her project – that survived the completion of the work. Le Doeuff expresses it in both minimalist and maximalist versions, and says that her reading of philosophical texts for images often oscillated between these two versions:

> The narrow version states that the interpretation of imagery in philosophical texts goes together with a search for points of tension in a work. In other words, such imagery is inseparable from the difficulties, the sensitive points of an intellectual venture.
>
> The broader version states that the meaning conveyed by images works both for and against the system that deploys them. *For*, because they sustain something which the system cannot itself justify, but which is nevertheless

1 There have been philosophers and cognitive scientists who have spoken of the role of images in thinking, but this is rarely directed at the practice of philosophy. An exception is Johnson and Lakoff 1990 and 1999 (the latter book looks at the practice of philosophy).

> needed for its proper working. *Against*, for the same reason – or almost: their meaning is incompatible with the system's possibilities. (Le Doeuff 1989: 3)

In the minimalist version, to locate an image in a text is to locate a tension – to find a wrinkle in the fabric, a place where the author has encountered something difficult. The maximalist version spells this out more explicitly, and makes it more about the text than the author: the image is not only a site of tension, but something that both supports and undermines the 'system'. Thus what Le Doeuff offers is not only a method for reading philosophy – that is, a method that looks for images in philosophical texts – but also a way of understanding what it is to think philosophically. In this view, to think philosophically is to create and then inhabit a tension between doubt and faith. To be a philosophical text is to both assert and undermine at the same time; to make a claim that cannot itself be justified, but that is believed in because everything else around it is presented as something to be doubted. In the imagination, doubt and faith are placed in dialogue: the former is required for the latter, and the latter is a brief respite from the former. The two need each other, and their interdependency is displayed in the role that an image plays in a philosopher's thinking or the way it holds a philosophical text together.

Le Doeuff is a wonderful reader of philosophy, and her method of paying attention to images offers not only new ways of seeing old texts, but also new ways of understanding the history of philosophy; that is, tracing precisely the echoes of images in philosophical debates.[2] In any such exercise, one could hardly begin in a better place than with the Ancient Greeks. As Nicholas D. Smith (2007) observes in a paper entitled 'Plato's Book of Images', Plato's work is replete with images:[3] there is not only the image of human beings as prisoners in a cave, but also, for example, 'that most famous image of the ship of state, whose brave ruler is compared to the ship's captain' in Plato's *Republic* (Smith 2007: 3). Jill Gordon mentions some others:

> the unruly, winged horse of the *Phaedrus* resists the bridled control of the charioteer and therefore fails to ascend to the heights; Socrates, the midwife in *Thaetetus*, aids in the birth of ideas and disposes of those ideas delivered stillborn or unfit; Aristophanes relates the story in the *Symposium* of our origins as double-sided humans, two joined as one, cartwheeling around with our other halves in erotic bliss; philosophy is depicted as medicine for the soul when it is

2 Lest one think that Le Doeuff chooses convenient examples, consider her discussion of the use that Kant makes of 'the island of truth', an image that appears in ch. 3 of Book II of Immanuel Kant's *Critique of Pure Reason* and which is taken by Kant from Bacon's *Temporis Partus Maximus* (where Bacon speaks of 'the island of truth … surrounded by a mighty ocean in which many an intelligence will drown in storms of illusion'; see Le Doeuff 1989: 8–17).

3 The irony of this, given Plato's banishment of image-makers from the ideal city, has been noted by many. See, for example, Murdoch 1991.

> in ill health; Alcibiades flaunts his striking and seductive beauty; and we might even say that Socrates flaunts his ugly visage. (Gordon 2007: 212–3)

Some of these images are less well-known than others, but there is no doubt that many of them have long had an influence on philosophy, and that they continue to do so. Consider, as just one example, the image of Socrates the midwife. One contemporary philosopher who has drawn on that image is Hannah Arendt (1971a, 1971b). In fact, Arendt noted that there were three images of Socrates the thinker in Plato's work: first, Socrates is a gadfly: 'he knows how to sting citizens who, without him, will "sleep on undisturbed for the rest of their lives" unless somebody comes along to arouse them' (Arendt 1971a: 172); second, Socrates is a midwife: he 'purged people of their "opinions", that is, of those unexamined pre-judgements that would prevent them from thinking' – in other words, 'because he is sterile himself … he knows how to deliver others of their thoughts' and he knows 'whether the child is a real child or a mere wind-egg of which the bearer must be cleansed' (indeed, for Socrates, it is always a wind-egg; ibid.: 172–3); and third, Socrates is an electric ray: he 'remains steadfast in his own perplexities and … paralyzed himself, paralyzes anyone he comes into contact with' (ibid.: 173). As a gadfly, midwife and electric ray, Socrates does not claim to teach anything or to make men wise (ibid.). But what he does is to remain thoughtful and teach thoughtfulness. As Arendt puts it, thinking á la Socrates 'is always out of order, [it] interrupts all ordinary activities and is interrupted by them' (ibid.: 197). Thinking, with the help of these images, helps you to 'see that you have nothing in your grasp but perplexities, and the best we can do is share them with each other' (ibid.: 175). Famously, Arendt then builds on these images of thought to develop what we might call 'an ethics of thoughtfulness'.[4] Arendt proceeds from an account of intellectual virtues to an account of the virtues of interpersonal morality and good polity. What allows her to do so, arguably, are precisely images; the journey is from images of thought (which are also, to some extent, images of the self) to images of the ethical and political life.

Le Doeuff inspired more philosophers to reflect on the role of images in philosophical thought.[5] Among them is Marguerite La Caze, whose work, *The Analytic Imaginary* (2002), focuses specifically, as the title suggests, on the role of images in analytical philosophy. La Caze clarifies early in her work that she is using the term 'image' in 'a very broad sense as an umbrella or cluster concept to cover notions from different disciplines', including notions such as 'metaphor', 'analogy', 'thought experiment', 'myth' and 'model' (La Caze 2002: 1–2). What attracts her to images – understood in this broad sense – is that, as she says, they 'are extremely important to the expression of philosophical thought, to the way debates are structured and assumptions are shared; [and] they can also work to

4 Recall that it was thoughtlessness that Arendt identified as a characteristic of Adolf Eichmann (see Arendt 1964).

5 See the papers collected in Deutscher 2000.

persuade and to provide support for a particular view and to exclude alternative views and methods' (ibid.: 1). Like Le Doeuff, La Caze covers a great variety of texts and identifies images where we might have missed them before: she speaks, for example, of Locke's talking parrot, and the cobbler and the prince, of Descartes' tree of knowledge or the shelter of morality, but also of other famous images of contemporary philosophy: 'Otto Neurath's ship of language', W.V.O. Quine's fabric of knowledge or belief (and web of belief metaphors), Hilary Putnam's Twin Earth thought experiment and his analogy between brains and computers, Frank Jackson's 'Mary' thought experiment, John Searle's Chinese Room, the ever-popular brain-in-the-vat, Donald Davidson's swampman, and David Chalmers' zombie' (see ibid.: 9 for references).[6]

It is important for La Caze that we realize that images of this kind are much more than rhetorical flourishes.[7] To combat this narrowing of the role of images, she argues that images can be embedded in philosophy in three different ways (these are what she calls the 'levels of embeddedness' of images): first, they can function at the level of expression – 'one needs the image to express the thought' (the 'expressibility' level); second, they can provide 'a framework that gives substance to the thought expressed' (the 'enframement' level); and third, they can help to make 'the thought be convincing' (the 'persuasiveness' level) (see ibid.: 11).

The first type of image runs deep – examples here typically involve basic spatial and temporal metaphors (such as, for example, the notion of the middle in Gillian Rose's work[8]), or metaphors of movement or of the senses (think only of the language of contemporary epistemology: 'seeing the point, accommodating points of view, perspectives, and so on', which rely so much on the sense of sight): ibid.: 12). La Caze includes in this level images that engender certain concepts, such as associating reason with the masculine (ibid.: 11–12). Her point, in general, is to note that the alteration of such images 'requires a rethinking of the entire field of endeavour, and perhaps an examination of our cultural understanding of the concepts in question' (ibid.: 12). The second kind of image (at the enframement level) is best illustrated with an example – the reliance on 'social contract myths … in liberal political philosophy' (ibid.: 12). Enframement images, says La Caze, 'guarantee the continuance of the framework, methodology, and objects of discussion' (ibid.: 12). Finally, the third kind – functioning at the persuasiveness level – 'often works in conjunction with the other two', meaning that an image that

---

6 Recently, Robert Brandom (2011, 204, fn. 19) endorsed Jeremy Wanderer's use of an image (that of a parrot) as an organising trope for his account of Brandom's work (see Wanderer 2008). Perhaps Brandom's use itself echoes Locke's.

7 Though already to use 'rhetorical' in this way is risky; what is needed is an acknowledgement of how rich the tradition of rhetoric was in the days when it was not disparaged.

8 See Rose 1992. See also, in this volume, Chapter 14, by James MacLean.

is deeply embedded or frames an issue or debate will also often be persuasive or striking in some way (ibid.: 12).[9]

La Caze's account of the role of images in philosophy is perhaps more prosaic – more analytical – than Le Doeuff's. The way that La Caze understands the role of images is much more constructive – it is about ways of building philosophies, and then ways of selling them, and it is not, as in Le Doeuff, an instrument for seeing where those philosophies are also vulnerable; where, to recall, they also undermine themselves, or at least reveal, perhaps unwittingly, a difficulty that cannot be expressed in any other way except through an image. There is no reason, however, why we cannot combine both La Caze's and Le Doeuff's insights. Images might indeed be the mortar – so to speak – of philosophies: they are what holds the arguments (the bricks) together. Images, one might say, are philosophy-makers. They can be philosophy-makers in various ways, as La Caze shows us, expressing, enframing and persuading. However, as Le Doeuff argues, the constructive role alone is not enough for philosophy: philosophy needs tension, an intermingling of doubt and faith. For Le Doeuff, images are certainly constructive, but they play a double role: not only enabling leaps of faith; but also introducing doubt. In that sense, somewhat paradoxically, what makes images philosophy-makers is that they are also philosophy-breakers: they leave many things unsaid, unjustified, to be believed in. Images, then, both enable and endanger thought. With these general points in mind, let us turn now to use images to read the work of Zenon Bańkowski.

The Imaginary of a Legal Theorist

What follows is a glimpse of Bańkowski's imaginary – that is, the stock of images that appears in his legal theorizing. By no means is it exhaustive. Quite the contrary, it is selective, and the majority of it is from what Bańkowski has called his 'middle period',[10] that is, the period between *Images of Law* (1976) and the current work on 'Beyond Text in Legal Education.'[11]

This middle period might be said to contain images that echo each other – all of them are unique in their own right and have their own autonomy to an extent, but they can also be said to be like beads on a string – that is, they may be taken to

9 Perhaps this works better with enframement images than with the deeply embedded ones (after all, something being upward/downward does not seem more striking than something being inside/outside).

10 For Bańkowski's self-periodization, see his Valedictory Lecture 'The Long Goodbye' (Bańkowski 2011), published in a revised form in this volume.

11 The 'Beyond Text in Legal Education' project began in 2008, under the auspices of an Arts and Humanities Research Council workshops grant. Bańkowski was the Principal Investigator of the project. The fruits of the project have been published by Ashgate (see Bańkowski et al. 2013, and Bańkowski and Del Mar 2013).

develop a theme that has been, and still is very strong in Bańkowski's work. This theme may be expressed in the following way: the sense, roughly, of an encounter that renews us, whether at the personal, systemic or institutional level (including the deleterious effect of the absence of such encounters). Accordingly, we will see (not in any particular order – for example, certainly not in chronological order) images of encounters with unresponsive ATM machines, hungry tigers, fellow students in a seminar, with people at a border, with friends or strangers with whom one exchanges gifts, and others. Images of such encounters also appear at supra-personal levels, such as the connections created in the sea of language by metaphors or the role of so-called 'bridging institutions' that infuse 'lay acid' into systems of regulation. It is these images of encounters that will be the focus of what follows.[12]

For the purposes of this chapter, then, the images in Bańkowski's work that will be engaged with are taken as, to some extent, allowing us to understand the importance of the encounter in his legal theory. We shall be attempting to see what work images do for Bańkowski's account of the importance of the encounter for legality, including legal professionals and legal institutions. This will build on what was said above about how La Caze approaches the role of images in philosophy: as ways of making philosophy, as useful tools. However, we shall also have one eye on how the images Bańkowski uses can be read both ways – that is, as both constructive *and* destructive of his theory; as ways in which his theory is both evocative and vulnerable. This is a side to images that, as discussed above, is most present in how Le Doeuff uses images to read philosophical texts. I hope that paying attention to both faces of images will help us get a little closer to the way Bańkowski thinks, and thereby articulate the uniqueness and importance of his theoretical work.

Finally, by way of preliminary matters, it ought to be noted that there are others who have noticed that Bańkowski has often drawn on – often thought in – images; indeed, often also taught in that way. Peter Goodrich, for example, observed that Bańkowski's 'teaching took place at the level of images' (Goodrich 2002: 441). Goodrich also observes, in relation to *Images of Law* (1976), that there is an

12 A more complete engagement with Bańkowski's work would look not only at the way he uses images to evoke encounters, but also at how he uses parables. That parables can be read as facilitating encounters in his work is clear from the way he himself talks about them; for example, 'The parable as an invitation to undertake a risky journey paying attention to the sometimes startling twists and turns of the stories – unsure of where they will lead us' (Bańkowski 2007b: 19). For more on parables, see also Bańkowski and Davis 2000, esp. p. 47, where Bańkowski and Claire Davis speak of 'parabolic discourse' as 'the discourse of mutuality', creating and maintaining a tension between law and love. Elsewhere, he also notes that the power of parables is that they are at once 'stories about mundane, ordinary, everyday events', and, at the same time, somewhat blasphemous, they unsettle, thereby opening up 'a middle' that we find both familiar and uncomfortable (Bańkowski 1998: 158–9). For a discussion of parables in legal reasoning, drawing in part on Bańkowski's work, see Chapter 13 in this volume by John Bell.

evocative image on the inside front cover of that book (an image of a faceless judge) – an image that Goodrich says makes room for 'graffiti' (see Goodrich 2002: 441). Goodrich's observations are helpful, but perhaps we should not make too much of either the use of the language of 'images' in the title of that book or the image of the judge.[13] It is arguably only later, when Bańkowski found his own distinctive voice (culminating in *Living Lawfully*, 2001), that images came to the fore in his style.

Masks and Robbers

In the early 1980s, Bańkowski was still a self-proclaimed anarchist, but already by then this was an anarchism that had matured over the years. In a paper delectably entitled 'Law Left Right Behind' (1984), Bańkowski noted explicitly that, as he saw it, jurisprudence was 'about the construction of morally acceptable societies' (Bańkowski 1984: 364), adding that both socialism and liberalism shared certain basic interests; that is, of 'looking at which ways of living together are morally and practically possible' (Bańkowski 1984: 375). It must, then, be remembered that Bańkowski's anarchism was never nihilistic, or even pessimistic: it was always a morally responsible, morally engaged, morally serious anarchism. But it was still anarchism, and in that vein, the view was one that expressed great suspicion (to say the least) of authority, or, more broadly, of ways of living together where the vision of a few was imposed on the lives of many.

This suspicion is best expressed in a range of images, but in particular via the imagery of masks and robbers. Consider the following:

> Law then is a robbery and involves the domination of the few over the many. As a way of organising social life it is itself corrupting. This is because it prevents sympathy and fellow feeling from coming through. It feeds on itself creating more crime and legal apparatuses which in turn solidify the power of those experts controlling them, preventing people from acting directly but rather through the coils and excuses of the law. It is, then, an aspect of domination and authoritarianism. Many legal ways of trying to change society are unhelpful because they retain the domination of law. This confirms the power of experts who would know best how to run a society and so prevents any direct political action leading to the anarchist ideal of a self-managed society. Action towards this end is prevented by going through law and the experts. People give up their own power to those who control the society and the law. (Bańkowski 1983, 272–3)

13 Both (or so it has been reported to me by Bańkowski) were instigated by the publishers: the book was originally to be called 'Perspectives on Law', and the title was changed partly as the result of inspiration from a book published at that time entitled *Images of Deviance* (Cohen 1975). The conclusion to this chapter returns to the issue of the differences between images (as thought objects) and pictures (such as precisely the 'image' in the inside front cover of *Images of Law*).

The imagery here is of robber-experts who exploit those below them – the workers, who are forced to work as slaves. But law is not merely a robbery, but also a mask, for it 'masks inequality' – indeed, its masking of inequality is 'what, fundamentally, is wrong with it' (Bańkowski 1983: 271). Again, notice that anarchism here is not the critique of order – any order, just for the sake of it – but only the kind of order that exploits and hides that exploitation, this being an order that is likely to be one where the ruler is positioned high above the masses, delegating his or her power to experts who maintain (for it is also in their interests to maintain) the ruler's ultimate and unassailable power.[14] Law, you might say, creates legal capital of which only the experts – the lawyers – can take advantage. Not only that, but law (so understood) is also 'morally corrupting for those who staff it' (Bańkowski 1983: 271). It does not matter how well-meaning those experts may be, or indeed how well-meaning any of the order's legal ideals may be: the point is that the very organisation of power is such that 'legal ideals ... create situations where solutions to political problems are taken outside of people and given to the external force of law' (Bańkowski 1983: 274).

Notice that the imagery here combines basic spatio-temporal forms – being on the outside of and below the order – with more specific images, namely those of robbers and masks. This top-down versus bottom-up opposition (precisely a kind of framing, to recall one of La Caze's functions for images) is still very much with us in theories of regulation, and indeed arguably, much depends in one's legal and political theory on whether one's temperament pushes more in the direction of qualifying and disciplining authority imagined to be top-down, or in the direction of enabling and respecting the emergence of order, bottom-up. Back in the 1980s, Bańkowski's emphasis was very much against top-down and in favour of bottom-up. He combined his critique of top-down authority with an argument for the virtues of a form of organization that emerges from the bottom up and focuses on the quality of horizontal (and not vertical) relations. What Bańkowski was searching for here was some kind of 'social anarchism'. He found it in anarchist-friendly communities, such as anarchist collectives and workers' councils. It is, he said, 'these "forms of sociality" that ... should be studied and emulated in order to see how a society might be democratised' (Bańkowski 1983: 288). Accordingly, the central problem was not (as Marxists thought) the mode of production, but rather 'domination':

> Domination is the central problem for it is domination, according to anarchists, that prevents the finding of the true community where objective human value can be expressed. A true human morality, they claim, is only possible when relations of superiority and inferiority no longer exist and shared community is possible. The more dominance is rooted out the more likely this community is to

14 As Bańkowski explains, the word 'anarchism' stems not from 'no order' but from 'no ruler' (Bańkowski 1983: 270).

> come into being and people will be enabled to live in groups which express both their individualism and their society. (Bańkowski 1983: 288)

The reference to democratization of governance, and to the importance of the 'participation of all actors, direct and indirect, from the community' (Bańkowski 1983: 287) again illustrates just how serious and responsible was Bańkowski's anarchism. It was not born out of a flippant or adolescent distrust of authority – it was no mere suspicion or some kind of hatred of power – but rather a deeply engaged, and characteristically personal, commitment to the construction of morally and practically defensible ways of living together, which Bańkowski then felt was best exemplified in the 'anarchist dream of an order of people taking part in their own solutions' (Bańkowski 1983: 285–6), protected from the theft and illusions of professionalized law.

The Attack of the Machines

Machines feature widely in Bańkowski's work. One finds, of course, computers and their programming codes, and these appear frequently whenever there is a discussion of what it means to live under rules (notice already here the shift from living under 'rulers' to living under 'rules'). Machines are present early on. For example, in the Bańkowski's paper entitled 'Anarchism, Marxism and the Critique of Law', he refers to lawyers as a 'skilled professional cohort ... running its machine' (1983: 285). Machines feature prominently not only in the title, but also in the substance of his Inaugural Lecture in Edinburgh: 'Law, Love and Computers' (1996). Perhaps the most famous of all machines to feature in his work is the ATM machine that does not care about you and your needs; the machine is not 'interested in your actual needs and wants', but 'just that representative of you, the card' (Bańkowski 1998: 145). You can beg and plead all you like with the ATM machine: it will remain there, motionless, expressionless, unable to respond to any of your gesticulations, ignoring all of your particularity. The machine, in short, does not care 'about you but only about you as represented in the rules' (Bańkowski 1998: 145).

Notice that this image of the unresponsive ATM machine is double-edged. It is true that the machine cannot hear people beg and plead and take their actual needs and wants into consideration. But it is also true that if it did do so – not only to us, but also to others in our situation – then the machine would quickly run out of cash, such that if you were in credit in your account, and you came – expecting legitimately for money to be given you – and the machine did not, you too would feel you had been treated unfairly (in your particular circumstances). Here you, the particular you in credit, would suffer as a result of those particular others who were not. Notice that it does not work to say that the person with credit in his account is likely to suffer less than one who has run out of money: both could be in a serious predicament. Here, what we see is the image leaking – that is, both promoting a certain message and at the same time undermining itself – this being an echo of what was said above, on the back of Le Doeuff's account, about images working both for and against any argument or position.

Writing later, together with Burkhard Schafer, Bańkowski acknowledges that 'sometimes not thinking about it and thus behaving like an automaton is in some situations appropriate and acceptable' (Bańkowski and Schafer 2007: 43). There are advantages in systems like the ATM machine: 'they can't be bribed, they are neutral, unbiased and consistent, they are predictable and so make it easier for us to live a life in accordance to the law' (Bańkowski and Schafer 2007: 46). But there are all the above-hinted at costs too: 'they are also crude and inflexible, often brutal and not open to critical reason' (Bańkowski and Schafer 2007: 46). The mature point, then, is that we need them – we could not govern on the basis of responsiveness to every single particularity – but also that we need to tame them; stop them from overtaking us or dominating to such an extent that particularity is lost sight of completely. This, of course, is the difference between legalism and legality: legalism is that realm of power exercised effectively by machines or machine-like processes, whereas legality is that form of organization where legal institutions are disciplined by rules and associated processes (that family of universals and universalization) but not so much as to collapse into legalism (Bańkowski and Schafer 2007: 49).

Is the ATM machine destined to be an image of legalism, or might it be revised to bring it closer to legality? One could imagine, perhaps, a system where, in the event one was out of credit, one could press a button and make a claim to a human bank official that one's life was in danger and one needed a certain amount (imagine that a limit was given of £100, repayable within three working days). This may still appear harsh, but the point is that an attempt is being made to prevent legalism from taking over – of combining the heartless application of universals, with the empathic respect for the particular. No doubt, this revised image too can be undermined, turned back on itself. We are back, once again, into the paradoxical realm of images that Le Doeuff identified.

Hungry Tigers

Tigers often crop up around the vicinity of ATM machines. There are those tigers that roam free in the wild, and those held in zoos. Those held in zoos suffer in two ways: first, they may suffer simply because they rely on the zoo staff to look after them and the staff perform their jobs negligently; or, second, they suffer because they lose their particularity – that is, they become an example of a species rather than a particular tiger.[15]

15 Typically, in zoos, animals are given names – for example, Tom, the tiger; perhaps Bańkowski would say that this is like a mask, an illusion, helping to make us feel better about stripping the animal of its particularity, though it could also be seen as an attempt to give back some of that particularity (as if it was ours to give or take).

The tiger appears in Bańkowski's work in the context of the difficulties involved in coming face-to-face with – rather than running away from – particulars. How do we confront the tiger? If we confront the tiger only in the zoo, it is likely that we shall be confronting that tiger precisely as a member – perhaps an exemplary member – of the species. If we do that, we shall not see the tiger – that particular tiger – but see only the universal. But how else can we confront not just the tiger as an exemplar, but that particular tiger? Well, we could do so in the wild, but then, as Bańkowski points out, this 'might be terrifying and frightful and not even good for us; the tiger could eat us' (Bańkowski 1998: 141). As he says elsewhere, 'If we were to meet a tiger [in the wild], standing in awe and marvelling at the mystery of its ontology would not be an option' (Bańkowski 2006: 30). Such encounters cannot be easy – if they are, it is likely we are standing too far back, protecting ourselves in some way from the sparkle or glare of the particular. But encountering the particular – as anxious as it makes us – is not all about bravery; it is in part about bravery (not standing too far back, or one would not be able to have an encounter at all), but also in part about avoiding foolishness, about being responsible, about taking care (standing back sufficiently to be out of the danger zone). Finding this balance between the glare of the particular and the protection of the universal is what is required – precisely, for example, in the case of judicial reasoning (see Bańkowski 2006).

It might seem at first that the universal is only about protecting oneself (for example, from the tiger). But, in fact, it is also about protecting the tiger. For tigers, like many other animals, are often more scared of human beings than human beings are of them; certainly, human beings – especially collectively – can do a great deal more damage to tigers than tigers can to them. It is not a good thing for a tiger to eat a human being: from that moment, that tiger is likely to be marked in the community as a threat to be destroyed, rather than a beautiful, wild animal with which to share one's environment (though at a respectful distance). We do not face a choice between being eaten by a tiger and putting one in a zoo. Of course, this is not at odds with the image in Bańkowski's work. But it does help us to see that striving for that balance (including among the judiciary) is not just about one's own personal growth, but about the protection of the vulnerable, and thus ultimately about the flourishing of care and respect for all in the community. Expanded in this way, the image of the (hungry) tiger is a particular fruitful one; a fertile image that orients the reader, while also remaining open to being further developed by the reader. Images, then, perhaps might also enable a philosophical work to be more interactive than is traditionally the case.

Robo-Judges, Robo-Citizens

What happens to people – whether officials, such as judges, or simply citizens – who do not face the anxiety of, and take care in, encountering the particular? The short answer is that they become Robo-Judges, or Robo-Citizens. The former feature often in Bańkowski's discussion of the virtues of judging, including the virtues of judicial institutions. For all of Bańkowski's sensitivity to the personal – to the 'existential', as he sometimes calls it (see Bańkowski 2006: 23) – this is never at the cost of neglecting the institutional. Indeed, his work is marked by asking a very distinct question – a form of question that really marks him out as a practical philosopher – namely: 'what sort of institutional arrangements this [or that life, e.g. the judicial life] can be embedded in so as to contribute to the good of that person and others?' (Bańkowski 2006: 23; see also Bańkowski 2007a). The personal and the institutional are merged in Bańkowski's work: the point is to examine – both critically and constructively – the form of life that certain institutions attract. There is no determinism here – but there is a warning, inscribed precisely in the image of the Robo-Judge (see Bańkowski 2006: 27), that there are certain institutional arrangements, and perhaps combined with certain frames of mind or certain attitudes, that can make it more likely than not that one will judge much too mechanically, and in the end simply badly. Not heeding the warning, a judge becomes a Robo-Judge when he or she is 'transformed into a machine that is the agent of the universal law, programmed to apply that law whenever the conditions for its application are met' (Bańkowski 2006: 27). This is a judge that can never hear – does not allow him/herself to hear – the call of justice (as Simone Weil put it: see Weil 2005 [1957]); and thus a judge that does not allow the system to encounter the particular – the particular call of the person pleading before the law – to help the system grow (a judge, you might say, that turns into an unresponsive ATM machine).

As we shall see shortly, this warning does not stand alone: it is mixed with an acknowledgment that we cannot have judges confronting such particulars perpetually; it also includes awareness of the fact that universals and universalization – disciplining oneself by universalizing one's behaviour (What if everyone did that? What if everyone did that to me?), and sometimes simply committing to certain rules (for example, the rules of chess) – is also required. As Bańkowski says, 'Kant's theory [with all its emphasis on universals and universalization] makes sense when we actually do find ourselves among a sea of desire and need to discipline ourselves' – but the point is, to paraphrase, that we can also become victims of discipline (see Bańkowski 2006: 28). The point, if you like, is that the answer is not available before the encounter: we have rules and the universalization process, and these are useful and often vital disciplining devices (which, to recall, not only help to discipline the judge, but can also protect the vulnerable), but we cannot enter into the courtroom determined to apply such, and only such, rules no matter what, or to look for only those facts we currently understand the rules to cover. What is wrong with the Robo-Judge is that he or she cannot experience anxiety – the anxiety of not being able to determine the outcome, of things being able to be changed precisely as a result of the encounter (Bańkowski 2006: 24).

The warnings addressed to judges can also be addressed aptly to citizens. As Bańkowski and Burkhard Schafer later wrote, legalism manifests itself not only in the 'judge or bureaucrat applying blindly the rule even if he considers the outcome unjust', but also in 'the citizen who accepts the restriction the law places upon him uncritically, even if he considers them damaging, and finally the claimant who insists on his rights even if he is not in need of a positive decision, and realises that his win is society's loss' (Bańkowski and Schafer 2007: 32).[16] We can have 'Legalistic rule obedience, legalistic litigation, and legalistic adjudication'; all these are 'facets of legalism' (Bańkowski and Schafer 2007: 32). The health of the community, if you like, depends as much on the wise courage of the judge, as it does on the wise courage of the citizen: both are prone to a disavowal of responsibility,[17] of hiding away from the need to exercise their critical-reflective practical reason *vis-à-vis* the law.[18]

Tuning In

What can judges and citizens, who do not wish to become Robo-Judges or Robo-Citizens, do? Well, it is important to see that part of the answer to this question is to ask a different question: namely, to ask what kind of institutional arrangements do we need to enable encounters with particularity, without destroying the protection offered by universals? We shall examine this throw-back question in a moment, but for now let us say that there is plenty that judges and citizens can do. As one example, they can prepare themselves to exercise 'attention' or 'watchfulness'.

Bańkowski's engagement with the notion of attention draws greatly on the work of Simone Weil and, after her, Iris Murdoch. The specific character of this attention is, in Bańkowski's own words, a 'caring and anxious attention', almost a kind of anxiety, though not a passive, defeatist anxiety, but rather a 'creative and loving anxiety' (Bańkowski 2006: 36). It is a kind of attention that lets 'the story speak for itself' and is not 'too quick to apply closure by imposing a principle or pattern on it' (Bańkowski 2006: 36). It is an attitude that can be genuinely surprised by what another says or does; it is not that tired complacency or world-weariness of someone who feels they have devoured all the books of wisdom. You might say it is an active waiting (connected, as Bańkowski notes, to the French verb 'attendre', to wait for: Bańkowski 2006: 32) – a looking out for, but not to be able to see only what one has always or previously seen. Watchfulness, in turn – a term that Bańkowski takes from the work of A.N. Shytov (2001), also points to the

16 There is a little paradox to mention here as to the very possibility of blind application. In his earlier writings – for example, Bańkowski (1983), he relies on the 'fact' that the law always requires interpretation to show that it can never be (as some of the proponents of liberal legality assert it can be) neutral and equal. Here, he relies on the 'fact' that the law can be applied blindly to argue that we must design institutions, and train judges, to have the ability and courage to face the particular. Perhaps the point is not that there can be blind application, but just that there can be thoughtless interpretation.

17 See Veitch (2007).

18 See Delacroix (2006).

importance of 'stillness and alertness', of this unique mix of the passive and the active (see, for example, Bańkowski 2006: 32).

At one point in the discussion of both attention and watchfulness, Bańkowski mentions the task of 'tuning in a radio' (Bańkowski 2006: 32). One can think of this image in a number of different ways (this being important, given what was said about Le Doeuff's take on images): first, as a way of tuning into one's favourite radio station, not bothering to listen to any others, rushing past them to find that familiar frequency (which would undermine the way Bańkowski presumably wishes the image to work); or second, as a process of moving the dial slowly, carefully, picking up on frequencies that are unfamiliar to one and tasting them (which would be much more – forgive the pun – in tune with his argument). The exercise of attention and watchfulness might be explored through this image: of the slow movement of the dial, of the occasional pause. Notice that this kind of tuning does not dismiss the particularity of the listener, because it combines the exploration of what is being heard with the listener's own tastes. The point is not to say that one must sit and listen to each radio station for half an hour at a time – that is a kind of moralism that is unhelpful. But there is something to be said for the listener who is able to move the dial slowly and explore different sounds, different tunes and different beats – and thereby to educate, and potentially transform, the range of his or her listening.

Acrobatics, Pyrotechnics

Bańkowski's judges are open – as Bańkowski's law is open – to what he refers to variously as 'leaps', or 'explosions', or 'flashes' or 'sparks' of 'love', or 'compassion', or 'brotherhood', or 'creativity'. He speaks, for example, of 'that spark of creativity that is necessary for a satisfactory existence and is represented by love' (Bańkowski 1997: 65). He speaks too of 'flashes of compassion', referring, in this case, to Raymond Gaita's (2000) description of the Soviet show trials, as depicted in *The Confession*, a film by Costa Gavras, in which a prisoner accidentally drops his trousers and there is, finally, some recognition of his humanity in the judge's sympathy (see Bańkowski 2007b). There are also 'explosions of love', which we need, he says, 'to get to the particular and be able to see the thing behind the rule' (Bańkowski 1998: 146). Finally, there is 'the creative leap of the imagination', which, he says, lies 'at the base of the system of reasoning' he advocates – leaps that may be facilitated, for example, by 'reasoning based on analogy, employing perhaps allegory or metaphor,[19] that enable us to move

19 For more on the importance of metaphor, as Bańkowski understands it, see Mary Hesse (Hesse 1987); also Bańkowski 1994. As Bańkowski says, paraphrasing Hesse, 'A metaphor is like a strange noise coming from the jungle. It has no meaning for us but it may advance our understanding. It might make us go into the jungle and discover a new species of bird' (Bańkowski 1994: 264). In a way, this is a little like a parable: we take the parable as we would a boat out into the unknown, potentially stumbling on new lands.

beyond a tradition and to import and export ideas between traditions' (Bańkowski 1995: 188–9). Leaps may also take another form, as when we take a leap of faith that others will give up their cars in the name of reducing traffic and pollution (in circumstances where we do not how others will behave), even though, in formal models of rationality, it would not be rational to do so (see Bańkowski 2007b).

We need courage to leap or to face the explosions of love, and it is a courage that must often give itself up, renouncing control of the outcome of the situation – only then might we receive that spark of creativity, or find ourselves responding, perhaps despite ourselves, compassionately (as was, arguably, the case with the judge in the Soviet show trial who at first mocked the prisoner with the rest of the crowd, but then found room for sympathy).

Bańkowski's vision of personhood and identity, then, is one where we must be continually open to change. At the heart of identity, perhaps somewhat paradoxically, is change – or better, an attitude of readiness to change.[20] If we care for ourselves – if we are lovingly anxious about our souls – we will be open to the explosions, flashes and sparks of others, of all that is unfamiliar to us. Care for the self is not a matter of keeping fenced in what one has accumulated, defending it proudly against all comers. Certainly, one can have the pride that accompanies keeping in good order what one has learnt (tending one's garden, as it were), but even this requires a sense of forward-looking development (preparing things, readying them). The mark of the self, in this view, is vulnerability, especially vulnerability to being transformed in unexpected ways (one might say, more strongly, that the self begins when it realizes that it is vulnerable to being affected by others). When we are not being so transformed, we are looking at ourselves – as honestly as we can, acknowledging the pain we might have – and preparing ourselves (for example, by being able, willing and ready to criticize how we came to the beliefs we hold) for transformation. This holds as much for ourselves as individuals as it does for ourselves in a community (for example, a community with certain beliefs about what is right or wrong, or what is just).[21]

Bridges and Acid

All this, you might say, is all well and good on the personal level, but what about the institutional? Here, as has already been observed above, is where Bańkowski comes into his own. It is in how he combines the personal, the existential, with the institutional that he finds his voice, and makes the greatest contribution to practical philosophy. There are two images we can speak of in this context. The first is

20 Bańkowski says: 'We must all be alive to the permanent possibility of changing our minds, that we can never take the rule as a fixed reason for our doing something' (Bańkowski 1995: 61). This attitude of readiness to change is closely connected with what we will consider later – namely, a process of exchange.

21 For a brief and insightful discussion of this theme in relation to Zenon's work, see Bell 2004.

that of a bridge, or, more accurately, 'bridging institutions'. The second is what Bańkowski refers to as 'lay acid'. The two are closely linked: the best examples of bridging institutions are those that infuse the system with lay acid.

Recall the argument institutions need to enable thoughtfulness, attention, watchfulness – to not allow its members to become mechanical, blind, automatic; the need for institutions to foster encounters with the particular, or the 'outside', as Bańkowski often calls it. How do we, as he asks in a different way, help the system to stop and 'rethink or recalibrate?' (Bańkowski 2006: 37). We can do this by incorporating lay justice into the system. Juries, for example, can be seen as

> a way of sensitising the court to the other impulse that comes in from the outside ... [they offer] something that would help the judges to pay attention and be watchful. The lay elements could be seen as ways of randomly stopping the inexorable universal logic of the law and forcing the court to reconsider, to reconfigure the system in the event of a decision that seems to subvert the system. (Bańkowski 2006: 37)

Institutional devices such as juries are precisely 'bridging institutions'; they are institutions that create the 'social equivalent of anxiety, the "moment of hesitation"' (Bańkowski 2006: 37) or 'the "interval of hesitation" when we see our common humanity, [when] we pay attention to the person' (Bańkowski 2007b).

Perhaps the best examples of these bridging institutions that infuse lay acid into the system come from the study conducted by Bańkowski, together with several co-authors, into 'lay justice' in Scotland (Bańkowski et al. 1987). In this book, as Bańkowski describes it later,

> we found that the lay justices did not subvert the official system, but rather by and large operated within its parameters. But that was not to be viewed as saying that we found that Lay Justice (the outside) was thereby subverted. Rather, one could see the whole thing as one with the lay element being seen as the opening to the outside and providing a constant steam of potential input. (Bańkowski 2004: 42–3)

Juries and lay justices are two examples of such institutions, but Bańkowski's work contains others – for example, he points to the work of Hugh Collins on how 'courts seek a climate of opinion' in their rules of standing, thereby introducing procedural devices (for example, class actions, *amicus curiae* briefs) that 'subvert[ ] the formal rationality of the law' (Bańkowski 1998: 162; see Collins 1986).

There is no doubt that Zenon's work on bridging institutions that infuse the system with lay acid is an important contribution to practical philosophy; it certainly deserves a great deal more attention than it has received thus far. Arguably, this contribution becomes clearer when we draw on the images of bridging institutions and lay acid – though, one might want to ask (in the spirit of Le Doeuff): do the bridging institutions not also need to be protected against complacency; do they not need internal bridges, as it were? Can the use of lay justice not become altogether too predictable, so that the system learns to incorporate it, without allowing it to shake its foundations? Can the system, in other words, become, over time, resistant to acid? Such questions suggest that no institutions or initiatives are in themselves bridge-like or acid-like, but that they can be, for a time, and then we need to exercise our institutional imaginations once again.

Finnish on the Loudspeaker

In his earlier work in the 1980s, Bańkowski was not complimentary about the contractualization of social relationships. He said, for example: 'Law helps to construct the automatic man necessary for the automatic production processes of modern capitalism. In this sense legal relations are the relations of a capitalist society and contractual relations of this sort best fit capitalist society' (Bańkowski 1983: 281). This was the stage in Bańkowski's thinking during which law was still being seen as opposed to, rather than as ideally in tension with, love. So contractual relations were false, illusory and morally corrupting, because they replace genuine love or fellow feeling with rights and duties, thereby forgetting or downgrading people's feelings (Bańkowski 1983: 282). This did not mean – even back then for Bańkowski – that 'all we need is love'; what we needed, he said, was 'a community where human feelings can be rationally expressed' (Bańkowski 1983: 283), with the punch-line being that the law could not create such a community: it gave people freedom (of a kind – for example, contractual freedom), but this freedom was gained 'at the cost of losing our souls' (Bańkowski 1983: 282).

Later, Bańkowski approached the issue differently. He began, as he did when he thought about judges – that is, with 'an individual's existential position' – and from there he looked at the 'institutional and social arrangements in commercial society' (Bańkowski 2007a: 194). This time, he argued that 'law is an essential element in the way we connect with people through our stepping outside our closed and circumscribed confines and giving ourselves to them. And it is in this mutual encounter that we also find good and value ... Law is inscribed in that giving and taking' (Bańkowski 2007a: 206). The imagery of giving *and* taking is vital: there must be mutuality of regard and vulnerability in the encounter/exchange. It is not enough, for example, for the exchange to be simply a matter of party 1 wanting party 2's B and party 2 wanting party 1's A. Rather: 'party 1 wants that s/he shall have B and that party 2 shall have A. The converse holds for party 2. It is in this exchange that equality is reached' (Bańkowski 2007a: 203).

Notice that this emphasis on mutuality in exchange also protects differentiation: it is neither assumed nor thought ideal that the parties are alike, or that they share underlying norms or values. The parties do not have to understand each other *ab initio*; on the contrary, they are different from each other, and it is those differences that bring communication alive between them. Even when we hear a language we do not understand – Bańkowski has a wonderful image here of hearing Finnish coming through a loudspeaker (see Bańkowski 1994: 264) – even then we do not experience it as 'pure noise, but an act of communication' (Bańkowski 1994: 264). Again, exchange protects differentiation, and communication is born not of sameness, but of difference. Of course, setting things up in a way that is protective of difference does mean that we are bound to misunderstand each other on occasion, but the likelihood of such occasional misunderstanding should not persuade us to scepticism about other minds: 'We have,' Bańkowski says, challenging the sceptic, 'direct access to each other. The fact that it is vague and prone to error does not mean it is not direct' (Bańkowski 1994: 264). Equally, though, our having 'direct access', does not mean our access cannot be questioned, that we cannot have doubts about it (this is not scepticism, but simply critical self-reflection). Furthermore, being protective of difference does not mean giving up on unity. Unity can (but does not have to) emerge from this network of exchanges. As Bańkowski says in a paper with Burkhard Schafer, 'The unity is the constant cross-cutting of these mutually interlocking spheres which do not have to be broken down into homogeneous states' (Bańkowski and Schafer 2004: 496). The emphasis, as so often in Bańkowski's work, is on the quality of horizontal relations: 'Union or collectivity is an emerging property, stemming from the interactions of the individual units and then changing and being changed by them in a flux of never-ending horizontal interactions' (Bańkowski and Schafer 2004: 499).

There are a number of ethical dimensions to any such encounter/exchange. It takes courage to be able to both give and take, and take in the sense of being ready and willing to be given anything by the other. It also takes courage to allow oneself to be vulnerable – not to try to control the exchange – while at the same time being active enough, curious enough, to pursue communication with another we may find difficult to understand. This is no idealistic picture, no 'love is all we need' version of interaction, no pure encounter with a particular – rather, it is the articulation of a careful, somewhat anxious, attitude, and one that is able to combine the 'actual experience of encountering' another (as other) with 'the ability of translating that into principle' (see Bańkowski 2004: 40).[22]

This image of thick exchanges, as we might call them, based on acts of communication and mutual regard that are respectful of mutual vulnerability in conditions of difference, with the contingent potential for the emergence of unity, is an important contribution to our understanding of social interaction, and deserves further theoretical attention.[23] It is, as so much of Bańkowski's work,

22 Here, Bańkowski draws on Scott Veitch's important observation that the encounter between Leo Tolstoy's Davout and Pierre (in *War and Peace*) is not just about encountering another person, but about being able to see that encounter in the context of 'a commonality of principle, that they are like brothers and that they should love brothers' (Bańkowski 2004: 40); see also Veitch 1998.

23 One sees it, arguably, in the work of Z.D. Gurevitch, who speaks of the way we need to have, in interaction, an ability to *not* understand each other (see, for example,

a unique blend of explanatory and normative layers: it looks at what is possible (often exploring that by letting images do the talking), and then selects, out of the realm of possibility, what is to be preferred (methodologically, then, we thereby do not have an opposition between the 'is' and the 'ought', but rather a creative dialogue between possibility and preference).

Curtains, Borderlands and Doorsteps

Bańkowski's work is peppered with a variety of images that can be understood as helping us to see the need for both law and love, for a dialogue and tension between them. One of the most arresting of these is the image of the very heavy curtain. Consider this passage:

> We can … think of the form of reasoning described here as operating in a sphere the middle of which is barred by a thick, almost opaque curtain. You sometimes dimly see through it other things that might be important. You lift the curtain to look but the curtain is extremely heavy and you cannot hold the curtain up for long. But the point is that it is one sphere altogether with this internal separation. It is not two completely separate spheres loosely joined together but each excluding the other. So law is both following the universal and rational rules and, at the same time, being open to the outside of passion and love. But the two elements articulate to make one whole and the outside is in an important sense inside. (Bańkowski 2004: 36)

The extremely heavy curtain lies in the middle of what is one sphere: what we call, for convenience, the 'outside', but is not really outside, for it cannot be; the point is that the system needs it as much as it needs the 'inside'. 'The system' is not an autonomous entity that is interrupted occasionally or brushed up against by another autonomous entity – rather, we have overlapping spheres, constant exchanges, purported acts of communication, surprises and renewals of expectations, and all this is as much a part of each sphere as anything that might more readily be identified with it.

Another related, and equally arresting, image is that of the borderlands: as the image suggests, it too is positioned in the middle, in that space between two lands. Here is how Bańkowski refers to this image in the context of theorizing identity:

> When I define myself as Polish, I appear thereby to exclude because I say that I am Polish and thus not German. But I also include Germanness into the definition

Gurevitch 1988; interestingly, Paul Schiff Berman has recently drawn on Gurevitch in his impressive account entitled *Global Legal Pluralism*, 2012 – this being another example of a theorist constructing a link between the personal and the institutional). It has also been seen, very recently, in the work of Anthony Simon Laden on reasoning, particularly in what he calls 'the authority of connection' (see Laden 2012).

> by calling myself a European (and we are both Europeans). In thinking of myself as a Polish European, I thereby include in myself that that I am not (German) because that is part of being European and that changes my conception of being Polish, German and European. And in this way my identity becomes one that is formed in its emerging from the fluctuating negotiations at the border posts of these identities (see Bańkowski and Christodoulidis 1998). So that which I am not is also part of what I am – that distinction however is not static but is subject to negotiation for at that boundary, that Grenzestelle, is where we might say that the outside is brought in; where what is not law, welfare, need, etc., comes in to leaven and change the law. (Bańkowski 2004: 37)

The borderlands are fertile – they are the forgotten or neglected spaces of modernity, for they disappear from our vision if we focus too much on who has what, or on defining, too sharply, where lies what you have and what I have, or on asserting too strongly – shouting, rather than whispering – who I am and who you are. And it is not just me and you, or all of us, who grow at the border; it is also law: 'Law is an institution which at its boundaries always tests itself by a creative encounter with the outside' (Bańkowski 2007a: 194). The image of the borderland is extraordinarily powerful one – I shall not dwell on it further here, for it is one that Bańkowski and I have thought about together, collecting images of borders of various kinds, identifying and examining the cultures and practices of what happens in those spaces.[24]

Consider, finally, one more image of 'the middle', that place that is 'ambiguous and tension ridden because it is there we stake ourselves and our vulnerability is exposed … [a space that] is risky and unsettled' (Bańkowski 2007b). This image is that of the doorstep ('na progu' in Polish). On the doorstep, one can either be looking in,[25] or looking out.[26] Ideally, one would have an image of a person looking both in and out on the doorstep (perhaps we would need René Magritte to portray that). In such a picture, we would have two faces, two kinds of courage: there would be the courage to look out, to face that anxiety and difficulty of all that we find unfamiliar and strange, uncomfortable and risky, and there would also be the courage to look in, and to allow that experience of the outside to transform us, to

---

24 This paper, which has been presented at a number of conferences, is entitled 'Images of Borders and the Politics and Legality of Identity' (Bańkowski and Del Mar, unpublished) and is available on request.

25 See http://commons.wikimedia.org/wiki/File:Bilinska-Bohdanowiczowa.BretonkaNaProguDomu.1889.jpg, accessed 21 December 2012. This painting (oil on canvas) is entitled 'Bretonka na progu domu [Breton Woman standing on a doorstep]', and is by Anna Bilińska-Bohdanowiczowa (1857–93). It is exhibited in the National Museum in Warsaw, Poland.

26 See http://jv.gilead.org.il/zydorczak/images/liw_%2820%29.jpg. This is a drawing that is part of a series by George Roux where he illustrated scenes from Jules Verne's *Sans dessus dessous [The Purchase of the North Pole]*, 1889. There are various contemporary editions of this with Roux's illustrations.

reflect and consider how it has changed us, to rummage about and confront what we have hidden away – often because it is too painful.

I finish there, with this image of the doorstep, because it is also one that Bańkowski and I have considered together,[27] and one that has stayed with me, and often returns to me, precisely as a result of thinking about it together with him.

Conclusion

The 'images' used in the preceding section were, strictly speaking, pictures rather than images. There is a difference: as thoughts rather than material objects, images are arguably more ambiguous and abstract than pictures. Of course, one can have pictures that are more like images than, say, photographs (though, equally, one can have photographs that are very ambiguous and abstract). A more rigorous metaphilosophy would systematize these terms, throwing in also examples and narratives, and analysing carefully the different roles these play in philosophy (both in the process and in the result of philosophical thinking). As used here, images can appear in a wide variety of forms – for example, they can be quite starkly and thinly spatio-temporal (bottom-up or top-down) or they can be thick and meaty (for example, hungry tigers or unresponsive ATM machines). Corresponding to this wide variety of forms, images also have a wide variety of functions they can perform – expressing, enframing or persuading, and perhaps also enabling greater interaction with the reader. In all these ways, images allow philosophy to be built – they are constructive; like islands of belief dotting the oceans of doubt. Understood in this way, images are powerful implements in the toolbox of the jurist. But images, as Le Doeuff has reminded us, are also sources of anxiety. Images can be read upside down and inside out, thereby to some extent undermining the theory that they helped to build. Images, then, can make a theory – and a theorist – particularly vulnerable: they expose the theorist, and the theory, just where it is most sincere, where it has struggled to bare its soul. Perhaps that is why there are so many images in Bańkowski's work. Bańkowski's philosophy is a deeply personal one. Even his most concrete institutional recommendations are shot through with the heady storms of self-scrutiny. Perhaps, then, it is because he has not shirked from confronting the anxieties of his soul that his theory is such a rich imaginary.

Bibliography

Arendt, H. 1964. *Eichmann in Jerusalem: A Report on the Banality of Evil.* London: Penguin.

Arendt, H. 1971a. *The Life of the Mind.* San Diego, CA: Harcourt.

27 See Bańkowski and Del Mar 2008.

Arendt, H. 1971b. 'Thinking and Moral Considerations: A Lecture'. *Social Research,* 38(3): 417–46.

Bańkowski, Z. 1983. 'Anarchism, Marxism and the Critique of Law'. In D. Sugarman (ed.), *Legality, Ideology and the State*. London: Academic Press, 267–92.

Bańkowski, Z. 1984. 'Law Left Right Behind'. *UNSW Law Journal,* 7: 362–76.

Bańkowski, Z. 1994. 'How Does It Feel to Be on Your Own? The Person in Sight of Autopoeisis'. *Ratio Juris*, 7(2): 254–66.

Bańkowski, Z. 1995. 'Analogical Reasoning and Legal Institutions'. In Z. Bańkowski et al. (eds), *Informatics and the Foundations of Legal Reasoning*. Dordrecht: Kluwer Academic Publishers, 177–90.

Bańkowski, Z. 1996. 'Law, Love and Computers'. *Edinburgh Law Review,* 1(1): 25–42.

Bańkowski, Z. 1997. 'Nie Pozwalam'. In A. Aarnio et al. (eds), *Justice, Morality and Society*. Lund: Jurisforlaget I Lund, 53–68.

Bańkowski, Z. 1998. 'Parable and Analogy: The Universal and the Particular in Common Law'. *Acta Juridica*, 138–63.

Bańkowski, Z. 2001. *Living Lawfully: Love in Law and Law in Love*. Dordrecht: Kluwer Academic Publishers.

Bańkowski, Z. 2004. 'Legal Reasoning from the Inside Out'. In T. Biernat et al. (eds), *Stressing Legal Decisions*. Kraków: Polpress, 27–46.

Bańkowski, Z. 2006. 'In the Judgement Space: The Judge and the Anxiety of the Encounter'. In Z. Bańkowski and J. MacLean (eds), *The Universal and the Particular in Legal Reasoning*. Farnham, Surrey: Ashgate, 23–38.

Bańkowski, Z. 2007a. 'Bringing the Outside In: The Ethical Life of Legal Institutions'. In T. Gizbert-Studnicki and J. Stelmach (eds), *Law and Legal Cultures in the 21st Century*. Warsaw: Oficyna, 193–217.

Bańkowski, Z. 2007b. 'The Risk of Reconciliation'. In S. Veitch (ed.), *Law and the Politics of Reconciliation*. Farnham, Surrey: Ashgate, 49–68.

Bańkowski, Z. 2011. 'The Long Goodbye: (a) Life In and Out of the Law', Valedictory Lecture, School of Law, University of Edinburgh.

Bańkowski, Z. and Christodoulidis, E. 1998. 'The European Union as an Essentially Contested Project'. *European Law Journal*, 4(4): 341–54.

Bańkowski, Z. and Davis, C. 2000. 'Living In and Out of the Law'. In P. Oliver, S. Douglas-Scott and V. Tadros (eds), *Faith in Law: Essays in Legal Theory*. Oxford: Hart Publishing, 33–51.

Bańkowski, Z. and Del Mar, M. 2008. 'Na Progu [On the Doorstep]'. *No Foundations: Journal of Extreme Legal Positivism*, 5: 142–4.

Bańkowski, Z. and Del Mar, M. 2009. 'Images of Borders and the Politics and Legality of Identity', Unpublished draft delivered at conferences in St. Andrews and Edinburgh, 2009.

Bańkowski, Z. and Del Mar, M. 2011. 'The Torch of Art and the Sword of Law: between Particularity and Universality'. In O. Ben-Dor (ed.), *Law and Art: Ethics, Aesthetics and Justice*. London: Routledge, 163–74.

Bańkowski, Z. and Del Mar, M. (eds) 2013. *The Moral Imagination and the Legal Life: Beyond Text in Legal Education*. Farnham, Surrey: Ashgate.
Bańkowski, Z. and Mungham, G. 1976. *Images of Law*. London: Routledge & Kegan Paul.
Bańkowski, Z. and Schafer, B. 2004. 'Emerging Legal Orders: Formalism and the Theory of Legal Integration'. *Ratio Juris*, 16(4): 486–505.
Bańkowski, Z. and Schafer, B. 2007. 'Double-Click Justice: Legalism in the Computer Age'. *Legisprudence*, 1(1): 31–49.
Bańkowski, Z., Del Mar, M. and Maharg, P. (eds) 2013. *The Arts and the Legal Academy: Beyond Text in Legal Education*. Farnham, Surrey: Ashgate.
Bańkowski, Z., Hutton, N.R. and McManus, J.J. 1987. *Lay Justice?* Edinburgh: T & T Clark.
Bell, J. 2004. 'The Perspective of the Ordinary Citizen on Law'. *Res Publica,* 10: 311–17.
Berman, P.S. 2012. *Global Legal Pluralism*. Cambridge: Cambridge University Press.
Brandom, R.B. 2011. *Perspectives on Pragmatism: Classical, Recent and Contemporary*. Cambridge, MA: Harvard University Press.
Cohen, S. 1975. *Images of Deviance*. London: Penguin.
Collins, H. 1986. 'Democracy and Adjudication'. In N. MacCormick and P. Birks (eds), *The Legal Mind: Essays for Tony Honoré*. Oxford: Oxford University Press.
Delacroix, S. 2006. *Legal Norms and Normativity*. Oxford: Hart Publishing.
Deutscher, M. (ed.). 2000. *Michele Le Doeuff: Operative Philosophy and Imaginary Practice*. Amherst, NY: Humanity Books.
Gaita, R. 2000. *A Common Humanity: Thinking about Love and Truth and Justice*. London: Routledge.
Goodrich, P. 2002. 'Zenotypes: On the Modes of Reproduction of Critical Lawyers'. *Social and Legal Studies,* 11(3): 425–43.
Gordon, J. 2007. 'In Plato's Image', in *Philosophy in Dialogue: Plato's Many Devices,* edited by G.A. Scott. Evanston: Northwestern University Press, 212–37.
Gurevitch, Z.D. 1988. 'The Other Side of Dialogue: On Making the Other Strange and the Experience of Otherness'. *American Journal of Sociology*, 93(5): 1179–99.
Hesse, M. 1987. 'Tropical Talk: The Myth of the Literal'. *Proceedings of the Aristotelian Society, Supplementary Volumes*, 61: 297–311.
Johnson, M. and Lakoff, G. 1990. *Metaphors We Live By*. Chicago, IL: University of Chicago Press.
Johnson, M. and Lakoff, G. 1999. *Philosophy in the Flesh: The Embodied Mind and Its Challenge to Western Thought*. New York: Basic Books.
La Caze, M. 2002. *The Analytic Imaginary*. Ithaca, NY: Cornell University Press.
Laden, A.S. 2012. *Reasoning: A Social Picture*. Oxford: Oxford University Press.

Le Doeuff, M. 1989. *The Philosophical Imaginary*. Trans. C. Gordon. London: The Athlone Press.

Murdoch, I. 1991. *Fire in the Sun*. London: Penguin.

Rose, G. 1992. *The Broken Middle*. London: Blackwell.

Shytov, A.N. 2001. *Conscience and Love in Making Judicial Decisions*. Dordrecht: Kluwer.

Smith, N.D. 2007. 'Plato's Book of Images'. In G.A. Scott (ed.), *Philosophy in Dialogue: Plato's Many Devices*. Evanston, IL: Northwestern University Press, 3–14.

Veitch, S. 1998. 'Doing Justice to Particulars'. In E. Christodoulidis (ed.), *Communitarianism and Citizenship*. Farnham, Surrey: Ashgate, 220–34.

Veitch, S. 2007. *Law and Irresponsibility: On the Legitimation of Human Suffering*. Abingdon, Oxon: Routledge-Cavendish.

Verne, J. 2001. *Sans dessus dessous*, illustrations by G. Roux. Toulouse: Editions Ombres.

Wanderer, J. 2008. *Robert Brandom*, Montreal: McGill University Press.

Weil, S. 2005 [1957]. 'Human Personality'. In S. Miles (ed.), *Simone Weil: An Anthology*. London: Penguin, 69–98.

Chapter 5
History in the Service of Life: Law's Authority and Dealing with the Past

Adam Czarnota

Introduction

In the essay 'On the Uses and Disadvantages of History for Life', written in 1874, Friedrich Nietzsche (1997: 47) argued that we need history, but only to the 'extent that history serves life'. Nietzsche distinguished between three human situations: acting, respecting others and suffering. On that basis he identified three different attitudes to history:

1. Monumental;
2. Critical; and
3. Archivist.

'Monumental' historiography presents history as an unbroken chain of great events, which together provides the basis for a glorious future. According to Nietzsche, that approach to history presents a danger – it distorts not only the past but through the past also distorts the present.

'Critical' historiography is a response to moral distress and represents a sort of 'tribunal' that 'judges and condemns' the past. This could also be a dangerous approach, since critical historiography runs the risk of becoming self-serving. After some time, critical historiography usually slides into becoming monumental. But the most important point made by Nietzsche is that preoccupation with a difficult past poses a danger to the present. Such a situation could block movement, paralyse people and endanger both the present and the future. So, it looks as though history in the service of life should find a delicate balance between remembering and forgetting.

An 'archivist' approach to history focuses on the detailed documentation of all the things that happened in the past.

At this point, someone might raise the question: what about history in the service of truth? It is a legitimate question but personally, since I am not professional historian, I do not believe that such a type of historiography can exist. This does not mean that I try to undermine the scholarly activities of professional historians, but I do believe that even their activities concerned with a reconstruction of the past is always based on some more-or-less spelt-out normative assumptions. These normative elements provide the criteria for the selection of facts. Forgetting is presupposed by the normative dimension of the world view at the same time, and the normative is about the present and the future, not so much about the past. Such an approach is similar to that of law. Law is an institutional mechanism for systematic remembering and systematic forgetting. But before I move on to law, and the role of legal institutions in dealing with the past, it is necessary to stress, following Nietzsche's suggestion that, if history's function is for life then forgetting cannot be the same as amnesia. Remembrance is there to remind us of the horrible atrocities committed in the past, in the service of life – that is, for the present and the future.

Modern political philosophy, especially liberalism, as a starting point accepted some timeless and abstract assumptions about human nature. This is true from John Locke through to John Rawls. Only one distinguished modern political philosopher, Judith Shklar, criticized such an approach and proposed instead to build liberal political philosophy on real historical experiences, and in particular on wrongdoing committed by people to people in peoples' name. Her proposal for liberalism is based on fear (Shklar 1984).

It looks as though the end of the twentieth century was a time for apologies for terrible things committed in that and former centuries. These are not only apologies for the Holocaust, genocide and war crimes, but also for colonization, the slave trade and so on. In. Central/Eastern Europe the ghosts of the past are still haunting people. This was noticed by external observers, such as Tina Rosenberg in her book, *The Haunted Lands* (1995). Some of these ghosts date from pre-communist times and new ones were added during the communist regimes. The question that nearly all societies asked themselves was: is it better to draw a line and cut off and forget the past, or to face the problem of the wrongdoing committed in the past?

Such a question is an important moral one, and answers to it differ in various societies. To a high degree the answer depends on the balance of political forces within the political elite. In each society there are usually mixed answers, which means that policies are adopted to cope with at least some elements of the difficult past. Nevertheless, it seems to me that if we think of history as in the service of life there must be a moral obligation to face in as open a way as possible the problems of the past. Each society, sooner or later, will be forced to acknowledge the ghosts of the past. Observing affairs in societies around the globe that did not face these problems openly at the outset, I came to adopt the historico-philosophical thesis that a difficult past can be suppressed for a time, but then will return and create more problems.

The Moral Obligation of Public Truth-Telling

There is always a problem with morality, especially now in late modernity or, as some people prefer to call it, postmodernity. Zygmunt Bauman, the eminent theoretician of the postmodern condition, has said that we live in a situation of 'ethics without morality' (Bauman 1993). What he meant is that it is nearly impossible to find moral norms that have universal status. Having said that, I want to propose an approach that is future-oriented. This is nothing new. Moral norms are always future-oriented – that is, they are norms of the vision of specific types of relations between people. Without making any a priori decisions about the substance of the norms, we could start from the point of view of democracy and civil society, asking the question 'What are the preconditions for such types of relations between people?' It seems that the idea of democracy is still alive in Central/Eastern Europe – but it is interpreted increasingly as a pluralism of political elites. The idea of civil society has disappeared in some way from political discourse – which is a pity. Nevertheless, if we enquire about the social roots of these two ideas (democracy and civil society), the answer is that they are in society: not only in its social and/or economic structures, which are certainly very important, but also in public morality.

Martin Krygier is a tireless advocate of the notion of civil society. He has been advocating that idea from Sydney and San Francisco/Berkeley to Warsaw and Toruń in Poland. Geography is important, but more important is Krygier's suggestion that we have to go back to basics – to the notion of civility. By civility he means 'routine non-predatory relations between people'.[1] They are not based on love, or other intimate relationships, but are simply civil. This means offering no violence or humiliation to others, including strangers. A similar idea was the essence of the Israeli philosopher Avishai Margalit's excellent book, *A Decent Society* (1996). The idea is good but still the question remains: what are the necessary but perhaps not sufficient preconditions for civility? I claim that one of the important elements is dealing with the difficult past for the sake of the present and the future.

Social relations based on civility exclude humiliation and hatred. A civil society based on civility must exclude social institutions which humiliate people. It is easy to decree such an institutional framework, but much more difficult to implement in real social life. What we learn from tragic recent history, especially in the twentieth century, is that average citizens were passive when the authorities implemented policies and laws against groups of fellow citizens. That is probably a dimension of what Hannah Arendt called the 'banality of evil'.[2] Such evil looks banal from the point of view of an external observer or analyst, but it is not banal for those who suffer. It means that victims, especially victims of so-called state crimes – which include the Holocaust, other genocides as well as killings, apartheid and abuse of the human rights and dignity of those who were victims, and also in some way the dignity of bystanders. The last category is the biggest one. The dignity of those who were just normal, average citizens was destroyed by the criminal regimes but also by their social passivity. By being passive, ordinary citizens acquiesce to state crimes. Such people usually did not commit any crime in an active way, and

1 See Krygier (1996–7); (1996a); (1996b); (1997 – esp. ch. 3: 'The Uses of Civility').

2 Arendt, H., *Eichmann in Jerusalem*, Penguin Classic, 2006.

they were not even always beneficiaries of the policies adopted by the criminal regimes. Nevertheless, by escaping to the comfort of their private life they did not save moral standards. That mechanism has been described by the Polish writer, Leon Kruczkowski.[3] I recall another Polish contemporary philosopher, Bronisław Łagowski, who coined the term 'reverse Machiavellianism' (Łagowski 2010). What he meant by this is that all victims, including bystanders, are corrupted by the public's non-morality.

We arrive, then, at the point where the distinction between public and private morality is important. In the contemporary world there is still value in such a distinction, but at the same time there is a growing connection between its two poles. In some situations, people cannot be moral in private without being active in public morality – that is, without adopting an *active* stance on principles of public morality.

At this point we arrive at the public morality issue. It is a big problem and I do not feel intellectually strong enough to solve it. Nevertheless, I think we can include some knowledge from psychoanalysis to support my claim about the necessity of public truth-telling.

To be brief, I shall recall some arguments put forward by a German scholar, a Professor of Political Sciences, Gesine Schwan (1998) in her article, 'The "Healing" Value of Truth-Telling: Chances and Social Conditions in Secularized World'. Schwan rightly argued that guilt-silencing has destructive potential in the form of what she called 'destructive splitting': 'perpetrators and bystanders who silenced their guilt were obliged to wall in, to various degrees, their emotional life, to deny parts of their past and present "reality". Their self-esteem and self-confidence were severely damaged, their personal relationships became cold and impersonal because they had to suffocate their spontaneity' (Schwan 1998: 728). Concerning the example of guilt-silencing in Germany after the Second World War, Schwan claimed that this 'destructive splitting' syndrome had been transferred to the next generation: children grow up in the distorted reality of their parents. Despite the fact that she focuses on private guilt-silencing, she draws public conclusions. The process of guilt-silencing

> undermined any possibility of an open perception of and confrontation with the 'real world' and a common understanding of social and political life, thus spoiling any chance of a new democratic common sense. This psychological legacy of the perpetrators' guilt-silencing diminished the readiness and capability of the next generation to take over responsibility, to practice their individuality as well as their sociability, to accept conflict as well as compromise, non-conformism as well as cooperation. It weakened or often destroyed their capacity to maintain reliable relationships, be they in the personal realm in their neighbourhoods, or for common political purposes. (Schwan 1998: 729)[4]

3 Kruczkowski, L., *Niemcy* (Germans), Sara, Katowice, 2003.

4 For an elaborated description and arguments, see Schwan (1997).

In other words, Schwan claimed that without facing a difficult past it is impossible to develop personalities suitable to expand and sustain democratic order. A necessary precondition for new personal and political communities is to face the past through truth-telling. Using Nietzsche's concept, history could work in the service of life. Truth-telling is not any type of talking about the past: it has to have a public character, and if possible also some degree of authority. Only such a type of repentance could create a proper structure for the development of new values and rebuilding a moral community that will be able actively to defend democracy and social and political freedoms.

For such a community it is not enough to preserve morality in the private sphere but it must also have public morality. By that I do not mean some new religion but rather an active involvement in public affairs. The best history book describing what has happened cannot do that – it is necessary to create the framework in which, through truth-telling, it would be possible to implant in collective memories subjective as well as objective reasons for what happened. Such a process will have therapeutic as well as democratic effects.

The late Adam Podgórecki, a renowned legal sociologist, for years proposed what he called global ethics – based on caring for all living beings and the Earth (1991: 59–61). I want to stress only one element it is possible to draw from his suggestions. The dominant moral norm is still about private morality: 'love your neighbour'. What we have learnt, especially in the twentieth century, is that to fulfil such a norm it is necessary to be active in defence of public morality. This is particularly important now in a time of globalization. Civil society is impossible without a certain, quite high, degree of civic society – that is, the active involvement of citizens in public life.

Avishai Margalit, in his Horkheimer's Lecture 'Morality of Memory', delivered at Frankfurt University (Margalit 2004), asked a very important question – is it possible to build on negative memory, to build on memory of wrongdoing? In other words, do not we always need some 'monumental' history in order to build a new political community? It is difficult to give one decisive answer, but we can say that if we start with the aim of reconciliation, it is necessary to remember as well as to forget and forgive. This is why legal institutions play an important role in such a difficult process as dealing with the past.

Legal Strategies for Dealing with the Past: An Overview

Law as a system of norms and institutions is a mechanism for systematic remembrance and forgetting. During the 2,000 years of the history of the Western legal tradition, a very impressive arsenal of techniques has been developed to remember, but also forget. One need only mention statutes of limitation, *nulla poena sine lege, nulla crimen sine lege*, principles of natural justice, and the Rule of Law. What is important is the fact that law possesses authority, and remembering as well as forgetting is approved by the authority of law. This means that individuals and groups can remember and not forgive, but will not be able to start a new legal action. That curious character of law, its peculiar institutional authority, plays an extremely important role in all possible strategies for dealing with the past.

After the change of regimes resulting from loss through war or negotiations, new elites have always faced the problem: what to do with wrongdoing in the past? The question is not so dramatic when the collapse of regimes is caused by revolution or defeat by an external power. The outcome is always condemnation of the past and the imposition of the victors' justice. Generally, criminal law is used in order to show the criminal character of the former regime, and show trials take the role of education for the new political and social community.

More interesting problems of dealing with the past are faced by the new political elites when a change in regime is achieved through negotiation. On the one hand, the old power is being recognized as a partner and is usually interested in granting itself general amnesty for past wrongdoing. On the other hand, there is pressure for justice and revenge coming from below, and from some factions within the new political elites. The adopted legal strategies are never perfect, but we could evaluate them from the above perspective – namely, their contribution to new normative values.

In every country there is a combination of retributive justice (criminal trials, lustration, decommunization) with restorative justice (reprivatization, rehabilitation of victims). It is impossible to point to any political and legal strategy that was focused on the creation of public discussion about the mechanism of operation of the communist regimes and the involvement of everyone in the sustaining of that regime. In other words, the focus is not on revenge and stigmatization, but on public truth-telling and reconciliation – on the entire society truly coming to terms with the past.

There is no doubt that those who committed crimes during the former regimes should face the law, and suffer punishment. At the same time, however, criminal law cannot play the role of public truth-telling and reconciliation. Mark Osiel (1997), an American socio-legal scholar, wrote a book in which he tried to show, on the basis of Argentinian examples, that criminal show trials (not in the Stalinist sense, but according to the rules of law, nevertheless with publicity) are able to implant liberal values in society and in particular the observance of human rights. He follows the theory of Emile Durkheim that, in modern societies, based mainly on organic solidarity (division of labour), the function of criminal law is the reinstatement of basic accepted values in society. I have doubts about this claim because of the limitations of criminal law and criminal procedure. Opening up the procedure would also open the space for the abuse of law. Even Osiel at one point confirmed that criminal law plays a limited role (1997: 230).

Communist regimes were based on control of society not only through the party cells in all factories and organizational units, but also permanent surveillance by the secret police and its collaborators. The scale was not the same in each country in the communist camp – some barracks were under more relaxed surveillance than others – but nevertheless the so-called 'problems of the files' exists. Legal strategies adopted by particular countries vary. The most radical was the strategy adopted in the former German Democratic Republic (DDR). Each person, and not only citizens, has a right to gain access to his/her own files with names of secret collaborators not erased. From the media we learn about the personal tragedies when brother spied on brother, or a husband on his wife. It is true that such a strategy cleans up the atmosphere but I do not think it stimulates public discussion about the mechanisms of the past and our involvement in sustaining the regime. It still has a private character. It is a private citizen having access to his/her file through the so-called Gauck Commission. In one of the interviews given to the Polish weekly magazine *Wprost*, Joachim Gauck (2000) said 'there is only one way to finish the problem with the files', meaning the way adopted by Germany. This could possibly stop the use of files in political battles and for short term political gains, but it does not have a healing potential for the entire society.

Other countries – such as, for example, Poland – adopted a middle-of-the-road approach, but already this seems to be too late. This approach is based on the separation of the archival substance of the secret services in the Institute for National Memory. Each citizen will have a right to apply to have access to his/her file, but the decision will be taken by some person on the basis of victimization. This will only create problems – how to operationalize that term victimization? Again, there is its private character – no national debate. Already, the nomination of the chairperson of the Institute is the object of purely political manipulation.

Other legal strategies such as decommunization and lustration also play a very limited role in societies dealing with the past. It is easy to understand security reasons behind the lustration of state officials, but generally the entire process has failed everywhere. For those not familiar with the term lustration in Central/Eastern Europe, it refers to the process of screening people from the point of view of their collaboration with communist secret services to prevent them from occupying certain public positions. It has been used mainly in political battles and for political gain. Lustration and decommunization also play the role of curtailing discourse on the operation of the communist system. Instead of serious societal discussion, it limits the discourse by showing a few scapegoats. Of course, the level of responsibility of the members of the Politburo was higher than that of members of the Communist Party, but if we think about facing the difficult past in the service of life, all levels of responsibility and operation of the system must be objects of the process on societal discussion. The question remains: is this possible? In some parts of the world there were attempts to do precisely that. I mean the so-called truth commissions, and in particular the most comprehensive process of facing the difficult past by South African society in the institutional form of the Truth and Reconciliation Commission (TRC), which last year tabled the report of its work.

Facing the Past as Constitutional Process

The Truth and Reconciliation Commission in South Africa was a unique institution for many reasons. From the legal point of view, because of its open-ended procedure and stress on reconciliation through public truth-telling, it represented what should be called a quasi-judicial body.

The TRC was established by an Act of the Parliament of the Republic of South Africa. I claim that from the very beginning the institutional design of the TRC was such as to prolong and extend the constitutional debate in South Africa. It is impossible to assess the role of the TRC outside constitutional politics and constitutional debate.

Transfer of power in South Africa took place in a negotiated transition. In the 'Postamble' to the Interim Constitution were suggestions regarding essential features of a future TRC. In the Postamble we read that facing the past should 'now be addressed on the basis that there is a need for understanding but not for vengeance, a need for reparation but not for retaliation, a need for *ubuntu* [a spirit of kinship] but not for victimization'.[5] The power of the TRC went well beyond any known model of truth commission. Its investigation was open and driven by public participation. It had a power to shape its enquiries and to enforce participation. The report released in 1998 (in five volumes)[6] was intended to lead to institutional reforms and reparation to victims. Once the TRC has been disbanded, its work will continue through a body known as the Institute for Change, Memory and Reconciliation.

The Commission was split into three committees: the Human Rights Violations Committee; the Amnesty Committee; and the Reparation and Rehabilitation Committee. In addition, the TRC has an investigating unit with police powers of search and seizure, and the TRC itself has the authority to subpoena witnesses to appear before it.

The TRC's activities were threefold:

1. To unveil the truth about how apartheid worked between 1 March 1960 and 10 May 1994.
2. To build a foundation for reconciliation through truth. From that position, retributive justice was put aside in the hope that the truth would emerge through a process of collective enquiry and debate.
3. To proceed so that knowledge received through enquiries would help to rebuild the institutional framework of government.

The work of the TRC was based not on retributive justice but on reconstitutive justice – a type of justice that seeks institutional change through an examination of past wrongs.

---

5 See http://www.info.gov.za/documents/constitution/93cons.htm; accessed 16 December 2012.

6 See http://www.justice.gov.za/trc/report/index.htm; accessed 16 December 2012.

This is not the place for a comprehensive assessment and evaluation of the work of the TRC. It is only to show that such a quasi-legal institution could play a very important part in dealing with the past in the service of life.

The TRC exposed many apartheid atrocities and provided many former victims with the opportunity to tell their stories and achieve a certain catharsis. One interesting fact is that the TRC was not content with what it termed 'factual and objective truth', and referred to 'social or dialogue truth' established 'through interaction, discussion and debate', as well as 'narrative truth' – victims' statements, including 'perceptions, stories and myths' – and, finally, 'healing truth'. 'Healing truth' – 'the kind ... that places facts and what they mean within the context of human relationships' – was, the TRC said, 'central' to its work.[7] In this way, the TRC was able to expand the public discourse. This was possible because of its character as a quasi-judicial institution. Normally, law by its nature restricts discourse. Only one commissioner, Wynand Malan, entered a minority report,[8] asserting that the TRC had not stuck to 'factual truth' but relied instead on its other three kinds of truth and a great deal of hearsay.

The TRC relied principally on the data provided by some 21,300 uncorroborated victim statements. There were 7,127 amnesty statements which did have to be verified, though only 1.4 per cent of them had been by the time the TRC came to its conclusions about culpability. The TRC itself actively sought out many victims and then concentrated all its attention on the 9,980 killings they proceeded to recount. Of these, the TRC concluded, the police were responsible for 2,700, the ANC for 1,300 and Inkatha for 4,500 – leaving 1,480 killings unexplained. It is interesting that the TRC also conducted so-called structural hearings regarding the role of business, media, the legal profession, the medical profession, the army, police and so on – on their role in the sustaining of apartheid.

To discover the really new element in the TRC as a special institution to deal with the past we have to remember that the Nuremberg Trials were an extremely flawed exercise. France's attempt to deal with its traitors and collaborators, and to face up to what was perpetrated by the Vichy Government and its allies was even more badly handled. The arrest of Augusto Pinochet for human rights' violations suggested that the Chilean counterpart of South Africa's attempt at Truth and Reconciliation had left some fundamental problems unsolved.

One critic wrote:

> Societies that try to resolve recent social traumas by quasi-legal procedures seem always to make a mess of it. The only satisfactory way to deal with such situations would be to assemble a large and expert task force of professional historians, lawyers and policeman, tell them to avoid grandstanding and give

---

7 See http://www.justice.gov.za/trc/report/finalreport/Volume%201.pdf, 115; accessed 16 December 2012.

8 See http://www.justice.gov.za/trc/report/finalreport/Volume5.pdf 436–56; accessed 16 December 2012.

> them ten years to report … There may be no way of disposing of painful history. The clerics tell us that we have to put it behind us if we want to get to heaven, but when it comes to history here on earth, maybe we have just got to live with it. (Johnson 1999)

Societies always have to live their lives with a difficult past but, for the reasons mentioned above, it is better to reveal than to embark on historical amnesia. The TRC did not fail. History is not something totally objective; there are always different historical narratives. The question is: how is it possible to cut off the most radical and antagonistic historical narratives? It appears that the authority of law is needed. South Africa embarked on the creation of a new type of quasi-judicial institution which at least attempted to face the problem – when at the same time other societies – richer, and perhaps more democratic – did not made any attempt to do that.

One of the commissioners expressed a widely-held opinion when he said that the aim of the TRC was to produce 'a publicly sanctioned history' which 'can be taught in schools' to the exclusion of 'contradictory versions'. This does not mean that such a history has to be necessarily a good thing, but my interpretation of that statement is that nobody will be able to deny what happened.

R.W. Johnson (1999: 23), who criticizes the TRC from a liberal, individualistic and legalistic position, also acknowledged that 'two great justifications for the existence of the TRC remain intact: that it allowed a good many victims and relatives of victims to tell their stories, and it made certain that no whites could be ignorant of what apartheid had meant'.

Conclusion

In conclusion, I would like to stress the point that law, because of its authority, has to play a role in dealing with the past.[9] Another point is that traditional legal mechanisms, based on retributive justice, are not good tools to deal with the past. There is a need for a new type of quasi-judicial institution.

Law as a mechanism for systematic remembering and forgetting in dealing with the past is always in the service of life – for a better present and future. The best way is to deal with the past as part of a constitutional process. As the moral and political philosopher, Hanna Fenichel Pitkin (1987: 168) says, constitutions are not only something that we *have* but they are also what we *are*, and more important, something that we *do*. By *do* she made reference to 'the action or activity of constituting – that is, of founding, framing and shaping something anew'. Legal dealing with the difficult past is part of 'what we do' – reshaping ourselves and our societies.

9 See the excellent summary of arguments in Sadurski (2001).

Bibliography

Bauman, Z. 1993. *Postmodern Ethics*. Oxford: Wiley Blackwell.

Gauck, J. 2000. 'Otwarty Rachunek' [Open Account]. *Wprost*, 36: 927.

Johnson, R.W. 1999. 'Why There Is No Easy Way to Dispose of Painful History'. *London Review of Books*, 21(20), 14 October: 23–5.

Krygier, M. 1996a. 'The Sources of Civil Society, Part 1'. *Quadrant*, October: 12–22.

Krygier, M. 1996b. 'The Sources of Civil Society, Part 2'. *Quadrant*, November: 26–32.

Krygier, M. 1996–7. 'Virtuous Circles: Antipodean Reflection on Power, Institutions and Civil Society'. *East European Politics and Societies*, Winter: 36–88.

Krygier, M. 1997. *Between Fear and Hope: Hybrid Thoughts on Public Values* (The 1997 Boyer Lectures). Sydney: ABC Books.

Łagowski, B. 2010. *Pochwala politycznej bierności* [Commending Political Passivity]. Warszawa: Sprawy polityczne.

Margalit, A. 1996. *The Decent Society*. Cambridge, MA: Harvard University Press.

Margalit, A. 2004. *The Ethic of Memory*. Cambridge, MA: Harvard University Press.

Nietzsche, F. 1997. *Untimely Meditations*, trans. R.J. Hollingdale. Cambridge: Cambridge University Press.

Osiel, M. 1997. *Mass Atrocity, Collective Memory, and the Law*. New Brunswick, NJ: Transaction Publishers.

Pitkin, H.F. 1987. 'The Idea of a Constitution'. *Journal of Legal Education*, 37: 167–71.

Podgórecki, A. 1991. *A Sociological Theory of Law*. Milan: Giuffre Editore.

Rosenberg, T. 1996. *The Haunted Land. Facing Europe's Ghosts after Communism*. New York: Vintage.

Sadurski, W. 2001. 'On the Relevance of Institutions and the Centrality of Constitutions in Postcommunist Transitions'. In Jan Zielonka (ed.), *Democratic Consolidation in Eastern Europe, Vol. 1: Institutional Engineering*. Oxford: Oxford University Press, 393–415.

Schwan, G. 1997. 'Politik und Schuld'[Policy and Debt]. In *Die uzerstorerische Macht des Schweigens*. Frankfurt/Main: Fisher-Verlag.

Schwan, G. 1998. 'The "Healing" Value of Truth-Telling: Chances and Social Conditions in Secularized World'. *Social Research*, 65(4): 725–40.

Shklar, J. 1984. 'The Liberalism of Fear'. In N.L. Rosenblum (ed.), *Liberalism and the Moral Life*. Cambridge, MA: Harvard University Press.

PART 2
Legality

Chapter 6
But to Live Inside the Law, You Must Be Honest[1]

Claudio Michelon

Introduction

A few years ago, when I was working at as a lawyer, I remember often being surprised by the ability that some of my more experienced colleagues displayed in finding solutions to complex problems that were far from obvious but which, in hindsight, seemed to everyone involved to be plainly correct. One of the many occasions on which I witnessed this happening was in the context of a meeting in which nine lawyers, from two different law firms, were discussing a trial court decision that ordered our common client to change aspects of its production line 'within 10 days of this decision's publication in the official gazette'. The decision was due to be published within a few days, but the client told us that implementing those changes would take approximately two months, which effectively meant that the company would have to halt production for at least 45 days (but possibly longer), at immense cost and competitive damage. We had spent the morning discussing how to deal with the situation. We pondered arguments about how to gain a staying effect for our impending appeal, and the timelines for obtaining the decision on that staying effect; we discussed the substance of competition law and how to bring it into the argument; we discussed procedural decisions by the São Paulo Appeal Court and by the Brazilian Federal Courts; and a plethora of other legal arguments. By 2.00 p.m. we had reached no conclusion on either how to proceed or how to advise our client on whether (and when) the company should halt production.

Then one of us thought of something. He realized the case had similarities with some aspects of the Brazilian law of injunctions (which was not, strictly speaking, applicable to the case at hand), according to which court orders that require a performance by the party needed to be notified in person, not by publication in the official gazette. If that could be extended to final decisions with the peculiar features of the one we were discussing, it would be safe to assume that our client would not need to halt production as ordered. We all thought that he was right, and the court later confirmed it, to the dismay of the other party.

1 I am thankful to Zenon Bańkowski, Felipe Oliveira de Souza and Maksymilian Del Mar for comments on early versions of this chapter.

What struck me then was that, after many hours of thinking, no solution had emerged, but as soon as this particular lawyer (one of the best litigation lawyers I have ever met) came up with the idea, it was clear to everyone that his thesis was not only a defensible argumentative line, but also the applicable law. As I said above, that was one of many occasions in which I witnessed that happening in legal practice. This chapter attempts to explain this capacity that the best lawyers and judges seem to develop, of perceiving what is not legally obvious, but turns out to be clearly correct.

I believe that one argument put forward by Zenon Bańkowski in *Living Lawfully* (2001) provides a crucial element for an appropriate philosophical account of legal decision-making that is able to explain that capacity. I am referring to Bańkowski's account of the dynamics between rule-following and the identification by the decision-maker of situations in which the rule should not be followed. The relevance of Bańkowski's account can only be properly understood if it is embedded within a more comprehensive, virtue-based approach to legal decision-making. In what follows I present the basic tenets of one such approach and, in doing so, hope to vindicate Bańkowski's claim that one needs to learn to break the law in order to fulfil it.

The chapter's argument starts with a brief discussion of the conceptual reasons why theories of virtue have had only a discreet impact within legal theory, and in particular, within the theory of legal decision-making. That brief account will help to identify the burdens of relevance a theory of virtue has to discharge in order to be taken seriously as being able to provide an appropriate account of legal decision-making. I then briefly explain, in the second section, Bańkowski's view on the relationship between rule-following and rule-breaking. In the third section, I introduce the conceptual tools I need to make sense of Bańkowski's suggestion in a legal context. I do so by analysing the perceptive aspect of prudence using the broader Thomistic 'inner senses', and by explaining how those inner senses generate both a zone of perceptual clarity and a peripheral perceptual zone. The final part of the chapter deals with some potential problems of translating this general model into the specific context of *legal* decision-making. I believe that much of the purchase of Bańkowski's theory comes precisely from its capacity to generate conceptual resources that allow for a smoother transition from the conceptual scaffolding that holds general *phronesis* (practical wisdom) together to a specifically legal conception of this.

Virtues and the Theory of Legal Decision-Making

The relatively weak impact that theories of virtue have had within the theory of legal reasoning relates to the widespread assumption that while virtues might be relevant as part of a more general theory of what constitutes a good moral character, it has little or nothing to say about right action.[2] Moreover, whatever it might have to say about right action seems to be derivative of a theory of good character. That is often seen, in turn, as a downplaying by virtue theorists of rule-governed behaviour. As Robert Louden put it almost 30 years ago when discussing virtue ethics: 'They [agent-centred accounts of ethics] are not concerned with portraying practical reason as a rule-governed enterprise which can be applied on a case-by-case basis' (1984: 229). This view of ethical theorists who attempt to offer a theory of virtue as a central (sometimes *the* central) component of ethics is not entirely unfounded. In fact, one does not have to go far to find passages within many canonical texts for virtue theorists that seem to support that reading. That seems to follow, for example, from Aristotle's opinion (expressed in many different contexts) that the moral perception/opinion of a good man is the measure against which actions can be regarded as being right or wrong.[3] In relation to practical wisdom (*phronesis*), in particular, most commentators rush to tell us that it is not to be understood as a rule-applying skill, as a capacity to grasp the right rules and apply them to the situation.[4] That said, one might conclude hastily: 'Theorists of virtue have no need for rules, then.'

If that were the case, one could see why legal theorists might have good reason to dismiss theories of virtue as being unable to shed any light on either law or legal practice. After all, if there is anything that most legal theorists can agree on, it is that rules, rule-following and action guidance are crucial features to the law. They might (and often do) disagree about what counts as rule-following, about what counts as a rule (or as a legal rule), about what lies beyond the rule, or about whether rule-following is only an appearance, but it is difficult to deny that accounting for rule-production and rule-following is a crucial part of what an explanation about the law would be. Hopes of using theories of virtue as tools to clarify law and legal reasoning would seem to lead to a dead end.

From the kind of picture painted by Louden, a third objection might be raised against using the concept of virtue as a tool to illuminate legal problems: virtue theorists focusing on character as a measure for right and wrong seems to go against the grain of the rule of law. One of the central aspects of the rule of law is that public authority is to be given only to officials reasoning from impersonal

---

2 Louden famously voices that opinion in no uncertain terms. He claims that 'it is commonplace that virtue theorists focus on good and bad agents rather than on right and wrong acts' (1984: 229).

3 See, for example, the following passages of the Nichomachean Ethics: III, 4, 1113a33–34; NE, X 5, 1176a16–18; and NE IX, 4 1166a13–14. In the first, Aristotle states that 'the good man differs from others most by seeing the truth in each class of things, being as it were, the norms and the measure of them'. In 1106b36, Aristotle affirms that the just mean is determined by the right reason, which is, in turn, defined by reference to the *phronimos* (Aristotle,1984: 1748). For an enlightening discussion of the *phronimos* as criterion, see Aubenque (1963: 33–41).

4 That often comes through in discussions of Aristotle's concept of deliberation (Russell 2011: 5).

normative standards, rather than from their personal opinion about right and wrong.

If Louden's account of virtue ethics were accurate, it might be appropriate to conclude that the conceptual tools generated by virtue theories would have very little to contribute to our understanding of the law. They would (i) have little or nothing to say about two of its central features (rule-following and the evaluation of actions); and (ii) would seem to go against a foundational value of modern law. The account is, however, inadequate.

As Daniel Russell has remarked, it is surprising that the idea that virtue ethics (and more broadly, virtue theory) deals only with character and not with criteria to judge the right action, was ever entertained (Russell 2009: 1). The canonical texts of virtue ethics are ripe with statements about the importance of performing the right action, as opposed to the idea of simply possessing virtue without acting (Aristotle 1984: 1732, at 1095b30), with the importance of action to learn virtue (Aristotle 1984: 1730, at 1095a1–6), and with actual criteria (at different levels of abstraction) of how to assess a wide range of possible actions (for example, the doctrine of the *mesotes*). I shall not dwell on this issue, as I believe Russell has already provided a clear account of how virtue ethics can deal with action (2009: 37–142).

In this chapter, my concern is to offer grounds to dispel the other two charges raised against virtue theory's potential to clarify law and legal reasoning, namely: (a) that it cannot offer any interesting insight about rule-following; and that (b) virtue ethics is too contaminated by personality and character to help us understand the impersonal ideals of the modern rule of law. To answer those charges, I will present in what follows a picture of legal reasoning (or at least of some of legal reasoning's central features), which explains how legal rule-following relates to (indeed, cannot be properly understood without) analytical tools provided by theories of virtue, and how this use of virtue theory can be made compatible with the necessary impersonality embodied in the ideal of the rule of law. Bańkowski in part anticipated this picture in the account of the relationship between rule-following and rule-breaking put forward in *Living Lawfully* (2001).

Rule-Following as a Pedagogical Concept

Unlike most contemporary legal philosophers, Bańkowski is not concerned primarily with solving minute technical problems that have been raised by a relatively narrow agenda, but is motivated by a deeply existential concern about the meaning of living a life dedicated, in one way or another, to 'the law'.

This question does not have a straightforward answer. Alasdair MacIntyre, one of the most influential contemporary theorists of virtue, and one of the few who has something to say about it, does not seem to believe that it is possible for contemporary lawyers to justify their professional engagement. According to him, the activity of a legal practitioner is one of the clearest examples of the fragmentation of the moral life that takes place in modernity (fragmentation that is even more perceptible in the experience of a citizen who tries to understand the juridical implication of his or her actions). In a culture largely dominated by experts, decisions about what to do are always connected to a certain activity (the activity of a bureaucrat, of a manager, of a lawyer) and, as MacIntyre argues, there would not be any overarching scheme capable of integrating these different activities. In his words, 'Ours is a culture dominated by experts, experts who profess to assist the rest of us, but who instead make us their victims. Among those experts by whom we are often victimized the most notable are perhaps the lawyers' (2000: 91).[5]

Bańkowski is not happy to explain the problem away by dismissing the life lived under modern law as a potential source of value. That, in turn, changes the way he approaches some of the many more specific problems he deals with in *Living Lawfully*. His discussions of, say, 'exclusionary reason' (a conceptual focus of many contemporary positivists),[6] integrity (a central concept in Dworkin's theory),[7] and institution (a central concept in MacCormick's theory)[8] are all considered to be unpacking aspects of the wider problem of a morally justifiable life. As John Bell put it:

> Much of analytical jurisprudence has focused on the limits of law – the distinctions between law and morals, legal rules and social rules, and so on. Bańkowski deliberately changes the focus. Instead of concentrating on the limits of law, he focuses on what it is like to live lawfully, to live in a manner which is fundamentally committed to the law and to the legal order. (Bell 2004: 311)

At the centre of Bańkowski's account of how to live lawfully lies the problem of the relationship between autonomy and heteronomy, and in particular, the way in which the legal decision-maker negotiates his/her way between them. This is not a question that has attracted much of virtue theory's attention. The superficial reason for this is that the problem, as it is perceived by those living within the political structures of most modern Western legal systems, is not a central concern of the classical sources used by contemporary virtue theorists. The deep reason relates to the particular context in which problems of autonomy and heteronomy appear

5 This was not the only occasion in which MacIntyre addressed the activity of contemporary lawyers as an expression of such fragmentation (see MacIntyre 2006: 198).

6 The literature on the so-called 'exclusionary reasons' stems from Joseph Raz's *Practical Reasons and Norms* (1990); and *The Morality of Freedom* (1986: 38).

7 The notion pervades Dworkin's theory of law, but is identified explicitly by him as the central value of the social practice we call law in *Law's Empire* (1991: chs 2, 6 and 7).

8 The notion of institutional fact as the central element to understanding law emerges in MacCormick's *Inaugural Lecture* at the University of Edinburgh (MacCormick 1974, reprinted in MacCormick and Weinberger 1986). One can find a revision and deepening of his institutional theory in his recent *Institutions of Law* (MacCormick 2007), esp. chs 1–4.

in modernity. One of the central features of the modern conception of law is that there should be a relatively strict institutional separation between law creation and law application, the absence of which is seen (from the seventeenth century onwards) either to contribute to the rise of despots[9] or else to be the very definition of despotism.[10]

The institutional context in which there is a relatively strict division of rational labour between law-creation and law-application institutions sits uncomfortably with the holistic conception of the virtuous rational agent. This uneasiness stems from the fact that any agent assigned a particular role in those institutions (say a judge in charge of applying the law he or she has not created) would have to outsource part of his/her decision-making process. If the traditional thesis of the unity of virtue[11] is correct, how can one be eligible to apply the rules, while being considered ineligible to create them? Moreover, how can the judge apply the rules whose creation he or she would not have supported? In this context, one aspect of the autonomy/heteronomy tension comes to the fore more saliently.

In fact, there are two paradigmatic ways in which the tension between autonomy and heteronomy manifests itself. It might present itself as (a) a competition between the best judgements of two agents. This tension is external to each agent's reasoning in the sense that each is charged with producing a complete process of reasoning (identifying/enacting principles they will themselves apply). Alternatively, it might also present itself as (b) a tension between agents deciding within the context of an institution responsible for the application of a (legal) standard created by another institution and over which the first institution has no revoking or re-creating roles. The division of reasoning labour mentioned above between law creation and law application, so prominent in the post-enlightenment political environment, brings the latter tension to the fore. That tension expresses itself in a number of different ways. The persistent problem of the limits of legal interpretation, and the corresponding (and oscillating) denunciations of judicial usurpation of political power and of judicial formalist passivity, are just the clearest manifestation of a deep anxiety caused by the need to insulate law creation from law application.[12]

Bańkowski's suggestion of how to reconcile the autonomy and heteronomy of the decision-maker in contexts in which rule-application and rule-creation are conceptually and institutionally separated lies midway between two opposite ideal

9 For example, in Montesquieu's famous discussion of the 'English Constitution' in Book 11, chapter of *L'espirit des Lois* (1748: 311–34).

10 Kant, for example, considers the central feature of the Republican (whose alternative is the despotic government) is the separation of executive from legislative power (Kant 1996: 324, at 8: 352).

11 For a discussion of the thesis, see section below, 'Virtuous Legal Decision-Making…'.

12 Other manifestations include the constitutional debate about judicial control of legislation, and the debate on the role of legal doctrine and the limits of its creativity.

types. On the one hand, Bańkowski's suggestion rejects the conception of legal reasoning as a set of interpretative methods aimed at purging the legal opinion of the subjectivity of the decision-maker. On the other hand, Bańkowski rejects the conclusion that there is no specifically legal form of practical reasoning (and the reduction of legal reasoning to other registers of practical reasoning such as political reasoning or economical reasoning). By contrast, Bańkowski argues that repeated rule-following would (*ceteris paribus*) generate in the agent the capacity to perceive in which cases the strict application of a rule would be at odds with the law. In his conception of legal decision-making, heteronomous rule-following shapes the agent's character in such a way that he or she becomes a *subject* capable of perceiving when the strict application of the rule should be excepted. As he puts it, when discussing Abraham's disquieting willingness to break the law and obey God's command to slay his son:

> Why and how does he know that it is right now to change and break that law? One of the reasons is paradoxical – it is precisely because he led a life of faith according to the law. Precisely because he was someone who followed the laws, who knew and applied them, was he able to recognise when there was an exceptional pattern and be able to change them. So his act of creation, his act of creativity, in breaking the law and recreating it, stems in the end from the structured life he led under the law. In that sense, his act of love makes the law, but that is only possible because he follows the rules and the laws. (Bańkowski 2001: 77–8)

In this passage, Bańkowski is not simply stating that, when following the rules, we internalise them and consequently become more able to discriminate in future cases because these rules are printed indelibly in our minds. He is claiming something bolder and more interesting: to follow the rules and principles faithfully affects the agent in such a way that he or she becomes able to recognize when cases that lie squarely within the semantic reach of the rule or principle should be placed outside its sphere of application.

Bańkowski's contention that one learns to discern patterns by behaving in a way that is primarily rule-oriented resonates with the Aristotelian pedagogy of virtue. For Aristotle, one does not learn virtue from teaching, but from habit (Aristotle 1984: 1737, at 1099b9 ff) and, while habit can be developed in a number of ways, it often evolves through a strict adherence to rules. In the tradition of virtue ethics, as we saw above, strict rule-following is not the final goal of human moral growth, but it can (indeed must) be a stage in the process of acquiring virtue, something that is useful for the *encratic* (continent) character, but not to the *phronimos* (the practically wise).[13] But Bańkowski's argument does more than make a simple translation of that aspect of virtue ethics into the legal context. It suggests a way to understand the role of *phronesis* in social contexts heavily marked by

13 On the distinction in Aristotle, see the interesting discussion in ch. 8 of MacIntyre's *Whose Justice? Which Rationality?* (1988, 124 ff, in particular 136–8).

the institutional division of labour between law-creation and law-application, in which the decision-maker working at the application level is partially insulated from the law-creation moment. That insulation generates the awkward situation of the decision-maker following rules which might not be conductive to the development of his/her virtue *tout court* (and whose observance, arguably, might even hinder the development of certain virtues or aspects of it). That situation is a result of the fact that the separation between law-creation and law-application, and the fractioning of practical reasoning in that way, serves an objective that is not related directly to the enhancement of the flourishing of the decision-maker. Instead, the separation is designed institutionally to make public decision-making less personal in at least two different ways: (a) the point of the separation is not the flourishing of the decision-maker; rather, (b) its point is to limit the role of the decision-maker's subjectivity in the application process.

In that context, Bańkowski's suggestion that rule-following teaches us to perceive patterns (and the deviation form patterns) beyond what is explicitly stated in the rule might help to explain how rule-application might be dependent on the decision-maker's subjectivity, while at the same time being impersonal.

Bańkowski does not, however, provide a complete explanation of *how* and *why* rule-following would be able to shape the agent's subjectivity in such ways. The next section provides the conceptual context (the *how* and *why*) that makes sense of Bańkowski's pedagogical conception of rule-following and, in doing so, I hope to produce a framework within which the subjectivity of decision-makers regains protagonism in theories of decision-making. I hope the next section will also make clear how the proposed framework opens up new possibilities for the pedagogy of legal decision-making beyond Bańkowski's suggestion.

The Construction of a Peripheral Conceptual Perception

My attempt to provide such a framework is centred on the unpacking of the concept of *phronesis*. Aristotelian practical wisdom is often thought to be a form of insight that allows the decision-maker to intuit the right answer to some practical predicament. This very general conception of practical wisdom is not very useful for our purposes here. The investigation of practical wisdom that is needed for the task at hand starts by identifying some of its component parts. In fact, practical wisdom is a combination of a number of faculties, abilities or forms of perception, which could, at least in principle, be understood separately and arguably be possessed separately. The bundle is held together in a division of reasoning labour whose *thelos* is the performance of the right action. For our investigation on how the experience of rule-following might help to sharpen the decision-maker's ability to identify when a case which apparently falls under a particular rule should be excepted (or when the rule should be extended to a situation not clearly covered by it), we should focus on one of practical wisdom's elements: its perceptual aspect (or, rather, one of its aspects).

Phronetic perception does not refer simply to raw data streams gathered by the senses (whatever those would look like), but to conceptual perception; that is, to the perception of something *as something*. In fact, within the Aristotelian tradition, the senses are not conceptually passive but instead have a preliminary ordering role that see the data streams *as something* even before the operation of our more specific reasoning capacities. Aquinas has provided a very useful account of that ordering role of perception in his theory of the inner senses, which I described in more detail elsewhere (Michelon 2012). In short, Aquinas believed that there were four inner senses that organise data streams into Gestalts – that is, into totalities of meaning, and which are, *mutatis mutandis*, shared between ourselves and other beings gifted with perception, notably animals (McCabe 2008: 123–7). So when a lamb looks at a wolf it sees more than simply the wolf's colour or shape: it sees a wolf and senses a source of danger. In those animals that reason, the inner senses provide the preliminary organization without which reason would not be able to deal with the particulars of the situation. For our purposes it is important to bear in mind that those inner senses are at least in part acquired. This becomes clear when we analyse each of the inner senses (*communis*, *imaginatio*, *aestimativus*[14] and sense-memory) and the interplay between them.[15] The *sensus communis* allows us to see Gestalts of meaning in what would otherwise be unordered sense data. It is responsible for our seeing a tiger (to use one of Bańkowski's favourite examples) instead of localized orangeness, blackness and whiteness. Those Gestalts on which the data streams are organized can change (both by addition and subtraction) through the subject's own experiences. Moreover, they include both physical objects and cultural and, in particular, institutional objects (we do not only see tigers, but contracts, courts and so on). But that evolution can only be explained because there is another aspect of our inner senses that is able to store the Gestalts as part of the individual's intellectual patrimony: that is the job performed by *imaginatio*. The remaining two senses perform similar roles in relation to assessments of the relationship between the Gestalts identified by the *communis* and the perceiving subject (an object might be perceived as 'valuable' or as 'dangerous') and the retention of those assessments. So, in conclusion, what Aquinas brings to this discussion is (a) a more active and ordering conception of perception; and one in which (b) perception can evolve through experience and training.

The investigation of the ways in which those changes to our perceptual framework occur, in particular in relation to perceiving aspects of complex social and institutional realities, is not a simple task. At the broadest level one might be satisfied with an explanation such as Aristotle's thesis according to which virtue

14 In humans, the *aestimativa* is called by Aquinas *cogitativa*, to emphasise the capacity that human beings have to acquire their *aestimativa* by comparisons (and not only by instinct, as it occurs in other animals).

15 What follows is a sketch of the relatively brief discussion in *Summa Theologiae* 1a, question 78, article 4 (Aquinas 1970: 134–43).

(and presumably also the intellectual virtue of *phronesis*) is acquired through experience. What that means is that we acquire our Gestalts primarily as a result of directly experiencing events in our lives. That is not the only route open to the agent, and one of the ways in which literature relates to the formation of a moral character is by providing narratives with which the reader can relate, such as those contained in novels and fairy tales (Nussbaum 1995: 4–10). Now direct experience, novels and fairy tales (and other human artefacts) are not specifically legal, and while they might have a role to play in legal decision-making, they would not be able to account for my law firm colleague's ability to perceive the instant case as being 'relevantly similar' to another set of legal cases in such a strikingly appropriate (yet previously unknown) way.

Before we go on to investigate the legal ways in which the sort of sense-perception I have been describing plays out in specifically legal contexts, it is important to keep in mind that it is not enough for the agent to be exposed to the transformative experiences that could potentially shape his or her perceptive framework: those events need to be engaged with in certain ways. The ability to engage with such events in appropriate ways is a result of the agent possessing certain intellectual virtues. Though this is not the place to provide a complete account of those virtues, it is important for my purposes here to understand from what those virtues guard the practical intellect. The enemy of intellectual virtues in general is 'perceptual rigidity' (Roberts and Wood 2007: 202–4).[16] As discussed above, an agent's sense-perception changes as the Gestalts through which his or her inner senses organize the world change as a result of experience. As those Gestalts accumulate and become progressively more complex, the temptation of the agent's practical intellect (and of the theoretical intellect, if Roberts and Wood are correct), is to find a resting place beyond which it becomes resistant to further change. This rigidity effectively prevents the agent from improving the ways in which his or her perception orders the particulars in a number of contexts. Though this prevents the agent's growth, perceptual rigidity might be functional in certain contexts. Bańkowski himself gives us a number of examples of situations in which the mechanical application of rules is functionally better than trying to reopen the discussions that informed the introduction of the rule.

Within the context of practical reasoning, there are two distinctly troubling consequences of that rigidity. First, perceptual rigidity inhibits the perceptual framework stored by *imaginatio* and *sense-memory* from changing, thus encumbering further elaboration of the perceptual scheme. Change is not impossible, as the rational agent might still perceive the need for further elaboration by the operation of reason on the materials gathered by the senses. However, other ways in which a stabilized framework could be challenged (in particular, what I will

16 16 While I borrow their phrase here, the overlap between what I mean by it and what Roberts and Wood mean is only partial, given the fact that there is only partial coincidence between what I call a perceptual scheme and what they call perception (or acquaintance).

refer to bellow as 'peripheral conceptual perception') are foreclosed by perceptual rigidity. Second, and more important for our purposes, that rigidity might prevent the agent from seeing an aspect of the case that could lead to a different conclusion about what is the required action. Those consequences (learning impairment and aspect blindness) are of different orders: the former is a problem for the pedagogy of practical wisdom, while the latter is a problem for practical wisdom as performed in particular decision-making. The avoidance of perceptual rigidity is a matter of the agent possessing the relevant intellectual virtues, but a detailed discussion of these virtues here would distract from my main argument.[17] It is more relevant to analyse further how those perceptual frameworks constituted by our inner senses operate.

My suggestion is that those perceptual frameworks generate both (a) a zone of conceptual perceptual clarity, within which stimuli are ordered according to familiar Gestalts; and (b) a peripheral zone of conceptual perception. The latter is what explains how practical wisdom is able to alert the agent to the oddness of a situation that seems to fall squarely within (or outside) the rule. This peripheral perceptual zone provokes an irritation in the inner sense's ordering of the sense data, which points towards a possible shortcoming on his/her perceptual framework. This peripheral perceptual zone develops in at least two ways. First, because an agent's overall perceptual framework is always developed by his/her experience, and that in turn occurs only within particular contexts, the peripheral perception might be triggered by perceiving something *relevantly* unusual in a new context on to which we project our perceptual framework. This, in fact, seems to be the core of Bańkowski's case for how repeated rule-following enhances an agent's ability to recognize when it is appropriate to challenge the ordering of the facts inherited by the habit of repeatedly applying the rule. Second, in complex perceptual frameworks it might be the case that one's peripheral perception is triggered by the excitement of parts of the conceptual framework which, while not being immediately relevant to the situation at hand, are perceived as being relevantly similar to it. This seems to be the way in which my colleague perceived an aspect of the law of injunctions that would not normally be relevant to the particular case under investigation.

Maksymilian Del Mar, commenting on an early version of this chapter, raised an objection that helped me to develop my argument further. His objection was essentially that both in my account of moral perception and, more specifically, in my running example, perception seems to have moved so far from sensory perception as to make it an ability of a different kind. My lawyer friend's insight does not seem to Del Mar to be connected primarily to something he perceives through his senses; it seems to be more akin to an intellectual requalification of something already perceived through the senses 'as something else'. That in

17 Aquinas not only put forward a list of the constitutive elements of *prudentia*, among which feature openness to be taught, and caution, but he also offered clear evidence of previous work attempting to identify those constitutive parts.

turn makes the example a case of a capability of identifying a non-immediate relevant similarity, rather than one of the perception of an irritation that moves the decision-maker beyond the available frames of reference, into the void, as it were. While I am not convinced that my friend was not relying on sense data (of *institutional* facts, such as the 'judicial decision', which he sees in the paper in front of him), I believe Del Mar is right in thinking that there might be two different abilities here (each of which points to different decisional phenomena). On the one hand, there is the requalification of certain perceived features of a situation; while on the other, the perception of an irritation that does not point directly to a requalification of the situation. Both occur, I believe, in the aspect of perception that sees something 'as something', rather than in the realm of argumentation, but the former is an example of re-qualification by the inner senses, while the latter, more radically, simply generates what I called above 'an irritation' (and Del Mar would probably qualify as an 'incongruity'), where the insufficiency of the current perceptual scheme is made apparent, but the new perceptual scheme is not yet available.

Now, if this rough picture of our perception is correct, some light is shed on how virtues can operate in contexts of legal decision-making and, in particular, on how one can 'creatively break the law'. This outline of a theory of perception explains why practical wisdom is a necessary component of any theory of rule-following, including, legal rule-following. However, this theory is not a complete answer to the second objection mentioned above to the suitability of relying on virtues and virtue theory to explain legal decision-making: if the decision-maker's character (or aspects thereof) were so crucial for an account of legal decision-making, would not legal decision-making be living short of the standards of impersonality set by the ideal of the rule of law? I turn to that question in the next section.

Virtuous Legal Decision-Making and the Rule of Law

One way to present the problem posed by the ideal of the rule of law to a theory of legal decision-making based on virtues is to place it against the background of the law-creation/law-application distinction mentioned in the first section of the chapter ('Virtues and the Theory of Legal Decision-Making'). If a theory of legal decision-making relies on the subjectivity of the legal decision-maker (or aspects of this) it would seem to happen at the expense of the guidance provided by the law-creating institution. It would seem, then, that the political community's self-rule would be mediated by a small number of virtuous individuals, and that in turn seems to go against the grain of the rule of law. That suspicion arises because the content of the law would then seem to hang on the subjectivity of legal decision-which, in turn, seems to render the process of law-creation either idle or at least a hostage to those decision-makers.

This appearance seems to gain traction if one looks into some of the features virtue theorists attribute to virtue; in particular, the thesis often referred to as the 'unity of virtue'.[18] According to this thesis, 'the fully successful exercise of one virtue depends upon other aspects of the person's character' (Annas 2011: 83). More precisely, no virtue can be fully possessed without the possession of other virtues (arguably, the *full* possession of other virtues). What makes it certain that virtues are thus reciprocal is their connection to an organizing virtue, namely, practical wisdom (originally in Aristotle 1984: 1144b33-1145a2; today, among many others, see Annas 2011: 86 and Hursthouse 1999: 153). Because practical wisdom is only one (or so it is claimed), all virtues cannot but evolve together. As Julia Annas (2011: 86) put it, '[t]he point here is that practical intelligence develops over your character as a whole, in a holistic way'.

If that is correct, a wise judge would also be just and know what is due to each party in a legal battle. Two questions might arise from this thesis: first, if the judge is so knowledgeable, why would he or she need created law to assess the rights and wrongs of the situation? If anything, it would seem that the law created by the community might distract the judge from what he or she knows to be the appropriate way to cope with the situation. The alternative would, of course, be that he or she does not know very well the rights and wrongs of the situation, but then his/her possession of the virtue of justice (and practical wisdom) would be defective and, in a theory of legal reasoning and decision-making that makes virtue a central aspect of it, one would have to accept that this particular decision-maker is not competent enough to apply the law. It looks like a Catch-22 situation for the theory of legal reasoning, which assigns an important role for virtues in legal decision-making.

In addition, the idea of how virtues operate in legal reasoning and decision-making seems to have difficulty in explaining the way in which my colleague found the non-obvious right answer in the situation I described at the beginning of the chapter. My colleague is a good man, but not noticeably more virtuous than any of the other eight lawyers who took part in the meeting. So on top of leading to a dilemma that seems to curb its explanatory usefulness, the conception of legal reasoning that assigns pride of place to virtues seems to be inadequate to explain the kind of problem I set out to explain.

This is the moment to take a step back and ask whether the framework within which the explanatory shortcomings of this conception of legal reasoning arose cannot be changed (or further elaborated) in such a way as to give it some explanatory purchase. If we rule out the possibility of giving up on the ideal of the rule of law (as I think we should), a limited number of changes would be possible.

First, we might think that perhaps the theory presented is too hasty to qualify the ability needed by legal experts in order to identify the relevant features of particular cases as a virtue. This ability might be something else that shares

18 There are different versions of the thesis in the literature (Hursthouse 1999: 153, Russell 2009: 335 ff). The version I present here is the one I consider most plausible, but the arguments that follow apply to many of the different versions of the thesis.

some features with virtues (in particular, the operation of conceptual perception), without themselves being virtues. The most obvious competitor here is what in the Aristotelian tradition is normally identified as a skill. Recent developments of virtue theory have stressed how much skills and virtues have in common, instead of focusing on the contrast between them, as does most of the relevant literature (Annas 2011: 1–3, 16–51). In fact, one thing that they do seem to share, at least in part, is the operation of the inner senses and the ability to project concepts to fields different from the ones in which the concepts were learnt. If this is the case, the picture of conceptual perception presented in the third section of the chapter ('The Construction of a Peripheral Conceptual Perception') might still be relevant to explain my colleague's ability to identify the non-obvious right answer. Moreover, without the added pressure of considering the legal decision-maker's skill to be a virtue, this approach to the role of subjectivity in legal reasoning does not need to comply with the unity of virtue argument – that is, one might have this particular skill without being a particularly just or practically wise agent. This is a tempting alternative, but before we can give it more attention, I must outline another possibility.

The second possible change in the explanatory model proposed would be to deny the thesis of the unity of virtue. As we saw above, the most common strategy to explain the unity of virtue is to do so by postulating a necessary connection between each virtue and practical wisdom. As practical wisdom is one virtue, it provides the umbrella that organizes all virtues into a cohesive scheme and provides the unity between them. But one might argue that different virtues are connected to different aspects of practical wisdom, which could develop independently of each other. Practical wisdom would then share a conceptual core, but would effectively break down into more specific wisdoms in more specific settings. I cannot argue at length for the unity of virtue here, but many of the arguments I would put forward if I could are already in print, and I hope that makes this gap tolerable (see, for example, Annas 2011: 87–99).

The third change operates by adding complexity to, rather than simplifying, the original picture of the relationship between legal decision-making and virtues. This complexity suggests an alternative economy of legal decision-making, in which practical wisdom is placed in the wider context of the virtue of law-abidingness. Law-abidingness is the subjective side of the Aristotelian general justice and part of justice. To display law-abidingness, the agent must possess practical wisdom in two forms: (a) practical wisdom must be able to discriminate when law should be followed in particular circumstances; and (b) it also must help the law-abiding agent to discriminate what the law requires in a particular circumstance. Those two functions of practical reason must work *in tandem*, as law-abidingness is displayed neither by someone following laws that should not be followed, nor by someone who is determined to follow the law, but is wrong about what the law requires. In relation to form (a), practical wisdom protects the law-abiding agent from two opposite temptations, namely (i) the temptation of replacing the judgement made by the community through law by the agent's own judgement; and (ii) the temptation to follow the law without paying attention to how the application of law in a particular situation relates to the context in which the action must be performed. In relation to form (b), practical wisdom guards the agent against the conceptual rigidity that blinds him or her to what the law requires in the particular circumstances. If this picture of the relationship between legal decision-making and practical wisdom is correct, much of what was described in the third section of the chapter was a more detailed explanation of the second relation between practical wisdom and legal decision-making. But the possession of this aspect of practical wisdom cannot in and of itself create the agent's law-abidingness. Both aspects are required.

In this picture, aspect (b) of practical wisdom's relation to legal decision-making is not simply an auxiliary skill to be possessed by the law-abiding agent. It is not comparable to horse-riding for the courageous agent. Aspect (b) is an integral part of law-abidingness. But it shares something with skills, in that the perception of the relevant particulars might be developed to a great extent by someone who does not have all the virtues harmonically developed. Zenon Bańkowski's explanation of how one learns when the presence of certain particularities in a case that falls within the semantic meaning of the legal source should be perceived as a legally relevant oddity refers precisely to that aspect of practical wisdom. The framework provided in the third section above positions Bańkowski's claim within the context of a theory of perception, which is its rightful place. So the development of the moral perception of the kind identified by Bańkowski is a result of being exposed to a particular set of 'legal experiences'. Those legal experiences range from the study of previous cases, of sources of law, and of doctrinal accounts of legal concepts, to the experiences of particular contexts of law-application as trainee, lawyer or judge.

The similarity between this aspect of practical wisdom to simple skills would allow us to explain how my friend might be able to come up with his non-obvious yet clearly appropriate legal solution to the case. On the one hand, he can possess this ability, at least up to a point, without possessing the whole of law-abidingness and hence the objection founded on the unity of virtue is bypassed. On the other hand, it is able to explain how my friend's perception can develop in relation to something that is not a requirement of justice (or any other good or virtue) considered independently of the specific legal context of a particular legal system. I am sure his insight, which seemed to be perfectly appropriate to Brazilian law, would not be relevant in the context of other legal systems, which, for example, regulate the law of injunctions in a different way.

But this crucial similarity to skills should not blind us to the fact that this ability is an integral part of the virtue of law-abidingness. This form of legal conceptual perception (both central and peripheral) is not an auxiliary skill to the virtue of law-abidingness in the way that 'bridle-making and the other arts concerned with the equipment of horses' (Aristotle 1984: 1729, at 1094a10-12) might be helpful to the militarily courageous agent. This form of perception is not something that helps the agent to be law-abiding, but it is a necessary element of being law-abiding.

This can be seen in the counterfactual case of an agent who entirely lacks this perceptive ability, yet acts as guided by the advice given by a third party who he or she believes has the skill of knowing what the law requires from him or her. In that case, the agent might be qualified as 'encratic', but not as virtuous, as a crucial part of virtue is to be able to respond to particular situations appropriately. The agent's dependence on a third party's judgement can only make him or her law-abiding in an imperfect way (that is, as an encratic, rather than a virtuous agent).

This way of conceiving practical wisdom explains why some of the most intuitive, and prima facie plausible, objections to the use the concept of virtue as a central element of an account of legal decision-making, are ultimately ungrounded. Though other objections might be raised to such use of virtue, the conception of practical wisdom presented above goes a long way towards justifying this explanatory use of virtue in a theory of law, by removing the most evident obstacles to it.

Bibliography

Annas, J. 2011. *Intelligent Virtue.* Oxford: Oxford University Press.

Aquinas, St. Thomas (1970; 1974) *Summa Theologiae*, Vols XI and XXXVI. London: Blackfriars.

Aristotle. 1984. *The Complete Works of Aristotle*, ed. J. Barnes. Princeton, NJ: Princeton University Press.

Aubenque, P. 1963. *La Prudence chez Aristote.* Paris: Presses Universitaires de France/Quatrige.

Aubenque, P. 1997. *La Prudence chez Aristote*, 2nd edn. Paris: Quadrige/PUF.

Bańkowski, B. 2001. *Living Lawfully.* Dordrecht: Kluwer.

Bell, J. 2004. 'The Perspective of the Ordinary Citizen on Law'. *Res Publica*, 10(3): 311–17.

Dworkin, R. 1991. *Law's Empire.* London: Fontana.

Hursthouse, R. 1999. *On Virtue Ethics.* Oxford: Oxford University Press.

Kant, I. 1996. 'Toward Perpetual Peace'. In M.J. Gregor (ed.), *Immanuel Kant: Practical Philosophy*. Cambridge: Cambridge University Press, 317–51.

Louden, R. 1984. 'On Some Vices of Virtue Ethics'. *American Philosophical Quarterly*, 21(3): 227–36.

McCabe, H. 2008. *On Aquinas.* London: Burns and Oats.

MacCormick, N. 1974. 'Law as Institutional Fact'. *Law Quarterly Review*, 90: 102–29. MacCormick, N. 1978. *Legal Reasoning and Legal Theory.* Oxford: Oxford University Press.

MacCormick, N. 2005. *Rhetoric and the Rule of Law.* Oxford: Oxford University Press.

MacCormick, N. 2007. *Institutions of Law.* Oxford: Clarendon Press.

MacCormick, N. and Weinberger, O. 1986. *An Institutional Theory of Law.* Dordrecht: Kluwer.

MacIntyre, A. 1988. *Whose Justice? Which Rationality?* London: Duckworth.
MacIntyre, A. 2000. 'Theories of Natural Law in Advanced Modernity'. In E.B. McLean (ed.), *Common Truths: New Perspectives on Natural Law*. Wilmington, DE: ISI Books, 91–116.
MacIntyre, A. 2006. *Ethics and Politics: Selected Essays, Vol. 2*. Cambridge: Cambridge University Press.
Michelon, C. 2012. 'Practical Wisdom in Legal Decision-Making'. In A. Amaya and H.H. Lai (eds), *Law, Virtue, and Justice*. Oxford: Hart Publishers, 29–51.
Montesquieu, Charles de Secondat, Baron de. 1768. *De L'Esprit des Lois Nouvelle Édition.* A. Londres.
Nussbaum, M. 1995. *Poetic Justice.* Boston, MA: Beacon Press.
Raz, J. 1986. *The Morality of Freedom.* Oxford: Clarendon Press.
Raz, J. 1990. *Practical Reasons and Norms*, 2nd edn. Princeton, NJ: Princeton University Press.
Roberts, R. and Wood, W.J. 2007. *Intellectual Virtues.* Oxford: Clarendon Press.
Russell, D. 2009. *Practical Intelligence and the Virtues.* Oxford: Oxford University Press.

Chapter 7
Living Under Dead Ideas: Law as the Will of the People

Fernando Atria

> When the state, on the eve of ruin, maintains only a vain, illusory and formal existence, when in every heart the social bond is broken, and the meanest interest brazenly lays hold of the sacred name of 'public good,' the general will becomes mute: all men, guided by secret motives, no more give their views as citizens than if the state had never been; and iniquitous decrees directed solely to private interest get passed under the name of laws.
>
> Jean-Jacques Rousseau, *The Social Contract* (2002 [1762])

We live under the domain of dead ideas. To a considerable extent, our political language seems to be meaningless. What is the meaning of, for example, 'Sovereignty rests essentially with the Nation, and it is exercised by the people'?[1] How can we say, without naivety, that law is the will of the people, and that the people are the bearers of constituent power? When and how (if at all) can we say that a Constitution imposed by a dictator or an occupying power is the people's? This is what I would like to discuss in this chapter: not the answers to these questions, but how to make them intelligible.

Living Under Dead Ideas

The Riddle of Every Constitution: The Ascription of the Rules of Ascription

Perhaps the last question I posed above, given its obvious political relevance in Chile, is a good place to start. Can the people appropriate a Constitution that was originally imposed? Or must we say, on the contrary, that the initial heteronomy is insurmountable? Can an originally heteronomous Constitution become autonomous? If the Constitution was imposed by a dictatorship, as the decreto ley[2] 3464 was in Chile (and I have no intention of joining the collective

---

1 Article 5 of the Chilean Constitution. All references to articles hereafter are to be understood as references to the Chilean constitutional text, unless stated otherwise.

2 "Decreto ley" (law-decree) is the name traditionally given to legislation passed by *de facto* regimes. They are decrees, i.e. presidential mandates, but regulate issues that are

amnesia that apparently affects our constitutional theory on this matter), would not 'appropriating' it be just a way of falling in love with our chains?

The starting point must be our initial observation: it seems as though these questions are difficult because their answer is problematic (one can imagine the 'realist' asking: 'Barring political rhetoric, how do the people go about becoming the owners of an alien constitution?'), while in truth the hard part is to understand it. We shall see that understanding and developing the question is to find an answer. Thus, our first stop must be to consider why it is difficult to understand. For now, we can say bluntly: appropriating the constitution is an action, and in that action we are supposed to read a volition. Hence, if the people are the bearers of constituent power they must be able to act and to have a will. But what, strictly speaking, is it for the people to act, to have a will?

The answer seems to be simple: law is the will of the people, and the institutional forms thorough which law is produced is the manner in which the people act, the way in which the people's will can be formed. Thus, according to article 5:

> Sovereignty rests essentially with the Nation. It is exercised by the people through the plebiscites and periodic elections, as well as by the authorities established by this Constitution. No sector of the people nor any individual may assume its exercise.

Thus the people act through institutional forms, and those forms identify what is to count as the will of the people.

There is nothing unusual in this. In fact, law can trivially ascribe a will to entities that, strictly speaking, seem incapable of willing anything. Thus the opinion of one or more human beings counts as the will of a corporation when the former has been formed in the appropriate way. This appropriate way takes the form of a procedure, so that any decision taken by following such procedure is recognized as the corporation's. The procedure is specified by law or by the articles of association. Regardless of its source, these are what we could call 'secondary rules of ascription'. To say that a corporation wills something is to apply to some facts a given rule of ascription. Such a statement looks like a description, but in truth is what Raz (1980: 217) called an 'applied legal statement' (that is, a statement, the truth of which depends on the validity of certain rules and the occurrence of certain facts).

Thus from a legal point of view there is a readily available answer to the question of how can the people will something. The people will whatever corresponds to the occurrence of certain facts in the world, as specified by certain constitutional rules of ascription. In the Chilean case, such rules are contained in articles 5, 6 and 7. When a bill is submitted to either chamber of Congress, it reflects only the will

---

reserved to legislation. In normal circumstances presidents do not have the authority to pass legislation.

of the individual Member of Parliament or political party who presented it. That is, it is the will not of the people but of a faction. Yet, when the bill is duly voted and approved, and later enacted by the president, it becomes the will of the people (it is recognized as the will of the people). It becomes the will of the people *because* it has been so enacted.

But this is too simple an answer, because what ought to be ascribed to the people is not only the rules formed through the procedure set by secondary rules of ascription, but the rules themselves. Here our analogy collapses: precisely because, in the case of a corporation, the rules of ascription (at least some of them) are previous to and independent of the corporation's existence, it is possible for the corporation to form a will. Without these secondary rules of ascription the corporation would not and could not have a will. And these rules were there before the corporation ever was. They are not valid because the corporation wants them. On the contrary, the corporation is able to will something because of the validity of these rules. But if the constitution contains the rules of ascription of a will to the people, how can we ascribe the constitution to the people; that is , how can the people will their own rules of ascription?

This is the paradox of the constitution, the 'riddle of all constitutions', the answer to which is democracy.

The People as Institutional Fact

How can democracy be the solution to the riddle of all constitutions if democracy itself presupposes a constitution? In fact, democracy is the idea that 'state power must be articulated in such a way that both its organization and its exercise derive from the will of the people or can be ascribed to it' (Böckenförde 2000: 47). The fact that the rules of ascription are part of what must be ascribed to the people suggests that the people have two modes of action, that there are, we may say, two concepts of 'the people': an institutional concept and a pre-institutional one. Institutionally speaking, 'the people' is what acts through the operation of the norms of ascription as mentioned above; and pre-institutionally speaking, 'the people' are what wills those rules of ascription.

Let us go back to article 5:

> Sovereignty rests essentially with the Nation. It is exercised by the people through plebiscites and periodic elections, as well as by the authorities established by this Constitution. No sector of the people, nor any individual may assume its exercise.

There are three rules here. According to the first, sovereignty rests essentially with the nation; according to the second, it is exercised by the people, but only through institutional forms (plebiscites, periodic elections and constitutionally established authorities); and the third rule forbids any faction not authorized by a rule of ascription to act as agents for the people. This last rule is complemented by article 7 (second paragraph) of the same text:

> No magistrature, no person or group of persons may assume, even on the pretext of extraordinary circumstances, any authority or rights other than those expressly conferred upon them by this Constitution or by law.

This seems, again, paradoxical: the constitution is willed by the people, but the people can only act in ways specified by the constitution or according to it. The former idea makes the constitution seem autonomous, the latter heteronomous. Yet how can the same norm, related to the same agent, be simultaneously autonomous and heteronomous?

There is a sense in which this is indeed paradoxical, but before we discuss it we have to notice that in these two apparently contradictory features (autonomy/heteronomy) resides nothing less than the explanation of the very meaning of law. Every legal concept is the formalization of a pre-legal concept.[3] The function of the legal concept is to make probable the pre-legal concept, which would otherwise be impossible, or at least improbable. This is as valid for concepts such as 'contract' and 'testament' as it is for concepts such as 'law' and 'constitution'. Thus, for example, co-operation is, without law, improbable. What is probable is for each individual to act towards another in an objectifying manner; that is, to try to force or manipulate the other into doing what the first wants. In other words, each individual will understand the other as an example of a much larger problem: that the world shows resistance to their will. The world's resistance has to be trumped somehow, and in this all that succeeds is success: 'if any two men desire the same thing, which nevertheless they cannot both enjoy, they become enemies; and in the way to their end (which is principally their own conservation, and sometimes their delectation only) endeavour to destroy or subdue one another' (Hobbes 1996: ch. 3). Since (if) there is law, each individual's way to his/her end does not lead to destroying or subduing the other. Without law (in Hobbes' 'natural condition of mankind'), there is no reason why I should refrain from using force or manipulation to obtain what I want, which is to say that the world is for me an instrument for my ends. The relation between self and the other will be purely instrumental, because the other does not appear before him or her as an other, but as part of a world that has to be manipulated to achieve his or her ends. The law of contracts makes my forcing or manipulating the other self-defeating: my using force or deceit to obtain your consent to a contract will be detrimental to me or,

3 This is what distinguishes institutions like law from institutions like games. That is why the analogy between legal rules and the rules of games, though useful in a certain sense, may confuse rather than clarify the analysis of law as an institutional system. This is thoroughly discussed in Atria, *On Law and Legal Reasoning*, (2002: ch. 1), where 'regulatory' institutions (such as law) are distinguished from 'autonomous' institutions (such as games).

at least, useless (not only will I be punished because of the illegal aggression, but I will also find out, when I want to enforce the contract, that my fraud or duress renders it void). Thus if I want something you have, trying to get it by destroying or subduing you will not be in my interest; I will have to contract with you, and for that contract to be valid I will have to treat you *as if* I recognize you as an equal (without fraud, duress and so on). By rendering my objectifying action self-defeating law makes it probable for me to relate to you as if I recognized that you are not just another parcel of the world that I can use to pursue my own ends, but an end in itself. It makes probable, in other words, that I relate to you as if I recognize you as an 'other'.

Very much the same can be said of other (indeed: all) formal concepts. Take 'testament'. The function of a testament is to make trivially ascertainable something that it would otherwise be hard to identify: the deceased's last will as to how his or her assets ought to be distributed. But the law does not accord the institutional status of 'testament' to any plan as to how my assets will be distributed after my death. It has to meet some requirements: the testator must be of sane mind, the testament must be given in the presence of a number of witnesses, or in writing and so on. These conditions are such that, if met, it is probable that the will expressed in it will actually be the last will of the decedent.

Both pairs (exchange between equals/contract, last will of the decedent/testament) show the relation between the pre-institutional ('brute') concept and its institutional correlate. They also show that the function of the institutional concept can only be achieved if it is opaque to its institutional correlate; that is, in so far as in its operation the institutional concept becomes autonomous from the pre-institutional concept: the claim that an unfair contract is immediately void and is not (because of its unfairness) legally binding is incompatible with the existence of the law of contracts, just as it is incompatible with the existence of a testament that it may be struck down proving by any means that the decedent's last will was in some way (any way) different.

Thus the three rules contained in article 5 reflect the structure common to every legal concept: the pre-legal concept (the first rule) is formalized (second rule), and then the formal concept becomes, in its operation, opaque to its pre-institutional correlate (third rule).

This is indeed part of the explanation, but it does not do away with the problem completely. As was noted above, there is something paradoxical in article 5, but to identify the paradox it is not enough to distinguish a pre-institutional and an institutional concept of the people, so that the second is opaque to the first, and in particular cases might even appear to be in opposition. This, for the reasons explained above, is common to every legal concept. To see the problem we have to notice that legal concepts are opaque in relation to their pre-legal correlatives, not in their *intelligibility* but in their *operation*: while 'contract' and 'testament' are opaque in their operation to 'fair exchange' and 'last will of the deceased', they are dependent on them (or, of course, any alternative possibility) as regards their intelligibility: understanding its relation to the notion of 'fair exchange' is necessary to be able to understand the concept of 'contract'; and to understand the concept of 'testament' we have to refer it to the concept of 'deceased's last will'. If these pre-institutional concepts were unintelligible, then the corresponding legal concepts would be equally unintelligible, an empty formalism. And the problem is that the very concept of 'the people' in a pre-institutional sense seems unintelligible. As Bruce Ackerman has said, in a passage we shall discuss later in the chapter,

> we all know what it is for an individual to decide something, but what is it for a collectivity so grand as the People to enter constitutional politics in a meaningful way? (Ackerman 1996: 209).

Yet if the pre-institutional concept of 'the people' is unintelligible, then the institutional concept of 'the people' is a mere formalism, a mystification contrived to deceive us, to make us believe that we live according to our own will when we are in fact subjected to an alien will. A dead idea.

A Pre-institutional Concept of 'the People'

If we are to say that the will of the people is whatever can be ascribed institutionally to the people, we must be capable, at least in principle, of identifying what it can possibly mean for the people to want something, to have a will, in a pre-institutional sense. Here, it seems, we must choose one of the following answers.

The first answer is that 'the people' is a physical entity, characterized by some pre-political feature ('pre-political' here does not mean 'metaphysical', but only 'not politically constituted'): by race, religion, language and so on. This is the sense in which the expression is used when we speak of 'native (or indigenous) peoples'. Here 'people' is an entity characterized by some natural feature, which defines an *identity*: 'the self-identity of the concretely present people as a political unity' (Schmitt 2008: 255).

The second answer is the one usually given by economists: 'the people' is the name we use to refer to the aggregation of individuals, and its will is the will that results from adding together all the particular wills. In this sense we cannot speak about 'the people' (*el pueblo*), but just about 'people' (*personas*).

The most salient aspect of these two explanations about what 'the people' are and what their 'will' consists of is that they are both incapable of making the democratic rules of ascription intelligible, in so far as democracy relies on institutions; in fact, both institutions imply a form of mediation the function of which cannot be, strictly speaking, making the identification of the people's will more probable, but rather less so. For the first, the identity between rulers and ruled is what is crucial, and this identity is hindered or denied by the institutions we recognize as democratic. Thus, in this sense, the people's form of expression *par excellence* is *acclamation*:

> Only the genuinely assembled people can do that which pertains distinctly to the activity of this people. They can acclaim in that they express their consent or disapproval by a simple calling out, calling higher or lower, celebrating a leader or a suggestion, honoring the king or some other person, or denying the acclamation by silence or complaining. (Schmitt 2008: 272)

Democratic political forms aim at 'directly ignoring the assembled people as such', because 'a distinctive feature of the bourgeois *Rechtsstaat* constitution is to ignore the sovereign, whether this sovereign is the monarch or the people' (Schmitt 2008: 273).This renders problematic the democratic forms of popular participation:

> The election or vote, more precisely, is a secret individual vote. The method of the secret individual vote, however, is not democratic. It is, rather, an expression of liberal individualism ... In the struggle against impermissible electoral influencing by the government and against other misuses, the demand for secret individual ballots makes sense and is relatively justified. Nevertheless, it is necessary to understand its nature correctly and to be clear that in principle it is part of the circle of ideas associated with liberal individualism and contradicts the political principle of democracy. For the logically consistent execution of the secret individual election and the individual vote transforms the distinctly democratic, or *political*, figure, the state citizen or *citoyen*, into a private man who, from the sphere of the *private*, whether or not this private sphere may be his religion or his economic interest or both together, expresses a private opinion and casts his vote. Secret individual ballot means that the voting state citizen is isolated in the decisive moment. (Schmitt 2008: 273)

With remarkable anticipation, Schmitt discusses what today appears as a manifestation of the so-called *e-democracy*:

> It is fully conceivable that one day through ingenious discoveries every single person, without leaving his apartment, could continuously express his opinions on political questions through an apparatus and that all these opinions would automatically be registered by a central office, where one would only need to read them off. That would not be an especially intensive democracy, but it would provide a proof of the fact that the state and the public were fully privatized. The result is only a sum of private opinions. In this way, no common will arises, no *volonté générale*, only the sum of all individual will, a *volonté de tous*, does. (Schmitt 2008: 274)

To Schmitt, therefore, the characteristic institutions of representative democracy do not have the function of making the identification of the people's will probable, but, on the contrary, *neutralizing* the people, making it politically irrelevant.[4] Thus, the idea of the people as a political concept is at least in tension and, strictly speaking, is in contradiction to democratic institutions, in so far as the first implies that the main function of these institutions is to neutralize it. Constitutional principles such as article 5 are empty declarations with no real political content. The only reason we would not say, on this reading, that they are dead ideas is that they were never truly alive.

This may be predictable, because after all Schmitt has gone down in history as Nazism's legal scholar. If one wishes to find an explanation of the political meaning of 'the people' that is compatible with democratic institutions, the plausible thing to do is to look for it in the work of those who have defended democratic institutional forms, and not in the work of those who have attacked them.

Bruce Ackerman, for example, criticizes Schmitt precisely because his comprehension of the idea of 'the people' is totalitarian. In fact, to return to a passage already partially quoted: 'The crucial problem is the People with a capital *P*. We all know what it is for an individual to decide something, but what is it for a collectivity so grand as the People to enter constitutional politics in a meaningful way' (Ackerman 1996: 209). Ackerman makes reference to the very same passages of Schmitt's *Verfassungslehre* that we have quoted, in particular to his statement that the people's mean of expression *par excellence* is acclamation, and continues:

> Once Schmitt "solves" the problema of identification in this brutalized way, his Nazism follows immediately: the rallies at Nuremberg are just the kind of remedy for the disease of modernity that Schmitt is prescribing in his *Verfassungslehre*. (Ackerman 1996: 209)

Notice the way that Ackerman claims to have found the connection between these two ideas: from an existential understanding of 'the people', Nazism is *immediately derived*. That is the reason why, as Schmitt says, the liberal wants to neutralize 'the people': the point of the institutions of representative democracy is to make politically irrelevant this existential reality, prior to institutions, which can acclaim. The liberal sees no political sense whatever in this notion of 'the people', so he or she replaces it with the second sense, based on what 'everyone knows' – namely, what it means for an individual to want something, adding that what is politically relevant is the sum of the preferences of the individuals who live in a specific territory. But then democratic institutions can only be seen as a pale *second-best* in relation to the idea of direct democracy, in which each individual can defend his or her own interest on his/her own, with no intermediaries. In fact, Ackerman believes that 'the people' expresses itself on rare occasions, which he calls 'constitutional moments'. These constitutional moments are characterized

4 This is the same thesis defended by left-wing intellectuals who advocate a 'participatory democracy' as opposed to a 'representative democracy'. In relation to this, see Moulian, *Socialismo del Siglo XXI* (2000: 121).

precisely by the divesting of institutional bonds, because during them the people express by means of what Ackerman once called, apparently without noting the contradiction, 'extraordinary institutional forms' (Ackerman 1984: 1022).

Since democracy is about aggregating what we all know; namely, what it is for an individual to decide something, in the most efficient way possible, to answer a much less obvious question ('What is it for a collectivity so grand as the People to enter constitutional politics in a meaningful way?'), the liberal agrees with Schmitt on just this point: the institutional forms that mediate – that is, that stand between individuals and their preferences or convictions, and the decisions that are accorded the institutional status of 'the people's', are problematic. And they are problematic because they mediate, because they perennially face the 'cut-out-the-middleman' objection. Their being problematic does not mean, of course, that they are unjustified (this is what Schmitt called a 'relative' justification, like that of the individual secret vote by reference to 'the struggle against impermissible electoral influencing by the government and against other misuses'). What this means is that they are forced upon us by the transition from ideas to really existing institutions. If this is so, the fact that it has become empirically possible to do away with them immediately challenges them. Hence e-democracy.

What is striking is that both Schmitt and Ackerman agree on this: Schmitt believes that popular acclaim is 'more democratic' than the result of an institutional process, because it is immediate; Ackerman believes that the people expressing through extra-institutional means (in 'constitutional moments') is a form of democracy superior to the institutional expression ('normal') of the people, because it is a form not mediated by institutions. The parallelism is too precise for it not to be meaningful.

In fact, in the broader public debate (I am leaving behind Schmitt and Ackerman now) the parallelism continues, and it is expressed in the proposals for institutional reform that nowadays have become common to both the left and right. In so far as mediating institutions are seen as hindering the people's expression, these fashionable proposals purport to diminish their mediating capacity, making them more transparent to what individuals 'really' (that is, without mediation, immediately) want. Direct democracy is, for both, the ideal situation: for some, because in this way the people may act directly and immediately, acclaiming in assembly (or protesting on the streets); for others, because the more direct that democracy is, the closer the decision will be to the preferences to be added (the less mediated the decision, the more precise the addition will be). And, of course, actually existing representative democracy and political parties defined by an ideology, and any association of citizens other than single-issue movements, are poor substitutes for direct democracy, for the immediate expression of the citizens' will through, for example, some form of e-democracy which was not technologically feasible in the past.

In my opinion this is our current predicament, especially after we look at what has occurred in some Latin-American countries: while direct appeal to the people is disqualified as a 'plebiscitary' or 'populist' form of democracy, our institutions suffer from an acute legitimation crisis, which (it is suggested) may be mitigated by reforms meant to make political decision-making more immediate: popular initiative, decisions by referenda, recalling, attention to the dominant preferences expressed in opinion polls, primary elections for selecting candidates, and so on. The malaise of democratic institutions is manifested in sharp scepticism towards them: can we say seriously that in any real sense law is really the will of the people? The law might be seen as will, but in that case it is anybody's but the people's: perhaps the will of economic groups, or of the 'political class', of those who practice influence peddling and so on (and that explains, by way of compensation, why it has become common to understand law in a way that devalues the role of legislation and understands the law as reason rather than will: a regression, in other words, to pre-modern forms of law, sometimes called neo-constitutionalism).

Signifying Imperfectly

Regarding Schmitt, Ackerman shows no disposition to engage with, or to be questioned by him. Schmitt can simply be excluded from the conversation by mocking him, because as a Nazi jurist he has become fair game. And that is so despite the fact that Ackerman has perceived the key to solve our riddle. Since he seems uninterested in understanding Schmitt, however, he misses it. The point is that, as Ackerman notices, Schmitt's *Theory of the Constitution*

> Is a piece of 'negative theology', with the crucial exception that Schmitt's god-term is the Volk: he tells us a lot about how the will of the Volk should not be confused with normal acts of political representation, but he is very weak in developing affirmative criteria for identifying the magical event. (Ackerman 1996: 209)

Ackerman's point here is not to understand, but to discredit ('not only he was a Nazi, but he also believed in magical nonsense', one could say). Saying that something is 'theological', in this context, is equal to saying that it is 'magical' – that is, irrational (as is believing in fairies or unicorns). The point has been correctly identified by Jeremy Waldron:

> Secular theorists often assume that they know what a religious argument is like: they present it as a crude prescription from God, backed up with threat of hellfire, derived from general or particular revelation, and they contrast it with the elegant complexity of a philosophical argument by Rawls (say) or Dworkin. (Waldron 2002: 20)

In the following pages I want to question the self-sufficiency of the 'secular theorist'. I want to explain that the reasons why we misunderstand our own political language are the same as why the 'secular theorists' Waldron refers to cannot understand theological language as anything but a language based on the discussion of magical events, of crude prescriptions from God, backed up with threat of hellfire, derived from general or particular revelation. This is the key to political theology.

Political Theology

The idea of political theology is much more radical than the thesis, interesting but nowadays transformed into a commonplace, that 'All significant concepts of the modern theory of the state are secularized theological concepts' (Schmitt 1985: 36). In its most powerful sense, the idea behind political theology is not a thesis about the genealogy of political concepts, but about their meaning, what we shall later call their *mode of signifying*. Since they use the same mode of signifying, the unintelligibility of the political concepts we have noted is the unintelligibility of theological concepts. This is concealed because, as opposed to political concepts, theological concepts do not seem unintelligible (they only seem plainly and ridiculously false: 'magical'). But theological concepts so rejected or accepted are theologically distorted concepts; they are forms of idolatry. This is why there is not much, in my view, to be said about political theology without going into theological questions (one cannot study political theology without also studying theology).

In choosing a point of entry into theological questions one can do far worse than paying special attention to the distinction between faith and idolatry, because this goes right to the heart of the problem of theological language. As Simone Weil said:

> There are two atheisms of which one is a purification of the notion of God. Of two men who have no experience of God, he who denies him is perhaps nearer to him than the other. Religion in so far as it is a source of consolation is a hindrance to true faith: in this sense atheism is a purification. (Weil 1963: 114–15)[5]

The thesis that political concepts are theological concepts and vice versa, implies something quite precise: it means that their *mode of signifying* is the same, and

5 Similarly Karl Rahner (1969) said that 'If we say "God" we must not imagine that everyone understands this word and that the only question is whether what all mean by it really exists. Very often the man in the street believes it to mean something, which he rightly denies, because what he imagines it to mean really does not exist. He thinks it is a hypothesis for explaining phenomena until science can give the true explanation, or someone to frighten children until they realize that nothing extraordinary happens if they are naughty.'

therefore that their pathologies are analogue. From the point of view of theology, the point has been brilliantly identified by Juan Luis Segundo:

> We are more interested in the (apparently dated) antithesis between faith and idolatry than in the (apparently topical) antithesis between faith and atheism. Furthermore, it has to be said at the outset that those who call themselves Christians can occupy, in the more radical antithesis faith/idolatry, either of these positions. In other words, we believe that men are more profoundly divided by their image of God than by the position they take as to whether that image corresponds to something real. (Segundo 1969: 22)

To explore the political meaning of the antithesis 'faith/idolatry' the best starting point seems to be precisely the idea of 'negative theology' that Ackerman mentions without even trying to understand it.

Negative Theology I: The Creation of the World

Rowan Williams has warned perceptively that 'theology is perennially liable to be seduced by the prospect of bypassing the question of how it learns its own language' (2000: 131). Perhaps it is possible to understand Thomas Aquinas's 'negative theology' (so-called 'apophatic' theology) as an attempt to make explicit his awareness of the danger of seduction identified by Williams. The sense in which Aquinas's theology is negative is expressed in one of his capital points about our knowledge of God:

> When the existence of a thing has been ascertained, there remains the further question of the manner of its existence, in order that we may know its essence. Now, because we cannot know what God is, but rather what He is not, we have no means for considering how God is, but rather how he is not. (Aquinas, Summa: q2)

The way I want to exploit this idea is that theology uses an *inverted language*. Thus the statement that God is 'our father' is a statement about universal human brotherhood. This is because

> when we speak of God, although we know how to use our words, there is an important sense in which we do not know what they mean. Fundamentally this is because of our special ignorance of God. We know how to talk about shoes and ships because of our understanding of shoes and ships. We know how to talk about God, not because of any understanding of God, but because of what we know about his creatures. (McCabe 2006: 104)

'God, maker of heaven and earth, of all things visible and invisible' is a good start, among other things, because it refers to the paradigm of 'religious' statements that Waldron's 'secular authors' have in mind. Richard Dawkins, for example, defines what he takes to be the 'more defensible' version of 'the God hypothesis' in the following way: 'There exists a superhuman, supernatural intelligence who deliberately designed and created the universe and everything in it, including us' (Dawkins 2008: 31). And of course, in these terms, 'God's existence or non-existence is a scientific fact about the universe, discoverable in principle if not in practice. If he existed and chose to reveal it, God himself could clinch the argument, noisily and unequivocally, in his favour' (Dawkins 2008: 50).[6]

But this is precisely 'cataphatic', positive theology: it assumes that we may know what God is: a super-wizard, which is idolatry (a super golden calf). The alternative to idolatry is negative theology. Therefore, we must understand that the meaning of the phrase 'God, maker of heaven and earth, of all things visible and invisible' is not to be found in what it positively affirms about God. But the statement seems to be about what God is (it has God as a subject: the maker of heaven and earth; that is, the world, in the sense of all that is the case), so in order to understand its way of signifying it must be inverted. It then becomes a statement, not about God, but about the world: 'God, maker of the world' implies 'the world is something created'. Notice, it is not that since we have independent reason to believe in God's existence that we believe it, since He is such a powerful person; He is the creator of all that is visible and invisible. We express our faith that the world is a created thing by saying that God made it *ex nihilo*. God is whatever is necessary to understand the world as something created.

If the claim that God created the world *ex nihilo* is understood in a positive manner, it seems hard to avoid some form of idolatry. It will have to be taken as a thesis about the (temporal) origin of the world: that there was a moment, at the beginning of time (as if this expression could possibly mean something), in which the world was created by a wizard of fabulous powers. But the (temporal) origin of the world (and the existence of such a wizard) is a fact about the world, and is difficult to deny that such a fact, like any other fact, is prima facie verifiable (a 'scientific' fact). The distortion contained in this interpretation becomes evident when one remembers that Aquinas, for example, believed that the idea of the world created by God *ex nihilo* was in principle perfectly compatible with the thesis that the world is eternal, that it did not have a beginning.

Now, what does the idea of creation, in its inverted meaning, say about the world? First, that the world is not sacred, that it is not God (it is the negation of every form of pantheism, which does not distinguish God from the world). But it also expresses confidence in the answer to what might be called 'the most fundamental question of philosophy': Why is there something rather than nothing? Or, in Wittgenstein's formulation, 'It is not *how things are in the world* that is mystical, but *that it exists*' (Wittgenstein 2001: §6.44). Not knowing anything affirmative about God implies ignorance of the answer (the believer does not have,

6 Dawkins does not explain to the reader what is a 'scientific fact' and how it can be distinguished from other, non-scientific facts.

qua believer, any special access to privileged knowledge), but faith in that there is an answer. This faith in the existence of an answer to the question about the meaning of the fact that the world *is* might be expressed in the following way: the world is like Beethoven's Ninth Symphony or Shakespeare's *Hamlet*, which exist because they are the expression of somebody's genius. Understanding the Ninth Symphony as a creation, namely, as someone's work, is to understand it as something with meaning. But it is clear that the Ninth Symphony or *Hamlet* only provide an analogy, because neither Beethoven nor Shakespeare could create *ex nihilo*. In fact, both *Hamlet* and the Ninth Symphony could only be created in the context of existing practices, and the genius of their authors is to be found in the way in which they were capable of organizing forms of artistic expression that were around when they arrive to the world (recall Hannah Arendt's (1958) insight that the fact that the world was there when we arrived and will continue without us when we leave, is a fundamental part of the human condition). This means that the sense in which we talk about the Ninth Symphony or *Hamlet* as being created things presupposes something prior to them that was not created: they are not, we could say, *radically* created. When we ask about the status of a parcel of the world the answer may be partial: when the question is 'why the world?' the answer has to be radical. Therefore Shakespeare and Beethoven are 'creators' in much less radical a way than is God. This implies that while theological language is an inverted language, the inversion is necessary, it is not dispensable. 'God is the creator of heaven and earth, of all things visible and invisible' *implies* but is not *reducible* to 'the world is something created'. The second statement gives us a hint about the way in which the first statement signifies, but the meaning of the first is not reducible to the meaning of the second.

Why insist, as Christian theology does, on the idea of a personal God instead of a cooler Hellenist unmoved mover? Is this not affirming something positive about God? A brief answer could be: because God cannot be the answer (or, strictly speaking: the name given to the confidence in the existence of an answer) to Wittgenstein's mystical question and be impersonal at the same time. If God were impersonal, then it would not be part of the explanation, but part of what needs to be explained: being the first does not stop a motor from being a motor. A motor is something that can be used, if we know how to use it. This is not the case with a 'person': to recognize something as a person is to recognize its character as an end in itself. The thesis that God is 'personal', thus, is also a negative thesis, not positive, because

> what this truly and blessedly means is that God cannot be less than man, endowed with personality, freedom and love, and that the mystery itself is free protective love, not an 'objective order' which one can, after all, possess (at least in principle), and against which one could insure oneself. (Rahner 1969)

Hence the idea that God cannot be an impersonal force (something that can be used instrumentally) may be expressed by saying that God is a person. As can be seen, in these terms the choice is also between a personal God and an idolatrous understanding of God. When we speak about ourselves, the way to express that human beings are ends and not means is to say that they are 'persons'. The idea of a personal God expresses the same about God, but in a radical manner. This means that the fact that God is a person does not entitle us to say of God what we say of us: that God has intentions, plans, wishes, will and so on. Almost all of our positive language related to the term 'person' is determined by the fundamental fact about human beings: they have (we have) *bodies* that develop and decay. And, of course, God does not have a body, because otherwise God would be part of the world. Therefore God is a 'person' like us in the same sense that he 'creates', like Beethoven or Shakespeare.

The point here is that our language about God is a language that cannot account for itself. That is why it must rely on analogies (such as 'creator') or metaphors (such as 'father'). In short, it must use what Hegel called 'representations'.[7] And, of course, the first representation is 'god'. Indeed, 'God' is a pagan word that was appropriated by Christian theology in order to say 'there are no gods'. But it is a word that shows no meaning at all, that operates as if it were a proper name (Rahner 1969). This is so because when we talk about God we are talking of what cannot be spoken. The fact that we cannot speak about God, however, is not a reason to remain silent, but to keep constantly in mind that when we do we are 'stretching language to breaking point', so that it is 'precisely as it breaks that the communication, if any, is achieved' (McCabe 2005: 177).

Negative Theology II: Negative Political Theology

I want to show now that everything we have been discussing can be understood politically. This task has been facilitated by Professor Carlos Pérez's notable book, *Proposición de un Marxismo Hegeliano* (2008). The reason Pérez gives in the Introduction to his book for 'recurring to Marx once again' are indeed negative: 'For his idea that the communist goal, the end of class struggle, is possible. For his radical critique against capitalist exploitation ... Against all forms of naturalism, against the idea of human finitude, so characteristic of the culture of defeat' (Pérez 2008: 9). Pérez postulates, as the basis of his Hegelian Marxism, what he calls a 'theory of alienation', which is, in turn, grounded

> on an absolute historicism, in which every object is objectified by the human action of producing its whole being. The political reason for affirming so counter intuitive a fundament is to avoid all traces of naturalism, all possibility of appealing to elements that, starting from human nature or the human condition, put limits to the possibility of ending class struggle. What is stated here, as the basis, is a radical affirmation of human infinitude ... Without these founding

7 On Hegel's idea of 'representations' (*Vorstellung*), see Taylor (1979: 480–509).

> statements we can project as an utopian horizon a better humanity, but never a humanity that is essentially free. (Pérez 2008: 71)

But the idea of alienation implies that there is no way of knowing what it is for humanity to be 'essentially free'. 'Essential freedom' cannot be seen from our alienated perspective; to talk about it is, again, talking of what we cannot talk. Pérez explains this point with his distinction between *lie*, *error* and *alienation*. What characterizes these three situations is the difference between discourse and action. But in the cases of lying and error this gap is a phenomenon of the conscience: he or she who lies may begin to recognize he or she is lying, and he or she who errs may come to recognize his/her mistake (Pérez 2008: 88). But alienation is different: it cannot be overcome simply at the level of consciousness, by just *acknowledging* that one is alienated:

> It is not the case that you are alienated. It is, rather, that you are your alienation. And you cannot overcome it until you change what you are … In a situation of alienation, there is no non-alienated point of view … Only from the point of view of other alienation it is possible to see the alienation. This means that overcoming it cannot be an epistemological process (making the truth appear) but only a specifically political process. (Pérez 2008: 89)

But how can we understand what it would be like to be in a non-alienated situation? If there is no non-alienated point of view in an alienated situation, how can we even describe the idea of a non-alienated life? What is important here is the experience of a *deficit*, a

> Suffering that drives us towards breaking the relation that constitutes it, in order to change life itself. The possible movement of the alienated conscience is given by the flagrant, existential, empirical contradiction, between that which is harmonized by conscience and that which is suffered in immediate experience. (Pérez 2008: 90)

What Pérez has called 'a suffering' is *an existential experience of deficit*. This experience of deficit flows from the contradictions in our forms of life, from the fact that they promise what they cannot give. We may be able to formulate the idea of a non-alienated life through a radicalization of such unfulfilled promises. What makes the conscience of alienation as well as its overcoming action possible is that what is experienced as a deficit may be identified as a deficit (that is, it is not harmonized). Refusing to regard this deficit as anything other than a deficit can be described as faith in human infinitude: in the possibility of non-alienated life:

> The anthropological thesis that is discussed here is that exploitation is, originally, a survival strategy against scarcity, a strategy progressively objectified through history …That human beings have no internal tendency to oppress … or

> subjugate …is not, and cannot be, an empirical thesis. It is a matter of principle, driven by the conclusion one wants to arrive at. If these tendencies existed (as part of the human nature, the human condition or as a biological basis of conduct) communism would be impossible. If one wishes to arrive at that conclusion it must be excluded from the premises. (Pérez 2008: 109)

The conditions under which alienation can be identified, however, are unlikely to be maintained. This is so because what allows the individual to identify his alienation is consciousness of a deficit, which implies that he or she must face a 'generally painful and catastrophic' situation. This condition appears as cognitive dissonance, a contradiction between what is harmonized by conscience and suffered by experience. The dissonance is reduced by denial, which neutralizes the deficit. This denial assumes one of two forms – the first is the liberal (or conservative) response:[8] there is no deficit, because a mature understanding of the human

---

8 In the politically relevant sense, the expressions 'liberal' and 'conservative' are equivalent. In the apparently most popular antithesis, these two terms are politically opposed: but in the radical antithesis, the two terms are analogous and are both opposed to 'socialism'. This may be one of the reasons why 'academic' discussions seem so detached from actually existing politics: those discussions do not capture the oppositions that are really important. This is the case, for example, with the so-called 'liberal–communitarian debate', labels that, in North American academic vocabulary, correspond to the liberal/conservative distinction. Paul Kahn (2005) has noticed very much the same point in his *Putting Liberalism in its Place*, where he claims that that liberalism and communitarianism are, concerning the relevant issues, analogous, a thesis as implausible at first sight as it is correct.

To express this larger point briefly, both liberals and conservatives settle for this world: the conservative because he or she ascribes normativity to the traditional order he/she discovers in the world, and the liberal because he or she believes that the subject, the human being (not the order), is natural, and therefore the only thing we can do is to order human interactions so they can live without attacking each other. Both liberals and conservatives deny human beings' infinitude, because they both think there is no hope in this world (the very idea of an 'essentially free' humanity is meaningless to them): for the conservative because he or she thinks that if there is hope it is in another world, completely alien to this one (thus it is politically irrelevant), and for the liberal because for him or her there is nothing more than the actually existing world.

The fundamental equivalence of liberals and conservatives makes its more concrete oppositions, about this or that legal reform proposal, pale in comparison. This equivalence is particularly pristine (*pace* its author, which gives it greater value) in Gray's *Black Mass*. Gray's thesis is that what characterizes modern political discourse is its apocalyptic dimension: 'Modern politics is a chapter in the history of religion' is the book's opening phrase. Thus this is the same thesis as is defended in this chapter. Gray nevertheless thinks this is modernity's curse, because all apocalyptic comprehension of politics leads to terror and totalitarianism: 'all societies contain divergent ideals of life. When a utopian regime collides with this fact the result can only be repression or defeat. Utopianism does not cause totalitarianism – for a totalitarian regime to come into being many other factors are

condition (enhanced nowadays by volumes of neo-Darwinism) will show us that human beings are 'naturally' wolves to each other, so that the only meaning of politics is to hold each person at bay in order to make our co-existence possible. The second form of denial (which is nothing but a symmetrical reflection of the first) is the one taken by those whom Engels called 'infantile communists'; those who

> imagine that, merely because they want to skip the intermediate stations and compromises, the matter is settled, and if 'it begins' in the next few days – which they take for granted – and they take over power, 'Communism will be introduced' the day after tomorrow. If that is not immediately possible, they are not Communists. (Quoted in Lenin 1940: Ch. 8)

The first denies alienation because it denies that reconciliation among really existing individuals is possible, either because there is a natural tendency to violence and domination within them, which may be controlled but not eliminated, or because reconciliation will be reached only in paradise, understood as something completely alien to this vale of tears. When they are optimists, they say we can expect a 'better humanity' (namely, one with a bigger GDP) but 'not an essentially free humanity'.

The second, on the other hand, denies alienation by treating it as a phenomenon of the conscience, which may be solved simply by 'realizing' that one is alienated (a state at which, in fact, he or she has already arrived, so that if 'it begins' in the next few days, communism will be introduced the day after). Pérez's idea of

---

necessary – but totalitarianism follows whenever the dream of a life without conflict is consistently pursued through the use of state power' (p. 53). Indeed, if this claim can be associated with someone in particular, the most obvious candidate is not a conservative but a liberal thinker – Isaiah Berlin.

Both liberalism and conservatism are defined by the idea that the actually existing world, with its conflicts as they appear to us today, *is as good as it gets*. Gray claims that this is only asserted by conservatives, but at the price of forcing an obviously implausible millenarist interpretation of liberalism. If Gray is right and totalitarianism is the consequence of pursuing a completely human form of life through politics, we shall have to choose between conservatism and liberalism (that is the reason why, after the fall of Berlin's Wall, so many leftists followed Isaiah Berlin and became liberals). But Gray is wrong, because he identifies the origins of totalitarianism incorrectly. Totalitarianism does not originate in the idea that a world is possible in which the unity of particular and general interest is transparent. It originates in the idea that to achieve this it is necessary to ignore actually existing human beings and their (our) forms of life, because they are completely worthless. It is the idea that, because they are alienated, the interests, wishes and beliefs of actually existing individuals are irrelevant, that they may be ignored in order to hasten the birth of the new man. Later, this will be discussed by reference to the idea of Revolution and what will be called the 'Portalian principle'. Because what Gray's argument legitimately brings into question is not the idea of a world free from alienation, but the idea of Revolution which, as we shall see, is where the main problem of Pérez's argument lies.

alienation as a foundation (or at least the way in which I interpret it here), implies that in a deep political sense liberals (conservatives) and infantile communists are equivalent, because neither understands the way in which actually existing institutions can legitimately claim our allegiance. The liberal, who settles for this world, must claim that law is not the will of the people, if by 'the people' anything greater than the sum total of individuals is meant. But then, of course, the obvious problem is grounding the obligation to obey a law one opposes but which was passed nevertheless because, for example, the lobbying of some particular pressure group was highly effective. Democratic theory says that, in a politically relevant sense, that law is still *my* will because it is *our* will, but for the liberal this is overheated rhetoric.

The infantile communist, on the other hand, will flatly deny the legitimacy of any actually existing democratic institution, because to him or her the function of institutions is always the same: to mask exploitation. For them, the idea that law is the will of the people is also overheated rhetoric, but in this case its function is *ideological*.

What is common to both is that they fail to understand political discourse and its particular mode of signifying. It is this mode of signifying that politics shares with theology. Political concepts signify, as do theological ones, imperfectly.

The idea of representation (metaphors or analogies) provides us with a new perspective from which we can try to understand our political institutions. Previously, the dilemma was that, to recognize their claim on our loyalty, we had either to deny that they embody a systematic deficit (to do this we must change our understanding of the institution – the point of democracy being that heads will be 'counted and not severed', in Norberto Bobbio's phrase) or we had to recognize the deficit and claim that because of it institutions are 'merely ideological' and thus false. The problem is that the infantile communist is right in claiming that there is a systematic deficit inherent in institutions: they exist because something must be made probable, and the obvious question concerning any institution is; Why is it necessary?: Why is co-operation unlikely without the institution of contract law? The existence of the institution, in other words, is in itself a deficit, and it is crucial to remain aware of this, because the experience of the deficit as a deficit is the necessary condition for identifying our alienation as such without assuming an impossibly non-alienated perspective.

Hence liberals are right in claiming that really existing institutions, with their really existing shortcomings, do have a claim on our loyalty. But since they will not admit signifying imperfectly, they believe that to say this, the deficit must be ignored or wished away. And with this they invite us to abandon the crucial perspective that stems from the experience of the deficit, to settle for the world as we know it.

Since existing institutions are in themselves the mark of a deficit, all institutions have two faces: one emancipatory and the other oppressive. The law of contract is an explication of what it is to co-operate for two individuals who recognize each other and refuse to behave instrumentally towards the other. Yet individuals can assume this position for instrumental reasons. Generally speaking, institutions are false (there will be no institutions in the kingdom of God or under communism) but in their falsehood they teach us: it is by living under them that we can see from afar what a non-alienated life looks like. For this reason, we can be loyal to institutions without denying their deficits. But this loyalty never loses its ironic quality, in so far as the form of life we live is necessarily dehumanized, insufficient. This ironic loyalty is based on faith: faith that what is inhuman in our really existing world can be overcome, because it is not a fatal and necessary consequence of our nature, but of our forms of life; forms of life that accustom us to show 'incredible levels of indifference towards the pain of others' (Pérez 2008: 62). And as it is a consequence of our alienated forms of life, it is possible, in principle, to live humanly, if we could only live under truly humane forms of life! What could these forms of life be like? The whole point of a theory of alienation such as the one defended by Pérez, or at least the sense I have of it here, is that we cannot answer this question: there is no point of view free from alienation in an alienated situation. But we may know some aspects of our forms of life that will not exist: there will be no opposition of class interests (which means, there will be no class differences), there will be no objectification, no exploitation. We know that because these are the conditions that lead to the existential experience of deficit. And as we cannot know affirmatively what these non-alienated forms of life will be like, we cannot truly talk about them. But here we have to follow Wittgenstein's example and disregard the advice he himself contradicted in the very act of giving it.

Sacraments

Once again the idea that we are speaking of what we cannot speak. Perhaps because of that we should remember Pérez's observation: speaking is not enough, because alienation is not a phenomenon of the conscience, but of life. In theological terms, this implies the notion of *sacrament* and of *sacramental practices*.

In Christian theology, sacraments are signs of God's presence among us. That is, they are signs of the possibility of radical reconciliation, of complete human fulfilment, in a world where reconciliation and such fulfilment are impossible. Therefore, they are signs that, as Aquinas said, 'signify imperfectly'. Their signifying imperfectly does not mean they are false, but rather that their full meaning is inaccessible to us given our forms of life (forms which Pérez would say are constituted by alienation, while Aquinas would say constituted by sin). And, of course, in the kingdom of God those signs will be unnecessary (and that is why in the kingdom of God the virtues of faith and hope will disappear). An understanding of politics that avoids the symmetrical errors of someone who believes that what we see today is *as good as it gets* and someone who thinks that a non-alienated life can be brought about just by seizing power and rearranging things 'the right way' is what we could call a *sacramental* understanding of politics; our institutions are (or at least may be) signs of what is unknown: living non-alienated lives.

Here it might be useful to phrase it differently: alienation consists in seeing the other's interest as opposed to one's own. Because our interests are (or appear to be) in conflict, it is unlikely that we shall spontaneously agree in our identification of what is in our common interest. What is likely is that I will try to use whatever means I have to get you to agree to what is in my interest (indeed, if I manage to convince you that your interests are served when you serve mine, I will have thoroughly succeeded) – and you will do the same. The function of democratic institutions is to make likely what is unlikely: that our norms serve everybody's interest, and not only that of the powerful.

A 'sacramental' understanding of those institutions allows us to show an ironic commitment to them. It is a form of commitment, because in our conditions it is the only way to express (and live according to) the idea that the only source of normativity is one common to everyone's perspective. But it is ironic, because we know that law as an institution does not live up to its own promises. And note that it does not live up to them because it *cannot* do so: if it could, the fundamental commonality of interests among humankind would be transparent to us; that is, we would have overcome our alienation. But had we reached that condition, the institution would no longer be necessary, because the necessity of this institution is the deficit of our alienated forms of life. This is the meaning of the Marxist idea that under communism, law would wither away, as well as the meaning of the Thomist observation that in the kingdom of God there will be no sacraments. Just as religion is the soul of a soulless world, law is the will of a community that has no community of wills.

The fact that both political and theological language cannot but use representations (metaphors and analogies) implies that their pathologies are also the same. Indeed, because of this pathology it seems as though we are living under the domain of dead ideas. The pathology is losing sight of the fact that representations are just that: representations, instead taking them as literal descriptions. The origin of this pathology lies in the temptation to deny the contradiction between promise and delivery on which they are based, and thus lose sight of the possibility of an ironic commitment, which if not resisted reduces our possibilities to naive devotion or cynical irony.

If the representations in which theological and political language recur must be understood literally, then they are evidently false and must be abandoned. Those who assume this position are likely to ask questions such as: Do you really believe the consecrated wafer is a piece of human flesh? That the world appeared magically in six 24-hour days? That the earth is no more than 10,000 years old? That law is truly everyone's will and not the will of an 'elite'? For this line of criticism, splendidly illustrated nowadays by the recent (and banal) books written by the high priests of neo-Darwinism, Richard Dawkins (2008) and Daniel Dennet (2006), as well as in the school called 'public choice', all theological language, in addition to the political language of the democratic tradition, is complete nonsense. Since these critics do not even understand the literary genre (that is, the mode of signification) of theological or political discourse, their admonitions are ridiculously irrelevant.[9]

Or, better, they are or would be for a self-conscious theology or political understanding. The reason why their admonitions might have sense today is the symmetric but inverse pathology of religion; if Dawkins and Dennett believe that metaphors and religious representations are meant to be literal descriptions, and that as such they are obviously false, the idolatrous agree with them in the former but disagree in the latter (believing they are true). They go to court to claim that the story of Genesis ought to be understood as a theory alternative to Darwin's about the origin of life on earth. Here religion becomes a way out of this vale of tears, and is eternally projected outwards: it tells us nothing about this life, except that we must endure it in order to gain access, once we have served our time down here, to a better and truer one. Thus this idea ignores that 'God' is a metaphor, that the meaning of God is that there are no gods, and worships an idol defined by its fabulous powers, whose most portentous demonstration has been the 'intelligent design' of everything that exists. Politically speaking, they correspond to the neo-constitutionalist who believes that injustice in our forms of life is a phenomenon of pure conscience, and that, were he or she appointed to the Constitutional Court, true justice would follow the day after tomorrow.

Here we must return to Juan Luis Segundo's antithesis. In the faith/atheism antithesis, Dawkins opposes those who condemn evolution because it contradicts the Book of Genesis just as the infantile communist opposes the liberal/conservative. But in the faith/idolatry (Varone: faith/religion) antithesis, Dawkins and those who see God as a super-wizard concur, and they oppose those whose faith is free of idolatry, in the same way that the infantile communist and the

9 These critics, who call themselves 'brights' (Dennett 2006: 21) define what they criticize by reference to the belief in representations literally understood: 'For some people, prayer is not literally *talking to God* but, rather, a 'symbolic' activity, a way of talking to *oneself* about one's deepest concerns, expressed metaphorically. It is rather like beginning a diary entry with 'Dear Diary'. If what they call God is really *not* an agent in their eyes, a being that can *answer* prayers, *approve* and *disapprove, receive* sacrifices, and *mete out* punishment or forgiveness, then, while they may call this Being God, and stand in awe of *it* (not *Him),* their creed, whatever it is, is not really a religion according to my definition' (Dennett 2006: 10). In other words, Dennett defines 'religion' on the basis of the literalness of its representations: religion, in his definition, is 'a social system whose participants avow belief in a supernatural agent or agents whose approval is to be sought' (ibid.: 9).

The ease of Dennett's move from 'him' to 'it' shows that he and those he criticizes occupy the same position in Segundo's 'more interesting' dichotomy (between faith and idolatry). Indeed, both of them take the language they use for granted (oddly enough, it is authors such as Dennett or Dawkins who are specially liable to forget Williams' warning). Therefore his stipulations are quite difficult to comment upon, since *in some sense* he is completely right. But not in the sense he imagines himself to be. It may be said about the idea of 'religion' that it is a corrupt notion, incompatible with faith. See Francois Varone's distinction between religion, atheism and faith in Varone (1987: 15–79).

liberal (conservative) are against those who exhibit an ironic (that is, sacramental) commitment to existing institutions.

The Protestant Principle

Political theology begins in the thesis that the modes of signifying of theological and political discourses are the same. We have seen that by adopting the theological–political point of view we can re-draw a familiar landscape in which traditional antagonisms are equivalent in an important sense. What makes them equivalent is their rejection of political theology; that is, their rejection of politics as a language structurally analogous to theology (as a language that signifies imperfectly). By ignoring this they are forced to deny the contradiction in which we live, and must then accept one horn while ignoring the other: it means either settling for this world or rejecting it altogether. Since the possible movement of alienated consciousness is grounded in the existential experience of this contradiction (as Pérez has said), this denial amounts to the radicalization of alienation, in so far as it hides what permits its identification. But none the less (or perhaps precisely because of it) these positions are attractive, as they reduce our cognitive dissonance and allow us to continue with our lives.

How can we maintain the tension in spite of normality's brutal levelling force? What I have called a sacramental understanding of our institutions is, of course, the first step. But, is this a *stable* understanding? Is it possible for a sacramental understanding of politics to subsist in normal times, in the face of the levelling force of normality? (The traditional leftist objection to social-democracy was precisely this: normality transforms citizens into clients, because the spirit that grounds social-democratic institutions cannot survive the normal operation of the institution; hence they create new forms of alienation, rather than emancipation. That the 'revolutionary' left has been defeated and that the social-democratic option is somewhat more attractive nowadays should not make us forget these objections, for they point to a truly fundamental problem.) In my opinion, the survival of our political practices depends on the answer to this question. This is what it means to live under the domain of dead ideas. Given the question's breadth, it would be derisory to pretend to give a full answer here, but we may try to move a step closer by availing ourselves of what Paul Tillich called 'the Protestant principle':

> Protestantism has a principle that stands beyond all its realizations. It is the critical and dynamic source of all Protestant realizations, but it is not identical with any of them. It cannot be confined by a definition. It is not exhausted by any historical religion; it is not identical with the structure of the Reformation or of early Christianity or even with a religious form at all. It transcends them as it transcends any cultural form. On the other hand, it can appear in all of them; it is a living, moving, restless power in them … [It] contains the divine and human protest against any absolute claim made for a relative reality, even if this claim

> is made by a Protestant church. The Protestant principle is the judge of every religious and cultural reality. (Tillich 1948: 163)

The last sentences here reveals that what Tillich calls the 'Protestant principle' is not really Protestant: it is the assumption made by all theological reflection that heeds Williams' warning – that is, it remains aware that it must always account for its own language: for the moment in which representations fossilize and claim to provide a full account of what they represent – specifically, the moment in which metaphors are no longer understood as metaphors but rather as literal descriptions – faith becomes a set of false, irrational and supernatural beliefs (that is, idolatry). It ceases to be faith in the possibility of a non-alienated human life and becomes a conspicuous sign of alienation.

In fact, the Protestant principle has to be a Catholic principle, because Catholicism insists on a politically central dimension. One of the distinctive characteristics of Catholicism is its insistence on tradition as a source of revelation, which in turn implies the special relevance of the institutional aspect of the Church. As Schmitt claimed, Catholicism is an idea of representation by means of institutions (Schmitt 1966). Institutions are formalized traditions. Tradition, on the other hand, is a common history, a collective biography.[10] But it is a biography, the meaning of which only appears when it is read according to the Protestant principle, for only then can revelation be understood not as a truth fallen from the sky and communicated to us from the outside, without denying its radical opposition to this world of sin (as was done by nineteenth-century liberal theology). The Protestant principle enables us to understand tradition as the effort of successive generations to give finite form to what is infinite, historicity to what transcends history. This is possible only to the extent that tradition itself does not seem alien; that is, that members of the tradition understand that they have a special responsibility towards it. Tradition becomes alien when it forgets the Protestant principle. Speaking of a tradition as the Christian tradition in general or Catholicism in particular, there is nothing strange about its being, in the same sense as Pérez's Marxism, opposed to this world. This is precisely the point: it is the sigh of the oppressed creature, the heart of a heartless world, the soul of a soulless environment. This opposition may be called eschatological, or anticipatory, because it has a sacramental dimension in the sense we have already seen. But since we are talking about actually existing traditions and institutions, it is possible and even likely that this opposition to the world will be caused, as

10 This is the reason why a tradition needs a principle of identity, something of which we can say that the tradition is the history. And the institutionalization that marks Catholic Christianity was precisely a compensation for the deficit of identity implied by Christian universalism: from its early days, Christianity was understood not as the religion of a (naturally defined) people, but of humanity as a whole. The lack of any natural feature that could provide a principle of identity is offset artificially by the institutional Church. See Segundo (1989: 1903).

least as much, by the fact that the institutional forms of the tradition, since they exist in this world, have become corrupted (McCabe 1968: 155). Distinguishing these two reasons for the opposition between tradition and the world is what it means to belong to a tradition that is not experienced as alien, a tradition for which one is responsible. Tillich's 'Protestant principle' is the modulation of this idea. It keeps the possibility constantly open that accepting what one receives is not showing loyalty, but rather betraying one's tradition. That is why the fact that the Church is a corrupt institution is not a reason to abandon it.[11]

Revolution

Now we are in a position to discuss one of modernity's most powerful ideas, whose development during the twentieth century was nevertheless very unpromising. Donoso Cortés called it 'the most terrible word of all': Revolution.

Pérez characterizes his Marxism as 'revolutionary':

> [I]n the specific sense that it claims that only violence can break the chain of violence, already installed by dominant classes. But also in the slightly more scholarly sense that the only way to finish the prevailing class domination is radically to change the rule of law and, eventually, putting class struggle to an end will imply abolishing any institutional kind of rule of law. (Pérez 2008: 67)

Later, Pérez will claim that the dichotomy 'reform-revolution' is 'one of the most sterile and destructive discussions in the culture of the left' (Pérez 2008: 182) because 'the difference between reform and revolution is one of degree, of range, it is not a disjunctive and least of all an antagonism' (ibid.: 183).

To some extent, the whole of this chapter's argument is contained here. The usual oppositions we have been discussing would understand that the difference between reform and revolution is a difference of type: the liberal and conservative would say, in fact, that only reform is acceptable (because revolution implies violence and it is, as a method of political action, 'immoral'), while the infantile communist will believe that only revolution is acceptable (because in order to end with alienation it is necessary to seize power and arrange everything anew). A sacramental understanding of politics may overcome this opposition because it understands that revolution is a radicalization of what is already present in our institutional forms of life; it is not about replacing one set of institutions for another, nor about doing away with them, but about radicalizing them.

But it is precisely because this point contains the whole argument that the way in which Pérez discusses it is so insufficient. Indeed, Pérez is not overly interested in the emancipatory dimension of our institutional forms of life. This emancipatory dimension does not lie (it is always important to remind ourselves) in the fact that institutional forms of life actually enable us to live non-alienated

11 See McCabe (1967).

lives, so that we could accept them naively. This is why their emancipatory dimension is not denied when we recognize that institutions are corrupt, that they have an oppressive dimension. Every actually existing institution possesses these two facets, one oppressive and the other emancipatory. When we discussed the institutional forms of our religious practices, we noted something that may be generalized: they belong to an alienated world. A non-alienated world is a world in which mutual radical recognition is no longer improbable, and therefore where there is no need to render it probable by means of institutions: it will have become second nature to us or, better yet, we will then have understood that non-alienated life was always our authentic nature. The point, however, is not what we might say about forms of life we cannot imagine, but rather how they inform our actions, even if we cannot actually imagine them. It is about identifying the forms of political action that are sacramental, not because they are instrumental to hasten the arrival of the kingdom of God (or communism), but because they anticipate it. As we have seen, the idea that alienation may be diagnosed from a non-alienated perspective makes no sense at all. It can only be identified from within alienation, as an existential experience of deficit. And it is this that must be coupled with an understanding of our institutional forms of life that shuns both cynicism and naivety. Cynics see only the oppressive face of institutions; and the gullible see only their emancipatory side. The former ignore the fact that institutions carry the promise of a non-alienated life (in contracts we find the idea of exchanges among subjects that fully recognize each other, in marriage the idea of a community based on love, and so on), while the latter ignore the fact that actually existing institutions can never live up to their own promises, and that the extent of their failure to do so is the extent of their being instruments of oppression.

I want to refer here to a little known exchange of letters between Karl Marx and Pierre-Joseph Proudhon. In 1846, Marx wrote to Proudhon, inviting him to become a member of a European socialist and communist network to link German, French and English socialists. The network was meant, on the one hand, to create a discussion forum that surpassed nationalist limitations and, on the other hand, to allow members in one country to be kept informed of developments elsewhere, to be prepared for 'when the moment of action comes'. Proudhon accepted the invitation unenthusiastically. Along with his acceptance, though, Proudhon included two remarkable substantive observations in response to Marx. The second observation is particularly relevant now:

> I have also some observations to make on this phrase of your letter: *at the moment of action*. Perhaps you still retain the opinion that no reform is at present possible without a *coup de main*, without what was formerly called a revolution and is really nothing but a shock. That opinion, which I understand, which I excuse, and would willingly discuss, having myself shared it for a long time, my most recent studies have made me abandon completely. I believe we have no need of it in order to succeed; and that consequently we should not put forward *revolutionary action* as a means of social reform, because that pretended means

> would simply be an appeal to force, to arbitrariness, in brief, a contradiction. I myself put the problem in this way: *to bring about the return to society, by an economic combination of the wealth which was withdrawn from society by another economic combination.* In other words, through Political Economy to turn the theory of Property against Property in such a way as to engender what you German socialists call *community* and what I will limit myself for the moment to calling *liberty* or *equality*. But I believe that I know the means of solving this problem with only a short delay; I would therefore prefer to burn Property by a slow fire, rather than give it new strength by making a St Bartholomew's night of the proprietors. (Proudhon 1846)

From our historical and spiritual moment it is hard not to see the sense behind Proudhon's observations. Particularly in the Third World, so much bloodshed, so many frustrated expectations of revolutions that in the end were 'nothing but a shock'. When one remembers the seizures produced by the Land Reform (agrarian reform) in Chile, and the fact that less than ten years later the most extreme neo-liberalism the world has ever known was instituted in storm of fire and steel (and this is not a metaphor), how can we fail to see the truth behind Proudhon's fear of giving property new strength by making a St Bartholomew's night of the proprietors.[12]

I think that Pérez's concept of revolution fails to take account of this. His suggested measures (reducing work time while keeping the wages fixed, decentralizing public services, reducing the cost of credit and so on (Pérez 2008: 188–9)) is a set of instrumental measures, the value of which can be reduced to its instrumental aptitude to bring about a better humanity, but precisely because of this aspect, not a humanity that is essentially free. It is not a programme of political action that strives towards a radicalization of the unfulfilled promises of our own institutions. Pérez leaves no space to explain the meaning of our current political forms in terms of their two faces. This double face explains the 'more scholarly' sense of revolution Pérez defends (though I am not sure he would recognize my reading). A revolution is in this sense a radical transformation of our forms of life, so radical, in fact, that pre-revolutionary discourse about post-revolutionary life cannot but avail itself of representations; that is, to analogies and metaphors. The reason for this is that post-revolutionary life cannot be explained in terms of a pre-revolutionary life:

> The revolutionary … proposes to change not merely this or that detail within society, but the structure, and hence the values of the society itself. The revolutionary does not propose something that in terms of *this society* is better; he wants to change the terms. He wants history to advance not simply further

12 I am not saying that the agrarian reform in Chile was such a St Bartholomew's night of the proprietors. But it is clear that they understood it as such, and that explains why there was to be, after the 1973 *coup d'état*, so much violence.

> along the established lines, but along new lines. Now such lines extend into the past as well as into the future. I mean that each society interprets its history as leading up to itself, as well as leading forward into the future. Indeed each society *is* its interpretation of its past, just as each person *is* his interpretation of his past; I hope this does not sound too enigmatic. I only mean that if you ask yourself the question 'who am I?' you answer by producing an autobiography. A radical change in society, a revolution, means a change in its interpretation of history, just as a radical change in a person, a conversion let us say, involves a change in the whole of his autobiography. He *now* sees that he was a miserable sinner even though while he was committing the miserable sins he was really rather cheerful about it all. (McCabe 1968: 28–9)

Hence Pérez is right when he says that revolution implies 'changing the rule of law radically' and 'abolishing any institutional kind of rule of law'. Those institutional forms are the sign of a deficit, so they will not be necessary when the deficit is overcome. Yet it is a mistake to conclude from this that 'revolution' implies fighting those institutional forms in order to abolish them. How will we know what we are fighting for, and how will we be able to distinguish revolution from a purely imaginary future, from an illusion? The question is the same as the one we already answered following Pérez: How can we know what it is like to live a non-alienated life? It is impossible, because post-revolutionary forms of life cannot be described in pre-revolutionary language. We can only know how it is *not* going to be, and it is crucial for that to assume the existential experience of deficit. Our institutional life (the 'rule of law'), keeps that existential experience alive. But, as we have seen, living with the existential experience of deficit is painful because it means living with cognitive dissonance. Certainly, this painful experience can be reduced through denial (false consciousness), whether it be by thinking that the rule of law as it actually exists fully guarantees freedom and autonomy (to do so requires the redefining of liberty and autonomy: negative liberty, for example) or by thinking that the institutions of the rule of law are *only* a mask of exploitation. While institutions (the 'rule of law') are indeed signs of deficit, the deficit is not in the existence of the rule of law, but in the conditions of our lives that make the rule of law necessary in order to live human lives. By making this dramatic mistake, Pérez seems to be in line with the twentieth-century revolutionaries who fought for revolution but did not achieve it, but what Proudhon (the utopian socialist) saw: an appeal to force, to arbitrariness; and ultimately a contradiction. For today it is hard to deny that, as Tomás Moulian has said: 'Socialist revolutions could never overcome their mark of origin and always needed coercion to affirm themselves. They could never build a participatory democracy because the 'all-out war' ('guerra a muerte') never ceases: it is endless' (Moulian 2000: 112).In other words, the objection to Pérez's less scholarly idea of revolution is not a *moralist* objection that condemns violence as a method of political action. It is a *political* objection, one that holds that violence is not a force that can be dominated, but is rather a force that dominates anyone who thinks he or she has dominated it,[13] and makes people forget what they were fighting for.

The People and Their Will

Now we can return to the question about the people, their will and the law. Our question was: how can the people will anything, and in particular, how can the people will into being the rules of ascription? The argument up to now implies that our problem can be solved by understanding the question or, more precisely, by understanding its mode of signifying imperfectly. This will lead to the observation that, like any theology free from idolatry, our understanding of these political concepts will have to be negative or 'apophatic'.

The Will of the People as a Double Metaphor: The Metaphor of the Will

To begin with it may be useful to consider the usual objection to the liberal idea of self-ownership, of the property of one's own person. This idea is the basis of liberalism (or at least some varieties of liberalism), because it grounds the natural rights that individuals want to protect by means of the social contract. The usual objection is that this idea rests in a Cartesian dualism of mind and body that is nowadays unacceptable: it assumes that behind this body there is 'me', its owner: that my body is an object possessed by a subject different from it, just as any owner possesses his things (a 'ghost in the machine'). And this, of course, is absurd.

The charge of dualism is an objection against a *positive* understanding of self-ownership: if the thesis is understood as an answer to the question of who owns my body, it seems to be unavoidably dualist. But the thesis finds a basis in a negative interpretation, according to which what is important about it is not the way it answers the question, but its self-evident negative implication: that nobody else (neither the lord, nor the king and so on) owns me, or my body: I am not a slave, I am free. In this negative sense, the idea of self-ownership is not only free of the objection of Cartesian dualism, but it also possesses content that is undeniably emancipatory: it marks the movement, to use Maine's (1906) celebrated expression, from status to contract.[14]

Just as the self-ownership thesis is distorted if it is understood in a cataphatic rather than in an apophatic way, so is the thesis of law as the will of the people

13 See Weil (1987) and Atria (2006).

14 The question, of course, is not only 'philosophical'. Gerald Cohen (1995) claimed that the self-ownership thesis that lies at the base of Marx's concept of exploitation, makes it liable to a neo-liberal critique such as the one deployed by Robert Nozick in Nozick (1974). Therefore, Cohen claimed, the thesis had to be abandoned. But what had to be abandoned is the thesis in its cataphatic sense only.

distorted if it is understood in a cataphatic way: it is the will of no one else. Thus the idea of the will of the people marks the transformation of subjects into citizens.

Let us try to move further ahead. To do this, we must use representations. Why a *will*? The answer becomes apparent if we acknowledge a fundamental fact about what we might call the grammar of the will. Compare what is sometimes called the 'direction of fit' of preferences and beliefs: while beliefs are directed to fit the world (thus having an intrinsic criterion of correctness) desires are directed to make the world fit to them (hence they are self-affirming). If I am challenged ('Why do you want X?') I can point to the fact that I want it ('This is simply who I am'). If I am challenged as to why I believe something I owe an explanation in terms of reasons; that is, in terms of the world.

Whoever invokes a belief appeals, then (correctly or incorrectly), to what is universal, to reasons that are, in principle, valid for everyone.[15] The particularity of the person speaking is, therefore, transparent. The speaker claims to be giving expression to something that is in principle universal, in the sense that it could be said by anyone; but he or she who expresses a will affirms his/her particularity – he or she claims (correctly or incorrectly) authority to decide the issue, to decide it in such a way that the decision is not made valid by its correctness, but rather because it is his/her decision. The particularity of the person who wants is not transparent: his/her wanting is contingent and thus it is valid because it is his/her will:

> What is sacred in science is truth; what is sacred in art is beauty. Truth and beauty are impersonal. All this is too obvious. If a child is doing a sum and does it wrong, the mistake bears the stamp of his personality. If he does the sum exactly right, his personality does not enter into it at all. Perfection is impersonal. (Weil 1950)

Because perfection is impersonal and truth universal, believing is transparent: the phrase 'I believe that p (is the case)' means the same as 'p (is the case)'. But willing is not transparent in the same way: a will is always somebody's will. To say that law is will is to say that the existence of law (its validity) is not something universal, that it is always somebody's law: it has been posited, rather than discovered. *Auctoritas, non veritas, facit legem* (Hobbes 1996: Pt II, ch. 16). The sense in which this is an emancipatory idea can also be found in Hobbes' *Leviathan*:

> And when men that think themselves wiser than all others, clamor and demand right Reason for judge; yet seek no more, but that things should be determined, by no other men's reason but their own, it is as intolerable in the society of men, as it is in play after trump is turned, to use for trump on every occasion, that suite whereof they have most in their hand. For they do nothing else, that will have every of their passions, as it comes to bear sway in them, to be taken for

15 This subject is discussed thoroughly in Atria (2009).

> right Reason, and that in their own controversies: betraying their want of right Reason, by the claim they lay to it. (Hobbes 1996: Pt I, ch. 5)

Law is volition because its validity does not depend on its conformity to reason. And the reason for this is that, ever since Hobbes, appeal to the authority of reason does not immediately constitute an appeal to reason's authority, but rather an appeal to the authority of the person making the appeal.

In this first sense, the apophatic content of the idea that law is volition is denial of the unmediated authority of reason. It is a mistake to understand the denial as a celebration of irrationality. It only means that reason cannot rest in any formal authority, and thus its strength is reducible, to use Habermasian jargon, to the unforced force of the better argument: to deny the unmediated authority of reason is to claim that when it is unmediated, the appeal to reason is not an appeal to reason. And this is related to the second sense in which law is will. To affirm that I want X is the same as saying that (I think that) X suits my own interest. Of course, I may be wrong. But if no one has authority over me, that means that only I can correct myself to reach greater clarity as regards my interests. My destiny is my responsibility, and my mistakes will be mistakes and will last until I correct them (this was the first sense: my will is valid because it is mine). Thus my decisions may be described as mine, and my history is my biography.

In this second sense, the fact that law is the people's will means that law is what goes in the people's interest; that is, in everyone's interest (we shall say more about this step from 'the people' to 'everyone' soon). But, of course, this is too ambitious; as Rousseau said in *The Social Contract*,

> In order to discover the rules of association that are most suitable to nations, a superior intelligence would be necessary who could see all the passions of men without experiencing any of them; who would have no affinity with our nature and yet know it thoroughly; whose happiness would not depend on us, and who would nevertheless be quite willing to interest himself in ours; and, lastly, one who, storing up for himself with the progress of time a far-off glory in the future, could labor in one age and enjoy in another. Gods would be necessary to give laws to men. (Rousseau 2002: 27)

By discovering the idea of 'general will', Rousseau founded the modern democratic tradition. But the moment in which he discovered the idea and the moment in which he identified its historical or political improbability were the same. Using the terms introduced above, though applying them to Rousseau is anachronistic, we may say that the improbability of the general will lies in the fact that it must be identified under conditions of alienation. In these conditions, what is ours appears alien. Thus the general will, that is, what goes in everybody's interest, seems to be different and opposed to our own, factious, particular interests. This contradiction between common and particular interest is what gives meaning to the idea of the 'state of nature' (the case proposed by Hobbes is, as always, the most perspicuous one): the state of nature was a literary resource to illustrate circumstances in which it was immediately evident to the reader that the individuals' interests of the moment were in conflict with their real interests. The paradox of the natural condition of mankind is not that there is *bellum omnium contra omnes*, a situation that is deplorable for all, but the fact that such a situation is brought about by the rational actions of individual people, each of whom is doing what, in those circumstances, in his or her individual interest, and because everyone is pursuing his or her individual interest, everyone loses. And note carefully that here 'everyone' does not mean a magical, mysterious supra-individual entity, but each individual.

The problem is not that there is no such thing as the interests of all; the problem is that, in the natural condition of mankind, identifying common interests is unlikely; what is likely is that each will pursue his or her individual immediate interest. This is why 'without a common power to keep them all in awe, [human beings] are in that condition which is called Warre', in which 'nothing can be Unjust' (Hobbes 1996: ch. 13, 88–9).

Thus the creation of a common power capable of keeping all in awe is what makes peace likely.[16] But though it makes peace likely it does not make freedom likely, because it makes us subject to a heteronomous will. The sense of democratic institutions is that they make it more likely that we shall only be subjected to what is in the interests of all. This they do by introducing formal criteria of recognition (just as we have seen that the law of contracts introduces formal criteria of recognition of fair exchanges, or the law of wills introduces formal criteria of recognition of the deceased's last will as to how his or her assets should be distributed). When those criteria are met, and because the criteria are met, then we can treat the relevant decision as one taken from the point of view of everybody. We can express this by saying that the decision has been taken in the name of everybody; that is, it is everybody's decision. But notice that the claim that it is everybody's decision is not based on the idea that the formal criteria are likely to produce a correct aggregation of preferences. Indeed, in times in which the number of citizens who fail to vote is considerable, there is no reason to assume that, if aggregating preferences were the fundamental point about democratic

16 That is why it is so naive to say that the function of the constitution is to 'limit' power. Not because it is naive to believe that power needs to be limited (that is obviously true), but because of the assumption that this is the first problem, the main function of a constitution. But the limitation of power is the second problem. The first problem, the fundamental one, is the creation of power. Constitutions create power, and so enable us to overcome the state of war among us, which is the sign of the absence of power (Hobbes' 'natural equality'). The case of Iraq's post-war situation is the most evident case of the dissolution of power and of the difficulty (or even, in these circumstances, the impossibility) of re-creating it (on this, see Gray 2007: 149–61), but there is no need for us to go this far: the problem in Latin America is precisely that: the creation of a power strong enough to submit the natural forces (sometimes called, using a contradictory expression, 'factual powers').

institutions, a sufficiently sophisticated poll would not produce a better report than a popular election. The point is not about aggregating preferences, but of assuming the proper perspective. And law's claim to be everybody's decision is based on the fact that, by advancing through the different stages of institutional procedure and thus causing the issue to be discussed in public by different people from different perspectives, when a decision receives the final, official mark that allows us formally to identify it as the will of the people, it is likely that it will have been purged of particular interests. Or at least more likely than alternative institutional arrangements such as four generals deciding what is good for an entire country.[17]

Let us not forget, the general argument about institutions involved two moments. The first was answering the question about the meaning of the institution: it was held to be a means to make something probable that would otherwise be improbable. The second was about the way in which institutions can achieve: a testament is an institutional device to identify the last will of the deceased as to how his or her assets should be distributed, but when asking whether a testament is valid we do not ask the substantive question: Does it truly contain the testator's final view on the subject? A contract is an institution, the function of which is identifying exchanges that are fair – that is, those in which none of the parties has been exploited by the other as if they were simply resources – yet in order to determine whether a particular instance of the institution is valid we do not ask the substantive question: is it fair? Legislation is an institution, the point of which is the identification of what is in everybody's interest, but when a given law has been passed its validity cannot be challenged by showing that it is not in everybody's interest; that instead in this case a particular lobby was especially effective.

Thus, we treat whatever is produced by the institution (laws in the 'formal' sense) as if it were what really is in everybody's interests (laws in the 'material' or 'substantive' sense). The gap between the formal and the substantive sense can only be properly breached by (something like) the notion of a *sacrament*, as explained above.

Law, then, is a sacrament of radical recognition. This implies that it has two faces, which correspond to the two senses in which law equates to will. To citizens, it presents itself as their will, as what we think is good for us. As happens with all our beliefs, it is fully reducible to our reasons for believing it is correct.[18] This is shown by the fact that it does not make sense to hold fast to a belief that one has come to accept is false. Our beliefs, in other words, are intrinsically connected to

---

17 In a Chilean summer festival in February 2011, a stand-up comedian performed a rather homophobic routine. The next artist was Puerto Rican band Calle 13, and its leader, Resident, criticized the comedian on national television. The next day the comedian said that he would not accept any criticism coming from a foreigner. Resident replied with a phrase that explains better than I could the reason why institutionally mediated democracy cannot be understood as a second best *vis-à-vis* direct democracy: 'I see from afar what you can't see from up close' ('Veo de lejos lo que no ves de cerca').

18 The point is discussed thoroughly in Atria (2009).

reason, they are transparent to reason (not in the sense, obviously false, that I can only have 'true' beliefs if they are rational, but in the sense that I cannot hold a belief once I have seen it to be irrational). That is why political deliberation knows no a priori limits: the fact that a will has been formed by means of legislative procedure does not constitute a reason to stop thinking or deliberating or campaigning about the issue, so if we come to the conclusion that the previous decision was wrong we can simply change it. This is the meaning of the old idea that law does not bind the legislator.

But if law appears to *the citizen* as his or her will, as what they believe from a universal point of view, namely, what they *really* want, it appears to *the individual* as pure heteronomy, as a decision that is valid because it has been adopted in accordance with valid procedures, and that will stay in force, even if he or she does not agree with it, until it is repealed in accordance with the same procedures. To a pharmaceutical company's CEO who negotiates collusive agreements according to the law of his competitors, it does not appear to him to be his own will, but rather as a norm that binds him regardless of his desire; that is, that coercively constrains his freedom.

This is why law is, like religion, the sign of an alienated world. In a non-alienated world there will be 'exchange but no market ... family but no marriage, government but no state, organizations but no institutions' and later Pérez added: 'order but no laws' (Pérez 2008: 20, 91). Each of these pairs is meant to rescue law's first dimension while denying the second. All of them express the idea that institutions make probable what is improbable: were it not for our alienation, family, government, organizations and order would be immediately probable (that is, probable without institutional mediation), because they would seem 'natural' and thus institutions would become redundant. But the question before us now concerns the sense in which living with markets, states, marriage, institutions and laws points to a non-alienated life in which exchange, family, government, organizations and order come about naturally. It is in this tension that the idea of the law as the will of the people exists.

Because there were gods before Christianity, and peoples before democracy. And just as Christian theology uses a pagan concept, god, in order to subvert it and express the idea that there are no gods, democratic tradition takes hold of an anti-democratic concept, 'the people', to subvert it and express the idea that there are no peoples. The mistake of thinking that God is a supernatural wizard is equivalent to mistaking the people for a group of individuals each distinguishable from the next, which is the mistake of using, as has become common these days, the word 'people' (pueblo) in the plural (as in 'indigenous peoples'). Pueblo, like God, is a word that can only be used in the singular.

The People, Bearer of a Negativity

Idolatry (theological or political) starts, as we have seen, in the movement from the negative to the positive, from the apophatic to the cataphatic. Positively characterized, God is a super wizard, and 'the people' is an existing entity, defined by race or some equivalent (natural) property. An apophatic idea of God understands it as the denial of all human deficits, and so we could say: God is love. This is not a statement about what God is, but one about what denies all human deficits (thus the argument discussed here is not a reformulation of Feuerbach's familiar argument, but rather its reverse: it is the reversal of the reversal). Correspondingly, 'people' is a denial of all political deficits, and so we are able to say that it is radical mutual recognition. Again, this is not so much a statement about what 'the people' is, as a statement that denies all political deficits. The contrary is political or religious idolatry.

Schmitt says that 'in a special sense', the people is a negative concept:

> In a special meaning of the word, the people are everyone who is not honoured and distinguished, everyone not privileged, everyone prominent not because of property, social position or education. Thus states Schopenhauer: 'whoever does not understand Latin is part of the people'. In the French revolution of the year 1789, the bourgeoisie as Third Estate could identify itself with the nation and the bourgeoisie was the people, because the bourgeoisie was the opposition to the aristocracy and to the privileged. Sieyès posed the famous question: what is the Third Estate? He answered that it is the nation. The Third Estate is nothing and should become everything. But as soon as the bourgeoisie itself appeared as a class that is marked by property and that dominates the state, the negation had to move. Now the proletariat became the people, because it becomes the bearer of this negativity. It is the part of the population that does *not* have property, does not participate in the productive majority, and finds no place in the existing order. (Schmitt 2008: 272; translation slightly amended)

And, to avoid the predictable *ad hominem* objection of the Nazi hunter, who will find a way to show that in some way Nazism follows from this, we may note that the same idea, albeit in somewhat different terms, is defended by Pérez: 'Our enemies have and must have the same universal rights we claim for ourselves. What we deny them are those particular rights which they claim for themselves, and which make them, structurally, our enemies: all those rights that have only been established to legitimate exploitation' (Pérez 2008: 186). This is why 'the people' is universal: because it is the bearer of a negativity. Any non-negative feature with which we were to characterize it would be a non-universal property. Hence the argument proceeds along the lines we have discussed: politics (rather than a *modus vivendi* on the one hand and management on the other) can only survive under a sacramental conception of our institutional life, and the Protestant principle is the negation of one of the main reasons why such sacramental understanding is unlikely: because of the normalizing effect of institutions; that is, its operative opacity. Political institutions will always be defective, for the very same reasons that we need them. Like the kingdom of God, which in Cullmann's celebrated formula is with us 'already but not yet', (Cullmann, 1962, 81–93, passim), law is the will of the people, but it will never be the will of the people until we can in fact have order but not law, in which case it will be made redundant; when, in other words, it will wither away.

Does this idea lead to a devaluation of our democratic institutions? At this point, the answer to this question needs only to be verbalized: since alienation cannot be 'diagnosed' from a non-alienated situation, it can only be experienced as a contradiction between promise and deliverance: between the idea of fair exchange between subjects that recognize themselves reciprocally, which gives meaning to the law of contracts and the strategic action it permits and, in a way, promotes; between the idea of gratuitous love which gives meaning to marriage and the spheres of abuse and domination it creates; and between the aspiration to radical and reciprocal recognition that lies in the idea that sovereignty rests essentially with the people and the imperfect institutional forms that allow factious interests to masquerade as common ones. By means of exploiting these contradictions we may understand what it means to overcome them. In Proudhon's terms, we have to put the theory of property against property; the philosophy of contract as an autonomous exchange among agents that recognize each other against the contract by means of which each individual uses the other as an instrument for his or her own ends; the idea of the family as a community constituted by love, against marriage as a sphere of patriarchal domination; and the idea of law as the will of the people against the negotiations of the 'political class'.

This implies the exclusion of what may be called the 'Portalian principle'. As is well known, Diego Portales was of the idea that citizens were 'full of vice ... lacking all virtues necessary for democratic governance'. The corruption of the citizenry implied the necessity of 'a strong, centralizing government', so that only 'once they have been moralized, the completely liberal government may come, free and full of ideals, where all citizens have a place'.[19] The objection to the Portalian principle need not be the denial of its premise; that is, that we are, in an important sense, full of vices and lacking all virtues. The objection is that living under institutions, the contradictions of which make their deficit clear, is the only way in which we can aspire to overcome alienation. Only if we live under imperfectly democratic institutions can we develop the virtues necessary for democratic governance.

The People as a Post-Institutional Concept

And now, at last, we can pull the strands of the argument together. Our starting point was to note that the intelligibility of our political institutions depended, as the intelligibility of every legal concept, on its relation with some pre-institutional concept, namely, a concept that does not assume the existence of any institutional correlative. But though they require a non-institutional correlative to become

19 Written in Lima, March 1822, and available in multiple sources. See, for example, Silva (1954: 15).

intelligible, in their operation they must be opaque to it. A legal concept may *operate* without a pre-institutional correlative, but it is, in fact, unintelligible: pure formalism, a meaningless ritual. One that in its operation is fully transparent to its pre-institutional correlative might be intelligible, but does not make any difference and is redundant.

However, unlike other legal concepts, the democratic concept of 'the people' could not be understood pre-institutionally, because that would force upon it a distorted content: the people as a naturally characterized group (in which case democratic theory would be inherently racist or ethnocentric) or as an aggregation of individual interests (in which case it would be inherently neo-liberal). But with no pre-institutional correlative to render it intelligible, democratic institutions can be nothing but form. Thus the options do not seem particularly attractive: democratic institutions are an empty formalism, an arrangement that is neo-liberal or plainly racist (ethnocentric). This is why nowadays we seem to be living under the domain of dead ideas; that is, ideas that operate, but are unintelligible.

But unlike all other legal concepts, and given its character as the founding concept of every other institutional form, the non-institutional correlate of the institutional concept of the people is not pre-institutional, but actually *post-institutional*: 'the people' is an anticipatory way of talking about the whole of humanity. We already live according to the will of the people, but not yet. Since it is an anticipatory concept, it rejects two opposite mistakes which should by now be familiar enough: the mistake of believing that, since in biological terms it constitutes a species, 'humanity' is an operative political category and that of believing that politics can only be particularistic (be that either a ground to reject them or to embrace them).

The people are the bearers of a negativity; it is the universal, bereft of everything particular. It is common humanity, universal community. However common, humanity does not truly exist, but is rather a goal of history. But from this it does not follow that it is an empty concept. It exists in an anticipatory or eschatological manner, within our political practices, which can only be understood as grounded on its will.

Thus, when we speak of the people, while we know how to use our words, there is an important sense in which we do not know what they mean. Fundamentally this is because of our special ignorance of universal reciprocal recognition. We know how to talk about infractions and contracts because of our understanding of infractions and contracts. We know how to talk about the people, not because of any understanding of the people, but because of what we know about the people's will.

Bibliography

Ackerman, B. 1984. 'The Storr Lectures: Discovering the Constitution'. *Yale Law Journal*, 93: 1013–72.

Ackerman, B. 1996. 'The Political Case for Constitutional Courts'. In B. Yack (ed.), *Liberalism Without Illusions: Essays on Liberal Theory and the Political Vision of Judith N. Shklar*. Chicago, IL: University of Chicago Press, 205–19.

Arendt, H. 1958. *The Human Condition*. Chicago, IL: University of Chicago Press.

Atria, F. 2002. *On Law and Legal Reasoning*. Oxford: Hart Publishers.

Atria, F. 2006. 'Reconciliation and Reconstitution'. In S. Veitch (ed.), *Law and the Politics of Reconciliation*. Aldershot: Ashgate, 33–48.

Atria, F. 2009. 'La verdad y lo político (i): La verdad y su dimensión constitutiva'. *Persona y Sociedad* (Santiago, Chile), 23: 21–50.

Böckenförde, E.W. 2000. 'La democracia como principio constitucional'. In W. Böckenförde (ed.), *Estudios sobre el Estado de Derecho y la Democracia*. Madrid: Trotta, 47–131.

Cohen, G.A. 1995. *Self-Ownership, Freedom and Equality*. Cambridge: Cambridge University Press.

Cullmann, O. 1962. *Christ and Time*. London: SCM Press.

Dawkins, R. 2008. *The God Delusion*. New York: Mariner Books.

Dennett, D.C. 2006. *Breaking the Spell. Religion as a Natural Phenomenon*. New York: Viking.

Engels, F. 1974. 'El Programa de los Emigrados Blanquistas de la Comuna'. In *Obras Escogidas de Marx y Engels*. Moscú: Progreso.

Gray, J. 2007. *Black Mass: Apocalyptic Religion and the Death of Utopia*. New York: Farrar, Straus and Giroux.

Hobbes, T. 1996. *Leviathan*. Cambridge: Cambridge University Press.

Kahn, P. 2005. *Putting Liberalism in its Place*. Princeton, NJ: Princeton University Press.

Lenin, V.I. 1940. *'Left-Wing' Communism, An Infantile Disorder*. Moscow: International Publishers.

Maine, H.S. 1906. *Ancient Law*. New York: Henry Holt and Co.

McCabe, H. (ed.) 1964. *Aquinas' Summa Theologiae, Vol. 3, Knowing and Naming God: 1a. 12–13*. Cambridge: Cambridge University Press.

McCabe, H. 1967. 'Comment', *New Blackfriars*, 48: 226–9.

McCabe, H. 1968. *Law, Love and Language*. London: Sheed & Ward.

McCabe, H. 2005. *God Matters*. London: Continuum.

McCabe, H. 2006. 'Signifying Imperfectly'. In H. McCabe (ed.), *St Thomas Aquinas, Summa Theologiae 1.12–13: Knowing and Naming God*. Cambridge: Cambridge University Press, 104–5.

Moulian, T. 2000. *Socialismo del Siglo XXI*. Santiago: LOM.

Nozick, R. 1974. *Anarchy, State and Utopia*. Cambridge, MA: Harvard University Press.

Pérez, C. 2008. *Proposición de un Marxismo Hegeliano*. Santiago: Arcis.

Proudhon, P-J. 1846. *Letter to Karl Marx*, 17 May. Available at http://www.marxists.org/reference/subject/economics/proudhon/letters/46_05_17.htm; accessed 17 December 1912.

Rahner, K. 1969. 'The Little Word "God"'. In Rahner, *Grace in Freedom*. London: Burns & Oates, 183–202.
Raz, J. 1980. *The Concept of a Legal System*. Oxford: Clarendon Press.
Rousseau, J-J. 2002 [1762]. *The Social Contract*. New Haven, CT: Yale University Press.
Schmitt, C. 1985. *Political Theology: Four Chapters on the Concept of Sovereignty*. Cambridge, MA: MIT Press.
Schmitt, C. 1996. *Roman Catholicism and Political Form*, trans. G.L. Ulmen. Westport, CT: Greenwood Press.
Schmitt, C. 2008. *Constitutional Theory*. Durham, NC: Duke University Press.
Segundo, J.L. 1969. *Teología Abierta para el Laico Adulto. Gracia y Condición humana.* Buenos Aires: Editorial Carlos Lohé.
Segundo, J.L. 1989. *El Dogma que Libera*. Santander: Sal Terrae.
Silva, R. (ed.) 1954. *Ideas y confesiones de Portales*. Santiago: Editorial del Pacífico.
Taylor, C. 1979. *Hegel*. Cambridge: Cambridge University Press.
Tillich, P. 1948. *The Protestant Era*. Chicago, IL: Chicago University Press.
Varone, F. 1987. *El Dios Ausente*. Santander: Sal Terrae.
Waldron, J. 2002. *God, Locke and Equality*. Cambridge: Cambridge University Press.
Weil, S. 1950. 'On Human Personality'. In Weil, *Utopian Pessimist*, ed. D. MacLellan. London: Macmillan, 273–88.
Weil, S. 1963. *Gravity and Grace*. London: Routledge.
Weil, S. 1987. 'The Iliad, or the Poem of Might'. In *Intimations of Christianity among the Ancient Greeks*. London: Ark Paperbacks, 24–55.
Williams, R. 2000. 'Trinity and Revelation'. in *On Christian Theology.* Oxford: Blackwell, 131–47.
Wittgenstein, L. 2001. *Tractatus Logico-Philosophicus*. London: Routledge.

Chapter 8
Iconoclasm Revisited: Zenon Bańkowski, Law, Love and *Antigone**

Emilios Christodoulidis

A

'How is a Greek chorus like a lawyer?' the chorus asks of itself in Anne Carson's fascinating retelling of *Antigone* – *Antigonick* (Carson 2012): 'They are both in the business of searching for a precedent/ … / so as to be able to say/ this terrible thing we are witnessing now is/ not unique you know it happened before/ or something much like it./ … / Now I could dig up those case histories, tell you about Danaos and Lykourgos and the songs of Phineas,/ they wouldn't help you/ it didn't help me/ it's Friday afternoon/ there goes Antigone to be buried alive.'

The last two verses shatter the pattern- and lesson-invoking narrative with a devastating attentiveness to the fate, not of transgressors of law, but of Antigone, the girl, the sister, on that Friday afternoon. The particularity is arresting.[1] No generalization, no rationalization, no lesson jars the concentration on the fate of this girl, whose resistance is and can only remain unique because the suffering is all hers. She stands, alone, before a responsibility she can neither shift nor renounce. On the axis of the particular and the general, of what remains human in its complexity against what is shorn of humanity in its reduction, of what yields against what resists insistently and fatefully, is played out the impossible dialectic of love and law, and on that axis it comes undone.

Now the reference to *Antigone* in this context is not incidental, and this is not just because Zenon Bańkowski's *Living Lawfully* (2001) contains a chapter on the play as well as a multitude of references to it throughout. In an important way the book itself is a variation on the same dialectic of law and love, and more significantly perhaps the continuity and discontinuity between this book and the earlier *Images of Law* (Bańkowski and Mungham 1976) can also be related to that dialectic. *Living Lawfully* situates itself in the unlikely space of a broken dialectic, the disjuncture that Gillian Rose (1992) calls the 'broken middle'.

* With many thanks for their valuable input to Scott Veitch, Johan van der Walt, Oren Ben Dor, the editors of the volume, and, of course, Zenon Bańkowski.

1 Detmold (1989) remains one of the most insightful analyses of the relation between particulars and universals in legal reasoning.

Put it this way: *Images* was on the side of Antigone, as Bańkowski reads her, smashing the imagery and insignia of authority, the power of the state and its edicts. It was uncompromising in its opposition to the law, to the play of ideology in all its manifestations, to the outwardly benign face of welfare laws that couple with the relentless extraction of value through property laws, as sanctioned, organized and justified by the capitalist state and its organs. *Images* is on the side of Antigone, albeit Sophocles' or Heinrich Boll's 'casting' of Ulrike Meinhoff in the role of Antigone,[2] with her bloody-minded, reductive, obsessive commitment to what is right. There is no room for concession here to the complexity and contingency of attachment and solidarity, no yielding to life; only relentless fidelity as becomes a cause of near-impossible furthering.

Living Lawfully marks a remarkable attempt to move the radical disjuncture on to a plane not – emphatically not – where a dialectic might redeem it, but on the site of brokenness, a 'middle' that is, in Rose's term, 'diremptive'. Bańkowski has in fact little time for the young 'Bańkowski and Mungham' as well as for the edict-defying hubris of Antigone. *Living Lawfully* is rather impatient with all this. The impatience, I want to argue, is unwarranted and the break with the early work exaggerated. This chapter looks at the continuities and, perhaps more important, the relative discontinuities, in Bańkowski's work by tracking the shift from the uncompromising early iconoclasm[3] of *Images of Law* to the more nuanced account of what it means to 'live lawfully'. How are we to understand this shift as a singular trajectory that captures something of the 'jurist's anxiety' not to compromise virtue and to protect the demands of a life lived in autonomy? There would be no anxiety if the continuity were guaranteed, if the legal and its rejection (in the name of love or solidarity) in *Images* were tied dialectically in the form of a transcendence that kept them both alive. But no such guarantees will deliver

2 In Heinrich Boll's 1979 script for the film 'Der Herbst in Deutschland'. There is a long history of *Antigone* in German post-war theatre, from Brecht to Julian Beck's Living Theatre, including also Peter Handke, Heiner Müller and Straub-Huillet. In his book *Antigones*, George Steiner suggests that there are no end of ways to interpret the play, and that inexhaustibility explains its classic status.

3 Iconoclasm – from the Greek *eikonoklasmos* ('image-breaking') – is the name of the movement against the worship of images that nearly tore Byzantium apart in the eighth and ninth centuries AD and became the significant first step in the severing of Eastern from Western Christendom. The emperors' (most notably among them Leo III, the Isaurian) zeal against representation of deity goes back to the old suspicion that the adoration of icons among certain Christians for many centuries before the Iconoclast persecution began was idolatrous. In the second half of the eighth century, persecution raged in the East. Monasteries were destroyed, monks put to death, tortured or banished, relics destroyed, shrines broken open and the bodies of saints that were buried in churches were burnt. Iconoclasm, while without a doubt also politically motivated, does in important respects reflect the radical schism between Eastern and Western world views surrounding the representation of the sacred.

us there. Instead, Bańkowski's 'living lawfully' is a dwelling in the law that must remain uncanny and ambivalent to remain true.

B

Images of Law is not a book in the tradition of critical legal theory but should be read, sometimes in spite of itself, as an anarchist manifesto. I insert 'in spite of' because there is a crucial ambivalence at the heart of the book, to which I will return. But why is this not a book in critical legal theory? Because if critical legal theory is understood as being popularized by the critical legal studies (CLS) movement – that is, primarily as a methodology that exploits and builds on the ambivalences that haunt legal practice – then the book's central insight is that reform and revolution are irreconcilable alternatives, and that reform, to repeat the revolutionary's standard indictment, makes the oppressive practice less heinous and thus more difficult to abolish. The dilemma is patently visible in Bańkowski's and Mungham's critique of legal aid and welfare law in the long, empirical analysis of chapters 3 and 4. In contrast to the impatient, staccato idiom of the rest of the book, this is a careful account of the 'legal profession in process' and the ideological workings behind 'bringing the law to the people'. This is a revolutionary's critique of reformism, of the ideological function that systems of signification perform in sustaining oppression. 'When we came,' Roberto Unger famously announced at the end of his CLS manifesto, 'they [the orthodoxy] were like a priesthood that had lost their faith but kept their jobs. They stood in tedious embarrassment before cold altars. But we turned away from those altars and found the mind's opportunity in the heart's revenge' (1983: 119). Unger finds the legal 'mind's opportunity' in the constant alertness to the possibilities of change, the revisability of those possibilities and the removal of all that falsely presents itself as unrevisable, undertaken variously as immanent critique, deviationist doctrine, negative capability, disentrenchment, critical legal politics and so on. In each case, the critical legal theorist resists that 'false necessity' of institutional straitjacketing, and reasserts the possibility that the political may draw its inspiration from the law's own powerful imagination.

But that, to repeat, is not the message of *Images*. For its authors, legal imagination stands depleted, assimilating the new to the old, rationalizing the incongruent into coherence. The political logic of disruption must resist the institutional; it finds its mode in the anarchic, in the iconoclastic. Wittgenstein (1967: 114–15) famously wrote this about pictures:

> One thinks that one is tracing the outline of the thing's nature over and over again, and one is merely tracing round the frame through which we look at it. A picture held us captive, and we could not get outside it, for it lay in our language, and language seemed to repeat it to us inexorably.

The iconoclastic is the defining moment in *Images,* resisting, as it does, Wittgenstein's image that both overwhelms and overdetermines what it means to imagine the new. In those few moments in the book where a faith in an alternative legal politics surfaces, the faith is misplaced. That is why I began this section with 'sometimes in spite of', and it is this that I shall elaborate further for a moment.

> [Capitalism has fixed the world in a certain way and the world that it created needs to be fought long and hard ... For the world of capitalism is the stage on which the struggle will be fought and this stage must be transcended, it must therefore not be ignored. (Bańkowski and Mungham 1976: 133)

There is a call for immanent critique here, one that locates itself in the institutions it seeks to transcend. It involves 'seizing the law' in a way that allows the playing out of politics in the courtroom; 'taking part in the trial is to become a political action in itself,' (Bańkowski and Mungham 1976: 115), 'a vehicle for self-actualisation in the courtroom' (ibid.: 117). Undertaken against law's 'act of nullification [which] depends on having "political acts" against the law redefined as "criminal" ones' (ibid.,: 114) the seizing of the law is an act of resistance for 'people caught up in the coils of the law, when they have to fight on the stage provided by it and their liberty is judged according to its norms' (ibid.: 112). The question the authors need to answer is, of course, 'On what template will these politics of law register?', given law's structural inability to host any politics worth the name. And I mean structural inability in the way that Bańkowski and Mungham meant it then, one that marks the withdrawal from political action of any point of purchase in a system, a withdrawal that operates to undercut possibilities at the deepest level, the level at which meaning is recovered.

There is no real 'seizing of the law' in all this except in the remote sense of seizing the opportunity to stage (in law) a protest that in legal terms defies locution. That is why the message of *Images* does not depend on a real articulation of politics with the law and nor does it depend on activating a real contradiction either, since there is at no stage any real 'constructive' engagement with the logic of the law. The legal stage is seized by legal activists in order to demystify the law: its insignia is ridiculed, and its speech emptied from within. The activists confront the legal idiom with ridicule and misuse, turning the logic of procedure, the channelling of communication, against itself; they create 'noise from order' (to reverse systems theory's oft-repeated formula). That is why the politics of the courtroom constitute no politics of law.

And how could it be otherwise for law's iconoclasts? For them, the critical legal scholars must assume a complicity with the institution they seek to place in doubt that comes from a certain logic of (legal) analysis that cannot at the same time be both deployed and challenged. Not simply because there is not enough time to do both in one operation, as Niklas Luhmann might have objected here, but more crucially because the analysis carries a certain 'logic of relationship' and a certain rendering of facts that are constitutive of how law fixes the social, or, closer to the idiom of *Images,* how capitalism fixes the world. To then argue that critique of the system and struggle against it will take place in terms of dislocations within this logic and opportunities it avails involves an impoverishment of struggle that *Images* in its more radical moments – and it is above all about this radicalism – has little time for: 'Our argument will take the form of showing that there is a praxis which itself denies the prevailing ideology. What it needs is an epistemology to explain it; to show that this is rational action in the world' (Bańkowski and Mungham 1976: 112).

To resist ideology is, of course, to place in doubt all that law presents to us as given, consensual, removed from contestation. Solzhenitsyn is quoted: 'On the threshold of the classless society we were at last capable of realizing the conflictless trial – a reflection of the absence of inner conflict in our social structure' (ibid.: 116). Making the trial political is a reflection of the inner conflict of the social structure, allowing it to re-emerge for what it is. The law's strategy, or counterstrategy when challenged, is to re-assert the givenness of the world, to define away or 'solve' conflict and establish order. That is why the success of the politics advocated needs a register that is *not* the law. But note also here the prophetic to some extent rejection of what the law presents as *rational*, the outcome of *procedure* aiming at *consensus*. The authors resist, on the one hand, law's translation of human need and want what is rational and reasonable, while on the other hand they are impatient – and this is typical of the impatience shown by many conflict theorists of the time – with consensus as the organizing principle of law. Law and rule-following both build on and aim at consensus. Consensus is false and thus ideological, operating to harmonize social relations and obliterate cleavages in society's conflictual self-reproduction.

C

The preoccupation with law as rule-following, with what it means to live in and by the law, the constructive and exclusionary aspects of that, the *ethics* of that, has remained at the core of Bańkowski's work and is what lies behind *Living Lawfully.* There are two things to note here. The first is that there has been a shift, clearly, from politics to ethics. The second is that the ambivalence that I argued underlies *Images* has in a certain sense become creative. What I mean is this: the question of whether one finds a faith in law at the basis of ethics and politics has become a different *kind* of question. What renews the faith in law is now, in the later work, an argument about aspiration, creativity, law's embracing of contingency. From *Images* there remains a critique of legalism, of blind rule-following, less political now, but still insistent on how it impoverishes the social. What legality, as opposed to legalism, holds up is the promise of a creative and 'risky' living by the law that will even stretch to breaking the law as a means of fulfilling its aspiration rather than of denouncing it:

> In conclusion I argue that a recognition of the centrality of the articulation of heteronomy and autonomy allows us to see how many debates have been trapped in structures which are in thrall to these oppositions ... My claim is that the tension between heteronomy and autonomy is part of the grammar of practical reasoning and an underlying premise of social organization and institutional design – accepting that is the way forward ... That is what gives our institutions integrity and dignity. (Bańkowski 2001: 12)

The work as a whole can be seen as a critique of binarisms and – as dialectically bound together – a critique of the promise of transcendence. Instead it asks: what does it mean to *dwell* in the tension that remains unresolved? What does it mean to remain in *media res*, and to cope between two poles, autonomy and heteronomy, law and love, that are not tied dialectically? In a formulation I think captures the book's central thesis, a 'zone' is suggested by Bańkowski that is 'analogous to what Gillian Rose calls the "middle", where the contingency of love breaks through the secure frontier posts of the law and yet only makes sense because of the law itself'. (ibid.: 135) Love's transgression is here a creative breaking of the law. Now this talk of 'breaking through' points in the direction of dialectical overcoming, but Bańkowski is not speaking of 'sublation'. What he is speaking of is rather the point at which the exclusionary language of law yields, the 'frontier posts' give, and what this moment holds open is a plane of tension, in which competing demands are placed on decision-making and in which, no matter how creative, legal imagination will be guaranteed redemption. The book is shot through with references to the anxiety of decision:

> We have to learn to inhabit the tension between particular and universal, autonomous and heteronomous, law and love. This is what Gillian Rose calls the middle. The place lies in the negotiation between law and love, particular and universal, autonomy and heteronomy. The area is an anxious place because it refuses to abandon either side of the equation. We cannot call it a contradiction because that implies that it can be transcended whereas we are dealing with and trying to hold together things that pull us in both ways. It is anxious because here there is neither an easy answer or guarantee that our solution has turned out right. (ibid.: 76–7)

Here is what Bańkowski says in this context about *Antigone*, and while the reading is perhaps too reliant on Nussbaum's critique, it is key to his main argument as it is also key to this account of his trajectory: 'Creon has created a world where there can be no conflict in values and tragedy cannot happen.' We might want to object here that tragedy does not happen, it frames the (impossible) choice within which hubris happens, and Bańkowski explains this hubris of Creon's as the reduction of practical reasons to reasons of state, a reductive commensuration of orders of reasons that only in their distinctness suspend tragic choice. Antigone too is guilty of simplifying 'a complicated world'; 'If we only listen to her ... all we know is that a brother rests unburied' (ibid.: 31); 'She transforms love of the family into a righteous certainty. The urge for that form of certainty transforms [love] into law and rules' (ibid.: 135). Though it is hardly the case that 'both Creon and Antigone have simplified their deliberative lives in the cause of safety' (ibid.: 31) Bańkowski's point is that they attempt to immunize deliberation against the irreducible pull of competing value systems and the messy business of attachments with all the contingency that entails. 'Living under rules' provides no refuge except at a cost of diminishing the fullness of attachment and thus of life.

The discussion is then uploaded to the field opened up by the key distinction of law and love, though, of course, Bańkowski is not implying any simple mapping here between that distinction and the respective positions of Creon and Antigone. Rather,

> the point seems to be that we cannot easily map them on to a distinction that seems to embrace all we have talked of, that of law and love. Why? ... [Because] if we see it as a distinction in the sense of a dichotomous contradiction, we map all the other distinctions on to it, lining up one set with love and good and the other with law and bad, and so we create a neat divide ... rather than seeing that ... distinctions run across each other and we have to hold them in a necessary and inevitable tension both in our individual and social moral lives' (ibid.: 41)

'Living in a creative tension of being in and out of the law' (ibid.: 41) becomes the key demand.

Such 'creative tension' is thought out and developed with the help of other key distinctions: duty and aspiration, as borrowed from Lon Fuller;[4] legalism and legality as borrowed and qualified from Judith Shklar.[5] There is no space here to account for the development of the argument, but suffice it to say that each reading offers a symmetrical move that reads the latter in the light of the former. In the same way that Fuller analyses it so well in the first chapter of *The Morality of Law*, the threshold of excellence could never as such be met by real practices and yet this did not diminish at all its function of guiding those practices by providing the internal standards of excellence for them, similarly 'aspiration' and 'legality' stand as the horizon. In the irreducible gap between the ideal and the real, the creative tension unfolds (and the anxiety of the judge installs itself). In each case, a move is repeated between inside and outside: stepping outside the comfort of rules and the certainty of law but only to fulfil the aspiration of law guided by love.

Universality and particularity are worth a special reference in this context. Attentiveness to particularity remains a central concern in the earlier and later work. Bańkowski follows Nigel Simmonds (1993) and Scott Veitch (1998) here. In an important early article on mercy, Simmonds had argued that mercy should

4 See Fuller, L.L., 1969.

5 See Shklar, J., 1964.

not be thought of as in some way taking place in the gap between particular cases and law's generality, as if mercy expressed 'fidelity to the unique particular'. From such a view, he says,

> mercy asserts the importance of particularity over and against the abstract universality of justice and law… On this view the value of mercy may be found significant as an indication of the extent to which, even within the context of juridical institutions, the concrete human being always partially escapes the all-pervading demands of justice: the subject is never fully subsumable under the categories of law. (Simmonds 1993: 61)

For Simmonds, this is misconceived because it postulates the particular or singularity as existing in itself. He asks: 'How should we think of unique particularity'? He sketches 'a view which seeks to oppose unique particularity to the abstraction and generality of law'; he argues against it, that 'in escaping all general categories and categorisations that which is irreducibly concrete turns out to be featureless and irreducibly abstract'. Instead '[s]ince a "total" description of any concrete situation is impossible and inconceivable, all descriptions must be more or less abstract' (ibid.: 61). Veitch too explains the construction of the particular as a matter of relations between such relative abstracts. It is epistemologically wrong, they both argue, to assume the existence of the 'particular facts of a reality-apart-from-thought' and thus falsely discern a rift between *that* particular reality and the categories of thought we employ to describe it. This radical contrasting – and the correspondence theory of truth that underlies it – cannot be sustained. And it is in this sense that one cannot be faithful to the particular (Simmonds), or 'do justice to the particular' (Veitch) because the particular as such does not exist.

Now Bańkowski (2001: 169–70) is in agreement with much of the above theorization as he aspires to navigate away from the deadlock between a 'nihilistic' (ibid.: 166) particularism and a blind rule-determinism. He is neither prepared to jettison the particular nor is he prepared to adopt the scale of 'more or less' abstract concepts or to rely on the logic of defeasibility of reasons. While he asks 'Don't we need criteria to think about [the decision]?' (ibid.: 159), he is not suggesting any 'meta-system of decision' but instead the exercise of judgement that will remain *attentive* 'to the infinite possibilities of the concrete particular before it', 'that cannot be captured by criteria' (ibid.: 184). The presence of infinite possibilities points to the inexhaustible nature of the judge's responsibility (though nowhere in Bańkowski's text is any reference to the 'aporia of judgement' made.) Instead, the solution is sought in Klaus Günther's[6] argument about a 'sense of appropriateness' that guides the justification of any application of law. In the process, Bańkowski will align – roughly – the two sets of distinctions: love/law, particular/universal, in a way that suspends them in tension and does not admit easy solutions. This is the

6 See Günther, K., 1993.

space of legal judgement as both inside and outside, as both realizing and creating the law, in which space the responsibility of the jurist and the law's debt remains unsettled and unsettlable. That is what makes the 'middle', the seat of judicial decision-making, an 'anxious place' (Bańkowski 2001: 166). And it is perhaps why, not only Jacques Derrida, but also Plato's Socrates in *Laches* might have been the obvious fellow traveller here, with his insistence that decision-making takes *courage*, understood as the exercise of reflexive judgement that persists in the face of risk and uncertainty.

But let us stay with what is perhaps most important here: that in this new formulation of the theory of *judgement* as proceeding in a space of ambivalence without warranty, the distinction between the visionary and the pragmatic, and the assumed contrast between the early and the later work, now begins to lose its sharpness. In each case, the theory of action taps both the visionary and the pragmatic. In *Images*, law's vision is crucially inadequate. It is ideological and, as such, places a wooden hand on praxis. The later work again measures the demands that the pragmatic places on us against the visionary. But as a practice that becomes meaningful only when measured against its aspiration, its vision, a striving for excellence is imported into the practice such that it forever questions its containment in any set of rules. In that, *in one act*, what makes legality possible also redeems it.

D

To end, let us return to *Antigone,* except that now I will venture some thoughts that place the play, against what was argued in *Living Lawfully*, on a plane that has *nothing* to offer law. Remember the question of the chorus with which we began: 'How is a Greek chorus like a lawyer?' And it answers its question thus: 'They are both in the business of searching for a precedent/ … / so as to be able to say/ this terrible thing we are witnessing now is/ not unique you know it happened before/ or something much like it./' But when *confronted* with the agony of Antigone it discovers, in the wonderful turn of Carson's opening phrase in *Antigonick*, that it can generalize nothing: 'it didn't help me/ it's Friday afternoon/ there goes Antigone to be buried alive'. There are no lessons for the law to be extracted from the agony of the girl walking to her burial site.

The question we might return to, then, is whether, in the distinction that organizes Bańkowski's book, Antigone stands on the side of love, or law? Why does her plight not add up to 'love'? Is it because it perhaps falls below love's threshold, too close to death, too unyielding to vulnerability, too protected from exposure to fraternal and romantic love, as represented – in Nussbaum's and Bańkowski's analysis at least – by Ismene and Haemon instead? If Antigone's *logos* is not like theirs, if it is too reductive, what does it reduce *to*? If not to love, to what?

Poor Antigone! She is barred from both love and law, we deny her both registers. If she misunderstood love, she also misunderstands law. Because what legal argument would qualify her to break into that watertight set of reasons, reasons of state, with which she is confronted? In Creon's confident statement of the law, the speech act carries perlocutionary effect *simpliciter*, his edict *is* jurisdiction. To this, Antigone can only counter a law of a different order, if it can be called that at all. How fragile this countering, more so when we see that her resistance presents itself as negation of Creon's totalizing appropriation, which includes and exhausts all alternatives: no conditionality enters the law-giver's verdict, no doubt clouds his concentration, no remainder haunts his law.

Such a totalizing coverage of reasons is what Alain Badiou[7] captures with the concept of the 'situation'. Like Luhmann, whose discussion of the operational closure of systems presents us with the spectre of a certain improbability as far as resistance is concerned, Badiou's account of the *situation*, to begin with at least, presents us with a similar totalizing closure. A situation contains all its reasons, it provides the full range of perspectives in terms of what can be observed and counted-in. Given a situation, where givenness over-determines, structures and enumerates, what are the opportunities of putting the situation to question, and where might they be sought? What does it mean to step back from the givens of a situation to allow that questioning? None, as Antigone finds out, condemned to be reciting the edicts of a 'higher' law without jurisdiction, and the demands of a 'higher' love without reciprocity. On both registers she is denied recognition; and on both counts she appears a fool. What denies her the meaning of her demands is this: that the situation sets the conditions of what can be asked meaningfully. These are the *conditions* of questionability, not its *object*. They determine what can be counted-in and accounted for meaningfully by the situation, and in this they establish and guarantee a *finite* responsiveness. This finitude is what underwrites the security of Creon's world. 'Love', too, from within Creon's world, will be thematized using the language and symbols of prudence and functionality; from within Haemon's and Ismene's it will be thematized as a plea – and only ever meaningful as such – to be *loved back*.

One could stop there and understand the tragedy as the impossible negotiation of the two situations, neither of which has the requisite openness to any aspect of the other, because the criteria of what counts – and 'counts-in' – cannot be generalized across the two. Yet, significantly for this other reading of *Antigone*, we might borrow from Badiou a more profound notion of *fidelity*. For Badiou, emancipatory praxis can claim truth for itself if it can capture in some way *the event* of its disclosure. The event marks the improbable surfacing of a truth, improbable because the situation does not allow it. But that truth can only be sustained if endorsed with a commitment to its promise, a promise that cannot be redeemed in the here and now, but that involves a commitment for which Badiou will reserve the term *fidelity*. For the event to irrupt at all in a space that has no place for it, Badiou insists that fidelity has a constitutive role to play: both in projecting a place for 'it', the event, and for holding on to 'it' as something that only retroaction

7 See Badiou, A., 1998 and 2003.

might bring about. Nothing underwrites the risk that there may be no redemption. But for she who assumes the wager, Antigone, the fanatic, the misguided, the fool, will have emerged instead as the subject of truth, of her own truth: of a *love* that had no place in this world. Without that (in every sense) unwarranted holding-on against the logic of the situation, the threats of authority, the appeals of Ismene and Haemon to give up the fatal stubbornness, to 'yield' to love, there would be no event because there would have come about no register to read it into. In retrospection and in diachrony, rather than in its momentary eruption, does the event register as the origin of something, as setting a certain sequence into action, as allowing causal links to be read *back* into the run of time, patterns to emerge. Only in this way does retroaction fully take effect. Only in this way does Antigone emerge as the subject of her own truth, as being committed to love.

Of course, a great deal more needs to be said about Badiou's theory, and I leave only tentative the connection to Antigone's plight. How, one might ask, are we to understand an emergent truth as in some way taking place *within* the situation but not being *of* it. Let us simply say that, for Badiou, a counter-factual fidelity to the event of this emergent truth constitutes the subject of truth. If this calls for a 'wager' it is because no guarantee is offered that this will not for ever remain a tragic commitment and the acting out of it will remain hubris. And we could generalize that across the spectrum of Antigones.[8] If Ulrike Meinhoff's (Heinrich Boll's 'Antigone') is indeed the story of a certain self-authorization, played out in the insistent claiming of a speaking position in a situation that afforded none, then with Badiou we could perhaps claim that both heroines were the subjects of a bitter truth, their fidelity to the event of truth exacted, for Antigone in the lonely burial site of her 'wedding chamber', and for Meinhoff in the white cells of the Stammheim prison.

But surely, one would object, what is the meaning of a 'wager' that seals fate irrevocably? Death, the consequence of a *certain* death, places an absolute limit that makes nonsense of the 'wager' – tragedy allows no space for it. What is there to risk when holding on to the event, holding on by returning for a second burial of the body of the brother, simply seals her fate? For this, final step, let us return to the play's much celebrated 'ode to man'. Here, halfway through the play, the chorus celebrates man as a '*deinon*' creature. The fraught meaning of this predicate, *deinon*, oscillating between 'wonderment' and 'horror', famously is what most befits 'man' in his ingenuity, his craftiness, his taming of beasts and of nature. And yet, for all that is brought into existence by him, *death* is the absolute limit.

In Elizabeth Wyckoff's translation:[9]

> Many the wonders but nothing walks stranger than man/ ... And she, the greatest of gods, the earth/ ageless as she is, and unwearied – he wears her away/ as the

8 The plural here is suggested by George Steiner (Steiner 1986).

9 See Sophocles, *Antigone*, translated by E. Wyckoff, 1954.

> ploughs go up and down from year to year / … Language, and thought like the wind/ and the feelings that make the town,/ he has taught himself, and shelter against the cold,/ refuge from rain. He can always help himself./ He faces on future helpless. There's only death/ that he cannot find an escape from.

And in Carson's freer rendition:[10]

> many terribly quiet customers exist but none more/ terribly quiet than man/ his footsteps pass so terrible soft across the sea/ down he grinds the unastonishable earth/ with horse and shatter … Every outlet works but one:/ Death stays dark.

Judith Butler writes this in her review of the book for *New Directions:* "Carson does not "rewrite" Antigone. Her text becomes the verbal and visual scanning of a prolonged scream or cry. Emphatic, elliptical, *Antigonick* is more transference than translation, a relay of tragedy into a contemporary vernacular that mixes with archaic phrasing, sometimes lacking commas and periods, a halting and then a rushing of words structured by the syntax of grief and rage, spanning centuries."[11]

And yet could we not imagine that even at this final 'outlet' there remains some ambivalence? For we observers, Antigone's determined walk to the burial chamber is unbearable. And, of course, for her, 'death stays dark'; how could it be otherwise? But in her obsessive commitment to honour her brother beyond any recognition that might redeem it, in fact anything that might even *count as recognition* – at no point does Antigone allow herself the illusion that those around her are capable of the requisite comprehension – does she not remain faithful to the event of a love that no worldly contingency can distract from or efface? It is a 'love for the dead', she kept reminding us, that commits her, faithfully, to her own. And maybe in that symmetry, that unlikely reciprocity, *darkness lifts,* if with Camus we ask the question that he has Sisyphus asking: 'What destiny cannot be defeated through contempt?' (Camus 1942: 161). With it her death-driving fidelity to Polynices, excessive, irrational, incomprehensible on all available registers, allows the event of love to break through, and herself to emerge finally as the subject of that love?

And perhaps, to come back to that improbable conjunction of love and law, the 'event' of Antigone's fidelity – her 'love for the dead' that endures despite all – could now be seen as marking the inauguration of a radically new articulation of love and law on a different, hitherto impossible, register of 'unwritten unchanging law'. This would be an articulation rather than an elision of the kind we find in Haemon and Ismene, whose yielding and sacrifice reveal nothing but the inconsistencies of human attachment. It is true to its 'eventness' that that conjunction, in the dilemma

10 Available at http://www.newyorker.com/fiction/poetry/2010/08/16/100816po_poem_carson.

11 Available at http://ndbooks.com/blog/notices/judith-butler-on-anne-carsons-antigonick.

before her, can only take the form of paradox, of a (double) denial of love and law coupled with a contempt for life as instantiated by her own (particular) death.[12]

As befits a book that ends on a note of 'divine folly to hunger and thirst for justice' (Bańkowski 2001: 230) let us think of Antigone as the heroine who dwells insistently in a space that denies her the justice she craves, and the love that she offers, though she is never graced with the epiphany of atheism that relieves Camus's Sisyphus. Here is Camus's famous final passage:[13]

> I leave Sisyphus at the foot of the mountain! One will always find one's own burden again. But Sisyphus teaches that higher sense of faithfulness that negates the gods. This universe henceforth without a master, appears to him neither sterile nor futile ... The struggle itself toward summits is enough alone to fill a man's heart. One must imagine Sisyphus happy.

Bibliography

Badiou, A. 1998. *Etre et évenement.* Paris: Seuil.

Badiou, A. 2003. *Infinite Thought.* London: Continuum.

Bańkowski, Z. 2001. *Living Lawfully.* Dordrecht: Kluwer Academic Publishers.

Bańkowski, Z and Mungham, G. 1976. *Images of Law.* London: Routledge & Kegan Paul.

Camus, A. 1942. *Le Mythe de Sisyphe.* Paris: Gallimard.

Carson, A. 2012. *Antigonick.* Tarset: Bloodaxe.

Detmold, M. 1989. 'Law as Practical Reason'. *Cambridge Law Journal*, 48: 457–71.

Fuller, L.L. 1969. *The Morality of Law.* 2nd edn. New Haven, CT: Yale University Press.

Günther, K. 1993. *The Sense of Appropriateness* (trans John Farrell). Albany, NY: SUNY Press (original in German 1988).

Rose, G. 1992. *The Broken Middle.* Oxford: Blackwell.

Shklar, J. 1964. *Legalism: Law, Morals and Political Trials.* Cambridge, MA: Harvard University Press.

Simmonds, N. 1993. 'Judgement and Mercy'. *Oxford Journal of Legal Studies,* 13: 52–68.

Sophocles, *Antigone*, translated by Elizabeth Wyckoff. 1954. In D. Greene and R. Lattimore (eds), *Complete Greek Tragedies.* University of Chicago: Modern American Library edition, 170–71.

---

12 Many thanks to Scott Veitch for our discussion of this.

13 The original passage in French: 'Je laisse Sisyphe au bas de la montagne! On retrouve toujours son fardeau. Mais Sisyphe enseigne la fidélité supérieure qui nie les dieux ... Cet univers désormais sans maître ne lui paraît ni stérile ni fertile ... La lutte elle-même vers les sommets suffit à remplir un cœur d'homme. Il faut imaginer Sisyphe heureux' (Camus 1942).

Steiner, G. 1986. *Antigones: The Antigone Myth in Western Literature, Art and Thought.* Oxford: Oxford University Press.

Unger, R.M. 1983. *The Critical Legal Studies Movement*. Cambridge, MA: Harvard University Press.

Veitch, S. 1998. 'Doing Justice to Particulars'. In E. Christodoulidis (ed.) *Communitarianism and Citizenship*. Farnham: Ashgate, 220–34.

Wittgenstein, L. 1967. *Philosophical Investigations*. Oxford: Blackwell.

Chapter 9

Fulfilling the Law by Breaking It? Formalism within Legality[1]

Francisco Saffie

In what follows I try to engage critically with insights and ideas contained in Zenon Bańkowski's *Living Lawfully* (2001). In particular, I analyse Bańkowski's notion of 'fulfilling the law by breaking it'. As I try to show, the consequences of fully developing that idea in the terms stated in *Living Lawfully* endangers the conception of law defended in it. The reason for this problem, arguably, is that there is still too much formalism in Bańkowski's notion of legality. This tension would make possible an instrumental use of the law, such as, for example, those described as 'tax avoidance', that endanger the political aspect of 'living lawfully'. I try to develop a solution for this problem by radicalizing some of the ideas contained in Bańkowski's conception of law.

The Setting

It seems to me that the best way to honour Bańkowski's work is to engage critically with (but not to oppose) some of his ideas. Blunt opposition is precisely a negation of what he is defending; that is, it would be a form of (false) certainty. The problem then is that in an oeuvre full of original and provocative ideas and images such as his, it is difficult to choose which of them to engage with, or even where to start. This is, of course, a benefit once we consider that his work tries to stand in 'the middle'. Or, to put it another way: by thinking through parables, his own work has become 'parabolic', open to continuous reinterpretation, and thus

1 I would like to thank Claudio Michelon and Maks Del Mar for inviting me to the seminar in which Zenon Bańkowski's work was celebrated. I would also like to thank Claudio Michelon, Zenon Bańkowski, Fernando Atria, Emilios Christodoulidis and Elisa Walker for their comments on the previous version of this paper, presented at that seminar. Claudio Michelon's detailed comments were particularly helpful in making the argument clearer and sharper. Any mistakes are my responsibility and expression of my intent to communicate in this community. I would like to give special thanks to Zenon as he has not only been a great teacher, but also a very good friend; I will always be indebted to him, as his company and advice helped me to give meaning to those things in life that seemed not to have it.

'invit[ing] us on a journey "beyond"' (Bańkowski and Davis 2000: 46). Trying to stop and fix the motion of thought and experience Bańkowski's work involves us in would be a mistake. However, to begin communication it is necessary to start from somewhere. For these reasons, I decided to visit Bańkowski's place by discussing the idea that puzzles me the most: what does it mean to fulfil the law once we embrace 'living lawfully'? This is, as I shall try to show, an idea where many of the tensions that Bańkowski analyses in his work meet. This will lead us to enquire what 'living lawfully' does (not) say about the law. In particular, I shall try to show that Bańkowski's idea of creatively breaking the law to fulfil the law is politically objectionable, as it disregards the idea that the law must be seen as a collective product of the political community and not as something that belongs to the legal interpreter or to the law-applying authority.

The Problem

We know what 'living lawfully' positively implies. The idea is that to live a good life we need to learn how to live with the law and at the same time know when to leave it behind, not to abandon it but to transform it. 'Living lawfully' implies knowing when to abandon the moral certainties we find in law and love that hinder our developing of a good life. According to Bańkowski, both extremes, that in principle seem to be opposed, share the same risk as they provide a place where we stop experiencing the difficulties of the particular. We do this by following rules, either of law or of love. When analysed in detail we realize that both extremes rest on the absolute, and that there we run the risk of falling into the universal. In Bańkowski's interpretation of Sophocles' *Antigone* we find a good example of the certainty of the universals. Following Nussbaum, Bańkowski shows how Creon and Antigone are unable to understand and see each other as they are strictly following rules (see Bańkowski 2001: ch. 2). While Creon rests on the universality of the law of the city; Antigone does the same but according to the universality of the love of *philia*. Both Creon and Antigone defined their ethical positions and reasons according to what the rules of law and love demanded; and as they were blindly following rules they were unable to see the particular. Anchored in their certainties, both ended tragically, following rules. The certainty of doing the right thing did not allow them to live good lives.

Bańkowski's attempt to address this problem is complex and original. Though he denies formalism, he rescues and shows the importance of the value of 'legality': the value that 'stands in the middle' between formalism and pure contingency. As we cannot live lives constantly open to contingency, legality allows us to rest on what has been decided and instituted in rules, while at the same time being open to the encounter with the particular. Legality therefore requires from us a certain attitude. We should be open to the encounter with the particular and the way in which this encounter can change us. According to Bańkowski, reasoning with rules cannot avoid the particular without running the risk of becoming formalistic. This shows us, therefore, that we cannot decide without the risk of being wrong, and at the same time we cannot avoid making a decision. The alternative Bańkowski argues for is to 'live lawfully'; to know when to follow and when to break the law, in order to fulfil the law. This is what Bańkowski calls, following Gillian Rose, to live in 'the middle' (Rose 1992). The 'middle' is the place where we cannot rest on the certainties of the universal; where we have to learn to live under the uncertainties we cannot avoid in life.

Against interpretations (Goodrich 2002), that rely on first impressions and consider Bańkowski's argument in *Living Lawfully* as breaking with his previous 'attack' against the law in *Images of Law* (Bańkowski and Mungham 1976), I claim that the argument presented in *Living Lawfully* should be read as a continuation of *Images of Law*. The common thread running through both books is that both are efforts to determine how we can develop proper human lives where individuality is a negotiation between autonomy and heteronomy. It is not difficult to interpret Bańkowski's work as an argument against those who see in law a substitute for ethics; the idea that we can avoid responsibility for our ethical decisions by following the law. What *Living Lawfully* does, and that is why it supersedes *Images of Law*, is to bring more complexity to the analysis of autonomy by assuming that we are not alone. That even if we did not choose to, we are thrown into a world in which we immediately become members of a political society (see, Walzer 2004: ch. 1; McCabe 1969).[2] That autonomy cannot be understood as being outside the world, because it would deny our dependency and vulnerability. (Or as the US rock band, The Doors, said, we are 'riders on the storm': born and thrown into this world). This is just another expression of the tension between law and love, between the law and the community. In other words, the argument in *Living Lawfully* starts from the premise that the individual is a social creation and that autonomy can be politically relevant only when it is part of a political project aiming at mutual recognition.[3] Therefore there are two aspects of our lives that come together in 'living lawfully' – that is, the ethical and the political.

The ethical aspect of 'living lawfully' has been captured very well by Claudio Michelon in the Preface to the Portuguese translation of *Living Lawfully* (Bańkowski 2007: v–xviii). According to Michelon, '*Living Lawfully* means precisely being able to know when to depart from the Law without throwing away the good that legality generates' (Bańkowski 2007: xi).[4] The obvious question that

2 'To be subject to law is to be a member of a community; law is, if you like, the bearing of the community as such on its individual members' (McCabe 1969: 36).

3 In this sense, Bańkowski's work could be understood to be along the same lines as that of Castoriadis. See, for example, (Castoriadis 1997: 77). I return to this idea in the final section of this chapter.

4 It is interesting to note here that Michelon talks about 'Direito', Recht, Derecho or the Law. Without making it explicit, he assumes the tension/equivalence in Bańkowski's work, to which I refer below, between rules and law.

follows is: How do we learn to do that? Michelon understands that Bańkowski's theory is one about the kind of subject that would have the ability to know when to transcend the law (Bańkowski 2007: xii). 'Living lawfully' would be a modern theory of an aspect of practical reason, heir of Aristotle's *phronesis* and Aquinas's *prudentia*. In this sense, following Michelon, 'living lawfully' would be a sort of virtue theory according to which we learn to 'develop certain skills of practical reason under modern law' (Bańkowski 2007: xv).[5]

Here I would like to stop and analyse Bańkowski's arguments in more detail. As mentioned above, a central aspect of Bańkowski's theory of legal (and moral) reasoning is the defence of the importance of learning when and how to leave behind – transcend – the rules. That explains why Bańkowski affirms that fulfilling the law might entail breaking the law. This can happen only once we know what it means to fulfil the law – something that, according to Bańkowski, we can only learn by following rules. At the same time, however, fulfilling the law is not just following rules or abandoning them for the love of the particular. 'Living lawfully' implies knowing when to follow and when to break the rules, being open to an encounter with the particular (Bańkowski 2001: ch. 7).

The reason I want to analyse this idea in greater detail is because this interpretation of 'living lawfully' arguably leaves unresolved the consequences that this theory of practical reasoning has for what I identified above as the political project in Bańkowski's work. As I shall show in what follows, it is relevant in political terms to determine who is the author of the law and how it is that we can modify it. This does not seem to me to be a matter that can be left open to the encounter with the particular. What is needed here is a distinction or a restatement of 'living lawfully', according to which the law is understood as the collective product of the political community and not as something that belongs to a legal interpreter or law-applying authority. If we focus too much on the ethical aspect of 'living lawfully', we run the risk of losing its political side.

The tension described above comes from what I consider to be a remnant of formalism in Bańkowski's theory. Formalism is an excessive identification of the right with rules; the reduction of ethics to nomianism (Shklar 1986: 1–28). This formalism appears in Bańkowski's idea that sometimes we have to break the law to fulfil it. There are at least two possible interpretations of this idea. The first is to understand that this breaking of the law takes place in law application processes; and the second, that the breaking and redefinition of the law is part of a political process.

In the first interpretation – breaking the law to fulfil it in the application of the law – the idea can only be possible once we assume that the law could be reduced

5 This is not to say that Michelon fully agrees with this idea. He argues that there are two possible interpretations of Bańkowski's conception of rules: they can either be causes for behaviour, or formal reasons. In the first interpretation, public agents have space for substantive reasoning, and Michelon would agree with this (for Michelon's argument, see Michelon 2006: 132–4).

to or fully contained in rules (and therefore, by breaking – getting out of – the law/rule, we recreate it anew). The problem therefore is that by breaking the rules, those who break them can redefine the law. Hence 'breaking the law to fulfil the law' is different from other non-formalist interpretation methods or instruments, as is the case, for example, of defeasibility. In cases of defeasibility the rule is not broken, but its terms are (correctly) interpreted (and redefined) to determine if they apply or not to the particular situation. Thus the law is interpreted correctly depending on the particularities of the case. On the other hand, 'breaking the law to fulfil the law' implies recreating it anew. This seems to me to contradict what 'living lawfully' aspires to: to live within the law (and not to redefine it constantly in its application because this would be pure contingency). Of course, in its best interpretation, 'living lawfully' would suppose that the decision to follow or not to follow the rules is a consequence of what is required by the law (what the law aspires to). But then again, in this case breaking the rule would mean that we are fulfilling the law and not breaking it. So, in a sense, the problem would be that we would rest on the rule or its redefinition to define what is legal when in fact we aspire to the reverse; that is, to redefine the rules in accordance with the law.

But there is another problem deriving from this first interpretation of 'breaking the law to fulfil the law' and its relation with the ethical reading of 'living lawfully'. This non-desired consequence is that it opens the door for an instrumental use of the law. If we are not able to distinguish between the law and the establishment of a rule, we could use the rule to go against the substantive content of the law without being able to distinguish between 'living lawfully' and 'living instrumentally'.[6] In other words, if we are not able to distinguish between 'living lawfully' and an instrumental use of the law, we can become a means for those individuals who can make the law an instrument of their will. I shall call this problem 'formalism within legality'.

In 'formalism within legality' the law becomes pure heteronomy and is no longer the expression of the general will or of the will of the people. Two important modern political ideas conflate in this understanding of the law. The first is concerned with determining who is (not) the people;[7] the second, the possibility of identifying and determining the content of the will of that people as what goes in the interests of all. Both ideas address the problem of explaining how the universality of the law can come to terms with individual freedom (see Pelczynski 1984; Taylor 2004: ch. 13; Laclau 2005: chs 4 and 5). But all of this is lost once we open the door to 'formalism within legality', because the law is

6 To use a traditional approach, understanding the law in this way solves the problem of the over-inclusiveness and under-inclusiveness of the rules that has worried legal reasoning for some time. The *locus classicus* is Schauer 1991: 31–4. The rule would be the law until the encounter with the particular. But the instrumental use of the law rests in making this encounter 'invisible'. The particular does not appear and the identification of the law with the rules helps in this.

7 I am not concerned with this issue in this chapter, but see Atria (2013).

redefined according to the will of the individual in the particular moment in which the law is applied.

This does not deny that there are other moments in which the law can be redefined by breaking it. In fact, this is the second possible interpretation of 'breaking the law to fulfil it' I mentioned above. I shall call this the 'political reading'. Hence, 'formalism within legality' must be distinguished from other cases in which the law is broken for political purposes, such as cases of civil disobedience. The difference between the 'political reading' and 'formalism within legality' is that, in the former, the redefinition of the law is part of the political and not a result of legal adjudication/application. In cases of civil disobedience, the law is broken and it should be so declared by those who apply the law. But in these cases, going against the law intends to show that the law is not considered the law of those who break it. In a case of civil disobedience, the breaking of the law has to have a political meaning. In other words, the law is broken because it is not considered any longer as 'my/our law' and breaking it expresses it as being oppressive.

In contrast, in 'formalism within legality' the law can become the will of an individual who does not agree with its content. This is, for example, what happens in cases of tax avoidance. In such cases, the individual uses the law for his or her own purposes, as it is taken to be a pure form. There is a formalist approach to the rules because tax law is understood to be an institution, the content of which is expressed and contained in tax rules. But we know that there is more than rules in the practice we call tax law, and where the content of tax law exceeds the formulation of the rule it is replaced with the will of the tax avoider. This is a good example, because we see the limitations of one of the presuppositions of 'formalism within legality': we cannot know or learn what tax law is about only by following its rules; we must interpret tax law as a practice that tells us something about, and is connected to, the general will. Tax avoidance is a clear example of the gap there is between breaking or following rules and fulfilling the law.

Therefore, 'fulfilling the law by breaking it' can only have meaning for those who do not 'live lawfully': those for whom there is identification between the law and the rules. Bańkowski's idea is to show that this is not the case; that is that rule-following does not encapsulate all there is to law. In other words, that law-abidingness may go beyond rule following. But for this idea to work there must be an interpretive instrument that reminds the law interpreter to consider law's collective authorship. On the contrary, if we use only formalistic interpretive instruments we welcome the instrumental use of the law. And this is precisely the reason why the unavoidable gap between the formulation of the rule and the content of the law does not seem to be fully captured by Bańkowski's approach to legal reasoning as an aspect of ethics. What we are missing here is the political aspect of modern law; that is, the idea that law is posited as part of a political process where the individual is the author of the law only through a political process. Otherwise, if we eliminate the political process and assume that each individual is the author of his or her own law without political mediation, or that the law is an aggregation of individual wills, we run the risk of losing autonomy (or political freedom), as the law would be imposed by those defining it or creating it anew by breaking it.

This is a topic that links with and underlies many of the ideas and arguments in *Living Lawfully*. How can we solve this problem without abandoning 'living lawfully'? I think that the solution for the tension I identified here can be found within *Living Lawfully*. What we need to do is not to abandon the 'middle', but rather to relocate it. As I shall try to show, the answer can be found by reconciling *Living Lawfully* with the main idea in *Images of Law* – that is, to assume that freedom (autonomy) can only be obtained in a political world. If the argument in *Images of Law* was anarchist because it understood that the law could be used instrumentally by the powerful to oppress the populace, *Living Lawfully* must avoid the opposite trap – that is, that law and love are unmediated synonyms, by assuming that we all 'live lawfully' without institutions. In the latter case, as we have seen here, the problem is that the law can be used instrumentally by any individual once 'formalism within legality' is a possible reading of 'living lawfully'. Otherwise the law becomes oppressive: we would be loving a false idol.

That the problem and the solution live together in *Living Lawfully* is captured in the following paragraph:

> Only by *obeying the law* will one know when the law is to be disobeyed or suspended, and it is only in this suspension, that the law itself is continually renewed. This creative breaking of the law can only be effective if it stems from a mastery of the law, in the sense of following and understanding it. But it is not the law that will guarantee the break. However, creativity cannot start *ex nihilo* for that would indeed be chaos. One cannot be a James Joyce and rework the conventions of English grammar without a mastery of those rules *but those rules would not guarantee the good of your new style*. (Bańkowski 2001: 78. Emphasis added).

The Sources of the Problem

We can go more deeply into 'formalism within legality' when exploring the sources of this problem in Bańkowski's work. This analysis will make explicit the lack of law's political aspect in *Living Lawfully*. As I shall show, there are two sources of this problem, and both are found in Bańkowski's notion of fulfilling the law: (i) the idea that the moral content of the law does not need to be mediated by political institutions; and (ii) the idea that we can be authors of law without institutional mediation. At the same time, these two problems at the genesis of 'living lawfully' show what Bańkowski's idea of the law is lacking: an understanding of institutions for living lawfully. I shall address this issue in the last section of this chapter.

For Bańkowski, to fulfil the law is not simply to apply a rule. Once we stand in 'the middle' there is what Bańkowski and Davis call a 'paradoxical means of discerning the path ahead'. In other words, fulfilling the law is a path and what is important is to learn to discern when to follow or to discard the rule. The way in which we learn to do this is 'paradoxical' because we can reach it 'only by obeying the law'. This is the only way in which we shall 'know when the law is to be disobeyed or suspended, and it is only on this suspension that the law itself is continually renewed' (Bańkowski and Davis 2000: 42). In this sense, any individual applying the law should be the recognized authority as a lawmaker. In Bańkowski's words: 'Once formed, the individual is itself a vehicle of the law which it has appropriated and will deploy in new and original ways in the diverse situations which it encounters. The individual, therefore, in turn becomes a lawmaker' (Bańkowski and Davis 2000: 43).

Morality Without Institutions

An important element in Bańkowski's 'living lawfully' is to know when to abandon rules. If we follow Bańkowski and Davis, we know when to abandon rules only once we know what it means to obey the law and to go through the encounter with the particular (Bańkowski and Davis 2000: 42 ff). If we follow another version, only once we master the rules (Bańkowski 2001: ch. 4). As I said before, this identification of the law with rules is a constant in Bańkowski's work. The difference between the way in which this identification is given meaning is what changes between *Images of Law* and *Living Lawfully*. In the first, anarchism was the answer to not living 'enslaved to rules' where 'the only way [to] cope with the cognitive dissonance of bad and corrupt rules is to abolish them entirely and have no rules' (Bańkowski 2002: 451–2). On the other hand, in the second, as long as we 'live lawfully' we do not need to abolish or have no rules, so far as we learn how to apply them. Or, in other words, by 'living lawfully' we incorporate rules to our lives, knowing we are the lawmakers. This is important because the content of the law is therefore a direct expression of what is good for us.

Thus, according to Bańkowski, we learn to follow the law when we master its rules. This is, following his example, what creative artists do: a painter can produce a ground-breaking work only once he or she has mastered the rules of painting, composition and colour. We can break the state of the art creatively only once we can manage its rules. Only once we know and have mastered the rules of the art, can we redefine the practice by breaking the rules (Bańkowski 2001: ch. 4).

This is similar to Herbert McCabe's ideas on morality and moral judgements. According to McCabe,

> [w]e have to go through a moral apprenticeship in which we learn to follow the moral laws that have been handed down to us, and this is a necessary stage if we are ever to learn to be free, to make our own judgements. Nevertheless in the crucial case, in the great choices in which we make our or unmake our lives, we may find that the truly loving act demands that we ignore or go beyond the rules. (McCabe 1969: 13)

But is this the best way to understand the law? In these examples we can see that there is a relative independence between the rule and the practice, and between the moral rule and morality. The rule can be a better or worse description of the content of the practice, or may be a better or worse description of what morality requires.

In its best reading, what Bańkowski and McCabe are trying to tell us is that we should be aware of this distinction because it might be the case that there is no identity between the substantive content of the law and the description contained in the rule, but that we shall only realize this in the encounter with the particular. Therefore, blindly following rules (that is, formalism or legalism) is adoring a 'false idol': it is equivalent to renouncing our moral autonomy, our freedom. In other words, the individual who has dominion over the art of applying and living by the laws, is his/her own master. This opens the possibility of transcending the polarities and making room for the 'third' – the 'singular' (Bańkowski and Davis 2000: 35, 43); that is, the space between polarities opened to the individual once he or she encounters the particular. Those who 'live lawfully' are able to experience the particular, suspend the ethical and decide to apply or re-create the law.

To sum up: if we follow Bańkowski, 'living lawfully' implies that the individual is to become the law-maker so there is no authority coming from the 'outside' imposing a rule or principle applicable to the particular case:

> Appeal to any authority, including God, external to this encounter [with the particular] and applied as a principle which determines its outcome, is illegitimate. The only legitimate authority is the authority of recognition which arises from the encounter itself. (Bańkowski and Davis 2000: 43)

But, as I said above, this reading of 'living lawfully' leads us to 'formalism within legality'. The law becomes oppressive, not for the law-maker, but for the rest of the citizenry. By identifying the law with its ethical aspect we forget its political aspect. So Bańkowski does not solve the tension between the laws and rules that endangers our freedom. What he seems to forget is that, in modern political societies, the individual, as a citizen, is a social construction (and therefore he or she is an individual because of social/heteronomous rules and not against them).

To put it differently, the reading of 'living lawfully' criticized here implies that whenever we are fulfilling the law in the encounter with the particular we are establishing its meaning. The meaning of the law would be settled and become the rule to be followed only after we applied it: '[I]t is in application that we make the law and not in the determination of its meaning' (Bańkowski and Davis 2000: 44). But when it comes to the law, how is it that *your* re-creation of it can respect *my* freedom and autonomy? Is it not that your re-establishment of the law requires my consent?

The identification of the law with rules (even in the antinomian sense; that is, even when breaking the rules is the right thing to do) allows room for oppression. The law can become the instrument for the will of particular individuals, with those individuals who use the law in their favour hiding behind the formality of the rules. This can happen when either fulfilling or breaking the law is reduce to following or breaking rules, and we forget the political reasons that explain the universality of the law. These reasons are those that can build a bridge between autonomy and heteronomy, the reasons that explain the need for political representation. I shall come back to this idea later.

To return to the example of tax avoidance. In these cases, the master of the rules – that is, the tax lawyer, follows the rules to (creatively) break the law. Avoiding taxes is so easy because tax law has been interpreted as a set of rules produced by the binary understanding of the law, derivative of the identification of the law with rules. The problem with tax avoidance is that, by following rules, the tax avoider redefines the content of tax law in its application. So, for those of us who consider tax avoidance a problem, we have a case in which the meaning of rules cannot depend exclusively on its application in a particular case. What we require here is a standard external to the rule, according to which we share the meaning of the rule. This is precisely what the understanding of the law as the will of the people achieves. We share the meaning of the rule because it is part of an institution, the content of which has been determined through a political process. Applying this approach to tax avoidance, we would have to provide an understanding of tax rules within a political decision concerning the definition of the right to private property, and which at the same time redefines the way that the tax is determined to make it independent of the will of any individual.

Bańkowski could answer that he provides a solution to this problem when he introduces the distinction between formal and substantive justice. He would agree that from the perspective of formal justice we cannot grasp tax avoidance and we can only see tax evasion, as we are either within or outside the law (Bańkowski 2001: 139 ff). It could be argued that the solution to tax avoidance could be found by introducing substantive considerations to overcome the dichotomous character of formal law. But then, who will determine the substantive content of the law? Should we assume a liberal, neoliberal, or socialist reading of tax law? Would this be left to those who 'live lawfully', even running the risk that they read it as 'formalism within legality'? It seems to me that the only way we can overcome this problem without risking autonomy requires a reading of tax law able to bring into it its institutional and political aspects.

Tax law should be explained as part of the autonomous decisions taken by a political society. Its legal aspect is an expression of the will of the people, and its substantive content should be determined according to that will. That content should show in some way that the political project is connected with the general interest or mutual recognition. There should not be room for an instrumental use of the law, because the law would continue to be a standard to evaluate the particular action and not merely a rule. The particular action would not redefine the law – as in 'living lawfully' – unless there was a political redefinition of the institution.

Who Is the Author of the Law?

The second source of the problem that has been called above 'formalism within legality' in Bańkowski's *Living Lawfully* is the identity between lawgiver and the interpreter/applier of the law. This problem comes from Bańkowski's use of the parables as a method of reasoning within the law. In the way in which Bańkowski uses the parables he misses the distance between them and our understanding of modern law. In the parables, the law is not part of the political, and the tension between autonomy and heteronomy disappears because there is identity between the law-giver and the interpreter/applier of the law. Jesus Christ is author and interpreter of the law; God in Jesus is authority. According to Bańkowski's interpretation, Jesus is not acting as a lawgiver but, on the contrary, he is teaching us to be free, to 'live lawfully' (Bańkowski and Davis 2000: 49–51; Bańkowski 2001: 99–104). Or, following McCabe, Jesus teaches us how to become law-givers of natural laws that reveal to us who we are – 'what we want' – as individuals who are part of the 'natural community of [the] human race' (McCabe 1969: 60). The problem is that I cannot be the author of my own law in these terms, being part of modern political societies. This could only happen in a place without politics, but with a community of meanings (where equal recognition would be part of our nature as human beings).

Institutions for Loving Lawfully

So far, the argument has attempted to show that the problem with 'living lawfully' is that, in its emphasis on our autonomous ethical law-making, it became an attempt to solve the unsolvable tension between autonomy and heteronomy that underlies the law in modern political societies. But I started this chapter by saying that the solution to this problem can be found in *Living Lawfully* if we radicalize some of Bańkowski's ideas. For this purpose, in this concluding section, I will suggest two ways in which the solution to 'formalism within legality' can be found. The first requires bringing to 'living lawfully' the political idea of representation; and the second, to show how institutions can evolve without breaking the law.

Representation and Politics

How can we bring together the general and the particular will/interests? We need to find an answer to this question to avoid falling into 'formalism within legality'. What we are looking for is a concept that will allow us to explain the political aspect of the law: in which my will is contained in the general will.

To put it in Bańkowski's terms, we need to relocate the 'middle'; to move it from adjudication to the process of formation of the law. As I said earlier, this is the way in which Bańkowski's work can be radicalized: what we are looking for is to fulfil the law by fulfilling the law, and this can be done '*[o]nly by obeying the law*' (Bańkowski 2001: 78. Emphasis added).

For this purpose, it is helpful to look at what Gillian Rose has said about political representation. In *Mourning Becomes the Law*, Rose built her argument showing how the polarization of the political debate between liberals and communitarians has left individuals subject either in 'the arbitrariness of the "libertarian" individual, and the arbitrariness of the "communitarian" interest group' (Rose 1996: 4, 15–16). For Rose, the abandonment of the universal by making it synonym with 'totalitarian' and at the same time the intent of liberating the individual or the community from domination 'disqualifies both the libertarian and the communitarian ... from any understanding of the actualities of structure and authority, intrinsic to any conceivable social and political constitution and which their opposed stances still leave intact' (Rose 1996: 4). What is needed is to build a third category able to relate the two opposites. This third category is, according to Rose, the universal. Only through the universal can we recognize the 'devastation between posited thought and posited being, between power and the exclusion from power' (Rose 1996: 10).

Rose adds further complexity. She argues that we shall never find a clear answer for the content of the categories and their relation, so we can only 'mourn' this loss. For Rose, 'mourning' is the process of not letting go. And 'mourning becomes the law' because we can only live in this uncertainty, constantly redefining the boundaries between the three categories (Rose 1996: 11–12).

For Rose, the universal – that is, the law – is neither the 'superior term' nor the 'symbolic', but the 'middle' that falls 'towards or away from mutual recognition', that is 'formed or deformed by reciprocal self-relations' (Rose 1996: 75). But as we shall never achieve mutual recognition in the law, we mourn and rediscover politics – that is, 'the risk of action arising out of the negotiation of the law' (Rose 1996: 85). So far we have not found an answer to the question with which we started this section, but we are coming closer to it by understanding that politics and the law do not stand in polar opposition to the individual. However, we know that 'the middle is broken'; that is, that we shall not find certainty in the universal. Here is when political representation becomes relevant as the place of 'the broken middle'. Only political representation can ensure that the inescapable universal consequences of political action are considered as such by those in power. Political representation 'understands all agents *in power and out of it*, to face the dilemma of asserting this moral will solely to guard their particular interest' (Rose 1996: 62). At the same time, it is only representation that can allow us to understand that law should also be an institution of 'the middle.' Only through representation does the law become *my* law; the law that I apply to myself is the law that someone else applies to him/herself. To put it in terms of what Fernando Atria calls in Chapter 7 of this volume 'a dead idea'; this political understanding of the law is the way in which the law is expression of the will of the people (of the general will).[8]

8 See Atria (2013).

To understand the law exclusively as part of the ethical is equivalent to missing its connection with the political aspect of our lives; that is, it is to understand the law as the particular and not the general will. If this is the case, relations of power become opaque to the critique of the citizen, and at the same time, for those who cannot take part in that redefinition of the law, it becomes more and more distant from mutual recognition.

To express these ideas in the traditional language of legal theory, we must bear in mind that a theory of adjudication is not independent of a theory of law (see Atria 1999; Atria 2002: ch. 7). And this also depends on a political theory able to explain the structure of power that underlies authority and law. Any political theory concerned with freedom and autonomy should assume that we are born in and become part of different groups, in which we have not chosen to be a part. In other words, we cannot avoid being born into, then being part of and subject to, structures of power to which we never freely decided to be born into or to belong. The law, therefore, should be understood in its connection with the general interest, as this is the only way in which we can ensure that everyone can be heard in an unavoidably alienated world,

> For politics does not happen when you act on behalf of your own damaged good, but when you act, without guarantees, for the good of all – this is to take the risk of the universal interest. Politics in this sense requires representation, the critique of representation, and the critique of the critique of representation. (Rose 1996: 62)

In politics, our particular interests can only appear through representation as expression of the general interest.[9]

Institutions for Loving Lawfully

One of the most important contributions to legal reasoning of Bańkowski's work is his argument in defence of the thesis that there is no certainty on which we can rest in our encounter with the particular. This is an important epistemological argument we should keep in mind in trying to understand the law;[10] and, as I have been attempting to argue, following Rose, we start from the same point in politics. What Bańkowski is saying here is that we should not live under the illusion that we shall find all the answers in the law. Accordingly, we have to remain open to the new possibilities that the particular can bring to the universal. I consider this to be a much better answer to the problems of adjudication than those who try

---

9 'Politics begins not when you organise to defend an individual or particular or local interest, but when you organise to further the 'general' interest within which your particular interest may be represented' (Rose 1996: 4).

10 This, the lack of an epistemological certainty in which the law rests, is another important common aspect between *Images of Law* and *Living Lawfully*.

to anchor the law epistemologically in principles of justice (such as Dworkin: see, in general Dworkin (2011), esp. ch. 19), or abandon the law in favour of different forms of judicial discretion (as legal positivists since Kelsen (1949) and Hart (1994) do), or subject it to a certain kind of privileged reasons (Raz 1999) or to a procedure (Waldron 1999; and Habermas 1998). What Bańkowski's epistemological uncertainty shows us is the radically contingent nature of law.

The criticism so far developed in this chapter tries to take this conclusion one step further by showing how this insight should be conceptually independent from rules (and its possible identity with the law) and adjudication. And this would require an understanding of adjudication that accounts for the fact that the norm contains and reveals a political decision and not just an opportunity to decide what is morally right to do.[11] In this sense, the product of the adjudicative process cannot but be understood as having political consequences. Not only because, to be effective, these decisions are backed by the power of the state, but also because the universality of this decision is necessarily in tension with our autonomy as individuals.

The work of Cornelius Castoriadis can be particularly helpful here to understand how we can maintain institutions open to change, taking Bańkowski's insights from adjudication to a general understanding of legal institutions. Castoriadis's analysis of the institution of society shows perspicuously how institutions can only be understood as part of the 'project of social individual autonomy' (Castoriadis 2007: 94). This project, in turn, underlies what he calls the political 'project of radical democracy' (Castoriadis 1997: 77); that is, the attempt to achieve mutual recognition. As a project it aims to achieve mutual recognition through the 'autonomous action of people and at establishing a society organised to promote the autonomy of all its members' (Castoriadis 1997: 95).

According to Castoriadis, society is instituted as a consequence of the work of the radical imaginary. An aspect of the radical imaginary is that it is social-historical. The 'social imaginary' is what 'in the social-historical is positing, creating, bringing into being' (Castoriadis 1997: 369). It is in the European or Greco-Western tradition where we find the seeds of the radical imaginary as the founding of philosophy and democracy (Castoriadis 2007: 93). This is important because, according to Castoriadis, it is only because of this socio-historical consciousness that societies can become autonomous; otherwise they are heteronomous societies: societies in which the individual is absorbed by institutions and does not have the disposition to contest them (Castoriadis 2007: 94). This project made possible the calling 'into question, in words and in deeds' (Castoriadis 2007: 93) the institutions that constitute the social. This is the way in

11 This is the way in which I interpret Claudio Michelon's very insightful defence of a conception of formality, in which 'formal reasons [are] guaranteed by strong substantive reasons' (Michelon 2006: 138). This allows Michelon to defend a conception of 'decision-making by public agents [which] must always be the result of comprehensive reasoning' (Michelon 2006: 174 and chs 2–5).

which what is instituted is open to constant transformation. Following Castoriadis, the law is the primal institution of society, without which society cannot exist. And for a society to be autonomous it has to accept that its laws are given by itself 'without the possibility of alluding to any nonsocial basis, to any norm for its norm, to any measure of its measure' (Castoriadis 2007: 93); and 'without the possibility of resorting (except by deluding itself) to some nonsocial source or foundation' (Castoriadis 2007: 94). For Castoriadis, the law has two aspects: it is both instituted and institution. And this means that at the same time that the law makes possible the existence of society, it also makes possible action – our doing. Within this schema we make sure that the law is our law and, at the same time, that if we want to change it we are not subject to any external norm.

Therefore, as long as we are open to this constant possibility of changing our institutions according to our social imaginaries, there is no risk of us falling into any epistemological certainty. But, and this is important, we no longer depend on bringing change through adjudication, as now the law is the product of an autonomous society committed to the project of radical democracy.

Conclusion

So where are we after the analysis developed in this chapter? We started by describing how 'living lawfully' is at risk in one possible reading of it – that is, as 'formalism within legality'. From there I attempted to show what I consider to be the two sources of that problem: (i) to assume that morality without institutions is all we need to determine the law; and (ii) that the author of the law is the individual who recreates it anew. Both of these sources derive from an excessive emphasis on the ethical aspect of 'living lawfully'. My argument is that this excessive focus in the ethical endangers 'living lawfully', because the law can become oppressive. The answer to this problem is to focus again on the political aspects that can make 'living lawfully' possible. For that, we need to start from a conception of the law that takes into account its political origin: the law as the will of the people, or the general will. So from the ethical we need to get to the political, from the individual to institutions. And here is where two political concepts are brought together to show how we can create 'institutions for loving lawfully': (i) political representation that connects politics with the general interest; and (ii) having institutions open to political change, the content of which depends on them trying to achieve mutual recognition. In this way, I expect to have removed from Bańkowski's 'living lawfully' the anarchist with no faith in the law.

Bibliography

Atria, F. 1999. 'Legal Reasoning and Legal Theory Revisited'. *Law and Philosophy,* 18(5): 537–77.

Atria, F. 2002. *On Law and Legal Reasoning.* Oxford: Hart Publishing.
Atria, F. 2013. 'Living Under Dead Ideas: Law as the Will of the People'. In M. Del Mar and C. Michelon (eds), *The Anxiety of the Jurist. Legality, Exchange and Judgement.* Farnham: Ashgate, 101–39.
Bańkowski, Z. 2001. *Living Lawfully: Love in Law and Law in Love.* Dordrecht: Kluwer Academic Publishers.
Bańkowski, Z. 2002. 'Images of "Images of Law"'. *Social & Legal Studies,* 11(3): 445–53.
Bańkowski, Z. 2007. *Vivendo Plenamente a Lei.* Rio de Janeiro: Elsevier.
Bańkowski, Z. and Davis, C. 2000. 'Living In and Out of the Law'. In P. Oliver, S. Douglas Scott and V. Tadros (eds), *Faith in Law: Essays in Legal Theory.* Oxford: Hart Publishing, 33–51.
Bańkowski, Z. and Mungham, G. 1976. *Images of Law.* London: Routledge & Kegan Paul.
Castoriadis, C. 1997. *The Imaginary Institution of Society.* Cambridge: Polity Press.
Castoriadis, C. 2007. *Figures of the Thinkable.* Palo Alto, CA: Stanford University Press.
Dworkin, R. 2011. *Justice for Hedgehogs.* Cambridge, MA/London: Belknap Press of Harvard University Press.
Goodrich, P. 2002. Zenotypes: On the Modes of Reproduction of Critical Lawyers. *Social & Legal Studies,* 11(3): 425–43.
Habermas, J. 1998. *Between Facts and Norms.* Cambridge, MA: MIT Press.
Hart, H.L.A. 1994. *The Concept of Law.* Oxford: Clarendon Press.
Kelsen, H. 1949. *General Theory of Law and State.* Cambridge, MA: Harvard University Press.
Laclau, E. 2005. *On Populist Reason.* London: Verso.
McCabe, H. 1969. *Law, Love and Language.* London/Sydney: Sheed and Ward.
Michelon, C. 2006. *Being Apart from Reasons.* Dordrecht, The Netherlands: Springer.
Pelczynski, Z.A. 1984. 'Political Community and Individual Freedom in Hegel's Philosophy of State'. In Z.A. Pelczynski, *The State and Civil Society. Studies in Hegel's Political Philosophy.* Cambridge: Cambridge University Press, 55–76.
Raz, J. 1999. *Practical Reasons and Norms.* New York: Oxford University Press.
Rose, G. 1992. *The Broken Middle.* Oxford: Basil Blackwell.
Rose, G. 1996. *Mourning Becomes the Law: Philosophy and Representation.* Cambridge: Cambridge University Press.
Schauer, F. 1991. *Playing by the Rules: A Philosophical Examination of Rule-Based Decision-Making in Law and in Life.* Oxford: Clarendon Press.
Shklar, J. 1986. *Legalism: Law, Morals, and Political Trials.* Cambridge, MA: Harvard University Press.
Taylor, C. 2004. *Modern Social Imaginaries.* Durham, NC: Duke University Press.
Waldron, J. 1999. *Law and Disagreement.* Oxford: Oxford University Press.
Walzer, M. 2004. *Politics and Passion: Toward a More Egalitarian Liberalism.* New Haven, CT/London: Yale University Press.

PART 3
Exchange

Chapter 10
The Ethical Character of Market Institutions[1]

Russell Keat

Moral Economies and Market Economies

In 'Bringing the Outside In' (2007), Zenon Bańkowski invites us to engage in the study of what he calls 'the ethical life' of legal institutions. These institutions, he says, should be understood not just in moral terms, as rules designed to prevent the worst excesses of human behaviour, but also in ethical ones, as enabling people to lead their lives in certain ways. The appropriateness of specific legal institutions for valued ways of living may then be assessed. In this chapter I shall argue that something similar can and should be done in the case of economic institutions, and of market institutions in particular, the relationship of which to law was a central focus in Bańkowski's earlier work, *Living Lawfully* (2001).

I shall begin by considering an influential school of thought that denies completely the normative character of market economies, and thus rules out the kinds of intellectual enterprise just noted. Market economies, it is claimed, differ radically from all other kinds of economy, and certainly from their historical predecessors, in their non-moral character, and in not being moral economies. In pre-market economies, economic activity is subject to moral constraints and governed by ethical goals; in market economies, by contrast, there is an absence of any such normative framework, and 'purely economic' considerations are the only ones that count.

This claim is associated in particular with the work of Karl Polanyi, most notably in *The Great Transformation* (Polanyi 1957[1944]), and is articulated there through the concept of *embeddedness*. Economic activity is said to be embedded when it takes place in a normative context provided by various social and political institutions and relationships, including those of kinship. It is thus seen and practised as a particular aspect or dimension of more broadly defined activities from which it cannot be separated, and is subject to the normative rules and distinctions recognized by the community. By contrast, when economic

1 This is a revised and modified version of a paper entitled 'Market Economies as Moral Economies', presented at the Political Thought conference in Oxford in January 2011; at the Institute for Social Research, Frankfurt, in February 2011; translated and published in German in *Deutsche Zeitschrift für Philosophie*, 60(4), pp. 535–56, 2012. I am grateful to Zenon Bańkowski, Lynn Dobson, Jonathan Hearn and Andrew Sayer for discussion of the issues it addresses.

activity is disembedded, it takes on a life of its own, as one might say: it no longer forms an integral part of the community's social and political life, but is conceived and practised separately from this, and hence from any normative order. Indeed, only in societies where economic activity is thus disembedded can there properly be said to be 'an economy' as such; that is, a separate sphere or domain.

In Polanyi's view, it is only when markets are used as the primary means of economic organization that this condition of disembeddedness obtains. Market economies differ from all others in being disembedded 'from society', and what Polanyi famously described as 'the great transformation' in modern European history consisted precisely in this disembedding of economic activity, and hence in the emergence of what he called the 'self-regulating' market economy. Thus the transition from pre-market to market economies can be characterized as the displacement of moral by non-moral economies.[2]

Closely connected with this view is a rejection of modern, neoclassical economics, or at least of its applicability to pre-market economies. The depiction of economic agents as self-interested, calculatively rational utility maximizers, and the definition of 'the economic problem' as one of choice between alternative resource-uses under conditions of scarcity, may perhaps be appropriate for the analysis of market economies, but is definitely not so when applied to the normatively embedded character of economic activity in pre-market societies. The universalistic pretensions of modern economics are thus rejected, and a 'substantivist' rather than 'formalist' approach to pre-market economies is endorsed, one that recognizes methodologically their actual embedded nature.

Polanyi's thesis (which provides part of the background to Alasdair MacIntyre's history of moral decline in *After Virtue* (1981) and is partly mirrored by Jürgen Habermas's (1987) claims about the modern decoupling of 'system' from 'lifeworld') has been discussed widely by economic sociologists, historians and anthropologists. Of particular interest to social, legal and political philosophers are the criticisms developed in a series of publications during the 1990s by William Booth.[3] Partly following Polanyi, Booth takes the ancient Greek household as the paradigmatic case of a pre-market economy, and Aristotle as its philosophical spokesperson. He then draws on the work of classical and contemporary liberal political theorists to argue, *contra* Polanyi, that market economies do in fact possess a distinctive *moral* character. He none the less agrees with Polanyi that market economies differ from their predecessors in their lack of orientation

2 Polanyi (1957[1944]); see also Polanyi's papers collected in Dalton (1968). I shall not try to justify the interpretation of Polanyi's views adopted here; it is their substantive correctness that is my concern, not the correctness of their attribution to Polanyi. For recent discussions of his work, see Harvey et al. (2007). Polanyi's concept of disembedding has proved especially contentious: see Krippner (2007).

3 I shall focus on Booth (1994a), but see also Booth (1991, 1993, 1994b).

towards substantive conceptions of the human good.[4] It is this latter claim that I shall be primarily concerned to challenge in this chapter.

Market Economies as 'Moral' but not 'Ethical'

Against Polanyi, Booth argues that market economies *are* moral economies: what distinguishes them is the specific content of the morality in which they are embedded, not their lack of any such morality. He does so by focusing on what he regards as the moral character of market *exchange*, as a contractual relation between 'free and equal' individuals, and argues that this can be seen, historically, as representing a challenge, and an alternative, to the morality of the household economy. In particular, he claims, the endorsement of voluntary contractual relationships between equals by classical liberal theorists, such as John Locke, was directed against the hierarchical, status-differentiated (and indeed patriarchal) nature of the pre-modern household. The specific normative embedding of household economies was rejected, and replaced by a differently constituted economy with its own moral embedding. As Booth puts it, drawing also on the concepts of more recent liberal theory:

> The mode of producing and distributing the means for human sustenance embodied in the market is expressive not of a human propensity to truck, trade and barter or of the desire to acquire ever more things but rather of a moral redrawing of the community and of the place of the economy within it. What that transition yields is a new form of moral embeddedness for the economy. The attributes claimed for it are familiar: an economy whose actors are considered equals and a system indifferent to their noneconomic attributes; a contractarian, voluntaristic institutional context for exchanges; and the view that the public authority should not decide among preferences – that one is entitled to live one's life "from the inside", selecting and ordering one's preferences according to the good as one understands it and seeking to engage the voluntary cooperation of others in one's pursuit of them.[5]

4 Booth treats Polanyi as the leading figure in a more broadly defined group of theorists, whom he calls 'the moral economists', including E.P. Thompson (1971) and James C. Scott (1976), though he recognizes important differences within this group. My reference to an 'influential school of thought' at the beginning of this chapter, and to Polanyi's place within this, is based largely on Booth's account.

5 Booth (1994a: 661). Indeed, Booth believes that economic activity is always normatively embedded, in any society: 'The economy, in short, is suffused by the norms of the community of which it is a part … In this sense, and contrary to Polanyi-type arguments, all economies, including the near-to-pervasive-market economies, are moral economies, embedded in the (ethical) framework of their communities' (ibid.: 662). However, to say that market economies are moral economies does not, in my view, entail that they share in

However, as this passage partly indicates, Booth's claim that market economies are, like their household predecessors, moral economies, is subject to an important qualification. He notes that something that is central to household economies is absent from this liberal account of the market's moral character, namely a clearly articulated and shared sense of the overall end or purpose served by the economy, of the substantive good(s) it is intended to achieve, and hence of the economy as an instrument for this purpose, open in principle to evaluation with respect to how well it serves it.

In the case of Aristotle's ancient Greek household, Booth argues, this ethical end consisted in providing (though only for *citizens*, of course) sufficient leisure-time and resources to engage in the activities seen as constituting 'the good life', including friendship, politics, private and public giving, and philosophical reflection. In contrast, market economies not only seem to lack any such ethical purpose, but the specific character of their normative basis *rules out* the subordination of economic activities to an overarching good. By endorsing voluntary contractual exchanges between equals who pursue their freely chosen goals, and refusing to discriminate between these through authoritative social judgements about their value, this central aspect of household economies (and their Aristotelian rationale) is excluded. As Booth puts it, from Aristotle's standpoint, market economies look like 'masterless households in which one can do whatever one wants ... One does as he wishes because the idea of a sovereign good (the master) is absent and in its absence all desires and pleasures, all life plans, are treated and honoured equally'.[6]

Booth regards this Aristotelian contrast between market economies and their household counterparts as being broadly correct. Taking this into account, one can, I suggest, articulate his overall response to Polanyi's thesis by making use of the distinction adopted by some moral and political philosophers between *ethics*, understood as being concerned with questions of the human *good*, and hence with the nature and sources of human flourishing or well-being, and *morality*, understood now in the more restricted sense as being concerned with questions of *right conduct,* and hence with the rules or principles that should govern people's actions towards one another.[7] Booth's position can then be stated in the following way: what is distinctive about market economies is that they are *moral* (in this restricted sense) but *not ethical*, whereas *non*-market economies

---

the morality of 'the community as a whole'; they might instead have their own normative character.

6 Booth (1994: 664). See also Booth (1993), where he explores the linkage between the internal hierarchy of households, headed by free males who do not work, and Aristotle's ethical hierarchy of ends.

7 Though the distinction is conceptually valuable, the terminology is awkward, given the more usual, everyday use of 'ethics' to refer instead to rules of conduct; that is, to what is now to be understood as 'morality', as *distinct* from 'ethics'. Both the distinction, and more recently this terminology, have played an important part in Habermas's work: see esp. Habermas (1996: 94–9, 151–68).

(or at least household economies) are both moral *and* ethical. Thus Polanyi's 'great transformation' was not from moral to non-moral economies, since market economies *are* moral economies; rather, it was from moral *and ethical* to moral *but non-ethical* economies.

This view of market economies would make them very attractive to those liberal political philosophers who endorse the principle of *neutrality*, according to which the state should not act with the aim of realizing or promoting any specific conception of the good, but should confine itself to establishing a just framework within which individuals could pursue their own such conceptions. Distinctively ethical judgements should thus be excluded from political debate. If market economies are moral but not ethical, the political choice of market institutions, and the use of state powers to support them, would be consistent with this principle of (ethical) neutrality.[8] And it is this understanding of markets that informs one of their most important philosophical defences, in the work of Friedrich Hayek.

Hayek argues that the crucial difference between markets, and other ways in which economies may be (and have been) organized, is the absence of any collective or societal-level decisions about the specific purposes to be served by economic activity. At least in modern societies, he argues, no genuine agreement about such purposes can be reached, given the great diversity in the kinds of goods that individuals value and wish to achieve. Markets enable societies to avoid attempting the impossible (and the highly undesirable consequences of such attempts). They do so, in effect, by devolving such decisions to individuals, pursuing their own, freely-chosen, goals through voluntary co-operation with others. The only societal-level purpose served by market institutions is what he calls the 'abstract' one of enabling individuals effectively to pursue their own 'concrete' purposes, whatever these might be.[9]

It might be argued that this defence (and characterization) of market economies should itself be seen as an ethical one, since it appeals to the ethical value of individual *autonomy*, and endorses the market precisely because of the ways in which it institutionally embeds this 'liberal good' (or at least facilitates its achievement in the economic domain). And it seems that Booth himself has something like this in mind when he eventually refines the contrast he has drawn between market and household economies by saying that the liberal *does*, in a way, have an answer to the Aristotelian question, 'For what end is the economy in this specific, market, form?', namely: 'So that within this sphere I may do with my things, my labour, and so on as I wish, consistent with a recognition of the rights of others to do likewise; in short, so that as far as is possible under conditions

8 For support of markets on neutralist grounds, see Dworkin (1985) and Arneson (1987); for criticism of the latter's arguments for the market's ethical neutrality, see Keat (2009a). On the exclusion of ethics from both liberal political philosophy and critical social theory, see Keat (2008b).

9 Hayek (1976, ch. 10); see also Hayek (1960, chs 10 and 15). On the relationship between Hayek's defence of markets and neutralist liberalism, see O'Neill (1998, ch. 2).

of interdependency, I may lead my life "from the inside."' Booth says that this answer expresses 'a more reflective form of liberalism – guided by the question of the good rather than by a theory of rights alone, but a liberalism nonetheless' (Booth 1994a: 664).

This 'more reflective form of liberalism' is of some significance, especially when the role of the state in supporting the good of autonomy through the institution of exchange is recognized. But given the peculiar nature of autonomy as a 'conception of the good', by comparison with its Aristotelian counterpart, what is implied is essentially a refinement of the 'moral but not ethical' thesis, rather than its wholesale rejection. According to this liberal ethic of autonomy, the good life consists in pursuing whatever (substantive) goods one regards as being worthy of pursuit, or chooses to pursue, on the basis of one's own judgement or decisions; any attempt (such as Aristotle's) to prescribe the content of these goods, and to subordinate economic activity to their achievement, is thus to be resisted. If the good of autonomy were all that the ethical character of market economies consisted in, the 'moral but not ethical' thesis would remain largely intact.

Later in this chapter I shall argue that we should reject this thesis in a more radical manner, and endorse instead the view that both market and pre-market (or household) economies are both moral and ethical; what distinguishes them is 'only' their specific character in these respects. To support this view will require us to move beyond the tendency in liberal thought to focus exclusively on *exchange*, and to direct our attention also to *consumption* and *production*. But before doing so, a good deal more needs to be said about exchange. In particular, I will argue that this may itself be seen as possessing an ethical character, 'over and above' its expression of individual autonomy.

Again, we can take our cue from Booth, who comments at one point that 'voluntary (contractual) relations among persons, whether in economic or other matters, represent a central *good* in liberal market society'.[10] These relations are, as we know from his earlier claims, relations between social equals (by contrast with the hierarchical relations within ancient households), and indeed equals who recognize one another as such. Their value, one might suggest, consists not merely in the exercise of autonomy by each party, but in the fact that, for both parties, they are 'freely entered into relations between equals'. They are goods *as relations of this kind*, and may be valued as such by the individuals concerned. And what enables them to be 'relations of this kind' is (at least in part) the specific set of obligations and moral constraints embedded in the rules that serve to define the market *institution* of contractual exchange.

---

10 Booth (1994a: 662) (emphasis added). Booth makes this comment in the course of criticizing Polanyi's account of the later 're-embedding' of market economies through the development of the welfare state, arguing that, when contractual freedom is overridden to achieve other goods, what is partly sacrificed is itself a good.

To explore further what is involved here, albeit by what will be a somewhat circuitous route, I turn now to some central claims made by the institutional economist Douglass North in his influential work, *Institutions, Institutional Change and Economic Performance*.[11]

Market Institutions and the Good of Exchange

North argues that the strikingly successful economic performance of modern Western societies has been a result primarily of the presence of specific institutional arrangements, and in particular of the institutions of private property, contractual exchange and the modern state. The existence and effective operation of these institutions, he says, is taken for granted by neoclassical economists, who fail to recognize their historical rarity and the great difficulties involved in establishing and maintaining them.

'Institutions,' says North, 'are the rules of the game in society or, more formally, are the humanly devised constraints that shape human interaction'; they 'are the framework within which' such interaction takes place. In some cases, these rules simply prohibit certain kinds of action. In others, they specify which agents (or agents occupying which positions) are permitted or required to perform which kinds of action, and under which conditions. In this and other respects they are, he says, 'perfectly analogous to the rules of the game in a competitive team sport'.[12] I shall return to this analogy later.

Institutions, North says, may consist both of formal rules that are specified in writing and enforced by the state, and of informal ones, such as (unwritten) codes of conduct, conventions and (socially sanctioned) norms of behaviour. Formal rules are especially important in modern market economies, which are characterized by highly impersonal exchange and third-party enforcement, though informal rules remain significant in modern economies. The remit of these formal rules includes the definition and enforcement of property rights, the specification of the requirements for legally binding contracts, and the procedures for enforcing such agreements and resolving disputes.

While North rejects some of the assumptions made by orthodox rational choice theorists, he shares their view that the chief function of institutions is to facilitate co-operation in situations where this would otherwise not occur, despite the benefits that would accrue to the parties concerned were it to do so. Institutions achieve

---

11 North (1990). While Booth's discussion of exchange addresses mainly the normative dimensions of embedding, he also emphasizes the importance of its institutional grounding.

12 North (1990: 3–4). My account also draws on Elinor Ostrom's (1986) analysis of the nature of institutional rules (to which North refers approvingly). See also the discussion of institutions in Rawls (1999: 47–50).

this by reducing the potential costs of such co-operation, including in particular the risks of defection, thereby overcoming standard game-theoretic problems.[13]

For North, then, the value of institutions such as contractual exchange is essentially instrumental: they increase the chances of each party satisfying goals whose nature and value are given independently of the institutional devices that enhance their prospects of achievement. These goals are assumed to have a broadly materialist, wealth-oriented character. North does, however, reject the orthodox rational choice theorist's view that individuals are *exclusively* wealth-oriented, that they are wealth (or utility) *maximizers*. Rather, he claims that moral, religious and ideological beliefs of various kinds are potentially significant influences on people's behaviour, including their willingness to co-operate with others, *provided* that the costs of doing so (in material terms) are not too great.[14] Institutions should thus be designed, *inter alia*, to reduce these costs sufficiently for what one might call 'moral motivations' to come into play in enabling mutually beneficial interactions.

This more nuanced view of economic institutions and individual motives has much to commend it, and – unusually, within economics – provides at least some minimal sense of market economies as moral economies. But it is indeed a quite minimal sense, by comparison with the *liberal* understanding of market exchange presented by Booth. In particular, there is no reference in North's account to the moral character of exchange as a relation between equals, nor to the 'freely chosen' character of the goals pursued. Nor is there any recognition of how the institution of exchange might be valued in anything other than an instrumental way.

To see what is at issue here we can return to North's conception of institutions as *the rules of the game*. For North, these rules facilitate the achievement of each player's aims, which can be specified independently of the institution itself, of the particular game that is being played. But suppose now that we take up his view that institutional rules are 'perfectly analogous' to the rules of a team sport: of hockey, for example. The rules of hockey, we might say, serve to define, or 'constitute', the game of hockey itself. Without these rules there *is* no game of hockey. The rules of this game are not rules that enable its players to achieve an aim that is specifiable without reference to the game, but make it possible for them *to play this game*, and hence also to have this as an aim.[15] They create the 'object'

13 On the distinctions between 'historical', 'rational choice' and 'sociological' forms of institutionalism, see Hall and Taylor (1996). North rejects the 'rational choice institutionalist' view that institutions can be *explained* by reference to their positive functions, rather than by contingent historical and political factors. He also rejects its conception of rationality and, as will be seen shortly, its motivational assumptions.

14 For criticisms of the morally unconstrained wealth-maximizing assumptions of orthodox economic theory, see Nelson (2006) and Ben-Nur and Putterman (1998).

15 Implicitly I draw here on Searle's view that 'regulative' rules may have a 'constitutive' role (1995: 27–9). But I do not accept the specific way in which he conceives

of this aim; they constitute it as a possible object of people's 'preferences'; that is, as something that they may desire or want.

Applying this to market exchange, with its liberal conception in mind, we could then say that the institution of exchange is a set of rules that serves to constitute the object of a possible aim or desire, namely to engage in relationships of voluntary co-operation with others who are one's equals. What is made possible by the institution of exchange – which relies on the powers of the state – can thus itself be seen as a (liberal) good, one that is quite distinct, and different in character, from the 'goods' that, according to North, are served by this institution in its instrumental role.

Further, the institutional rules that constitute, or make possible, this liberal good of exchange are themselves *moral* rules, at least in part: rules about fair disclosure, the absence of fraud, the competence of the parties, the discharge of obligations and so on. The good of exchange can thus be seen as an important case of what Joseph Raz has described as (partly) *duty-constituted goods*, or in the terms I am using, *morally*-constituted goods. Raz applies this concept to intrinsically valuable relationships that cannot be specified without reference to the obligations and responsibilities towards one another of the parties concerned. The example he uses is the good of friendship, but the concept is equally applicable, I suggest, to the good of exchange.[16]

Of course, whether exchange *is* properly judged to be a human good, as liberals have generally argued, or instead as (at least in part) an *ill*, as many socialists have, is open to serious debate. But the argument I have presented does not depend on the outcome of such debate, any more than Booth's argument that market economies are moral economies depends on the judgement made about the specific content of their 'morality'. To claim, *contra* Polanyi, that market economies are moral economies is not to endorse their moral norms, the ways in which they define the duties of the parties to contractual exchange, and so on. Nor, presumably, should Polanyi's view of household economies as moral economies be taken to imply his endorsement of *their* moral character. Normative judgements are, by contrast, crucial in making political decisions about what kinds of economic institutions should be established, and in evaluating those that already exist. But here, as throughout this chapter, my main concern is to provide an analytical framework that enables us to understand what these judgements should address.

---

of that function, and hence more generally of institutions, as presented, for example, in Searle (2005).

16 Raz (1994: 40–2). My argument here depends partly on supplementing North's analysis with elements drawn from Durkheim's account of the normative presuppositions of contractual exchange (1984/1893: Book I, ch. VIII). Bańkowski (2001: 86) makes use of Searle's conception of constitutive rules to explicate Pashukanis's (1980) view of the law's constitutive role for markets. One might suggest that once the moral character of the relevant legal rules is recognized, a less *legalistic* understanding of markets can emerge.

From Exchange to Consumption

I have argued so far that market economies should be understood as both moral and ethical. But the latter has been established (if at all) in only a rather attenuated form. We can get a good deal further if we now shift our attention from exchange to consumption. That we should do so is suggested by the possibility of a quite different (and much simpler) reply to Booth's Aristotelian question, 'For what end is the economy in this specific, market, form?' This is the reply that Adam Smith gave when he said that 'the sole end and purpose of production is consumption', and went one to explain why market economies are so effective in achieving this aim (Smith 1979[1784]: Book IV, ch. VIII, 660).

As Debra Satz has emphasized, Smith valued the exchange relations of commercial society highly because they replaced the servility and deference of feudal society with relations of social equality (Satz 2010: 41–2). But he also, and more familiarly, argued that exchange is an extremely effective means both of encouraging the development of human productive powers, through the division of labour, and of ensuring that these dynamic, wealth-creating powers are deployed for the benefit of consumers, enhancing their well-being through a continually developing array of innovative products whose value is realized through the uses to which they are put (and which, for the most part, they are able to acquire the means of purchasing).[17]

Marx, of course, thought it a serious mistake to attribute the aim of consumption to production in market economies. He regarded the replacement of production for *use*-value by production for *exchange*-value as the distinguishing feature of (capitalist) market economies, and – arguably following Aristotle in this respect – saw this as disqualifying market economies from properly being said to have any ethical goal. But this does not follow from the fact that productive enterprises in market economies 'aim only at exchange-value'. Supporters of Smith could surely respond by saying that, looked at from a systemic point of view, the market is an institutional arrangement that fosters the production of use-values precisely through its productive units aiming only at exchange-values, and indeed does so more effectively than systems in which producers aim directly at use-values.[18]

It might be objected that this does not justify regarding use-values as the (ethical) goal of market economies, since this teleological concept should be restricted to cases involving conscious human purposes, as distinct from unintended systemic effects. But even if this conceptual restriction is accepted, the critical force of the objection can be removed in the following way. Imagine that members of a political community are deciding what kind of economic system to 'institute',

17 As Bańkowski notes, the Hayekian rationale for markets may easily lead one to 'forget that at some level the market is justified in terms of outcome' (2001: 101).

18 The issue here is not whether this is true, but whether, if it were, it might legitimately be used to justify attributing this ethical goal to market economies. It is the latter claim I wish to defend.

or whether to accept or replace their current system. They become convinced of the merits of Smith's claims about the market, and therefore agree to institute (or retain) such an economy in order to generate use-values (through consumption) for their members. By doing so they will, as it were, transform the unintended systemic goal into a consciously intended purpose: 'their' market economy will now have an ethical goal or purpose, one that has been conferred on it.[19] They will also, presumably, wish to ensure that if and when the market fails to achieve this communal purpose, by leaving some members without these intended benefits, their welfare will be secured by some other institutional means.

However, to make such a decision in favour of market institutions, they must not only believe that a market economy is the best generator of consumer goods – and this is something that neoclassical economics cannot demonstrate through its well-known proofs of the market's *efficiency*, which has no bearing on the *dynamic* powers of the market – but also that these 'goods' are indeed valuable, that they do contribute significantly to human well-being.[20] That is, judgements have to be made about the ethical value of what the economic system actually generates, and it is by reference to these kinds of judgements that the use of the state's powers to support the institutions of a market economy has to be justified.

On what basis can and should such judgements be made? They cannot be based on a liberal ethic of autonomy, of the kind discussed earlier, since this has nothing to say about the *substantive* value of consumption, of the 'goods' that people purchase and use, as distinct from the value of their being acquired through voluntary exchange between individuals pursuing freely chosen purposes. To show that consumption itself has some ethical value – that what is acquired through exchange is valuable, as distinct from its mode of acquisition – clearly requires more than this. Further, this additional element cannot be provided by appealing to the neoclassical conception of welfare, defined as 'the satisfaction of preferences, whatever these may be', since it is the specific content and character of the kinds of preferences satisfied through consumption whose value (whether positive or negative) is at issue here.

A somewhat more useful resource for making these judgements is provided by recently burgeoning studies of happiness and life-satisfaction, which includes a good deal of work on their relationship with income levels and economic growth. But these suffer, as plausible criteria for human well-being, from the impact (whether positive or negative) both of expectations and of inter-personal

---

19 A similar suggestion, though not specifically about consumption, is made in Miller (1990: ch. 8). The point is not that such episodes have actually occurred, but that an ethically based political endorsement of the market on the grounds of its power to generate use-values is perfectly intelligible.

20 On the inability of neoclassical economics to explain the dynamic character of production in market economies, see Nelson and Winter (1982) and Lazonick (1991).

comparisons on people's levels of satisfaction.[21] They also fail to address the specific ways in which the use of consumer goods may – or may not – contribute to 'living well'. A more promising approach, I suggest, would be to apply to the evaluation of consumption the kind of Aristotelian conception of well-being developed by Martha Nussbaum. This would require one to examine the specific ways in which various kinds of consumer goods are used and enjoyed, and the extent to which these contribute – or fail to contribute – to the various human 'functionings' (or 'capabilities') that she identifies as essential elements in a flourishing life.[22]

I shall make no attempt to conduct such an evaluation here, nor to speculate about its likely outcome. Instead, I want only to insist that, even if a strong justification for the ethical value of consumption *can* be provided, and market economies can be shown to be better than others in generating such goods, it would not follow that the market is the best ethical choice for economic institutions. This is because there may well be other kinds of goods of equal or greater value to human well-being than those made possible through consumption, and markets might operate in ways that are antithetical to *their* existence, or indeed generate positive *ills* of their own. Environmental impacts are an obvious example here, and there are many others. But the case I shall focus on is the impact of market economies on the ethically relevant features of people's *work*.

From Consumption to Production

In *The Market Experience*, Robert Lane argues that the potential contributions to people's well-being from engagement in the *processes* of production are much greater than those deriving from its *outputs* – from the acquisition of income and its use for consumption. More specifically, he argues that this potential can be realized by the kind of work that involves: 'self-direction, substantive complexity and challenge, variety, little supervision, and intrinsic satisfaction of excellence or self-determination' (Lane 1991: 302). I shall call this 'good work'. But market economies, he argues, are not very effective in generating opportunities for good work. They are essentially *consumer* economies: they tend inherently to prioritize consumer-satisfactions over producer-satisfactions. In doing so they display a fundamental defect, since they sacrifice potentially greater goods for lesser ones.[23]

21 See, for example, the discussion of how and why increases in income, above a certain level, have little positive impact on people's happiness, in Layard (2005).

22 Nussbaum (1990). The evaluation of consumer goods in relation to the social practices in which they may enable people to engage is discussed in Keat (2000c: 154–7).

23 The analysis of work here, and in what follows, is restricted to paid employment in the formal economy, thus excluding *inter alia* the unpaid (and largely female) work performed in the modern household. Lane's 'prioritization' thesis is examined in Keat (2000b).

An argument with broadly similar conclusions is developed by Alasdair MacIntyre, who claims that the institutional character of modern market economies is inimical to the conduct of economic production as a *practice*. A practice, he says, is a 'complex form of socially established cooperative activity' in which goods that are *internal* to the activity are realized 'in the course of trying to achieve those standards of excellence that are appropriate to' and partly define the nature of that activity (MacIntyre 1981: 175). A wide range of social activities can potentially be practices, including the various arts and sciences, sports and games, and 'productive' activities such as fishing, farming or building. The primary aim of those involved in a practice is to perform well, and contribute to, the activity concerned, as judged by its standards of excellence. By learning how to engage in the practice, individuals will become able to appreciate and enjoy its internal goods: for example (mine, not MacIntyre's), the truthfulness and affective power of a theatrical performance, or the elegance and explanatory power of a scientific theory.

The internal goods of practices, says MacIntyre, are to be distinguished from the *external* goods of money, power and status. These external goods can potentially make a positive contribution to practices, since practices require *institutions*, and institutions require the use of external goods. But for practices to flourish, external goods must be subordinated to internal ones, and to the standards and purposes of the practice. In particular, they must be prevented from undermining the various *moral virtues*, such as justice, truthfulness and courage, which the conduct of practices depends on. For example (again mine), practitioners must be able to trust the honesty and fairness of the judgements made by others about the competence or value of their performances or contributions, and must have the courage to listen to these judgements.[24]

But in MacIntyre's view, the institutions of market economies (including the modern business corporation) are antithetical to the conduct of production as a practice. The internal goods of practices are subordinated to the external goods of money, power and status, and the moral virtues on which the integrity of practices depends are undermined. The potential value of work as a practice is thereby lost, and the possibilities instead provided for consumption, through the acquisition of money, can do relatively little to compensate for this loss.

So both Lane and MacIntyre can be seen as rejecting Smith's view that 'consumption is the sole end and purpose of production', and that, as he immediately goes on to say, 'the interests of the producer ought to be attended to, only so far as it may be necessary for promoting the interests of the consumer'.[25]

---

24 Thus the internal goods of practices are *morally-dependent* goods, and dependent also on the institutions that sustain these practices and the virtues of their practitioners.

25 Smith (1979/1784: Book IV, ch. VIII, 660). The passage continues: 'The maxim is so perfectly self-evident, that it would be absurd to attempt to prove it. But in the mercantile system, the interest of the consumer is almost constantly sacrificed to the producer; and it seems to consider production, and not consumption, as the ultimate end and object of all

Their response to this might be as follows: if this is a claim about what *should* be the ethical aim of production, it should be rejected, since there are other, more valuable, goods that can in principle be achieved through production; but if it is a claim about what purpose can be served by production *in a market economy*, it may well be true, and provide a strong reason for choosing some alternative to the market that is more conducive to good work, or to work as a practice.

But what are the grounds for believing that market economies subordinate good work to consumption, or internal goods to external ones? Lane argues that, in market economies, firms necessarily base their decisions on criteria that make no reference to the character of their employees' work; given the way that market economies operate, this is something that cannot and does not count as a relevant consideration. Thus:

> It is inherent in the market that it give consumer welfare priority over worker welfare because consumers are the source of profits and workers are costs. Inasmuch as exchange is central to the market network of transactions, giving price signals for the self-regulating system, it is inherent in the market that intrinsic satisfactions, none of which can be exchanged, should lack consideration (Lane 1991: 609)

However, this argument (and others like it) is problematic. It is true that the provision of good work is not something that the market requires firms to take into account, and that it has no market-established price or 'value'. But this does not rule out the possibility that an effective means by which firms can meet the requirements imposed by markets is by acting in ways that in fact provide such work. That this is actually so has recently been argued by the business economist John Kay. Markets may require firms to be profitable, but firms may best achieve this, he argues, not by aiming directly at profits but instead at organizing and conducting their production in ways that closely resemble a MacIntyrean practice.[26]

Kay presents his argument specifically as a response to MacIntyre's well-known contrast between two types of fishing crew. The first kind, which MacIntyre regards as typical of business enterprises in capitalist market economies, is described by him as follows:

> A fishing crew may be organized and understood as a purely technical and economic means to a productive end, whose aim is only or over-ridingly to satisfy as profitably as possible some market's demand for fish. Just as those managing its organization aim at a high level of profits, so also the individual

industry and commerce.' Smith was none the less concerned about the damaging effects on workers of mindless and repetitive tasks.

26 Kay (2010: 19–28). Kay presents this argument as an important case of the principle of *obliquity*: that, very often, the most effective way of achieving some objective is to aim at something else.

> crew members aim at a high level of reward. Not only the skills, but also the qualities of character valued by those who manage the organization, will be those well designed to achieve a high level of profitability. And each individual at work as a member of such a fishing crew will value those qualities of character in her or himself or in others which are apt to produce a high level of reward for her or himself. (MacIntyre 1994: 284)

The second kind of crew, which MacIntyre regards as engaged in fishing as a practice, is described thus:

> Consider by contrast a crew whose members may well have initially joined for the sake of their wage or other share of the catch, but who have acquired from the rest of the crew an understanding of and devotion to excellence in fishing and to excellence in playing one's part as a member of such a crew. Excellence of the requisite kind is a matter of skills and qualities of character required both for the fishing and for achievement of the goods of the common life of such a crew.[27]

Kay argues that while the first kind of crew may *seem* to be just what firms are like in a modern market economy, this is not because they actually *are* like this, but because of their widespread misrepresentation as such (in business economics textbooks, for example) by the proponents of what he calls 'the American Business Model'. He accepts that some firms of this kind exist, or at least operate in this kind of way for certain periods of time, but insists that they are generally less successful (in terms of longevity, profitability and so on) than those that resemble MacIntyre's second kind of crew, exemplifying the practice-model.[28]

However, the view I shall now present differs both from MacIntyre's (and Lane's) and from Kay's. It is that the American Business Model is a reasonably accurate depiction of the type of firm that predominates in *one* kind of market economy, whereas the practice-like firm is more typical of another, *different* kind. The institutional differences between these kinds of market economy, I shall suggest, are such that they will 'favour' different types of firms (that is, firms that differ in the ways presented above), so that those that conform to the American Business Model will be more likely to succeed in one kind of market economy, and those conforming to the practice-model in the other kind.

This suggestion requires one to reject something that has so far been tacitly assumed, namely that there is just one kind of market economy, that 'market economy' refers to a single, reasonably determinate, set of institutional arrangements. But there are good reasons for rejecting this assumption. For not

27 MacIntyre (1994: 285). Note also MacIntyre's view that, when fishing is conducted as a practice, what matters is not only the successful catching of fish, but also the 'perfecting' of the lives of the fishing crew.

28 MacIntyre's 'pessimism' about the possibilities for production as a practice in modern businesses is also questioned in Moore and Beadle (2006) and Keat (2000a, 2008a).

only can there be both capitalist and *non*-capitalist market economies (such as *market socialist* economies, in which capitalist firms are replaced by co-operative enterprises),[29] but even if we restrict ourselves to the former, capitalist category, there is a widely held view among comparative political economists that there are significantly different kinds of capitalism. It is the implications of this view that I shall now explore.

Ethical Varieties of Capitalism

In *Varieties of Capitalism*, Peter Hall and David Soskice set out to identify the institutional differences between what they call 'Liberal' and 'Coordinated' Market Economies (LMEs and CMEs).[30] Taking the UK and USA as exemplifying the former, and Germany as the paradigmatic case of the latter, they argue that the different institutional arrangements that characterize LMEs and CMEs impact significantly on the organization and behaviour of firms.

These institutional differences include, centrally, those concerned with forms of ownership and the provision of finance; with the internal governance of firms; and with the nature of inter-firm relationships. The first set of differences makes firms in CMEs much less vulnerable than those in LMEs to the pressures of short-term profitability (so-called 'patient' as compared with 'impatient' capital); the second reduces considerably the extent of intra-firm hierarchy and 'managerial prerogative' in CMEs, by comparison with LMEs; and the third enables various forms of co-operation between firms in CMEs, through industry-wide associations that are relatively undeveloped in LMEs, and that play a major role in research and development, in technology transfer, and in systems of education and training.

Among the effects of these institutional differences, they argue, is that, in comparison to their LME counterparts, firms in CMEs are more likely to compete in terms of quality, rather than price, and to make extensive use of skilled labour. They are also better suited to engage in long-term processes of what Hall and Soskice term 'incremental innovation', something that is achieved most easily if 'the workforce ... is skilled enough to come up with such innovations, secure enough to risk suggesting changes to products or process that might alter their

29 Arguments for market socialist economies based on competition between worker co-operatives are presented in, for example, Selucky (1979) and Miller (1990). For an argument that such systems would be conducive to production as a MacIntyrean practice, see Mason (1996).

30 Hall and Soskice (2001). Similar contrasts, but with different terminology, are drawn in Crouch and Streeck (1997) and Whitley (1999). Notice that these are conceived primarily as differences between *production* systems, whereas the more familiar distinction between 'neoliberalism' and 'the European Social Model' is primarily between *welfare* systems. I make use of Hall and Soskice's work in discussing Habermas's criticisms of neoliberalism in Keat (2009b).

job situation, and endowed with enough work autonomy to see these kinds of improvements as a dimension of their job'. Corporate organization in CMEs makes this more feasible than in LMEs, since the former, unlike the latter, 'provides workers with secure employment, autonomy from close monitoring, and opportunities to influence the decisions of the firm', and the skill system provides them with 'high levels of industry-specific technical skills'.[31]

If this argument is correct, we can see how CMEs might well be more favourable than LMEs to the various elements of 'good work' identified by Lane, which, as noted earlier, consist in 'self-direction, substantive complexity and challenge, variety, little supervision, and intrinsic satisfaction of excellence or self-determination'. But we can also see how they might similarly favour the conduct of production as a MacIntyrean practice, taking our cue from Lane's reference here to *excellence*. The satisfaction that comes from excellence, he argues, is quite different from that arising from self-determination, and is essentially connected to the shared *standards* of excellence to be found, *inter alia*, in the work of various professional groups.[32]

It is here that the industry-wide associations that Hall and Soskice emphasize as a feature of CMEs become particularly important, for my purposes. MacIntyrean practices are not just a matter of the development and exercise of complex skills and judgement, but also of the presence of shared standards of excellence and the appreciation and enjoyment of internal goods that are dependent on these. If one considers, for example, the kinds of vocational training and apprenticeship in industry-specific skills that are provided through the associations characteristic of CMEs, and the ways in which these may be expected to foster a sense of participation in a shared practice that goes beyond the boundaries of individual firms, it becomes plausible, I suggest, to regard CMEs as being especially conducive to the conduct of production as a MacIntyrean practice.[33]

Political Choices and Institutional Design

Though the argument that CMEs are more conducive than LMEs to production as a practice has only been sketched here, enough has perhaps been said to support the claim that varieties of capitalism (and hence of market economies) may well

31 Hall and Soskice (2001: 39–40). Industry-specific skills are those that can be used across different firms in the same industry, by contrast with firm-specific skills (relevant only to particular firms) and generic skills (usable across firms in different industries).

32 Lane (1991: 388–9). What this implies is that the various features of 'good work' identified by Lane and others typically depend for their existence on complex forms of social practice and institutional arrangement, and hence also on the moral virtues or norms involved in these.

33 This argument is developed in much greater detail in Keat (2008a); see also Keat (2011), in which the relationship between economic institutions and social goods, and the implications of this for liberal political philosophy, are explored.

differ significantly in the extent to which they 'favour' work that has certain ethically relevant features, features it possesses by virtue of the kinds of social relationships it involves. They differ in this respect because of the different array of institutions that define or constitute them as a specific kind of capitalist market economy, and which encourage or discourage the conduct of economic production in specific ways.

One might put this by saying that, in this respect at least, these two kinds of capitalism, and the institutions that define them as such, differ in their *ethical character*: in the kinds of goods they make possible, and hence in the kinds of lives they enable people to lead. But they do not differ in *having* an ethical character. Nor does the way in which I have depicted these differences imply any judgement that one is ethically preferable to the other. To endorse CMEs because they favour work as a practice, one would need, *inter alia*, to defend the ethical value of practices, and to consider what ethical case might instead be made for the different character of work in LMEs. And ethical judgements of this kind should, I suggest, play an important part in any political choice that might be made between these two kinds of capitalism. That is, they are relevant to the decisions that might be made, by members of a political community, about how they wish to 'institute their economy'; or, in the terms that emerged from my discussion of North's account of institutions, about the state-enforced rules that will constitute this as one 'game' rather than another.

This is the same kind of political choice or decision as the one that, earlier on, I imagined being made about the possible adoption of market institutions on the grounds of their impact on consumption. In both cases, ethical judgements about the value of the kinds of goods concerned need to be made. In making these judgements, what is thus at issue are the specific ethical purposes that are to be achieved through economic institutions (and how to prioritize these if not all of these valued purposes are institutionally co-realizable). And if this is so, the hope expressed by Hayek that the market is an institutional arrangement that obviates the need for collective decisions about the purposes to be served by an economy is unfounded.

Hayek insists that market institutions have no purpose apart from the abstract one of enabling individuals to pursue their own concrete purposes, whatever these may be, through voluntary co-operation with one another, and he limits the scope of collective decision accordingly. But this cannot be quite right. By no means every kind of concrete purpose can be achieved through voluntary co-operation in markets, nor is market exchange the only kind of voluntary co-operation; the case of friendship illustrates both points. Thus an ethically *liberal* justification of markets, in terms of individual autonomy or the ethical character of exchange, is at the very least seriously incomplete. Something must also be said about the substantive value of the kinds of benefits that may be achieved through markets, and once this is admitted, the relevance of other kinds of goods that may or may not be generated, or impacted upon, by markets, including those related to work and production, cannot be excluded.

If Hayek is wrong about this, then so too is Polanyi. Admittedly, Hayek would reject Polanyi's view of market economies as non-moral economies, since he regards the rules and conventions of market institutions as having, at least in part, a *moral* character. (His view is, in this respect, quite close to Booth's.) But the ways in which Hayek contrasts markets with households is otherwise very close to Polanyi's, in denying that markets, unlike households, are governed by any substantive ethical purpose. Their only disagreement is whether this makes markets more, or less, desirable than households. My view, by contrast, is that both markets and households are both moral and ethical, and that 'we must choose between them' by making substantive judgements about their moral and ethical characters.

Polanyi, as I noted at the outset, makes use of the concept of *disembedding* in articulating the historical transition from household, or pre-market, to market economies. Economic activity becomes disembedded from the moral constraints and ethical goals that had previously applied to it, constraints and goals that themselves reflected how this activity formed an integral part of the normative and institutional order of society. 'The economy', as such, did not exist; the emergence of the market goes hand-in-hand with the separation of 'economy' from 'society'. But this way of conceptualizing 'the great transformation' is misleading. A better account can be given in terms of *differentiation*, rather than disembedding (Holton 1992). 'The economy' becomes differentiated from other institutional domains, including those of politics and kinship. But in doing so it does not lose its normative character; rather, it gains one of its own.

Broadly speaking, this is the picture we find in Hegel's *The Philosophy of Right* (Hegel 1967), and rather more recently, in Michael Walzer's *Spheres of Justice* (Walzer 1983). In the latter, at least, it comes with a conception of social goods, and of their location within institutionally distinct spheres or domains, which has important implications for the kinds of judgements about economic institutions that I have assigned to political communities. In particular, the qualitatively distinct and plural nature of these institutionally-specific goods implies that, to regard market exchange as a good is compatible with there also being other goods, such as friendship, whose partly-constitutive moral duties and responsibilities differ significantly from those of exchange. The reverse also holds: both may be goods, within their respective spheres. Hence the failure of market exchange to demonstrate, in its moral character, the same obligations of mutual concern that friendship displays, is not necessarily an objection to economic institutions that rely on exchange rather than on friendship (or on kinship or political relations).

This does not mean that the very limited nature of 'the obligations of exchange' are beyond criticism, and hence that we might not quite reasonably prefer a different basis for economic transactions. Further, if the account I have suggested of how political choices between economic institutions are to be made is at all plausible, there must be some much wider, and deeper, sense of mutual obligation among members of a political community, for them to choose market institutions, based on the limited obligations of exchange, as the means by which 'the well-being of all' is to be secured. And if they are to decide in favour of market institutions, on these kinds of grounds (including a pluralistic understanding of social goods), they must also be concerned to ensure that these institutions, and the goods they make possible, are kept firmly in their place: that they are not permitted to 'invade' or 'colonize' other institutional spheres, undermining the integrity of the (quite different) goods that these make possible.

Admittedly, this picture of institutional (and ethical) differentiation is too simple as it stands, not least because it assumes a distinction between the normative character of market exchange and friendship that is more radical than may easily be justified. Bańkowski, in his work on the ethical life of legal institutions, has argued that exchange may take different forms, in some of which the salience for both parties of the *mutually* advantageous nature of their relationship significantly reduces its normative separation from friendship (Bańkowski 2007; see also Bruni and Sugden 2008). But it would take (more than) another chapter to explore the issues raised by this.

Bibliography

Arneson, R. 1987. 'Meaningful Work and Market Socialism'. *Ethics*, 97: 517–45.

Bańkowski, Z. 2001. *Living Lawfully*. Dordrecht: Kluwer.

Bańkowski, Z. 2007. 'Bringing the Outside In: The Ethical Life of Legal Institutions'. In T. Gizbert-Studnicki and J. Stelmach (eds), *Law and Legal Cultures in the 21st Century: Unity and Diversity*. Wolters: Kluwer Polska, 193–217.

Ben-Nur, A. and Putterman, L. (eds) 1998. *Economics, Values and Organization*. Cambridge: Cambridge University Press.

Booth, W.J. 1991. 'The New Household Economy'. *American Political Science Review*, 85(1): 59–75.

Booth, W.J. 1993. *Households: On the Moral Architecture of the Economy*. Ithaca, NY: Cornell University Press.

Booth, W.J. 1994a. 'On the Idea of the Moral Economy'. *American Political Science Review*, 88(3): 653–67.

Booth, W.J. 1994b. 'Household and Market: On the Origins of Moral Economic Philosophy'. *The Review of Politics*, 56(2): 207–35.

Bruni, L. and Sugden, R. 2008. 'Fraternity: Why the Market Need Not Be a Morally Free Zone'. *Economics and Philosophy*, 24: 35–64.

Crouch, C. and Streeck, W. (eds) 1997. *Political Economy of Modern Capitalism: Mapping Convergence and Diversity*. London: Sage.

Dalton, G. (ed.) 1968. *Primitive, Archaic, and Modern Economies: Essays of Karl Polanyi*. Boston, MA: Beacon Press.

Durkheim, E. 1984[1893]. *The Division of Labour in Society*. Trans. W.D. Halls. London: Macmillan.

Dworkin, R. 1985. 'Liberalism'. In *A Matter of Principle*, Oxford: Oxford University Press, 181–204.

Habermas, J. 1987. *The Theory of Communicative Action*, Vol. 2. Trans. T. McCarthy. Cambridge: Polity Press.
Habermas, J. 1996. *Between Facts and Norms*. Trans. W. Rehg. Cambridge: Polity Press.
Hall, P.A. and Soskice, F. 2001. 'An Introduction to Varieties of Capitalism'. In P.A. Hall and F. Soskice (eds), *Varieties of Capitalism: The Institutional Foundations of Comparative Advantage*. Oxford: Oxford University Press, 1–70.
Hall, P.A. and Taylor, R. 1996. 'Political Science and the Three New Institutionalisms'. *Political Studies*, XLIV, 936–57.
Harvey, M., Ramlogan, R. and Randles, S. (eds) 2007. *Karl Polanyi: New Perspectives on the Place of the Economy in Society*. Manchester: Manchester University Press.
Hayek. F. 1960. *The Constitution of Liberty*. London: Routledge & Kegan Paul.
Hayek. F. 1976. *Law, Legislation and Liberty*, Vol. 2. London: Routledge.
Hegel, G. 1967. *The Philosophy of Right* (1821), trans. by T.M. Knox. Oxford: Oxford University Press.
Holton, R.J. 1992. *Economy and Society*. London: Routledge.
Kay, J. 2010. *Obliquity: Why Our Goals Are Best Achieved Indirectly*. London: Profile Books.
Keat, R. 2000a. 'Markets, Firms and Practices'. In *Cultural Goods and the Limits of the Market*, Basingstoke: Palgrave Macmillan, 111–32.
Keat, R. 2000b. 'Consumer-Friendly Production or Producer-Friendly Consumption?'. In *Cultural Goods and the Limits of the Market*. Basingstoke: Palgrave Macmillan, 133–48.
Keat, R. 2000c. 'Justifying the market *and* its limitations'. In *Cultural Goods and the Limits of the Market*. Basingstoke: Palgrave Macmillan, 149–71.
Keat, R. 2008a. 'Practices, Firms and Varieties of Capitalism'. *Philosophy of Management*, 7: 77–91.
Keat, R. 2008b. 'Social Criticism and the Exclusion of Ethics'. *Analyse und Kritik*, 30(2): 229–53.
Keat, R. 2009a. 'Anti-Perfectionism, Market Economies and the Right to Meaningful Work'. *Analyse und Kritik* 31(1): 121–38.
Keat, R. 2009b. 'Habermas on Ethics, Morality and European Identity'. *Critical Review of International Social and Political Philosophy*, 12(4): 535–57.
Keat, R. 2011. 'Liberalism, Neutrality and Varieties of Capitalism'. In N. Smith and J-P. Deranty (eds), *New Philosophies of Labour: Work and the Social Bond*. Leiden: Brill, 347–70.
Krippner, G. 2007. 'The Elusive Market: Embeddedness and the Paradigm of Economic Sociology'. *Theory and Society*, 30: 775–810.
Lane, R. 1991. *The Market Experience*. Cambridge: Cambridge University Press.
Layard, R. 2005. *Happiness: Lessons from a New Science*. London: Penguin.
Lazonick, W. 1991. *Business Organization and the Myth of the Market Economy*. Cambridge: Cambridge University Press.

MacIntyre, A. 1981. *After Virtue*. London: Duckworth.
MacIntyre, A. 1994. 'A Partial Response to My Critics' In J. Horton and S. Mendus (eds) *After MacIntyre*. Cambridge: Polity Press, 283–304.
Mason, A. 1996. 'MacIntyre on Modernity and How It Has Marginalised the Virtues'. In R. Crisp (ed.), *How Should One Live?*. Oxford: Clarendon Press, 191–219.
Miller, D. 1990. *Market, State and Community*. Oxford: Oxford University Press.
Moore, G. and Beadle, R. 2006. 'In Search of Organizational Virtue in Business'. *Organization Studies*, 27(3), 369–89.
Mulhall, S. and Swift, A. 1996. *Liberals and Communitarians*, 2nd edn. Oxford: Blackwell.
Nelson, J.A. 2006. *Economics for Humans*. Chicago, IL: University of Chicago Press.
Nelson, R.R. and Winter, S.G. 1982. *An Evolutionary Theory of Economic Change*. Cambridge, MA: Harvard University Press.
North, D. 1990. *Institutions, Institutional Change and Economic Performance*. Cambridge: Cambridge University Press.
Nussbaum, M. 1990. 'Aristotelian Social Democracy' In R.B. Douglass, G.M. Mara and H.S. Richardson (eds), *Liberalism and the Good*. London: Routledge, 203–52.
O'Neill, J. 1998. *The Market: Ethics, Knowledge and Politics*. London: Routledge.
Ostrom, E. 1986. 'An Agenda for the Study of Institutions'. *Public Choice*, 48: 3–25.
Polanyi, K. 1957[1944]. *The Great Transformation*. Boston, MA: Beacon Press.
Pashukanis, E.B. 1980. *Selected Writings in Law and Marxism*, P. Beirne and R. Sharlet (eds). London: Academic Press.
Rawls, J. 1999. *A Theory of Justice*, revd edn. Oxford: Oxford University Press.
Raz, J. 1994. *Ethics in the Public Domain*. Oxford: Oxford University Press.
Satz, D. 2010. *Why Some Things Should Not Be For Sale: The Moral Limits of Markets*. Oxford: Oxford University Press.
Scott, J.C. 1976. *The Moral Economy of the Peasant*. New Haven, CT: Yale University Press.
Searle, J. 1995. *The Construction of Social Reality*. New York: The Free Press.
Searle, J. 2005. 'What Is an Institution?'. *Journal of Institutional Economics*, 1(1), 1–22.
Selucky, R. 1979. *Marxism, Socialism, Freedom*. London: Macmillan.
Sher, G. 1997. *Beyond Neutrality: Perfectionism and Politics*. Cambridge: Cambridge University Press.
Smith, A. 1979[1784]. *An Inquiry into the Nature and Causes of the Wealth of Nations,* 3rd edn. Oxford: Oxford University Press.
Thompson, E.P. 1971. 'The Moral Economy of the English Crowd in the Eighteenth Century'. *Past and Present*, 50, 76–136.
Walzer, M. 1983. *Spheres of Justice*. London: Martin Robertson.
Whitley, R. 1999. *Divergent Capitalisms.* Oxford: Oxford University Press.

Chapter 11

The Law of Contract and the Limits of the Welfare State

David Campbell

Introduction

This is the second time I have been privileged to be asked to write a piece in recognition of the career and achievement of Zenon Bańkowski. The first time, some 11 years ago, was to mark the 25th anniversary of the publication of *Images of Law* (Bańkowski and Mungham 1976). The paper I wrote at that time attempted to celebrate the 'liberating feel' that followed from the book's 'refreshing anarchism'. I contrasted this to the 'increasingly … statist quality of current left-wing legal thinking … that is being drawn towards authoritarian views about the law' (Campbell 2002: 413, 413–14, 422). In this chapter, I would like to take up this theme again, though whereas my earlier piece addressed general constitutional issues, I would now like to return to my last and discuss the law of contract, or, at least, the law and economics of the law of contract.

In a pan-European research project completed in 2006, some results of which were published in 2009 in *Capacitas: Contract Law, Capabilities and the Legal Foundations of the Market*, a collection of papers edited by Simon Deakin and Alain Supiot (2009),[1] the 'capabilities approach' developed principally by the enormously distinguished welfare economist and political philosopher, Amartya Sen, was applied to the law of contract. The aim of this project was to determine whether it is 'possible to identify the elements of a new concept of *capacitas*, one that goes beyond purely formal guarantees of market access, to encompass the conditions needed for effective participation in the complex economic orders

1 Of the nine papers published in this book, I have been able to read only the first three, by Deakin (2009), Martin Hesselink (2009) and Alain Wijffels (2009), which are in English, the other six papers being in French. I am also unable to read a companion volume of results of the research project as it is entirely in French (De Munck and Zimmerman 2007), though Sen's own contribution is a translation of an article originally published in English (Sen 2004). Deakin and Frank Wilkinson had earlier discussed the capabilities approach in relation to labour law (Deakin and Wilkinson 2000, 2005) and in relation to the single market generally (Browne et al. 2004). Deakin (2011) takes up the issue of the implications of the capabilities approach for the autonomy of the economic actor, the issue on which this chapter focuses.

which characterise our time' (Deakin 2009: 1). One cannot overestimate the importance of the attempts that have been and currently are being made to identify the institutions necessary for what I shall, in Hegelian vein, call the actualization of market order. In this chapter, I want to review this particular attempt and assess what it tells us of the current state of left-wing thinking on the law of contract.

Over the past 30 years, the capabilities approach has excited a considerable amount of interest in a range of intellectual disciplines, and has had a significant influence on policy at the international level, where it has been taken up with enthusiasm by UN agencies seeking to promote development. It has played an important part in an 'ethical' shift in development policy, away, not merely from aid as emergency relief, but from aid as the provision of basic needs when these are understood as, as it were, technical infrastructure, to aid as investment in the capabilities of the poor to engage in economic action to their advantage.

Based on theoretical welfare economics and the modern political philosophy of equality, the capabilities approach generally has an abstract quality which is only exaggerated by the attempts of mathematical economists to 'operationalize' it by measuring welfare, equality and capability in ways that are generally found to be incomprehensible or fantastical by other than initiates. That the UN can spend considerable sums on development policies that purport to put these metrics into practice tells one more about development politics than about development. When reading what development economists say of institutions, one must remember that it is normally the case that the writer will be possessed of scant empirical information about his or her subject matter. It is not so much that he or she knows little or nothing of extant institutions and that his/her abstract economic methods tend to preclude learning about them. It is that he or she is consciously or unconsciously averse to knowing anything about any institutions other than the novel ones he/she intends to impose on the societies that are targeted for improvement, as such knowledge would gravely limit the scope of development policy.

Now, Sen (1999b: 142) has regularly said things that acknowledge the importance of institutions and has given institutionally sensitive accounts of the development possibilities for India, his native country (Drèze and Sen 1995, 2002). In his more recent work, of which *The Idea of Justice*, published in 2009, is the centrepiece, he has made a point of insisting on a 'realization focused' approach which requires an assessment of the actual possibility of implementing the conclusions of abstract theorizing about justice, and so concentrating more on empirical rather than on 'transcendental' arguments about institutions (Sen 2009: 7–8).[2] But Sen does not seem to me to have acknowledged remotely adequately the implications of this for his own previous work, which, as I shall argue, is open to this recently formulated criticism.

The *capacitas* argument is a serious consideration of the application of the capabilities approach to the law of contract by some of our leading contributors

2 Sen (2012) is a recent summary of the argument.

to the legal and socio-legal understanding of that law and, as such, one would anticipate that it would take a very different attitude towards institutions, one that should rightly command the attention of those interested in the empirical operation of the law of contract.

Unfortunately, I cannot think of a more unsuitable current theory than the capabilities approach on which an attempt to develop a law of contract could draw. Though it is often interpreted as an argument for the universal provision of something like Rawls' primary goods, that approach is quite different from Rawls' liberalism, and is, in fact, as thoroughly authoritarian a form of welfare economics as has ever been conceived. As we shall see, even a figure so sympathetic to left-wing interventionist policies as the late Ronald Dworkin has described government action based on the capabilities approach as 'frightening', and what Dworkin was discussing merely as a theoretical speculation, the *capacitas* argument seeks to put into practice. This is symptomatic of the way that much current left-wing thinking about the market economy is so far out of sympathy with market values that it thinks those values can be realized only by the implementation of policies that, if carried through, would certainly destroy them. I shall show – in, I am afraid, stark opposition to the *capacitas* argument – that the application of the capabilities approach to the law of contract is wholly inimical to freedom of contract.

The Capabilities Approach Applied to Contract

The general idea that lies behind the capabilities approach will be familiar to anyone who has ever given sustained thought to the problem of inequality in the capitalist economies, and can be stated briefly. Let us allow that the ideal type of market economy is a system of formal, legal equality between citizens as economic actors. This will not mean very much to an economic actor who does not possess the practical capability to take action within that system to his or her advantage. The outcomes of market exchanges reflect, not only the initial endowment of resources that an economic actor is able to commit to an exchange, but also the capacity to conduct that exchange in such a way as to convert 'endowment' to 'advantage', which is a function of certain 'conversion factors'.

Some of these factors are personal, but some are social,[3] and an unjust distribution of social conversion factors will undermine the justice of market outcomes. A consumer who would like to have a comfortable retirement pension will not be able to buy one if he or she does not have sufficient wealth to do so, which raises its own issues. But even if he or she has otherwise sufficient wealth, he/she may not be able to contract to his/her advantage if he/she is, as a matter

3 It is arguable that a third category of environmental factors should be distinguished. These factors are not personal, but are not amenable to human control in the way that social factors proper are. This category, and the problem of whether it should be recognized, are not of relevance to us.

of his/her own personality, feckless, or much more important to us, if the retail pension market is so ill-functioning that, regardless of their own inputs, consumers are systematically 'mis-sold' poorly performing products and are compelled to pay excessive commissions. One way to describe the latter problem is to say that the social conversion factor of reasonable knowledge of the operation of the retail pension market is unequally distributed between the consumer and the financial institutions, and this must be addressed by effective regulation of the contract negotiations aimed at improving the former's bargaining capability. A market economy that will actualize the promise of formal, legal equality must, then, be underpinned by institutions that justly distribute social conversion factors and so furnish economic actors with the capability to enter into exchanges to their advantage. A market economy that does not do this is unjust. The actually existing capitalist market economies are unjust in this way.

I will give a preliminary account of the capabilities approach based on its three principal formulations of relevance to us:[4] Sen's 1979 Tanner Lecture (1982a); his 1982 Hennipman Lecture (1999a); and his 1984 Dewey Lectures (1985b). But though it uses some of the terminology peculiar to that approach, this account, as we shall see, by no means captures its specific qualities. Nevertheless, it will allow us to begin our discussion of the *capacitas* project. The way that project brings the capabilities approach to bear on the law of contract is highly ingenious and interesting. It is settled law that contract has a doctrine of capacity in the sense that it recognizes incapacity as one of the vitiating factors which may be pleaded in defence of a failure to perform a contractual obligation (Deakin 2009: 6).[5] A party may, for example, lack the capacity to enter into a contract because he or she suffers from mental disability. A contract such a party has, by the general rules of contract formation, agreed, may be voidable for incapacity, though there is a statutory power in certain cases to require that party to accept goods and to pay a reasonable price for them, determined by the court.

The *capacitas* argument is that this doctrine has two severe limitations. First, it is an, as it were, doctrine of exception. Most parties are assumed to be capable, and incapacity is relevant only to exceptional cases. Second, the incapacity doctrine is a negative one, with the predominant remedial response in English law being to, in

4 The literature I am largely putting to one side includes the outright development work, though *Development and Freedom* (Sen 1999b) must also be read for its contribution to the capabilities approach generally; the econometric attempts to measure welfare, equality and capability; some of the political theoretical offshoots of the capability approach, including the joint work with Martha Nussbaum, and, indeed, Nussbaum's own work; and what appears to me to be Sen's attempt to, at least in part, rethink his ideas *ab initio* in *The Idea of Justice* (Sen 2009), though I shall comment on some of what Sen says there in this chapter.

5 As Deakin (2009: 3) points out, full discussion of the doctrine of incapacity, which cannot be undertaken here, must be related to the background understanding of 'public policy' in contract law.

various ways, make the contract unenforceable against an incapable defendant. As such, the doctrine only scratches the surface of the real issues of capacity, which are to ensure that an economic actor has the capability to conduct exchanges to his/her advantage, which is a matter, not of vitiating certain contracts, but of providing positively for capacity to enter into all contracts:

> *capacitas*, or capacity, should be thought of as the juridical concept through which the legal system defines the conditions of access to the market by human persons ... In a narrow conception, capacity is defined as the ability to engage in rational economic action ... In a wider conception, capacity, or *capacitas*, is the sum total of the preconditions of effective participation in market relations, and the role of the law shifts from the selective enforcement of contracts to the insertion into contracts of mandatory and default terms ... contractual regulation also has a wider remit, which is to protect and enhance the capability of the individual, understood as the substantive freedom to realise, through participation in the market, a range of desired end states and activities. (Deakin 2009: 28)

In sum, if, in Deakin's opinion, 'we lack, today, a convincing theory of the role of law in enhancing and protecting the substantive contractual capacity of market agents' (Deakin 2009: 4), then the widened concept of capacity or *capacitas* will remedy that situation, and provide a coherent rationale for much of the existing law:

> one reason for taking the capability approach seriously ... is that it offers a more complete and coherent account of the structure and functioning of the modern law of contracts ... This is an account in which the capacity-enhancing role of contractual regulation is recognised as an ordering principle for the law of contracts. (Deakin 2009: 22)

In the neoclassical conception of the operation of the market, economic actors reveal their preferences through the choices they make and, if the market conforms to the conditions for general competition, a Pareto optimal equilibrium representing a perfectly efficient allocation of goods will be established. But, of course, once it is acknowledged that the conditions for general competition will never obtain empirically, the efficiency of actually existing markets becomes wholly questionable. In a thoroughgoing rejection of the 'standard (in the sense of orthodox or generally accepted) law and economics approach', in which 'resources, endowments and preferences are all taken as given' and so 'are exogenous to the operation of the market mechanism' (Deakin 2009: 19), the *capacitas* argument asks whether the neoclassical economic actor should normally be regarded as self-sufficiently capable of revealing his/her preferences through his/her choices and, giving a negative answer to this, interrogates 'the process by which preferences and endowments are formed' (Deakin 2009: 19). This leads, as we have seen, to an attempt to identify the 'conditions needed for effective participation in the complex economic orders which characterise our time'.

At a very general level, I am in agreement with this, and, indeed, in my own work on the law of contract, I have rejected the concept of revealed preference (Campbell 2003b) as part of a more general criticism of the conception of the economic actor in the classical law of contract and in neoclassical economics (Campbell 1997), and insisted that the public provision of a socially self-conscious, public institutional framework, in large part made up of a fundamentally reformed law of contract, is necessary for welfare-enhancing private exchange (Campbell 1999). I nevertheless believe that the *capacitas* argument is very ill-advised. To explain why, I need to say something at a more detailed level about the specific nature of the capabilities approach.

The Capabilities Approach and Welfare Economics

The claim on which the capabilities approach is based is that, to use Sen's excellent coinage in this connection,[6] 'opulence' is not necessarily an accurate measure of welfare (Sen 1999a: 19). Save in exceptional cases, which themselves are largely indicative of a pathology, there is a significant correlation between opulence and welfare, and, for Sen, recognition of this obvious truth has a particular importance as it is the way he has been able to introduce consideration of the possession of Rawlsian primary goods (Rawls 1999: 54–5) as essential to well-being into his thinking (Sen 1985b: 199). Nevertheless, to regard the correlation between opulence and well-being as perfect, or very close to it, is to take 'an alienated, commodity fetishist view, which is, ultimately, a confusion of "well-being" with being well off', and a confounding of 'the state of a person with the extent of her or his possessions' (Sen 1999a: 16). In calling this mistaken view 'commodity fetishism' (Sen 1999a: 16), Sen is not using this term at all in the way Marx intended, but one can see what he is trying to say. Save again in exceptional, typically pathological, cases, an economic actor does not value wealth as such: '[c]ommodity command is a means to the end of well-being, but can scarcely be an end in itself' (Sen 1999a: 19). The economic actor values wealth for the well-being it might bring, which Sen insists is in large part a matter of 'functionings', 'to wit, what the person succeeds in doing with the commodities … at his or her command' (Sen 1999a: 6).

Sen calls 'the set of functionings a person actually achieves' 'the functioning vector', and '[a] person's capability set can be defined as the set of functioning vectors within her or his reach' (Sen 1985b: 200–201). In this way, Sen dramatically moves the focus of the analysis of well-being away from commodity command, for what is essential at the end of his argument is no longer opulence, even as it

6 Rothschild and Sen (2006) sets out the more conventional usage of opulence in Smith's thinking.

includes primary goods, but the extent of an economic actor's capability set, which Sen claims is a measure of her agency or freedom. An economic actor will not be able to achieve a functioning vector that maximizes his or her advantage if he/she is subject to social conversion factors that limit her 'freedom to achieve well-being', which is a matter of 'checking whether one person did have the opportunity of achieving the functioning vector that another actually achieved' (Sen 1985b: 201).

Even from this brief account, which does not remotely capture the extent to which Sen has pursued his ideas into the conceptual and methodological foundations of welfare economics and the modern political philosophy of equality, we can see that the *capacitas* argument is right to maintain that Sen's views yield the conclusion that the capability of an economic actor to convert his or her wealth in a way which is to his/her advantage is in some way fundamental to well-being (Deakin 2009: 20). What, unfortunately for the *capacitas* argument, goes wrong is that the capabilities approach would be unavoidably thoroughly authoritarian in practice, and the *capacitas* argument is, precisely, an attempt to reform the law of contract so as to put it into practice.

Though there are numerous brief statements about the great value of market freedom to be found in Sen's writings (for example, Sen 1999b: 6, 112), I am unaware of any substantial engagement with how the market constituted of exchanges legally institutionalized in contract actually works to produce that freedom. The entire section of *Development as Freedom* headed 'Markets and Freedoms' (Sen 1999b: 25–31) is vacuous.[7] It is necessary to say something about some important aspects of this that relate to the shortcomings of the left-wing criticism of markets which Sen exemplifies (Campbell 2003a, 2011). Ideal typically, an economic actor brings material resources to market and exchanges them on terms he or she voluntarily agrees with another actor. The necessity and possibility of exchange follows from two things. First, it is an existential condition that human beings must engage with the natural environment, and that resources derived from that environment are scarce in part because, when in pursuit of individual betterment and collective, civilizing progress, human desire is infinite. Second, in market economies, the legitimate form of allocating these resources is to recognize private property in them and to obtain the property of another by persuading him or her to sell it in return for property of one's own on which he/she places a greater value. Exchange is a very earth-bound, corporeal process, but that is not because of the nature of the market; it is because of the nature of life. No doubt Sen is right to say that the ultimate motivation of this process is not, or should not be, the resources themselves, but the well-being they might convey. But for sensuous rational beings the process inevitably is focused on material resources, or, perhaps better, on their scarcity.

7 Sen has commented on Adam Smith on a number of occasions, especially recently, but he grossly misrepresents the balance between self-regarding and other-regarding sentiments in Smith's thought, to the point where the absolutely essential role of self-interest in Smith's conception of the working of the economy almost disappears (Campbell and Loughrey, forthcoming 2013).

At its best, market exchange is a system of mutual advantage. For a seller to persuade a buyer to buy, the seller must be able to convince the buyer that he or she will increase his/her well-being by exchanging his/her goods at a ratio that the seller also believes will increase his/her own well-being. This is simultaneously an intrinsically private and an intrinsically social process. What properties of the seller's goods are relevant to the buyer's choice to buy, and what the buyer will do with those goods are private matters for the buyer.[8] The seller might attempt to persuade the buyer to choose differently, but the autonomy of the buyer rests entirely on the privacy of his/her choice, which the seller must recognize socially by confining him/herself to persuasion as the means of obtaining the buyer's consent to the exchange. A fortiori, the state must normally enforce the voluntary contractual agreement that expresses that exchange legally, not second-guess it, and the core value of the law of contract, expressed in all its principal doctrines, is neutrality about the intentions of the contracting parties.

Much criticism of the market economy turns on a criticism of the selfishness of market actors. Sen's variant, the criticism of the fetishization of opulence, is a criticism of selfishness as a degrading narrowness of focus. But selfishness does not really capture the essential property of market action, which is autonomy. A market actor may buy goods to increase his/her well-being by, say, gratifying a desire to smoke, or to read Homer, or to feed the family, or to equip a foundlings' hospital. Why the actor wants to buy the goods is irrelevant to the process of exchange. What is essential is his/her autonomous choice to do so. When one says a market actor is selfish, all one is really saying if one is speaking of what is analytically essential to market action is that the actor makes up his or her own mind about the choice he/she will make. Of course, that may be a selfish choice in the commonly understood, pejorative sense.

If one identifies freedom with an absence of constraint, then the market is not a system of freedom. But, given the existential condition of scarcity we have noted, no economic order is a system of freedom in this sense. Freedom viewed in this way is bliss, and this is not vouchsafed to human beings. Once one acknowledges this, then the ideal typical market may properly be regarded as a system of perfect freedom, for in contractual exchange economic actors must mutually recognize the autonomy of each, and therefore of all, to make their choices within the ineluctable constraint of scarcity. The satisfaction of the economic actor is mediated by the voluntary alienation of private property in material resources, but it is this very mediation that posits the existential relationship with nature in such a way as to allow private choice, which produces a social order. Market exchange is a social system that allows economic order to be the product of voluntary choice. No other

8 I cannot go into the issue here as it would take us further into the problem of identifying a 'commodity' in the theory of general competitive equilibrium than would be of interest to the readership of this book, but the entire capabilities approach may be said to rest on a use of the concept of commodity characteristics diametrically opposed to the sense in which it is used in that theory (Sen 1999a: 6).

form of economic order that human beings have devised reproduces the autonomy of economic actors in this way. This is the basic claim to legitimacy of the market economy.

Sen has no understanding of why this claim to legitimacy is so strong,[9] though he has done much to demonstrate the ways in which it is weak.[10] In essence, the capabilities approach seeks to show that the claims I have just made for freedom of choice carry little weight (Sen 1988, 1993, 1994). The market is the means by which economic actors pursue their well-being through commodity command. One might say that to get to well-being via commodity command is to take an indirect route, and that one might get lost on the way; in essence, this is what Sen is saying when he identifies the conversion factors. He would have us take a more direct route, or at least ensure we do not get lost. But how does one take a more direct route?

In respect of the personal conversion factors that allow one to identify a functioning vector that is really to one's advantage, this is in the first case a question of personal moral philosophy. One should make one's choices in a way that aims, not at commodity command as an end, but at the reproduction and expansion of one's autonomy as the end of moral economic action. Sen has said quite a bit about this, which, in my opinion, adds nothing of fundamental interest to Kant. But while Sen, seemingly unknowingly, reinvents the Kantian wheel on a number of occasions, to say he has not fundamentally added to Kant is hardly a criticism, as who has done so since Hegel? But what about the social conversion factors? As Kant himself found (Campbell 1991: 511–14), arguments that might work for personal morality cannot possibly work in the same way for economic policy, which is a legal and political matter of coercion, and Sen does not come to terms with this at all.

Though developed with unusual philosophical acuity, the capability approach was developed within the specific discipline of welfare economics, and its particular qualities can be understood only in the context of that discipline. That opulence does not necessarily correlate with well-being is Sen's variant of the claim that underlies all 'social'[11] welfare economics: even perfect market outcomes do not necessarily correlate with welfare. Like Deakin and Sen, I do not doubt that this is so. But how can we know when the two diverge? To do this we must be able to

9 His most sustained effort in this regard of which I am aware is Sen (1975). But even this paper treats questions of optimization as informational problems and shows no real appreciation of the value of private, voluntary choice, which no planning authority can in principle reproduce.

10 If we treat Sen's explicit work on inequality and his work on the capabilities approach as together mounting one form of attack on the foundations of market economics, then to this must be added two others that have enjoyed similar success, one on the behavioural assumptions of neoclassical economics (Sen 1982e) and one on the problem of reconciling liberal politics with market order (Sen 1982b).

11 I take this term from Ogus (1994: 4).

identify a social welfare function independent of market outcomes. Sen (1982c, 2002a, 2002b) has gone into the abstract economics and philosophy of this at some length, discussing extensively the problems of 'partial solutions', 'incomplete rankings' and the like, which theoretical attempts to determine that function inevitably encounter, but he has never properly faced up to the fundamental issue. In terms of practical policy, the social welfare function can be identified only by government action. However we define it, we must use governmental computation processes to identify social welfare, and if we are to put our welfare conclusions into practice, we must use government power to alter the outcomes of voluntarily agreed exchanges. Sen responds to the undoubted lack of freedom in the formally free capitalist market by turning to a system which can work only by government action; that is, by coercion and by coercive transfers, both backed by a monopoly of violence. If this is not to be regarded as a leap from the frying pan into the fire, it requires some justification.

The core of modern welfare economics is an attempt to distance those economics from utilitarianism. Utilitarian economic and social policy has what I believe to be the immense virtue of making it explicit that it involves trumping economic actors' own judgements by coercively imposing the judgement of the policy-maker. This is very difficult to reconcile with the values of liberal market economics and democratic politics, and modern welfare economics typically try to deny that they are inherently coercive by claiming that they realize the outcome economic actors would realize for themselves, were they able. Sen has been a profound critic of utilitarianism,[12] and in this sense the capabilities approach sits squarely in the tradition of welfare economics; indeed, it is arguably its *ne plus ultra*.

To say this is, however, to some extent unfair. The Kaldor–Hicks compensation criterion, which has been the principal theoretical rationale of welfare economics, claims to identify economic actors' subjective satisfactions better than they can themselves, so identifying a state that would be the same as the Pareto optimum yielded by general competitive equilibrium, were it possible to establish general competitive equilibrium through the operation of the market, which it is not. This argument implies that government action capable of realizing an optimum is possible. But this is not possible either, and it is good that it is not possible, for it could be done only by an omniscient and omnipotent state that is unavailable to us, and, were it available, to the extent that saying this makes any sense, would be appalling.

The consequence of this is that no Kaldor–Hicks transfers are ever actually attempted, the basic idea of doing better than economic actors can do themselves being operationalized through cost–benefit analysis. Cost–benefit analysis replaces the claim to know subjective satisfactions with ultimately arbitrary assumptions

12 One can very clearly see the influence of the emerging capability approach in the 'Introduction' Sen and Bernard Williams provided to their influential 1982 collection of criticisms of utilitarianism.

about hypothetical willingness to pay, and gives up any claim to optimize the sum of satisfactions across the economy with a very much second-best claim that a transfer within a specific sector will produce surplus welfare assessed by looking only at that sector. The results of cost–benefit analysis are always unsatisfactory; indeed, despite the patina of technical sophistication in which they are typically expressed, these results are usually ramshackle. No justification of any merit has ever been given for cost–benefit analysis other than that, if we are going to engage in government intervention, this is the best we can do to guide it. This *petitio principii* has rationalized Pigouvian welfare economics and therefore piecemeal,[13] if now general, intervention in the capitalist economies.

Sen has rejected all of this as 'welfarism' (Sen 1982e: 248–51), an approach that is restricted informationally in that it regards 'social welfare to be [a function] only of ... individual welfare vectors ... without admitting ... description of social states' (Sen 1982e: 258), and the capabilities approach is an attempt to expand the range of information that welfare economics can deal with. It purports to move away from a focus on subjective outcomes and to address the structural opportunities that economic actors actually have to achieve outcomes that are to their advantage. The significance of this is that it is a clever response to the successful neoliberal critique of the command and control imposition of desirable end states, now regarded with suspicion because of its inevitable inefficiency, which Coase has called 'government failure' (Coase 1964: 195), and, more important, because what Nozick (1974: 155–60) has called 'patterning' is acknowledged to be inherently repugnant. The capabilities approach purports to move away from comparison of end states to the assessment of opportunity to participate in the market. But, in the course of the development of the capabilities approach, this move has been revealed to be unsuccessful.

When Sen's 1979 Tanner Lecture posed the question 'Equality of What?', his reply at that time, when his thinking was still very clearly Rawlsian, was equality of basic capability, which essentially was a matter of the primary goods, albeit 'shifting attention from goods to what goods do to human beings' (Sen 1982a: 368). It must be appreciated that a great part of the attractiveness of the primary goods is that, because of their nature, they embody a respect for restrictions on the reach of the state, despite Rawls' aim being to ensure that these goods are universally provided, as the goods are limited and they are to facilitate, emphatically not to prescribe, market participation. Rawls (1999: 6) was extremely anxious to establish a 'division of labour' in which prescriptive rules of justice should be applied to what he called the 'basic structure', and not to the 'particular transactions' of 'individuals and associations': 'if this division of labour can be established, individuals and associations are then left free to advance their ends more effectively within the framework of the basic structure' (Rawls 1996: 268–9). Much approving comment on the capabilities approach seems to imagine this was also Sen's intention. Dworkin (2000: 302) calls this the '"natural" reading' of Sen.

13 I take this term from Popper (1966: 157).

But this is exactly what the capabilities approach does not do. Sen did not remain with some idea of basic capability, and indeed, the capabilities approach requires the possibility of second-guessing all choices, without any limit in principle. This failure to sustain Rawl's respect for liberal limits, is, I am afraid, the aspect of the capabilities approach that is seized on by the *capacitas* argument.

Viewed from the perspective of addressing inequality, the difference between the capabilities approach's conception of equality of opportunity and the conception of equality of opportunity which is, it should be remembered, also central to liberal market notions of justice as deserts, has been, not only the critique of fetishization of commodity command, but the capabilities approach's stress on engineering the social conversion factors for equality. The difficulty for the capabilities approach, and for other modern political philosophies of equality, has been to put a limit to this engineering, because the steps it can seem desirable to take to advance equality of opportunity seem to know no end – an argument can be mounted coherently that even luck should be equalized. In those other philosophies, of which I shall single out Dworkin's, what seems to me to be a trick has been played. By conflating the equality of equals and the equality of unequals, which have been distinguished since Aristotle (*Nicomachean Ethics*, V, 3, 1131a; *Politics*, III, 9, 1280a), thinkers have attempted to identify a distribution of resources that will so skew the starting positions that the exercise of opportunity will lead to the desired end state of equality of well-being, however defined. Now, this may well be legitimate for non-market spheres, but it is destructive of the allocation of goods by deserts in the market sphere and must be handled with great caution.

Dworkin at least tries to observe Rawl's liberal constraint. But Sen would equalize, not the opportunity to make choices, but rather the opportunity to make choices to one's advantage. This is, as Dworkin (2000: 302) recognizes, 'frightening'. If putting a break on the reach of the state charged with engineering the distribution of endowments an economic actor uses to make choices is hard, this is as nothing compared to the unlimited power to second-guess and re-engineer those choices when, in principle, we are obliged to look behind them to assess the advantage, as identified by the government, those choices realize. Theoretical discussion of the adequacy of 'resourcism', as opposed to Sen's focus on realized advantage (Pogge 2004), has not, to my knowledge, contrasted any of the results of this opposition to the virtue of earth-bound economic exchange's ability to respond to the existential necessity of engagement with the natural environment with a system of in principle general freedom.

Dworkin asks us to imagine the frightening steps that the capabilities approach would require a government to take. The *capacitas* argument makes the act of imagination in large part unnecessary, for that argument illustrates the main way we could extend the capabilities approach beyond a concern with basic capability on to a concern with an economic actor's particular transactions: we should engineer the law of contract in the interest, not of freedom of choice, but of the optimization of advantage.

Let us take 'competitive markets' to be one part of Rawls' (1999: 6) basic structure. Primary goods allowing meaningful participation in those markets, which we can call opportunities (Rawls 1999: 54), must be distributed by the structure. It is undeniable that the argument I regard as a trick is latent in Rawls: one can go on with the specification of opportunity so as to actually eliminate the form of equality of opportunity that leads to the distribution of goods according to deserts and end with equality of welfare. It is also undeniable that Rawls did not want this. He wanted particular transactions to be governed purely by procedural fairness (Rawls 1999: 74). Rawls' wisdom is nowhere more evident than in his repeated acknowledgements that establishing the division of labour necessary to establish pure procedural justice is inevitably difficult. The core of what must be done is that, 'at least within a certain range', we must eschew thinking that there is a correct outcome to procedures governed by pure procedural justice, including exchange:

> pure procedural justice obtains when there is no independent criterion for the right result; instead there is a correct or fair procedure such that the outcome is likewise correct or fair, whatever it is, provided that the procedure has been properly followed. (Rawls 1999: 75)

This disregard for outcome is precisely what the modern philosophy of equality after Rawls has both pursued and found difficult to maintain, and is what the capabilities approach absolutely cannot maintain. Now if, in the course of abstract discussion, the goal of government policy is described in a general, amorphous way, such as the promotion of the capability to realize advantage, it seems that no objection can possibly be raised. Sen's increasingly common association of capacity with freedom is an extension of this persuasive rhetoric. But how exactly can we promote capability by government policy? If we focus on the provision of positive freedoms, which we allow are necessary, we can see that, even at the level of primary goods or basic capability, it is possible (but difficult) to maintain neutrality, despite one insisting that one is merely pursuing equality of opportunity. But if we move from the basic structure to particular transactions, as the *capacitas* argument about the operation of the law of contract, following the logic of the capabilities approach, urges us to do, it becomes clear that it is not possible to have a concrete policy towards specific choices that is amorphous in this way. One must have a policy that pursues a particular goal of advantage to the economic actor in respect of a particular pattern of consumption. There is no other way to proceed. One has to second-guess the economic actor's specific choices.

If, for example, one identifies smoking as not being to the economic actor's advantage, one must modify the capability set to change the actor's pattern of consumption of cigarettes. One can call this policy one of expanding the actor's freedom if one wishes. But, going beyond basic capability and assessing the advantage that results from a particular contract, one can carry out the policy only by coercively setting up a system that brings the actor's choices into conformity with advantage as the government defines it. The attraction of this as a form of governance after the success of neoliberalism is that one is not commanding the actor, but more cunningly controlling him or her. To my mind, the frankness of command is an infinitely superior conception of the proper relationship between government and citizen in the capacity of economic actor in circumstances such as these, but most left-wing thought on regulation now celebrates the sophistication of various soft law ways of manipulating the economic actor to make choices to his/her advantage, as defined by the government.

The problems we are bound to encounter in doing so illustrate vividly the wisdom of George Stigler's (1943: 355, 359) criticism of the new welfare economics: '[i]n the nature of things, the wideness with which any end is accepted depends on the specificity of that end'. The overwhelming majority of the citizens of the advanced capitalist countries would agree, for example, that some form of argument for the universal provision of education is successful, even though it inevitably involves coercive transfers. But surely 'education' is doing too much work here. I am of the opinion that seeking to provide a university education for 50 per cent of 18 year olds is a very bad policy. I imagine that most of those agreeing with the capabilities approach would disagree with me, however. We can debate this at interminable length, but collective decision-making requires an end to theoretical debate, and the point is that, even in this clearest of cases, the application of the capabilities approach yields a political choice which must, *ex hypothesi*, involve a coercive transfer in support of public policy. This has a bad smell about it even when a goal such as the universal provision of education is justified, and when we become more precise, the less likely the goal is to be widely regarded as justified. I, for one, regard universal education as one of the most desirable of policies, but bitterly resent the coercive imposition of the '50 per cent of 18 year olds' policy.

And things get much worse if we turn to particular transactions. If an educated adult chooses to smoke, it is trivially easy to make out an argument that his/her functioning vector reflects shortcomings in his/her capability set such that his/her choice is not to his/her advantage, and that social conversion factors such as advertising play a part in this, with the implication that educational programmes and restrictions on advertising should be supplied through coercion and coercive transfer. But why is smoking selected? It is possible to frame a critique based on the capabilities approach of all empirical choices, from taking heroin or drinking alcohol to excess through to buying a set of books, the reading of which does not improve the reader's critical faculty as well as another set would have done, because with a better education, a free public library service, government advice on what to read, and, the *capacitas* argument might add, the adoption of rules of contract guiding specific purchases, one might realize a better functioning by one's reading.

Smoking currently occupies an intermediate position between taking heroin and an unfortunate preference for supermarket pulp fiction over *The Iliad*, along with watching soap operas, going to boxing matches, wearing revealing clothes, reading a newspaper for the horoscopes, listening to jazz or pop music, getting a very short haircut, buying a four-wheel drive car, eating salty food and so on.[14] The only choice the capabilities approach cannot criticize is one made with perfectly efficient conversion factors that truly optimize well-being, and this is a purely theoretical postulate implying a repugnant perfectionism[15] that fails to understand the wisdom of the maxim *de gustibus non est disputandum* when applied to the actions of the state.[16] Leaving aside that one successful attempt to shift one element of a pattern of consumption will shift the entire pattern, the insuperable problem arises that all choices can be questioned, but not all can be questioned simultaneously, and the commitment of public resources to the cultivation of particular capability sets is a political choice which necessarily implies the downgrading or suppression of other, voluntarily chosen ways of living.[17] Though it is theoretically stated in general terms of an expansion of capability, the practical application of the capabilities approach can do no other than take the form of successive promotions of approved consumption choices (which must involve the relative lack of promotion, or even outright repression, of others). As such, it is a patterning, and, apart from the ingenious but frightening refinement in the techniques of promotion, we are back where we were before the neoliberal revolution.

---

14 I cannot consider the application of the capabilities approach to particular choices without guessing just how many of them Adorno would have despised for reasons which, to my mind, often amount to self-pastiche: on horoscopes, see Adorno (1994). For a humane and sensible perspective on these issues, see Orwell (2001a).

15 It is significant that the capabilities approach seems to have no way of accommodating people's mistaken judgements other than as defects in a capability set which are to be eliminated.

16 Deakin (1999: 19 n55) cites Becker and Stigler's (1977) famous paper: 'De Gustibus Non Est Disputandum' in support of his claim that 'the standard economic model does not concern itself with the process by which preferences and endowments are formed'. This is not entirely correct. Becker and Stigler (ibid.: 76) themselves reject what they call 'the traditional view [that] an explanation of economic phenomena that reaches a difference in tastes between people [regards this as] the terminus of the argument: the problem is abandoned at this point to whoever studies and explains tastes (psychologists? anthropologists? phrenologists? sociobiologists?)'. This paper actually is one of the foundations of Becker's extreme economic imperialism, because it stakes the claim that the rigorous economist 'never reaches this impasse' but rather 'continues to search for differences in prices or incomes to explain any differences or changes in behaviour' (ibid.). See also n32 below. Personally, I hold to the standard or traditional view.

17 With regard to the application of the capabilities approach to development, the point has been made acutely by Bliss (1993: 432): 'Consider the motivation of governments, World Bank officials, and various do-gooders. The intentions with which they are armed are impeccable: better health, longer life, less hunger, etc. Yet there exist life-styles that cannot receive these goods without disappearing. Can we be sure that it is good that they should disappear?'

The *Capacitas* Argument as a Practical Realization of the Capabilities Approach

What can be said of the *capacitas* argument in light of this criticism of the capabilities approach? When one looks at the current law, the position is interestingly complex. In a sense, the *capacitas* argument runs completely opposite to the direction taken by the English law of incapacity (Deakin 2009: 6). There has been so substantial a reduction in the nineteenth-century common law categories of incapacity that the common law doctrine is now of such diminished significance that it does not even feature in a number of well-regarded textbooks. However, in his *Capacitas* paper, Wijffels (2009: 61) tells us that the grounds of incapacity have proliferated in the twentieth century with the predominantly statutory recognition, especially in European consumer law, of 'new protected interests for which one of the instruments of legal protection has been the creation or extension of incapacities'. We are in a doctrinally difficult area here, because these 'incapacities' tend to be given a different jurisprudential basis, such as duress or unconscionability, rather than incapacity, and Wijffels' position is rather circular in that he identifies a wider law of incapacity only if one accepts the *capacitas* argument that widens what we should think of as capacity. In his *Capacitas* paper, Hesselink (2009: 33–5) is able to deal with the awkward fact that the most influential pattern so far produced for a European contract code, the draft *Common Frame of Reference*, contains no express law of incapacity, much less capacity, by saying it does the necessary work in other ways.

It is this thinking that allows Deakin (2009: 22) to, very acutely, pose and answer the following question:

> what would a contract law system look like if it encapsulated the capability approach rather than the standard approach to the conceptualization of economic exchange? The answer is that it would look very much like the kinds of contract law regime that are observed in European (and other) systems today – that is to say, regimes in which the classical principles of freedom of contract and *pacta sunt servanda* are complemented by mandatory and default norms of various kinds, mostly originating in legislation.

How plausible is this relationship of complementarity? On the basis of the adoption of the capabilities approach, it is not plausible at all. That entire approach is critical of commodity command and has no positive role for the private dimension of exchange. Sen has accommodated markets, saying positive things about them in passing, but only because he has had to reach a compromise with the way of the world. The autonomy of economic actors expressed in market choice is not to be respected in principle. It is to be assessed. If it passes the assessment, well and good. Reading Homer and equipping foundlings' hospitals will be found to be to the economic actor's advantage. But smoking will surely lead, in addition to restrictions on manipulative advertising, to bans on advertising that amount to suppression of knowledge of the product; taxes on cigarettes intended to prevent an activity it is not democratically possible actually to ban; restrictions on notionally universal public health care services for smokers; the prevention of smoking in public places, including open spaces; the prevention of smoking in one's car and so on. For the sake of argument, one may allow that all of these measures might in principle be defensible, if they are assessed as coercive measures. But it is repugnantly authoritarian to avoid such assessment by depicting those measures as not really being coercive because they are an expansion of the smoker's agency.

The *capacitas* argument, 'mostly originating in legislation', seizes on the capabilities approach's in principle unlimited second-guessing of economic actors' choices in order to sanction the development of 'mandatory and default norms' which guide 'freedom of contract'. Deakin is able to say that the result of this 'would look very much like the kinds of contract law regime that are observed in European (and other) systems today' only because that regime has at its heart an unlimited receptivity to framing the economic actor's choices in such a way that they produce well-being, as defined by those who decide cases and formulate legislation. Paternalism of this sort certainly is to be found in the common law of contract, the doctrine of incapacity arguably being one example (Deakin 2011). But even now paternalism remains an exception to the general principle of freedom of contract on which that law turns, to which it is, in my opinion, anathema. Paternalism is, however, the defining characteristic of journals such as the *Journal of Consumer Policy* and the *Journal of European Consumer and Market Law*, which are compendia of the techniques needed to frame law and policy to induce consumers to act to their advantage.

A ten-minute leafing through recent numbers of the former journal has, for example, led me to an argument for the sophisticated manipulation of householders into buying more home insulation in order to realize a (claimed) potential contribution to the reduction of CO_2 emissions (Zundel and Steiss 2011). Addressing the 'energy efficiency gap' created by the 'energy paradox' that householders do not buy as much insulation as theoretical projections of the savings in household energy expenditure to be obtained by doing so would justify, the authors convincingly show that householders, *inter alia*, both doubt the projections and are reluctant to get into debt to make the necessary investment. All this seems perfectly sensible to me, and, in fairness to the authors, they often seem to admit this. But, driven by their improving goal, the authors' response is to urge those wishing to promote insulation to couch their sales pitch in different ways, such as overemphasizing – 'in most cases it will be sufficient to show a perceivable positive effect' (Zundel and Steiss 2011: 104) – the laughable belief that 'energy-saving measures grant protection against energy-supply problems and the volatility of fossil fuel prices' (ibid.: 103). The beauty of all this, presumably necessary to those who wish to do good in this way, is that it allows the pursuit of a desirable social goal 'by changing behaviour' (ibid.: 92) to be depicted as 'trying to enhance the agency of homeowners' (ibid.: 104).

Hesselink's (2009: 40–47) account of the way that 'the idea social justice' should be pursued in European contract law envisages extensive positive rights and a form of the fair price rule, that is, a general power to set prices. This policy could not really have less sympathy for freedom of contract, and it comes as no surprise that Hesselink sees the effective prevention of parents choosing to buy a mobile phone for their teenager as a perfectly legitimate step to be taken under the *capacitas* argument; nor is it a surprise that he portrays this as an expansion of the parents' freedom (ibid.: 44). Being now a grumpy, middle-aged, middle-class intellectual who hardly ever watches TV, has a mobile phone – the least functional model it is possible to buy – only because his wife has insisted on it, and holds the conduct of many young mobile phone users in utter contempt, I have every sympathy with what I imagine is Hesselink's thinking. But, really, his inability to distinguish between persuading the parents not to buy the phone and using the law to stop them by devious means when an outright ban is impossible, or, even worse, identifying the two, is unacceptably authoritarian.

Three further points emerge. First, there is simply no integral way of taking the costs of a legal policy based on capability or *capacitas* into account. There is now a large theoretical literature seeking to identify capabilities and to rank them. It is all assessed from the point of view of expanding the capability set, and no consideration is given to the costs of doing so. This, of course, makes a very large part of the discussion of this expansion worthless even on its own terms, as it means there can be no proper cost–benefit analysis of any measure taken, either in itself or in comparison to other possible measures, for promotion of one capability can only be at the cost of the reduced promotion of another. It is an unfortunate aspect of the ethical approach to development, of which the capabilities approach has been such a part, that seeing these matters as fundamentally ethical, rather than economic or political, undermines consideration of the resource implications of choices about which capabilities to enhance (Schmidt 2010). The balancing of price and demand integral to market choice is not reproduced in the capabilities approach and typically no assessment of the costs of the implicit collective decision-making procedure that lies behind the abstract reasoning is made. One hardly needs to be told that Sen (2004, 2006) has come increasingly to see the issues in terms of positive human rights,[18] or reminded that Hesselink also takes this view.

Second, in the absence of such an assessment, a completely irrelevant choice between the extant market which is claimed to be failing and some situation inevitably improved by criticism of that market is postulated. But if we are comparing the results of the extant market and government action as actual alternative decision-

18 This relatively recent work engages with some of the specific issues regarding positive freedoms as legal rights, but predominantly in terms of using the rhetoric of law to increase the political efficacy of the implicit resource claims. The burden of Sen's argument remains, as it has always been, to decouple such freedoms from carrying any of the implication of being a Hohfeldian claim right, or, indeed, of being law in Austin's sense (Sen 1985a).

making procedures, then it is simply not enough just to concentrate on the failings of the market. After Coase, we must now recognize the possibility of government failure and take this possibility into account.[19] In a way that is indicative of the unfortunate compartmentalization of much economic thought, Sen's enormous contributions to collective choice theory in the tradition of Arrow's impossibility theorem did not lead him to posit serious questions about the likelihood of the capabilities approach as implemented failing actually to identify superior welfare, or to ground policies that realize it. In his development work, a beneficent state was the only real agent involved in policies claimed to expand the agency of the poor, this faith in the benevolent despotism of development programmes not really being sufficiently mitigated by his later awareness, in itself creditable, of course, that issues of democracy and participation had to be raised (Sen 1999b: ch. 5).[20] Nothing like this awareness has ever disturbed the basic statism of his views about the market in the advanced capitalist economies. His work has, in a strong sense, avoided the basic issue, which is not choosing between a failed market and an intervention that it is assumed will rectify the failure, but between a failed market and a government intervention which will also fail (Coase 1964: 195), and comparing the possible results. However, a 'comparative approach' of this sort has featured as part of the recent criticism of what he now calls transcendental institutionalism. But though Sen (2009: ch. 4) has now taken on board some public choice issues in the course of making this criticism, he has not considered their implications for the basic plausibility of the capabilities approach.

No appreciation of government failure troubles the *capacitas* argument at all. Government failure is acknowledged in Deakin's (2009: 15) paper, but only in passing, and it does not feature in the core formulation of that argument. This is bad enough, but the unproblematic way in which Hesselink, who is a great authority on European consumer legislation, thinks that social justice will be promoted unproblematically by *capacitas* – that is, by policy-making led by the EU Commission, makes one despair.[21] The logical error that characterizes the

19 Coase has applied his thinking to the operation of consumer groups in an insufficiently well-known, indeed obscure, paper (Coase 1972).

20 No argument derived from Rawls' conception of the primary goods and the basic structure, such as I am advancing here, can easily be made of Sen's views of development, or development policy generally. Rawls (1971: 152) saw the liberal limits to which I refer as a 'special' case of his 'general' conception of justice, the special case being applicable only to, in essence, the established liberal democratic societies, and was prepared to accept trade-offs between liberty and growth that would be unacceptable in those societies if this was 'necessary to raise the level of civilisation' in other societies, to the point where those societies would themselves become special cases. This language was changed, at some cost to the clarity of expression of the underlying idea, which Rawls (1999: 132) maintained, in the revised edition of *A Theory of Justice*.

21 On the gross defects in the welfare reasoning behind the harmonization of the contract laws of the member countries of the EU, see Halson and Campbell (forthcoming 2013).

Pigouvian tradition, of taking evidence of market failure be sufficient to justify intervention, characterizes the *capacitas* argument.

I do not want to belabour this point. I want instead to turn to the recovery of the core of sense in the *capacitas* argument once the fundamental wrongheadedness of the capabilities approach is acknowledged. For the third point that emerges from this criticism of the *capacitas* argument is whether it is, in principle, possible to integrate a limit into it that would stop it from overriding freedom of contract. I turn to this in the next section.

The Capability Approach and the Welfare State

Though Sen is rightly applauded for the degree of philosophical erudition he brings to his work, which is most unusual in economics, my principal reaction to reading his Tanner Lecture was, I am afraid, to think that its argument was to a considerable extent the product of a narrow focus evidencing disregard or ignorance of the wider history of its subject.[22] The point that is central to us is that, while one would not know it from this Lecture, recognition of the hollowness of formal capability to contract has a very long pedigree, so long, indeed, that Hart (1983: 207) called it 'an ancient insight'.

Let us roughly distinguish between communist criticisms of capitalism, which seek to replace commodity production with something superior, from socialist criticisms, which, by critique of capitalist institutions, seek to actualize the abstract promise of freedom made possible by market economics. Accepting this, then Sen's is a socialist argument, though he himself has not put it that way. As I have said, Sen's criticism of commodity fetishism owes little to Marx's own thought, but his use of the term surely signifies his radical intent. But if Sen's is a socialist argument, it is not the first such. One could without effort call to mind a score of unarguably first-rate, explicitly socialist contributions to the argument that is expressed in a nutshell in Anatole France's (1908: 95) ironic observation that: '[t]he law in its majestic egalitarianism forbids the rich as well as the poor to sleep under bridges, to beg in the streets and to steal bread'.[23] One might, in particular,

22 I should not wish to imply that Sen is alone in this. I am puzzled by the way that the modern political philosophy of equality after Rawls has largely proceeded without much reference to the socialist tradition or to the experience of the universal welfare state. I find the contribution, including his criticism of the capabilities approach, of the late G.A. Cohen (1993), a highly distinguished commentator on Marx, particularly disappointing in this respect.

23 France is placing in the mouth of a fictional character views clearly traceable to Louis Blanc (1848: 20): 'the poor man has the free right to ameliorate his position … And pray what of that if he has not the power? … This free right, considered in the abstract, is the mirage which since 1783 keeps the people in delusion. This right is the metaphysical and lifeless protection which has replaced the active protection the people are entitled to. This right, pompously and barrenly proclaimed in charters, has but served to mark all the

think of T.H. Marshall's (1992) claim that 'social' citizenship is needed to make formal 'civil' or 'political' rights, and therefore freedom, real. Sen makes little reference to this socialist tradition in his writings on the capabilities approach, or on welfare economics more widely,[24] and if this is puzzling, given the parallels between some of Sen's theoretical arguments and practical proposals to those made explicitly in the socialist tradition,[25] it does at least spare him the labour of distinguishing what he says from what has already been said by the likes of Marshall, which would be awkward in at least one way.

The avowedly socialist formulations of something like the capabilities approach have a quality that this approach does not have. They have been tested by long experience gained through implementation in the advanced capitalist economies, as they are one of the intellectual pillars of the welfare state. Marshall's work is perhaps the principal theoretical statement of the rationale of the British welfare state, which has been the pattern for the most important form of universal welfare provision. The general aim of the British form of welfare is to ensure that citizens enjoy basic conditions, such as good health and a decent education, for general welfare-enhancing participation in market exchange, principally through work (Esping-Anderson 1999: 74–7).

To the considerable extent that it has established these conditions, the British welfare state represents, in my opinion, an important development in the entire history of civilization. But even such grandiloquence cannot hide the fact that the welfare state has been in one crisis or another since before I was born – Marshall (1952: 92) gave 1952 as the date of its first – and is in deepening crisis at the time of writing. While it is unarguable that the most pressing problem is fiscal, the more fundamentally important problem is the one Hayek (2007) identified at the time of the birth of the universal welfare state in Britain: the difficulty of maintaining

injustice of a system of individualism, and all the barbarity of abandoning the poor to their own resources. It is because liberty has been defined by the word right that men have come to be called free who are in fact the slaves of ignorance and the slaves of chance. Let it be said once and for all. Liberty consists not only in the rights accorded, but in the power given to men to exercise and develop their faculties under the empire of justice and the safeguard of the law'. As Orwell has told us (2001b: 262), France's views amounted to a socialism in which, not the spirit of collectivism, but the spirit of nineteenth-century radicalism prevailed, and this is, I think, overall also true of Blanc.

24 Sen's most substantial discussion (1997: ch. 4) is an attempt to distinguish between desert and need based on reflections on *The Critique of the Gotha Programme*, which is repeated throughout his work. Though of interest in themselves, Sen's (2009: 14, 163) reflections are based on attributing to Marx a belief that bourgeois right is illusory, which emphatically was not his opinion.

25 For example, Marshall's (1992: 16) opinion about the public provision of education was based on his view that '[t]he right to education is a genuine social right of citizenship [a]nd there is no conflict with individual rights as interpreted in the age of individualism [f]or civil rights are designed for use by reasonable and intelligent persons, who have learned to read and write. Education is a necessary prerequisite of civil freedom'.

personal liberty as one expands welfare, which, in the area of concern to us, takes the form set out by Wieacker (1995: ch, 28) as 'the disintegration of private law' in the face of the expansion of 'social law'. Without argument here, I will simply say that I believe this crisis is profound and getting worse, as we are finding it extremely difficult to constrain a welfare state that appears to know no limit. If the welfare state is maximalist[26] in this sense, it has no future, and we must be glad that this is the case.

If what has been said so far is allowed to have weight, then the capabilities approach clearly is the wrong way to go. It is statist in principle and knows no intrinsic limit to the second-guessing of economic actors' choices. The reasons why actors choose – that is, why the allocation of goods takes the form of a market legally institutionalized in the law of contract – play no part, apart from as obstacles, to an approach that wants to focus directly on advantage. I do not remotely want to deny that explicitly socialist contributions to the criticism of the market have often taken the wrong tack and actively pursued authoritarian welfare economic policies without regard for their diminution of freedom.[27] Pigou, who sought only to make piecemeal interventions in a market he believed to be 'generally beneficent' (Pigou 2002: 128, quoting Cannan 1913: 333), clearly lost control of what has become the Pigouvian tradition.[28] Beveridge (1942: para. 294) would be appalled by the reach of a welfare state he insisted should observe the 'principle of a national minimum, above which citizens shall spend their money freely', and at all costs avoid 'adopting instead the principle of regulating the lives of individuals by law'. But, nevertheless, the socialist tack that seeks to locate the market sphere within a welfare state which facilitates participation in the market, allowing economic actors to make autonomous choices that are not second-guessed, and providing a safety net when those choices turn out to be bad, is, in my opinion, a far better way in principle than the capabilities approach. This way of addressing the issues can sustain close comparison to Rawls, and, indeed, I am of the opinion that the modern political philosophy of equality would have done well to replace a good part of the logometric and logomachic speculation characteristic of it with a more thorough examination of the practical experience of maintaining a neutral law of contract within the welfare state. However, I must now add that, given the current extent of piecemeal intervention and the current

26 I take this term from Barry (1990: 105).

27 I have tried to describe the administrative law aspects of this in Campbell (2010b: 507–31).

28 To take just one instance of resonance here: a major, founding contribution to the development within the Pigouvian tradition of a measurement of inequality believed to be superior to the mere measurement of the distribution of income, the background to Sen's welfare economics, was made by Hugh Dalton, Chancellor of the Exchequer in the immediate post-First World War Labour government (Dalton 1920). Sen has made repeated reference to Dalton in his own work on inequality.

size of the welfare state, the real issue for those who think the balance of freedom and welfare is wrong, undermining both, is the expansion of the market sphere.

It was obvious to Marshall (1992: 48–9) that the way of conceiving matters I believe is right involves a rejection of 'monism'[29] in political philosophy in an attempt to maintain quite opposed principles of justice, all of which are necessary in a good society, and which, in particular, must have market and welfare spheres. It is equally obvious that the *capacitas* approach is a monist one of progressive subsumption of the values of the market by the values of welfare, a subsumption that might best be called elimination because the conception of welfare in the capabilities approach is thoroughly authoritarian and knows no limit to second-guessing.

There is a passage in Hesselink's *Capacitas* paper that is very instructive on this. Having outlined Sen's views, Hesselink (2009: 43–4) goes on to say:

> of course, the most fundamental policies which can … contribute to giving people substantive freedom to choose the lives they want are probably to be found in the areas of the health service, education, security, etc. The different market transactions which a person is free to choose … may be seriously limited if he or she is poor or ill, or belongs to a minority who are systematically discriminated against or even attacked. Or – to give a less dramatic example – the capabilities of market actors to make informed choices crucially depends on the education that they have received. Nevertheless, it still makes sense to examine how contract law can contribute to improving the capabilities of people.

The welfare state provision of health, education, security and so on is effected by coercive transfers. To all apart from anarchists, this does not necessarily mean that this provision is unjustifiable, only that it needs a strong justification to rebut the presumption that, because it is based on coercion, it should not be done. But that Hesselink can see no difference in principle between welfare provision on this basis and interference in what should be the neutral process of exchange institutionalized in the law of contract really tells us enough about the nature of the *capacitas* argument's application of the capabilities approach to contract.

Conclusion

Perhaps the fundamental mistake on which the capacities approach is based, which the *capacitas* argument reproduces, is to aim its criticism, not merely at

29 I take this term from Miller (1989: 4). Marshall (1982: 104) called a good society encompassing quite different principles of justice a 'hyphenated society' – for example, 'liberal-democracy', 'welfare-capitalism'. For reasons I do not think it would be justified to discuss here, Sen's (1980–81) conception of the capabilities approach as a 'pluralist' evaluation of well-being composed of numerous vectors turns on quite different issues.

a straw man, but at the wrong straw man. The commodity fetishism criticized by Sen and the standard economic view criticized by Deakin are of no real interest when one is trying to formulate a welfare-enhancing policy towards the issues addressed in the *capacitas* argument. For we are not faced with choosing between a complete disregard of capability issues in the classical law of contract and in classical liberal economics and a law of *capacitas* that takes those issues on board. Apart from libertarian anarchists, no advocate of liberal market economics of any substance has ever failed to pay attention to the necessity of publicly providing a legal institutional framework for a welfare enhancing market, and almost none of those advocates saw this in purely negative terms – Bastiat seems to be the clearest exception. To put the point in the context of neoclassical economics, it is perhaps worth mentioning that Alfred Marshall (1966: 115) held to a position indistinguishable at a general level from Sen's own, apart from being expressed in a period language, of the necessity of transforming the working man into a gentleman,[30] that is not, of course, the way that Sen would express himself. T.H. Marshall (1992: 7) regarded his own views as an explicitly socialist restatement of the views of Alfred Marshall. Bearing all this in mind, one cannot but sympathize with, for example, Berlin (1969: xlv–xlvi), who, looking back on his work a decade after 'Two Essays on Liberty', told us that he had not pointed out, because he 'thought this too obvious to need saying', that the:

> failure ... of unrestricted *laissez faire*, and of the social and legal systems that permitted and encouraged it ... to provide the minimum conditions in which alone any degree of significant 'negative' liberty can be exercised ... and without which it is little or no value to those who may theoretically possess it. For what are rights without the power to implement them?

It is my opinion (Campbell and Klaes 2005: 277–80) that liberal economic attempts to determine the appropriate role of the state tend to give it an implausibly small role, but it would be quite wrong to say that they posit no role, or that there are no good reasons given for positing a small role. These reasons boil down to a generalization of the concern I am trying to apply specifically to the capabilities approach, that a larger role will undermine freedom, including economic freedom. The concept of freedom of contract in the classical law of contract is the legal expression of this concern. This concept is inadequate, but reform of the law must actualize, and not eliminate it.

Deakin (2009: 3) is perfectly well aware of all this, and in his *Capacitas* paper he acknowledges that 'the classical core of contract law gave expression to a theory of the institutional preconditions of a market economy, albeit a rather

30 These views of Alfred Marshall were heavily influenced by the socialism of J.S. Mill and Harriet Taylor expressed in the chapter on the 'On the Probable Futurity of the Labouring Classes' in Mill's (1965: bk 4, ch 7). Sen (1988: 273) is wrong to attribute to Alfred Marshall a commitment to 'the negative perspective of freedom'.

minimalist one'. Deakin (ibid.: 16–18) makes some fair comments on Hayek,[31] who, of course, not merely accepted but is to the fore of those who have insisted on 'the need for a legal-normative order to underpin market relations'. I am bound to say that I think Deakin would have done better to persevere with engagement at this level rather than getting his argument to work by directing his fire at the implausible views Becker maintained in the 1970s (Deakin 2009: 8, 19),[32] and at a law and economics argument for deregulation one associates with Posner, though Deakin does not mention him by name, that is truly feeble (ibid.: 14–16).[33] But it is possible that, if he had not posited deregulation as the opposite of *capacitas*, Deakin would have encountered considerable difficulty in setting out the *capacitas* argument. Deakin is certainly one of the leading commentators on these issues, and he, equally certainly, is conscious of the tension between freedom of contract and *capacitas*, and that he so fully goes over to the latter that it obliterates the former shows, I think, just how inimical the capabilities approach is to freedom of contract.

Individuals would have to be much further to the right in their political thinking than I am not to have sympathy with the *capacitas* argument. The law of contract does reproduce unjust inequalities in contemporary capitalist societies, and the *capacitas* argument is a sincere and highly thoughtful attempt to address this in a novel way. But I am afraid that seeking a foundation in Sen's capabilities argument is completely the wrong way to go about an argument that seeks to respect freedom of contract, and therefore freedom. The capabilities approach is an exaggerated form of welfare economics, simply incapable of respecting freedom of contract in a principled way, though it may, of course, as a practical matter seek to accommodate it. That approach is based on second-guessing the voluntary choices of economic actors in order to lead them, by means of coercion and coercive transfers, to an advantage they cannot realize for themselves. I do not doubt that in some cases something like this has to be done by the welfare state. But it is inherently repugnant and should not be undertaken as the normal case, which should be governed by a neutral law of contract.

There are a great many defences of necessary second-guessing in the socialist tradition, and, while Sen makes little no reference to them, his work overlaps them to some extent. This part of the capabilities approach, which retains some of the colour of the provision of Rawlsian primary goods, is the most attractive part of Sen's argument. But that argument cannot respect the liberal constraint that is at the heart of the Rawlsian concept of primary goods or the socialist

31 See also Deakin (1997: 288–94).

32 Ibid.: 8, 19. I have set out my own evaluation of Becker's views on which Deakin comments (Campbell (1996: 492–4). Becker has, unconvincingly in my opinion, moved away from these views in a way of which Sen (2009: 189–90) approves, though also finds inadequate.

33 I have set out my own views on this aspect of Posner's work (Campbell 2010a, 2012).

practice of welfare provision, and Sen has not merely intended to go beyond that approach explicitly, but has actually done so. He therefore has sanctioned theoretically unlimited second-guessing, leaving no proper sphere of private contract. It is therefore disastrous for a theory of contract that intends to respect freedom of contract to base itself on Sen's approach. In eagerly seizing on an approach that is authoritarian at its core, the *capacitas* argument poses the very difficult question of just how far left-wing contract scholarship actually does respect that freedom.

Bibliography

Adorno, T.W. 1994. *The Stars Down to Earth.* London: Routledge.

Bańkowski, Z. and Mungham, G. 1976. *Images of Law.* London: Routledge.

Barry, N. 1990. *Welfare.* Milton Keynes: Open University Press.

Becker, G. and Stigler, G.J. 1977. 'De Gustibus Non Est Disputandum'. *American Economic Review*, 67: 76–90.

Berlin, I. 1969. *Four Essays on Liberty.* Oxford: Oxford University Press.

Beveridge, W. 1942. *Social Insurance and Allied Services.* Cmd 6404 (London: His Majesty's Stationery Office).

Blanc, L. 1848. *The Organisation of Labour.* London: H.G. Clarke.

Bliss, C. 1993. 'Life-Style and the Standard of Living'. In M.C. Nussbaum and A. Sen (eds), *The Quality of Life.* Oxford: Oxford University Press, 417–36.

Browne, J., Deakin S.F. and Wilkinson, F. 2004. 'Capabilities, Social Rights and European Market Integration'. In R. Salais and R. Villeneuve (eds), *Europe and the Politics of Capabilities.* Cambridge: Cambridge University Press, 205–21.

Campbell, D. 1991. 'Individualism, Equality and the Possibility of Rights'. *The Connecticut Journal of International Law*, 6: 507–27.

Campbell, D. 1996. 'On What Is Valuable in Law and Economics'. *Otago Law Review*, 8: 489–514.

Campbell, D. 1997. 'The Relational Constitution of Contract and the Limits of "Economics": Kenneth Arrow on the Social Background of Markets'. In S.F. Deakin and J. Michie (eds), *Contracts, Co-operation and Competition: Studies in Economics, Management and Law.* Oxford: Oxford University Press, 307–36.

Campbell, D. 1999. 'The "Hybrid Contract" and the Merging of the Public and Private Law of the Allocation of Economic Goods'. In D. Campbell and N.D. Lewis (eds), *Promoting Participation: Law or Politics?* London: Cavendish, 45–73.

Campbell, D. 2002. 'Bringing Law and Lawyers to the People: Statism and Anarchy in Left-Wing Legal Thought'. *Social and Legal Studies*, 11: 413–23.

Campbell, D. 2003a. 'The Critique of Bourgeois Justice After the Failure of Marxism'. In A. Kerner, J. Priban and J. Young (eds), *Current Legal Issues in the Czech Republic and the United Kingdom*. Prague: Charles University Press, 9–25.

Campbell, D. 2003b. 'The Relational Constitution of Contractual Agreement'. In P. Heugens, H. van Oosterhout and J. Vromen (eds), *The Social Institutions of Capitalism: Evolution and Design of Social Contracts*. Cheltenham: Edward Elgar, 38–65.

Campbell, D. 2010a. 'The End of Posnerian Law and Economics (Review of R.A. Posner, *A Failure of Capitalism*)'. *Modern Law Review*, 73: 302–27.

Campbell, D. 2010b. 'Gathering the Water: Abuse of Rights After the Recognition of Government Failure'. *The Journal Jurisprudence*, 7: 413–59.

Campbell, D. 2011. 'How Sensible Is the Left-Wing Criticism of Money, Exchange and Contract?'. *Social and Legal Studies*, 20: 528–39.

Campbell, D. 2012. 'Welfare Economics for Capitalists: The Economic Consequences of Judge Posner'. *Cardozo Law Review*, 33, 2233–74.

Campbell, D. and Klaes, M. 2005. 'The Principle of Institutional Direction: Coase's Regulatory Critique of Intervention'. *Cambridge Journal of Economics*, 29: 263–88.

Campbell, D. and Loughrey, J. forthcoming 2013. 'The Regulation of Self-Interest in Financial Markets'. In G. Gilligan and J. O'Brien (eds), *Regulating Culture*. Oxford: Hart Publishing.

Cannan, E. 1913. 'Review of N. G. Pierson'. *Principles of Economics, Economic Review*, 23: 331–3.

Coase, R.H. 1964. 'The Regulated Industries: Discussion'. *American Economic Review (Papers and Proceedings)*, 54: 194–7.

Coase, R.H. 1972. 'Discussion'. In W.J. Samuels and H.M. Trebing (eds), *A Critique of Administrative Regulation*. East Lansing, MI: Institute of Public Utilities, Division of Research, Graduate School of Business Administration, Michigan State University, 311–6.

Cohen, G.A. 1993. 'Equality of What? On Welfare, Goods and Capabilities'. In M.C. Nussbaum and A. Sen (eds), *The Quality of Life*. Oxford: Clarendon Press, 9–29.

Dalton, H. 1920. 'The Measurement of Inequality of Incomes'. *Economic Journal*, 30: 348–61.

Deakin, S.F. 1997. 'Private law, Economic Rationality and the Regulatory State'. In P. Birks (ed.), *The Classification of Obligations*. Oxford: Clarendon Press, 283–304.

Deakin, S.F. 2009. '*Capacitas*: Contract Law, Capabilities and the Legal Foundations of the Market'. In S.F. Deakin and A. Supiot (eds), *Capacitas: Contract Law and the Institutional Preconditions of a Market Economy*. Oxford: Hart Publishing, 1–29.

Deakin, S.F. 2011. 'Contracts and Capabilities: An Evolutionary Perspective on the Autonomy–Paternalism Debate'. In A. Ogus and W.H. van Boom (eds), *Juxtaposing Autonomy and Paternalism in Private Law*. Oxford: Hart, 127–44.

Deakin S.F. and Supiot, A. (eds) 2009. *Capacitas: Contract Law and the Institutional Preconditions of a Market Economy*. Oxford: Hart Publishing.

Deakin S.F. and Wilkinson, F. 2000. 'Capabilities, Spontaneous Order and Social Rights'. Working Paper 174, ESRC Centre for Business Research, University of Cambridge.

Deakin S.F. and Wilkinson, F. 2005. *The Law of the Labour Market*. Oxford: Oxford University Press.

De Munck J. and Zimmermann, B. (eds.) 2007. *La liberté au prisme des capacities: Amartya Sen au-delà du libéralisme*. Paris: Editions de l'EHESS.

Drèze, J. and Sen, A. 1995. *India: Economic Development and Social Opportunity*. Oxford: Clarendon Press.

Drèze, J. and Sen, A. 2002. *India: Development and Participation*, 2nd edn. Oxford: Oxford University Press.

Dworkin, R.M. 2000. *Sovereign Virtue*. Cambridge, MA: Harvard University Press.

Esping-Anderson, G. 1999. *Social Foundations of Post-Industrial Economies*. Oxford: Oxford University Press.

France, A. 1908. *The Red Lily*. London: Bodley Head.

Halson, R. and Campbell, D. forthcoming 2013. 'Harmonisation and Its Discontents: The Transaction Cost Argument for the European Contract Code'. In J. Devenney and M. Kenny (eds), *The Transformation of European Private Law: Harmonisation, Consolidation, Codification or Chaos?* Cambridge, Cambridge University Press.

Hart, H.L.A. 1983. 'Between Utility and Rights'. In H.L.A. Hart, *Essays in Jurisprudence and Philosophy*. Oxford: Clarendon Press, 198–222.

Hayek, F.A. 2007. *The Road to Serfdom*. Chicago, IL: University of Chicago Press.

Hesselink, M.W. 2009. 'Capacity and Capability in European Contract Law'. In S.F. Deakin and A. Supiot (eds) *Capacitas: Contract Law and the Institutional Preconditions of a Market Economy*. Oxford: Hart Publishing, 31–47.

Marshall, A. 1966. 'The Future of the Working Classes'. In A.C. Pigou (ed.), *Memorials of Alfred Marshall*. New York: Augustus M Kelley, 101–18.

Marshall, T.H. 1952. *Social Policy*. 1st edn. London, Heinemann.

Marshall, T.H. 1982. 'Value Problems of Welfare-Capitalism'. In T.H. Marshall, *The Right to Welfare*. London: Heinemann Educational Books, 104.

Marshall, T.H. 1992. 'Citizenship and Social Class'. In T.H. Marshall and T. Bottomore, *Citizenship and Social Class*. London, Pluto, 1–51.

Miller, D. 1989. *Market, State and Community*. Oxford: Clarendon Press.

Mill, J.S. 1965. *Principles of Political Economy*. Toronto: University of Toronto Press.

Nozick, R. 1974. *Anarchy, State and Utopia*. New York: Basic Books.

Ogus, A.I. 1994. *Regulation*. Oxford: Clarendon Press.

Orwell, G. 2001a. 'The Art of Donald McGill'. In G. Orwell, *All Propaganda Is Lies*, revd edn. London: Secker & Warburg, 23–31.

Orwell, G. 2001b. 'As I Please'. In G. Orwell, *I Have Tried to Tell the Truth*, revd edn. London: Secker & Warburg, 2001, 261–65.

Pigou, A.C. 2002. *The Economics of Welfare*, 5th end. New Brunswick, NJ: Transaction Books.

Pogge, T.W. 2004. 'Can the Capability Approach Be Justified?'. *Philosophical Topics*, 30, 167–228.

Popper, K.R. 1966. *The Open Society and Its Enemies*, 5th edn. London: Routledge & Kegan Paul.

Rawls, J. 1971. *A Theory of Justice*. Cambridge, MA: Belknap Press.

Rawls, J. 1996. *Political Liberalism*. New York: Columbia University Press.

Rawls, J. 1999. *A Theory of Justice*, revd edn. Oxford: Oxford University Press.

Rothschild, E. and Sen, A. 2006. 'Adam Smith's economics'. In K. Haakonssen (ed.), *The Cambridge Companion to Adam Smith*. Cambridge: Cambridge University Press, 319–65.

Schmidt, E.A. 2010. 'The Missing Squirm Factor in Amartya Sen's Capabilities Approach'. In S.E. Esquith and F. Gifford (eds), *Capabilities, Powers and Institutions*. University Park, PA: Pennsylvania State University Press, 33–9.

Sen, A. 1975. 'The Concept of Efficiency'. In M. Parkin and A.R. Nobay (eds), *Contemporary Issues in Economics*. Manchester: Manchester University Press, 196–210.

Sen, A. 1980–81. 'Plural Utility'. *Proceedings of the Aristotelian Society*, 80: 193–215.

Sen, A. 1982a. 'Equality of What?'. In A. Sen, *Choice, Welfare and Measurement*. Cambridge, MA: Harvard University Press, 353–69.

Sen, A. 1982b. 'The Impossibility of a Paretian Liberal'. In A. Sen, *Choice, Welfare and Measurement*. Cambridge, MA: Harvard University Press, 285–90.

Sen, A. 1982c. 'Interpersonal Aggregation and Partial Comparability'. In A. Sen, *Choice, Welfare and Measurement*. Cambridge, MA: Harvard University Press, 203–21.

Sen, A. 1982d. 'On Weights and Measures: Informational Constraints in Social Welfare Analysis'. In A. Sen, *Choice, Welfare and Measurement*. Cambridge, MA: Harvard University Press, 226–63.

Sen, A. 1982e. 'Rational Fools: A Critique of the Behavioural Foundation of Economic Theory'. In A. Sen, *Choice, Welfare and Measurement*. Cambridge, MA: Harvard University Press, 84–106.

Sen, A. 1985a. 'Rights and Capabilities'. In T. Honderich (ed.), *Morality and Objectivity*. London: Routledge & Kegan Paul, 130–48.

Sen, A. 1985b. 'Well-Being, Agency and Freedom'. *Journal of Philosophy*, 82: 169–221.

Sen, A. 1988. 'Freedom of Choice: Concept and Content'. *European Economic Review*, 32: 269–94.

Sen, A. 1993. 'Markets and Freedoms: Achievements and Limitations of the Market Mechanism in Promoting Individual Freedoms'. *Oxford Economic Papers*, 45: 519–41.

Sen, A. 1994. 'Markets and the Freedom to Choose'. In H. Siebert (ed.), *The Ethical Foundations of the Market Economy*. Tubingen: JCB Mohr, 123–38.

Sen, A. 1997. *On Economic Inequality*, revd edn. Oxford: Clarendon Press, 1997.

Sen, A. 1999a. *Commodities and Capabilities*. Oxford: Oxford University Press.

Sen, A. 1999b. *Development as Freedom*. Oxford: Oxford University Press.

Sen, A. 2002a. 'Internal Consistency of Choice'. In A. Sen, *Rationality and Freedom*, Cambridge, MA: Harvard University Press, 61.

Sen, 2002b. 'Maximisation and the Act of Choice'. In A. Sen, *Rationality and Freedom*. Cambridge, MA: Harvard University Press, 158–205.

Sen, A. 2004. 'Elements of a Theory of Human Rights'. *Philosophy and Public Affairs*, 32: 315–56.

Sen, A. 2006. 'Human Rights and the Limits of Law'. *Cardozo Law Review*, 27: 2913–27.

Sen, A. 2009. *The Idea of Justice*. London: Penguin.

Sen, A. 2012. 'Values and Justice'. *The Journal of Economic Methodology*, 19: 101–8.

Sen, A. and Williams, B. 1982. 'Introduction'. In A. Sen and B. Williams (eds), *Utilitarianism and Beyond*. Cambridge: Cambridge University Press, 1–22.

Stigler, G.J. 1943. 'The New Welfare Economics'. *American Economic Review*, 33: 355–9.

Wieacker, F. 1995. *A History of Private Law in Europe*. Oxford: Oxford University Press.

Wijffels, A. 2009. 'Rationalisation and Derationalisation of Legal Capacity in Historical Perspective: Some General Caveats'. In S.F. Deakin and A. Supiot (eds), *Capacitas: Contract Law and the Institutional Preconditions of a Market Economy*. Oxford: Hart Publishing, 49–62.

Zundel, S. and Steiss, I. 2011. 'Beyond Profitability of Energy-Saving Measures: Attitudes towards Energy Saving'. *Journal of Consumer Policy*, 34: 91–105.

Chapter 12
What's Love Got to Do with Development?

Oche Onazi

Introduction

Zenon Bańkowski posed the following question to me at our first meeting shortly after I had arrived at Edinburgh to begin my doctoral degree: why did you choose to come to Edinburgh Law School (not Warwick, where I completed a Master degree) for your Ph.D.? I really was not sure what to answer, since the decision to come to Edinburgh was more intuitive than rational. Regardless, I muddled a response that I wanted to learn and also to work in an environment where I could distance myself from my convictions (particularly those that had been imparted to me at Warwick) without losing them. I was not surprised by the question, since this was something I had also thought about, despite being a little anxious about moving to a new country and place of study where I was not only a stranger, but also not an orthodox legal theorist. It seemed like a good time to find out from Bańkowski why he chose to supervise me. His response was quite reassuring. He said that there were aspects of my Ph.D. proposal that rekindled memories of his days as an anarchist. Though I was (and am still) not an anarchist, the reassurance was that I was going to be supervised by someone who spoke, or at least understood, my language and convictions.

Looking back, I have often wondered what my experience in Edinburgh would have been like, or how my Ph.D. would have turned out, if I had not encountered Zenon Bańkowski. As a true hallmark of his personality, he welcomed me with warmth, love, affection, friendship and laughter, making the time I spent in Edinburgh filled with fond memories. I will always remain indebted to him for his support, kindness and generosity. As a modest way of expressing my gratitude to him, this chapter seeks to relate the emphasis on love in Bańkowski's writings to particular aspects of international development discourse.

Bańkowski's work does not fall within the genre of development studies, but it can certainly be interpreted in the light of core debates about development. For example, the relationship between law and love that features so prominently in his writings is another way of understanding debates over the state or the market, or trade or aid, which remain unsettled controversies in development discourse. His work on the ethical life of institutions can undoubtedly be used to assess the moral quality of the work of development institutions and other organizations.

This chapter takes as its point of departure the introduction of human rights as the normative language for discourses, approaches, policies, practices and institutions of development. It aims to draw on the work of Bańkowski to illustrate the limitations of the widely held view that human rights can serve as the ethical or moral basis for different aspects of development work, especially in the attempt to recognize and respond to various forms of human suffering. What is unique about Bańkowski work (and what makes it stand out from other critiques of human rights), is that it shows the inadequacy of human rights themselves. It shows us why we cannot depend too much on human rights, for they are not sufficient as a conceptual medium that can encourage a proper understanding or articulation of how people suffer. In doing so, Bańkowski allows us to appreciate the importance of love and the constitutive role it should play in creating laws and institutions that can meaningfully address various forms of human suffering. In conclusion, I demonstrate how these ideas can contribute to the aspects of the practice of participatory development, something that is also affected by rights-based approaches.

Development

The origins of contemporary notions of development can be traced to the early parts of the post-Second World War international order, which led to the somewhat arbitrary classification of nearly two-thirds of the world's population as being poor. From its very beginning, development was conceived in economic terms, placing economic growth at the core of all efforts to alleviate poverty. Development and poverty came to exist as twin concepts. Poverty was measured according to gross domestic product (GDP) per capita. Countries, particularly those in the Third World, whose GDP averaged below US$100 income per capita, for the first time, became poor (Escobar 1995; Sachs 1992). Poverty was never properly understood, as it should be, as a multiple phenomenon: it was only an economic phenomenon and a characteristic of Third-World countries. Poverty became the object of intervention by a throng of experts, bureaucrats, planners, business people, economists, lawyers and anthropologists, among others, who sought to transform the lives of the Third World inhabitants through various economically determined policies, programmes and strategies. Poverty, to put it simply, gave birth to the whole enterprise of development.

The advantages and disadvantages of the GDP approach are well known. The main advantage of the GDP approach is that it is easy to calculate and to compare the monetary value of different goods and services (Nussbaum 2011: 47–50). GDP is also transparent, since the approach makes it difficult for the countries involved to paint false pictures of themselves. Overall, it is much easier to rely on economic growth as a variable for measuring the economic health of a nation. Economic growth, especially in the 1980s and 1990s, was adjudged to have a trickle-down effect on the poor – an assumption that was soon proved wrong, yielding to the most obvious limitation of the GDP approach today. GDP growth has often failed to translate into an equitable distribution of wealth or give an accurate reflection of quality of life within any given country. By aggregating and reducing various things that make life worthwhile into a single measure, the GDP approach cannot explain variations in the quality of life within any nation. The approach reduces the plurality of life by assimilating incommensurable aspects of life into a single and narrow monetary measure. In addition to this, it is not easy to distinguish the internal differences between countries with similar levels of GDP. For example, countries with similar GDP levels often have different standards of health care or public education, which also vary on their degree of accessibility.

Given the narrow opportunities for a distribution of wealth provided by the GDP approach, it is no surprise that the idea of development itself has been subject to criticism, both internally and externally. Since the early 1950s, when the problems with the GDP approach began to become evident, counter-approaches have both been proposed and resisted. The alternatives to the growth-led approach have been expressed in different terms, all with the objective of trying to expunge the economic bias from development. This is the common theme with concepts of social development, human-centred development, endogenous development, sustainable development, and very recently, human development.

Another significantly influential factor behind the shift in development thinking beyond its traditional economic dimension is the introduction of human rights to the situation, something that became a reality with the emergence of the United Nations (UN) Declaration on the Right to Development (Baxi 2009; Sengupta 2002). While the Right to Development did not expand the notion of development itself, it had the effect of assimilating human rights into development practice, yielding to what has become known as rights-based approaches (Cornwall and Nyamu-Musembi 2004). There is a conflict of opinion about why development theory and practice has resorted to human rights. Some see it simply a question of legitimacy; the legitimacy derived from the moral appeal of human rights, which is in turn used to validate (controversial) development policies, practices and approaches (Rajagopal 2003). On the other hand, others suggest that the resort to human rights was an attempt to provide a new normative language for development practices and institutions aimed at providing the necessary moral alertness to generate more awareness and appropriate response to novel forms of suffering and vulnerability (Rittich 2004; Del Mar and Onazi 2008). It would seem that both views are correct, apart from being interrelated, if one understands the rights-based approaches as an attempt to give a normative framework for development based on principles of international human rights law. Apart from the much needed normative and ethical dimension this brings, the practice of development was in need of some legitimacy, which the moral weight of the language of human rights has in turn been looked upon to provide (Rittich 2004).

Around the same time, Amartya Sen (1999) provided arguably the most influential internal critique of development, which contributed to an expansion of the notion of development by further anchoring it in ethics and values. He departs from the economic-growth-oriented approach to show that development has multiple dimensions, including, very importantly, an ethical one. For Sen, development is freedom; it is 'a process of expanding the real freedoms that people enjoy' (Sen 1999: 3). The pursuit of freedom should serve as the means and ends of development. Sen encourages us to think of development in multidimensional ways and not only associate it with the lack of GDP growth, the rise of personal incomes, industrialization or technological progress.

While Sen's work is not an example of a human rights approach, it nevertheless complements rights-based approaches. As Marta Nussbaum (2011) explains, while expanding on her own version of the capability approach, the concept of human dignity unites both approaches. Like human rights, the capability approach seeks to provide useful guidance for the protection and attainment of acceptable standards of human dignity. It is, as she says, 'one species of a human rights approach and human rights are often linked in a similar way to the idea of human dignity' (Nussbaum 2006: 160). Human rights and the capability approach both recognize that individuals should be accorded certain basic goods to safeguard their dignity. The rationale behind Nussbaum's list of capabilities is that (just like human rights) they provide some guidance of the basic rudiments necessary to live a life with dignity. Like human rights, it is possible to generate cross-cultural agreement on what these capabilities ought to be, and the processes of definition should always be left to open-ended regular processes that will be subject to constant revision.

Looking at the state of much of the Third World today (especially if the alleviation of poverty is the central objective of development), it is not difficult to conclude that development has clearly failed. The hardships and gaps within and between Third-World countries have deepened since the introduction of the post-Second World War development discourse. In short, development has failed, and continues to fail, the majority of the poor in the Third World. It fails to recognize the poor who suffer and to meet them at the point of need. Development's resort to human rights, in spite of the appeal and the perceived benefits, has not prevented suffering, which remains unabated across the world today.

Some problems with development and the different approaches to it (including the human rights approach) have invited criticism from several scholars. Upendra Baxi (2002), to give one example, highlights two related problems with the human rights approach to development. More generally, he points to the corporate capture of human rights by the advocates of neoliberal globalization through the emergence of what he calls a trade-related, market friendly discourse. A more relevant point, for the purposes of this chapter, is that Baxi criticizes human rights discourse for being unable to grasp human suffering. He says that this can be seen in many ways, including the distinction between international laws of war and laws of peace, yielding to stronger obligation to ameliorate suffering in times of war than in peace. Nevertheless, several problems in peacetime, such as 'conditions of extreme impoverishment, forced labour, systematically organised rape through sex trafficking, child labour, planned displacement of peoples in the name of development' (Baxi 2002: vii), demand a higher standard of obligations to alleviate human suffering and pain. As a response, Baxi proposes an approach situated from the standpoint of the victim/sufferer (communities of suffering) to make human rights more amenable to the alleviation of suffering. To pave a way for this possibility, he makes a distinction between modern and contemporary human rights discourse, even though he acknowledges that these discourses are not mutually exclusive. Baxi is more critical of modern human rights discourse, influenced by an extreme liberal individualistic ideology, for failing to take human suffering seriously. He decries modern human rights discourse for even sustaining various forms of pain and suffering through colonial and neocolonial discourses. In contrast, contemporary human rights discourse, which is diverse, inclusive (and emerges from the voices and communities of suffering), is more responsive to alleviating suffering and hardship.

While Baxi's work importantly draws our attention to how human rights seem blind, or might sometimes contribute to such problems, it seems that there is a prior question, which Baxi's critique does not touch upon. It does not question the capacity of human rights to enable the recognition of and response to vulnerability and suffering. The kind of responses to suffering that Baxi demands depend on how we are capable of recognizing that people are suffering in the first place. We need to know whether human rights can actually carry out this objective; that is, whether they are able to provide a sufficient foundation from which to recognize and respond to different types of suffering. If human rights are inadequate or inherently deficient in this sense, it would be too much to expect them to respond to human suffering. I turn now to Bańkowski's ethic of love, seeking a better understanding of precisely this point.

Bańkowski's Ethic of Love

An appropriate grasp of Bańkowski's ethic of love hinges on understanding a common theme in most of his work (Bańkowski 2001a). Any attempt, as Bańkowski says, to create law, or legal and political institutions, would ultimately fail if such arrangements are organized in a way that does not recognize and respond to deep cries of suffering. In particular, he argues that the stability often sought from law, and other institutional arrangements, would depend on whether they can enable the recognition and response to pain and suffering (Bańkowski 2001a). Love is central to how we recognize and respond to human suffering. Bańkowski defines love as an action-guiding principle, one that is not based on reason or rational universalizing principles (Bańkowski 2001b: 199). Love is a reason unto itself. It is derived from paying attention to particular or concrete circumstances. Love is a grace, which is neither predictable nor definable by rules. Love is at the basis of our passionate or contingent human natures. Love is about the present; the future does not matter. Love is self-questioning and spontaneous. It is, 'the spontaneity of autonomy … of doing something on your own responsibility because it is "right" and you feel it [is] so' (Bańkowski 2001b: 200). The principle of welfare is the closest and most concrete approximate description of love in contemporary political settings. Welfare is a response to particularity, something that cannot be anticipated by devising or adhering to general rules. Welfare is the act of giving according to need rather than ability. The demands of welfare, like love, are impossible to determine or constrain by rules.

Bańkowski develops these themes from the seminal work of Simone Weil (1962), who decried law and rights vociferously for inadequate provision of the kind of moral resources necessary to recognize and respond to those in pain and suffering. Bańkowski expands on this point from Weil's vivid depiction of the cry of a distressed girl forced to work in a brothel, to show the limit of law and the importance of love in paying attention to human suffering.

My understanding of the story is that it allows us to question whether the language of human rights reveals the marvel and the preciousness of human individuality. Her point is that the violent nature of the harm being done to the girl cannot be appreciated through the language of human rights. Rights do not get across the nature of the suffering, a proper understanding of which is necessary to determine the appropriate response. All that results from rights is property- or contract-related legal claims, which are inappropriate when trying to comprehend or convey the defilement of the young and vulnerable girl. After all, the girl's cry, as Bańkowski says, is not one for improved wages or for a better deal. Weil is ultimately suggesting that we should not rely entirely on human rights as conceptual tools to articulate such types of suffering.

In another sense, Weil decried the contentious, hostile or antagonistic nature of rights-based claims. She warned that '[R]ights are always asserted in a tone of contention; and when this tone is adopted, it must rely upon force in the background, or else it will be laughed at' (Weil 1962: 18). Weil's point here is that to insist on one's rights is to prevent warmer, affectionate, informal or less antagonistic modes of interaction between people. To make a claim for rights is like, as Jeremy Waldron describes in another context, the 'opening of hostilities' (Waldron 1998: 628).

By depending on human rights, not only will our capacity to articulate the gravity of this kind of suffering be inadequate, but our ability to respond to it will also be limited. Weil's analogy can indeed be read and applied more widely to different forms of suffering, the types upon which the whole enterprise of development has been founded to resolve. Only the spirit of love, she says, can draw our attention to grasp and respond to the cries of pain, hunger, disease, war and other humanitarian tragedies across the globe today.

To develop these points further, Bańkowski turns to Raimond Gaita's (2000) story of a nun he met while working as a ward assistant in a mental hospital. Most of the patients were diagnosed with incurable diseases and had lived there for more than 30 years. They had lost everything, and life meant nothing to them. They had no friends and were abandoned by their families. At the hospital, some of the staff treated the patients as animals, while others were humane, but condescending. Gaita, however, noticed something remarkable when a nun visited the hospital. The way she looked and spoke to the patients, her demeanour and facial expressions; everything she did was different. The nun exhibited something unique and pure; it was an example of love, the type of love of saints. It was the type of love

> which builds on and transforms that sense of individuality, and in doing so, deepening the language of love which compels us to affirm that even those who suffer affliction so severe that they have irrecoverably lost everything that gives sense to our lives, and the most radical evil-doers, are fully our fellow human beings. (Gaita 2000: xix)

It is no surprise that Gaita develops these insights from Simone Weil's belief in love as a conceptual resource to grasp the preciousness of human individuality. The nun embraced the affliction of the patients in a way that revealed the sanctity of their humanity. Bańkowski builds on this argument to contend that our legal, social and political institutions can only become more responsive to suffering if they are accompanied by bursts of love. As such, Bańkowski takes a different view from Immanuel Kant, who shows a preference for duties. Kant was wary of love. Our respect and care for others, he says, should not depend on love. Love, for Kant, cannot be commanded or generally guaranteed. He says that we must not have to love people to be able to assist them.

Bańkowski finds support for his disagreement with Kant from Gaita, even though they appear to have slight differences of opinion regarding their use of love. For Gaita, it seems that love should ground everything, from the political community to the laws, rights and institutional arrangements within them. With particular emphasis on rights, Gaita says it is impossible to begin to consider an obligation or the respect for others outside some notion of love, however minimal this may be. Without the language of love, we cannot adequately understand the preciousness and sanctity of individuals. Our inability to love or cultivate habits of love determines how and why we should respect the rights of others. Love must underpin human rights; otherwise 'rights talk' would be meaningless. As Gaita says, it is only through the language of love that we can build 'a more tractable structure of rights and obligations':

> If the language of love goes dead on us, however, if there are no examples to nourish it, either because they do not exist or because they are no longer visible to us, then talk of inalienable natural rights or of the unconditional respect owed to rational human beings will seem lame and improbable to us. (Gaita 2000: xix)

While agreeing with Gaita, I would like to add that the possibility of grounding rights in love would only arise if the perception of rights is altered, from traditionally individualistic claims to claims for mutual recognition or respect between human beings (Douzinas 2000: 274). It is only from the standpoint of mutual recognition that we can see how rights can be grounded in habits of love and affection, of those who share the same human condition. Human rights would then be more disposed to ethical claims based on love, identification and mutual respect of our shared humanity. Human rights become the inextricable link between each human being, something that is derived from love.

Bańkowski position is not a straightforward substitution of rights or law for love. Neither is it a claim that everything must be built on love, since Zenon understands that love has limitations because of its exclusive and unpredictable nature. He shows this through discussions on the administrative and unpredictable nature of the welfare state, where there are no clear rules to guide the distribution of resources. Distribution rests on administrative or bureaucratic discretion. The satisfaction of individual needs are dependent on contingent judgements, which are unpredictable or lead in different directions. But Bańkowski is also not saying that we should seek stability from law instead, mainly for the reasons that were outlined from Simone Weil's work. This lack of sensitivity to the cries of suffering that she speaks so eloquently about is one way of understanding Bańkowski's notion of legalism. Bańkowski decries legalism – a theme developed from Judith Shklar's work. Legalism is described as a legal mind-set, which is synonymous with rigid, if not blind, adherence to rules. Legalism denies the kind of contingency necessary to change laws, especially when they have exhausted their capabilities or outlived their usefulness.

Bańkowski's ethic seeks to maintain the attention to particularity that comes from love, without denying the universality and rationality of law: he is suggesting that we maintain a strong commitment to love without necessarily forfeiting law. Our moral life, he says, should not depend on a choice between love or law (Bańkowski, 2001a). Law and love are not separate, but mutually reinforcing concepts. We can understand this by paying closer attention to what is entailed by an act of love. It often begins within an explosion followed by a series of rational acts. He uses cosmology as an analogy to explain this point. The loving act is analogous to the big bang, which explains that the universe began with a sudden, arbitrary and singular explosion. As unreasonable as this explosion might be, it is, none the less, accompanied by certain rational actions, such as time and scientific laws. This is what Bańkowski means by saying that there is a degree of rationality inherent in an act of love. What he means is that law is present in love, and love is present in law. The loving act comes first, and it is accompanied by the rationality of law. The process is, however, not an endless undulation between law and love.

The relationship between law and love is risky, tense and uncertain, and it is negotiated in a space called the middle. The middle is an anxious space, where unpredictable and open-minded decisions are made about dichotomies. It makes us aware of the complacency that might arise from maintaining too strong an attachment to one conviction or another. This is how Bańkowski would suggest that we approach the relationship between human rights (law) and love. They should not be seen as opposites; rather, each concept has to be carefully considered and negotiated in the light of their merits and demerits. The importance of love is surely how it can renew human rights by allowing them to embrace contingency and change. The middle is ultimately the space that facilitates this. It is a space for rehabilitation, ethical imagination and creativity; a space, however, where one does not unreasonably hold on to or relinquish one's convictions. The idea of the middle provides an insight into what is entailed in all types of decision-making processes. It applies to judges and ordinary citizens alike, who encounter all sorts of dichotomies on a daily basis and in different spheres of life. In the end, Bańkowski is saying that rationality is not sufficient for deliberation and to reach sound judgement. Rational decisions cannot be reached without love.

The Space for Decision-Making

It is possible to read some of the above insights from Bańkowski in relation to the concept of participation, an integral part of development discourse and one of the fundamental principles associated with the rights-based approaches. Apart from revitalizing the moral and ethical aspects of development, another attribute of the introduction of the rights-based approaches is how they lend weight to the importance of participation in development discourse (Cook and Kothari 2001; Chambers 2002; Cornwall and Nyamu-Musembi 2004; Kapoor 2005).

Participation is one of the core principles of rights-based approaches, the aim of which is to involve ordinary citizens, especially the poor, in various decision-making processes concerning development. The idea of participation itself pre-dates the rights-based approaches, going back to the 1960s and 1970s (Sachs 1992). Participation is now central to the policies and practices of the major development organizations. The importance of participation emerged against the background of an era of failed development projects. Participation seeks to increase the involvement of citizens in decision-making processes and wider processes of social transformation. Participation carries a promise of empowerment and the social transformation of lives of ordinary people, a promise nevertheless, the fulfilment of which leaves much to be desired today (Onazi 2012).

In the current climate, there has been a good deal of experimentation with participatory methodologies; in the same way that new participatory institutions have been created to augment traditional models of political participation. Participation serves different purposes, from distribution of resources and local governance to the delivery of public goods and services. Participation can be distinguished between top-down processes (initiated by mainstream development organizations and policies) and bottom-up processes (initiated spontaneously and identifiable with people at the grassroots level).

Participation is about space; the kind of institutional spaces (old and new, ad-hoc and permanent) that facilitate deliberation on a range of issues by a range of people. The transformative potential of participation depends very much on the nature of practices that take place within any given institutional space. By focusing on such spaces, we are able to explore how accessible they are; that is, whether they are closed or open, inclusive or exclusive. This allows us to learn about the variety of participants, the power dynamics involved, the interaction between those who convene (representatives of government, donors, non-governmental organizations and so on) and those (often the poor) who are invited to take part. It helps us to explore the communicative processes, and the kind of listening involved, among other things.

Reflect[1] (Hickey and Mohan 2004, 164), an extensively used participatory methodology developed from the work of Paulo Freire (1972) and techniques of participatory rural appraisal, allows us to explore some of the themes above and below, including how Bańkowski's work might be relevant to it. Reflect is an approach to adult literacy and empowerment that creates spaces for participation and enhances the communicative ability of the poor. After successful pilot studies in Uganda, Bangladesh and El Salvador in the early to mid-1990s, Reflect is now used by an estimated 350 organizations in over 60 countries around the world (Archer and Cottingham 1997), by local, national and international non-governmental organizations, social movements, grassroots organizations, district and regional governments. It is used to pursue different objectives, ranging from peace and reconciliation, local planning, accountability, capacity building to school management, to give just a few examples.

Reflect is not ambivalent as to its vision of development. Its commitment is to improve the material conditions of the poor by providing interim responses to their basic needs. Reflect is also committed to assisting the poor in the struggle to claim their rights and alter their place in society. Without doubt, Reflect identifies with the poorest and most marginalized. Reflect gives primacy to giving power and a voice to the poor by enhancing their communicative ability.

Communication is a pivotal aspect of Reflect, and this means two related things. First, it means the inclusive nature of participatory spaces. Therefore, it entails the creation of spaces for scrutiny and reflection; spaces where people, without intimidation, can determine the subject of communication, the mode of communication, and the participants involved. Here, individuals need to develop the capacity for critical understanding and perception of the subject matter of communication. Second, communication is seen as a reciprocal process, meaning to transmit and receive, to listen, to be listened to, to interpret and reinterpret. Communication allows us to see how the participatory process works, the various actors involved, from representatives of institutions to participants, and how they speak, listen and try to understand one another.

If the overall objective of the Reflect approach entails delineating spaces where people, particularly the poor, can articulate their problems and be listened to, then this is something that Bańkowski's work can certainly strengthen. From his perspective, we cannot listen effectively in any given space for decision-making without cultivating what Simone Weil called 'attention':

> Attention consists of suspending our thought, leaving it detached, empty and ready to be penetrated … Above all our thought should be empty, waiting, not

1 Reflect is not an acronym. Its means 'reflect' in the ordinary sense of the term.

> seeking anything but ready to receive in its naked truth the object that is to penetrate it. (Weil 1951: 59)

Attention helps us to discern what we have often taken for granted. Attention is a habit that we all have the capacity to cultivate; that is, the aptitude to listen, look, be still, patient, and ultimately, to embrace the other with compassion and offer help. This act of helping is an act of participation, in the sense of taking part in the suffering of the afflicted. This makes attention difficult, as it places a very high demand or responsibility on those who are not afflicted. But there is a reason for this kind of strong obligation. It is an attempt to eliminate self-serving motives or the condescension that is often disguised through the act of helping. It is an attempt to avoid being paternalistic or treating those that suffer disdainfully, something typical of the rights-based or other development approaches. It seeks to avoid the act of helping from being concealed by power, or prevent situations where the reason for helping is different from the actual cry of pain.

Attention is novel in the sense that it places the afflicted and non-afflicted on the same plane. They become equal in pain from the moment the non-afflicted take part in the pain of the afflicted. Attention is literal, not metaphorical; it is both a spiritual and a political act. Attention can further be illustrated by the biblical parable of the Good Samaritan. In Bańkowski's words, the parable illustrates the 'creativity of "attention" to the cry of pain, of affliction' (Bańkowski 2013: 19). Attention is like a journey, where everyone is possibly a victim, an oppressor or oppressed. Bańkowski says the significance of the parable is that it is the 'constitutive act of making the other a neighbour by the act of helping' (Bańkowski 2003: 20); it is not merely discovering who your neighbour is. It is a risky and transformative journey, and the consequences are unpredictable.

If Reflect, as shown earlier, is a practical communicative process that requires us to cultivate the habit of listening, among other things, then it certainly can be enhanced by the concept of attention described above. The processes of communication can be improved if participants develop a listening, tranquil, serene and open attitude to embrace the other with compassion and give help. While the act of deliberation itself is an act of love, it does not by any means exclude rationality. Bańkowski's thought shows us more generally the need to, and how to, strike the right balance between our emotions and rationality.

What attention can help to achieve the most is the recognition that all participants are equal in pain. In doing so, it restores the afflicted to a position of equality with the non-afflicted, thereby challenging dominant perceptions of participation as top-down exercises, where the conveners engage with the convened from a position of superiority or at a distance. Attention reconciles and unites all participants in suffering, the conveners and convened, the victim and helper, the institution and non-institution, the donor or recipient, the government representative and ordinary poor citizen, the rich and poor. If the overall goal of Reflect is to enhance the capacity of people to act for themselves, then it is not difficult to see attention as being integral to how to nurture, foster or establish capacities and practices for communication, collaboration, shared learning and self-determination.

Conclusion

This chapter has been an attempt to relate the role that love plays in Bańkowski's work to moral–philosophical approaches to development and global poverty. If there is a single or overall contribution that can be extrapolated from Bańkowski's work, it is how it guards against the complacency that often comes from depending too heavily on human rights (law) as the normative resource to encourage recognition of and response to suffering and vulnerability. Love, according to Bańkowski, is pivotal to how we respond to people who are suffering. Our capacity to respond to suffering with love is inexplicably linked to the ability to cultivate the habit of attention. Attention is an act of helping. It is transformative, yet also a risky and unpredictable encounter. It is an act of participation, in the sense of the exchange between the afflicted and non-afflicted. Attention is giving and taking, to borrow another phrase from Bańkowski. It is an act of communication; it requires us to listen and to be heard. Attention restores the afflicted to a position of equality with the non-afflicted. In many ways, Bańkowski's ethic of love is best not described as a step-by-step guide or principle for certain actions, or the design of institutional arrangements. Instead, his ethic provides us with the space for critical reflection and imagination through which we can examine whether our actions and institutional arrangements pay sufficient attention to vulnerability and human suffering.

Bibliography

Archer, D. and Cottingham, S. 1997. 'REFLECT: A New Approach to Literacy and Social Change'. *Development in Practice*, 7(2): 199–202.

Bańkowski, Z. 2013. 'The Space to See: Law and the Ethical Imagination'. In Z. Bańkowski and M. Del Mar (eds), *The Moral Imagination and the Legal Life: Beyond Text in Legal Education*. Farnham: Ashgate, 11–32.

Bańkowski, Z. 2001a. *Living Lawfully: Law in Love and Love in Law*. Dordrecht: Kluwer.

Bańkowski, Z. 2001b. 'Law, Love and Legality'. *International Journal for the Semiotics of Law*, 14: 199–213.

Baxi, U. 2002. *The Future of Human Rights*. New Delhi: Oxford University Press.

Baxi, U. 2009. *Human Rights in a Post-Human World: Critical Essays*. New Delhi: Oxford University Press.

Chambers, R. 2002. *Participatory Workshops: A Source Book of 21 Ideas and Activities*. London: Earthscan.

Cook, B. and Kothari, U. 2001. *Participation: The New Tyranny*. New York: Zed Books.

Cornwall, A. and Nyamu-Musembi, C. 2004. 'Putting the Rights Based Approach to Development into Perspective'. *Third World Quarterly*, 25(8): 1415–37.

Del Mar, M. and Onazi, O. 2008. 'The Moral Quality of Work: Resisting Complacency'. *International Journal of Law in Context*, 4(4): 352–3.

Douzinas, C. 2000. *The End of Human Rights*. Oxford: Hart Publishing.

Escobar, A. 1995. *Encountering Development: The Making and Unmaking of the Third World*. Princeton, NJ: Princeton University Press.

Freire, P. 1972. *Pedagogy of the Oppressed*. London: Penguin.

Gaita, R.A. 2000. *A Common Humanity: Thinking about Love and Truth and Justice*. London: Routledge.

Hickey, S. and Mohan, G. 2004. *Participation: From Tyranny to Transformation?* New York: Zed Books.

Kapoor, I. 2005. 'Participatory Development: Complicity and Desire'. *Third World Quarterly*, 26(8): 1203–20.

Nussbaum, M. 2011. *Creating Capabilities: The Human Development Approach*. Cambridge, MA: Harvard University Press.

Nussbaum, M. 2006. *Frontiers of Justice: Disability, Nationality, Species-Membership*. Cambridge, MA: Harvard University Press.

Onazi, O. 2012. 'Legal Empowerment of the Poor: Does Political Participation Matter?'. *The Journal Jurisprudence*, 14: 201–44.

Sachs, W. (ed.) 1992. *The Development Dictionary: A Guide to Knowledge as Power*. London: Zed Books.

Sen, A. 1999. *Development as Freedom*. Oxford: Oxford University Press.

Sengupta, A. 2002. 'On the Theory and Practice of the Right to Development'. *Human Rights Quarterly*, 24: 837–9.

Rajagopal, B. 2003. *International Law from Below: Development, Social Movements and Third World Resistance*. Cambridge: Cambridge University Press.

Rittich, K. 2004. 'The Future of Law and Development: Second Generation Reforms and the Incorporation of the Social'. *Michigan Journal of International Law*, 26: 199–243.

Waldron, J. 1988. 'When Justice Replaces Affection: The Need for Rights'. *Harvard Journal of Law and Public Policy*, 11: 625.

Weil, S. 1962. 'Human personality', in *Simone Weil: Selected Essays 1934–1943*, edited by R. Rees. Oxford: Oxford University Press, 9–34.

Weil, S. 2009. *Waiting for God*. New York: Harper Perennial Modern Classics.

PART 4
Judgement

Chapter 13
Analogy and Parable in Legal Reasoning

John Bell

Introduction

The anxiety of the jurist is to come to a just decision in the immediate case, even though he or she knows that he/she has imperfectly thought through the rules that should apply, and their consequences. This chapter suggests that analogy and parable are important ways in which lawyers undertake practical reasoning in such situations of uncertainty.

In his writing, Bańkowski has made much of the place of analogy and parable in both the way that lawyers think and the way the wider community thinks about law. He is concerned that analogy simply leads us to reproduce existing patterns of thought (Bańkowski 2001: 179): 'This is not to say that within the tradition analogy does not produce rich and new solutions. But the solution we go to is one which in a sense we already know' (Bańkowski 2001: 180). By contrast, a parable is there to produce something in the hearts and minds of the listeners; to prepare them for a journey which is itself transformed by their response (Bańkowski 2001: 100–101). So analogy is conservative and parable is radical. Parable is openness, analogy is closure. But we should not be too quick to apply the parable. We need to continue to listen to the story from the inside until we know how it works (Bańkowski 2001: 180–81).

My argument will be that, in lawmaking, both are positive ways of taking the law forward. Both parable and analogy are capable of offering justifications for new rules. They are not just heuristic devices, as some, like Posner, would argue. They show the richness of legal reasoning, which is not confined to deductive reasoning from principle or pragmatic reasoning from consequences. This chapter seeks to show that both are distinctive justifications for decisions, but that judges are institutionally more likely to use analogy.

Everyone accepts that reasoning by analogy is natural among lawyers. But not everyone agrees that analogy offers a justification. My argument will be that analogy serves to provide a limited justification for a decision, and also serves to lend force to the argument that the judge is not engaged in inappropriate lawmaking. Briefly, I shall argue that an analogy offers an argument as to why it is fair to treat the current parties in a particular way, even if no binding rule governs the situation. The analogy also demonstrates that the 'jump' in reasoning that Peczenik (1989: ch. 3) identified is not excessive as a way of developing the law.

Analogy

A good example of reasoning by analogy is Lord Buckmaster's speech in *Donoghue* v. *Stevenson* [1932] AC 561 at 567–71. He searched through a large number of decided cases to see if they would help Mrs Donoghue. I shall group the cases here. First, there were the fraud cases, such as *Langridge* v. *Levy* (1837) 2 M. & W. 519 (1838) 4 M. & W. 337, where a plug in a gun barrel was covered up when sold to the father, and so the son was able to recover for injuries which he sustained when it was used. The second were the consumer cases. In *Longmeid* v. *Holliday* (1851) 6 Ex. 761, a man bought a lamp which was used by his wife and it injured her, but she could not recover in tort. There was no liability for latent defects, merely where there was a dangerous product (as in Langridge). Third, there were the specific ginger beer cases. In *Bates* v. *Batey & Co* [1913] 3 KB 351, the High Court held a manufacturer of ginger beer was not liable to the consumer for an injury caused by the bottle bursting owning to a negligent defect in the manufacture. *Mullin* v. *Barr* 1929 SC 461, the Court of Session found the manufacturer not liable to a consumer for harm caused by a mouse in a ginger beer bottle, and there was no recovery. *George* v. *Skivington* (1869) LR 5 Ex 1 was the exception, in that there was liability by the manufacturer of shampoo when the wife of the purchaser was harmed by it. But he examined the reasoning and found it unconvincing.

So the method is to identify key facts that are similar to the case before us: a non-purchaser suing a manufacturer over harm caused by the contents of a product and alleged lack of care by the manufacturer. The fraud cases lacked this last element, which was sufficient to explain their different outcome. But the consumer cases alleging negligence, and in particular the ginger beer case, nearly all pointed in the same direction of no liability. In this example, a new situation is resolved by looking at non-binding decisions in similar sets of facts and seeing how a new situation can be resolved in a way that is consistent with the established pattern.

But, of course, as we know that this was not the successful use of analogy. Lord Atkin reviewed a number of these cases, but concluded, for example, in relation to one that, 'With all respect I think that the judgements in the case err by seeking to confine the law to rigid and exclusive categories: and by not giving sufficient attention to the general principle which governs the whole law of negligence in the duty owed to those who will be immediately injured by lack of care' ([1932] AC at 594–5). His approach was to appeal to principle and to show that the principle was well-supported by leading dicta, and that the analogous cases had not been properly decided. But, while he needed the argument of principle, he also needed the analogy of the shampoo case, *George* v. *Skivington* and to identify in the other cases a relevant fact (for example, 'lack of intermediate inspection': [1932] AC 584 and 595). Principle alone was not enough.

Taking Lord Atkin's statements as an argument of principle put subsequent English judges into deep water. In the first place, the decision by Lord Wilberforce in *Anns* v. *Merton* [1978] AC 728, 751–2 to treat the dicta as a set of principles generated a good deal of unwanted litigation, especially in the areas of nervous shock, economic loss, and the liability of public authorities. The principle created a presumption in favour of liability from which the courts had to depart explicitly by raising arguments of policy. After much criticism, the approach was reversed in *Caparo* v. *Dickman* [1990] 2AC 605, in which an approach based on proceeding by analogy and incrementally was seen as being preferable to proceeding by way of general principle (see Lord Bridge at [1990] 2 AC 616-8). Lord Atkin's idea of reasonable foreseeability was only one element, alongside proximity and the idea of what is fair, just and reasonable. As Lord Oliver said, rather than proceed on the basis of one general principle, 'the most that can be attempted is a broad categorisation of the decided cases according to the type of situation in which liability has been established in the past in order to found an argument by analogy' [1990] 2 AC at 635. Analogy is preferred to potentially over-inclusive principles. It allows a step-by-step approach in situations where the consequences of a general rule are difficult to predict. Given the limited standing rules that apply in many civil and criminal proceedings, judges cannot easily receive argument on the wide-ranging consequences of particular general rules, and so an incremental approach to decision-making is sensible, and this is what analogy facilitates.

Parable

How does parable work? Bańkowski makes much of New Testament (Jerusalem Bible) parables, such as that of the Good Samaritan (Luke 10: 25–37). But the genre belongs very much to the prophetic tradition, and the most famous legal example concerns King David. David has committed adultery with Bathsheba and covered up her pregnancy by arranging for her husband to be killed in battle. The prophet Nathan comes to David and tells a story:

> There were two men in a certain city, the one rich and the other poor. The rich man had very many flocks and herds; but the poor man had nothing but one little ewe lamb, which he had bought. And he brought it up, and it grew up with him and with his children; it used to eat of his morsel, and drink from his cup, and lie in his bosom, and it was like a daughter to him. Now there came a traveller to the rich man, and he was unwilling to take one of his own flock or herd to prepare for the wayfarer who had come to him, but he took the poor man's lamb, and prepared it for the man who had come to him.
>
> Then David's anger was greatly kindled against the man; and he said to Nathan, 'As the LORD lives, the man who has done this deserves to die; and he shall restore the lamb fourfold, because he did this thing, and because he had no pity.'
>
> Nathan said to David, 'You are the man.' Thus says the LORD, the God of Israel, 'I anointed you king over Israel, and I delivered you out of the hand of Saul; and I gave you your master's house, and your master's wives into your

> bosom, and gave you the house of Israel and of Judah; and if this were too little, I would add to you as much more. Why have you despised the word of the LORD, to do what is evil in his sight? You have smitten Uriah the Hittite with the sword, and have taken his wife to be your wife, and have slain him with the sword of the Ammonites.'(2 Samuel 12: 1–9)

A parable uses a story to enable the hearer to see their present situation in a new light. Like analogy, it uses similarity to draw the hearer in, but is more elusive. This parable encouraged the hearer (David) to develop an analogy with the law on theft (Exodus 22: 1–3). Having been drawn into the story, he is then confronted with its application to himself.

In advocacy, the hypothetical story can draw the hearer into a line of thinking and see a situation differently. The question for me, however, is whether a parable also provides a justification for a legal decision.

Is analogy a satisfactory reason? In the established jurisprudential literature, there are two criticisms of the justificatory force of analogy in law. The first suggests that it does not belong to the realm of justification at all: it is a rhetorical device or, at best, it gets the hearer considering the right way of solving a problem. The second argument is that the force of any justification that uses analogy lies not in the analogy itself, but in the reasons that make the original decision and the present situation similar in the first place – some underlying principle or rule.

Posner (2008: 186) has argued that '[analogy] belongs to legal rhetoric rather than to legal thought'. It is a device to make the hearer think. Its force is to create an environment in which the hearer is more willing to accept the new decision. It is easier to appreciate the force of a rule if one is presented with a concrete application. That is what a previous decision does. It draws the hearer into a world in which his or her previous commitments force him/her to admit the rightness of the proposed decision in the immediate case – 'if you are committed to that outcome, then you have to be committed to this one'.

Even if it is not a purely rhetorical device, others would suggest that it is a device of legal heuristics – pointing the hearer to the place where a proper rule can be found, or the issues about which he or she needs to think. MacCormick (2005: 208–9) argued that analogy, seeing fact patterns, is an important logical step in the process of discovering legal solutions. There is often a dialectic between the process of developing a hypothesis and coming to a decision. The reflection on similarity enables the principle to emerge from the facts of cases. This is a different process from simply identifying a rule and then applying it by deduction to the situation at hand (MacCormick 2005: 209). However, the justification is to lie elsewhere.

In their different ways, Posner and MacCormick argue that the justificatory arguments for decisions based on analogy lie elsewhere. Posner argues that 'analogies cannot resolve legal disputes intelligently' (Posner 2008: 181). In his view, as a justification, reasoning by analogy does not work. In analysing the work of Weinreb, he suggests that a lawyer may well identify a set of fact patterns, but then proceed to ask whether any relevant similarity reflects an underlying rule. In such a case, the justification is actually provided by the underlying rule and not by the analogy (Posner 2008: 183). In the passage that Posner criticizes, Weinreb (2005: ch. 2) discusses the *Adams* v. *New Jersey Steamboat Co.* 45 NE 369 (1896) case at length, where the problem of the liability of a steamboat owner to a passenger robbed while asleep was resolved on analogy with the rule governing innkeepers. At best, Posner (2008: 180–86) suggests, Weinreb is appealing to a rule of a higher level of abstraction that does not distinguish between inns and tugboats. The key problem that he (and Brewer 1996) identifies is the criterion by which a similarity is identified. Analogy does not authenticate itself. Either the similarity is found in an existing rule (in which case that rule decides the case) or one is appealing to a notion of equal treatment (in which case that principle decides the case). As MacCormick (2005: 210–11) put it, 'once [analogy] is placed in a justificatory perspective, there is need for formulation of some principle that captures what the similarity is'. He then continued, 'In considering how arguments can be made to justify a decision, it does seem correct to say that analogies that work as justifications do so because of the way they instantiate the implementation of some general legal principle that covers both (or all) cases' (ibid.: 201). In many ways, MacCormick was wedded to the importance of syllogistic reasoning as a test of justification. Whichever way the principle is discovered – by the interpretation of statutes, examining cases or seeing fact patterns in analogies – the principle is then to be applied deductively to produce the result in the immediate case (see MacCormick 2005: 207–9).

Even those, such as Raz (1979: 203), who favour analogy reasoning, suggest that the justification for seeing a similarity between two situations lies in the rationale that underlies the first rule. Similarly to MacCormick, Raz argues that the justification for the decision in the instant case is the rationale for a previous rule that the analogy has helped us to discover. The analogy itself has some partial force, but is not binding, because there might be incompatible analogies between which the judge has to choose (Raz 1979: 205), as the speeches in Donoghue illustrate very well.

Posner and MacCormick are at root idealists. Posner wants the judge to decide new cases pragmatically by debating the policy implications for the solution to this new case. (By 'pragmatism', Posner means basing decisions on a consideration of consequences, rather than the deduction from previous rule or principles: Posner 2008: 40–41). MacCormick, like Dworkin (1986: 239–50) wants the judge to find some deep principle which rationalizes the solution of this case as well as previously rightly-decided cases. For them, only the policy or the principle will fully justify the solution in this immediate case. Raz perhaps points towards a different approach. He is right that analogy on its own does not provide more than a partial justification. But that does mean that it provides some justification, even if it is incomplete. In the end, the justification has to be completed by a leap of imagination, a choice, which involves human responsibility. In the next section, I shall argue that the distinctive feature of analogy is that it is a form of imperfect justification, but one belonging to the realm of practical reasoning that lawyers inhabit.

Analogy as Imperfect Justification

In my view, it is important to conceive analogy as a reason that is tentative and offers a potentially defeasible justification for a decision on how to deal with a new case. On the one hand, it demonstrates that the decision-maker, judge or legislator, has exercised the power of choice responsibly. By demonstrating similarities with previous cases, he shows that the decision he is taking is not idiosyncratic, but part of the legal tradition. Given the institutional position of the decision-maker, conservatism and consistency are virtues in such a person. Second, analogy offers a justification in its own right that is different from an appeal to the consequences of decisions or to legal principle.

Connectedness as a Justification

Schauer (2009: 98–100) points out the basic difference between precedent and analogy. Precedent is a constraint on an otherwise preferred outcome, or it provides a rule that can be applied deductively to a new situation. Analogy is an expansion of a previous decision based on the judge's choice. Again, he considers analogy to be a method of thinking. In analogy, the reasoning moves from particular to particular by way of an intuition, a mental leap. It differs from precedent or rule-based decision-making, because there is no need to proceed from one particular to another through the mediation of a generalized rule (ibid.). The pattern of analogy suffices to demonstrate the connectedness of the proposed solution to the existing norms of the legal system (ibid.: 101–3). This connectedness provides the justification.

Sunstein (1993: 746) articulates this idea of connectedness as a justification at some length. He argues that 'analogical reasoning has four different but overlapping features: principled consistency; a focus on particulars; incompletely theorised judgements; and principles operating at a low or intermediate level of abstraction'. It is a different way of working compared with the top-down, deductive application of a rule. Analogy is a process, similar to Rawls' 'reflective equilibrium' through which we try to develop considered judgements about the correct way to deal with a new problem (Sunstein 1993: 751–4). As a method of resolving problems, analogy contrasts with a resort to general principles: 'our considered judgements about particular cases have a kind of priority in deciding what the law is or should be … correct answers plausibly consist not of deductions from general theory, but instead of coherent convictions about particular cases' (ibid.: 775-6). The fixed starting points for reasoning are thus the considered judgements we have already reached.

Sunstein's work is a helpful way of understanding not just the method of discovery, which MacCormick identified, but also the character of the justification offered. In analogy, we identify the commitments we have, which are often rather fragmentary. We make considered decisions as and when we need to confront problems. We do not necessarily start with a fully developed set of principles, and even less of rules. As a result, our moral lives and those of our institutions, such as the law, are a mosaic of examples of matters on which we have reached considered judgements, and blanks to be filled in, as it becomes necessary.[1] We try to see patterns in the judgements we have already reached and assess whether these patterns can cover the case in hand.

We can justify working in this way to achieve answers to particular problems, even if we do not search out whether there are general principles we can apply. First, we have limited time and capacity. Dworkin's Hercules is an ideal (Dworkin 1985: 239–50), but we have to deal with the reality of our time and abilities. In practice, we cannot look at the whole canvas and produce a general theory that is fully consistent. We take decisions with adequate, but incomplete, consideration. Second, it is more likely that there will be agreement on the solution to a particular case than there would be to the formulation of a general principle. Rawls acknowledges this with his later development of an 'overlapping consensus'. We may have different world views, but this does not mean there are not significant points on which we do reach agreement. Third, Weinreb (2005: 78) argues that this method allows for moral evolution over time – we do not become locked into a general principle. We know that we have only thought through part of the picture. We may well find that, on reflection and faced with new situations, we are called to revise some of our existing considered judgements. For example, we may once have thought that it would be a good idea that barristers and those involved in the trial process should be immune from suit for professional negligence. But then we think about what they do out of court and we restrict the immunity to what they do in relation to their involvement at trial. But we then cheerfully go on to apply this not only to advocates, but also to expert witnesses (Bell 1983: 56–7). And then we think again about our principles of a fair trial, and perhaps we then do not think the immunity was a good idea in the first place.

This approach may seem to be an apology for not being able to be more intellectually ambitious. But there is a larger idea. Deciding by analogy is a 'second-order' strategy for reaching decisions. Working by analogy enables the decision-

1 Such an analysis applies to many of the Codes common in civil legal systems. They consist of provisions of varying levels of detail: some are general principles and others are very precise rules. As Portalis (1989: 47) said, 'The science of the legislator consists in finding for each matter principles which are most favourable to the common good; the science of the judge is to put these principles into action, to develop their ramifications, to extend them by a wise and reasoned application to individual situations, to study the spirit of the law where the letter kills; and not to run the risk of being from time to time, its slave and its rebel, and to disobey it by a spirit of servility.'

maker to proceed by incremental steps, to examine their consequences, and then to reverse the decision if the consequences prove to be unwelcome (Sunstein and Ullmann-Margalit 1999: 26–7). The strategy of proceeding by limited steps is the alternative to the Herculean project, and is certainly less ambitious (see Bell 1983: 17–20, 226–46).

So the basic argument arising from these authors is that analogy is a defensible form of justification. It privileges previous decisions on concrete situations and incremental development of the law in conditions of uncertainty, in preference to the search for general principles. The anxiety of the jurist is met by encouragement to focus on the task ahead of him/her and leave the formulation of general rules to the future.

Weinreb and the Process of Analogical Reasoning

Weinreb (2005) has produced the most developed recent presentation of this process of reasoning by analogy as a justification for legal decisions; he criticizes the view of Brewer (ibid.: 78) that analogy is deductively unsound, by suggesting that analogy is not about deduction from a higher order principle, and is not designed to generate a rule of general application. The reasoning process is different from any explicit, or even implicit, reasoning from rules. Analogy is reasoning based on experience. Within a context of professional experience, a lawyer is able to produce intuitively a practical solution to a new problem. Weinreb (ibid.: 92) suggests that the lawyer has to narrow the gap between the rule of law and the facts. On the one hand, an attempt is made to produce the application of a rule in ever-decreasing generality, while on the other, analogy serves to strip away the specificity of the particular situation of the case. You then reach a point where the gap between what is known about the rule and what is known about the facts are not so dissimilar that it seems reasonable to make the jump in the imagination to apply the rule to the facts of the case. Analogy provides a lens from which to examine the fact situation in the light of the law. But this analysis shows that the application of the previous decision to the new case is not logically ineluctable. A choice is being made to bridge the gap between the established rules and the facts.

While Weinreb, Sunstein and Schauer defend the rationality and desirability of analogy as a method of decision-making, they pay less attention to the justificatory power of its results. There are two distinct features of justification: formal and substantive. Looking at the form of the decision, we can accept that judges have behaved properly and professionally in reaching their decision if they offer reasons based on analogy, because they are showing a serious effort to find principles within the legal system to support their decisions, but, substantively, we may not be persuaded by the result. Schauer (2009: 94) places the most emphasis on 'fit' – connectedness to previous decisions. It requires a leap of faith to see the consistency, and it is not illogical for observers to say 'I just don't see the connection.' Seeing a pattern is not the same as a syllogism – it does not just require logic, it needs shared imagination. Seeing patterns in which the present case and a previous or hypothetical analogous case are connected requires more of a narrative in which the different features are connected, rather than logical deduction.

The lawyer decides that the appropriate method of solving problems is to proceed incrementally. Unlike applying an established principle deductively to the present case, or identifying one inductively from a number of previous instances, the method requires that the lawyer assembles analogies into patterns and picks the one that is most consistent with his/her experienced judgement about the purpose of the law. This method contrasts with the Dworkinian ideal of Hercules, who tries to produce an argument of principle in favour of the solution to this new case, which fits all the other considered judgements we want to make. It also differs from the Posner method of pragmatism, which looks prospectively at the best outcomes flowing from the decision. Authors favouring analogy prefer to stress the importance of consistency with the past, rather than future welfare.

My Own View

If one develops the idea that analogy is a distinctive form of justification, it is necessary to explain how seeing patterns has justificatory force. My argument would be that the justificatory force of analogy does not lie in the appeal to any underlying (but implicit) rule or policy. That is the point that was being made in *Caparo* v. *Dickman* [1990] 2 AC 605. Appeal to a principle leads to the opening of the floodgates of claims that the courts do not want to satisfy. A more cautious approach was considered to be more satisfactory to resolve the variety of circumstances presented to the court. It is sufficient that the judge argues for a connection between the immediate case and an analogous one, even though he or she does not explain how far the pattern might extend.

The core of the character of analogy is seeing fact patterns. Sunstein (1993: 747, 775) and Weinreb (2005: 78–81) both draw attention to the role of identifying facts and articulating rules at a low level of specificity. As they and Bańkowski (2001: 163) point out, analogy takes the known as a starting point. Provided these existing starting points are not called into question, then analogy works by identifying patterns within the existing law that are capable of covering the situation that has occurred in the present case. Similarity is perceived because a particular focal meaning has been chosen, to which everything else is related. This is what Tracey (1981: 423) calls 'relative adequacy' – the connection between two items is adequate within the context of a particular focal meaning. Thus 'analogy is a language of ordered relationships articulating similarity-in-difference. The order among the relationships is constituted by the distinct but similar relationships of each analogue to some primary focal meaning, some prime analogue' (Tracey 1981: 408).

Bańkowski (2001: 179) argues that we find patterns by imposing on the picture 'a template to which everything else conforms'. I don't think analogy works in quite that way. The approach is more inductive than deductive. It is much more like seeing patterns in coloured glass. You are identifying something that was not intentional, but that emerges and makes sense of the present configuration of light shining through the individual fragments of glass. Those fragments may have been put together with one particular intention in mind, but the onlooker sees in them something different. Rather as Sunstein (1993: 776–8) suggests, analogy is a rational source of justification that does not need to pass through the intermediate stage of a generalization. At some later point, we may want to generalize, but not immediately. We don't need to produce a generalization now in order to make a rationally justified decision.

There is a similarity between this account of the logic of analogy and the account that Wittgenstein (1953: paras 179–80) gives of understanding. He offers the example of someone continuing a series of numbers. the person shows that he or she understands what is expected by giving the next number, not by articulating (or even being able to articulate) the rule. I show I have learnt a language by speaking words correctly in appropriate places, not by explaining the rules of grammar that underlie my usage. When you know a language well enough, you know how to use the right word, even though the grammar rule may be complex or may be an exception. You know that to say 'eat of this bread' is not English, even if that grammatical construction is perfectly normal in French, Italian, Dutch, German and Latin. On the other hand, to use the subjective 'Be that as it may be...' is correct, but unusual. Think about telling a non-native speaker about when to use 'thus' and when to use 'therefore' in a sentence. Experience helps us find the right words. There may well not be a book like *Hart's Rules* (Ritter 2005), which sets out what is 'correct' usage, but an experienced user of English knows what sounds right. In the same way, experience in the law enables us to make a sensible judgement about how to continue the pattern of the law. As Weinreb (2005: 132, 137–8) suggests, we are dealing with a professional intuition, based on training and experience. The context for analogy as a justification is the legal community, what good lawyers find acceptable.

In such a situation, the justification proffered by the judge is not conformity to an existing rule or principle. The immediate case does not fit exactly under the rule as established in the precedent case. Rather, the justification for the decision in the immediate case is in equal treatment – like cases should be decided alike. The analogical argument is that, since we have found liability in situation A, we ought also to find liability in case B, since the two are sufficiently similar, even if not exactly the same. This is not a binding rule, but it creates a strong argument that is only defeasible in limited circumstances. Waldron (2010: 114) calls this the 'bottom-up demand for consistency'. Equal treatment is not confined to simply giving the same treatment in similar cases. It involves a margin of discretion to make adaptations. If I am treating my children equally, I do not necessarily give them all exactly the same. For example, if one likes beetroot and another courgette, then when I am serving vegetables, I show equal favouritism by giving to each of them a larger portion than the other of the vegetable they like. Equal treatment requires respect for difference, as well as for similarity. This is not a binding argument, but one that has a strong persuasive authority among those who have similar experience.

So how do we perceive 'similarity'? Wittgenstein usefully explained that similarity does not mean that there are some features that are identical in every case. He used the term 'family resemblance' (Wittgenstein 1953: para. 67) to suggest that we look for traits that recur, but are not found in every case in exactly the same combination. Finding adequate similarity in analogy works in much the same way. The judge points to some common features within the pattern of features that makes the immediate and previous situation similar.

In what way does this argument differ from pragmatism? Pragmatism, as explained by Posner (2008: 40–41) is essentially forward-looking. In new cases, we decide on the basis of what will produce the best results in the future. By contrast, analogy shares with principle and precedent a desire to be consistent with what has been done in the past. That is the appeal of equal treatment. Sometimes, judges talk about making decisions 'pragmatically' on a 'case-by-case' basis, but that simply means that they are not wanting to develop a general principle at this stage, as was shown by Lord Oliver in *Caparo* [1990] 2 AC at 635.

Bańkowski (2001: 179–80) objects that this is inherently conservative. It is an illustration of 'path dependency' in legal development. My view would be that analogy and re-interpretation go hand in hand. It is possible to use analogy to expand the range of solutions. On the whole, there is not much difference in practice between legislators and judges in dealing with new situations (Raz 1979: 199); both need to rely on analogy, even if legislators have more formal freedom of decision. Take the problem at the beginning of the twentieth century with motor cars (see Ibbetson and Bell 2012) – the newly invented machine that was causing deaths across Europe. Analogy was used to develop rules to deal with the question of how to compensate through tort law the victims of accidents caused by the motor car. Cars travelled fast and caused accidents often because of malfunction in the complex mechanism of the vehicle, which drivers did not fully understand and so they had difficulty in preventing accidents. The potential focal cases in the existing law were liability for animals or liability for railway engines and steam traction engines. The problem with liability for animals was that it depended on the dangerousness of the animal and, in any case, it was not in use for normal accidents caused by the horse and cart, or horse and carriage, driven by a coachman. Accidents caused by a horse-drawn vehicle gave rise to liability on the basis of the fault of the driver or the vicarious liability of the owner in all systems, so it was difficult to use the liability for dangerous animals to provide compensation without the victim having to prove the fault of the driver in relation to motorized vehicles. That left the analogy of railway accidents. The problems of the difficulties of proof in relation to complex and fast machines had arisen in relation to railway engines and to steam-powered traction engines. In Germany, the Imperial Liability Act of 1871 created liability without fault on the part of the operator of a train, unless the harm was the result of an external cause to the operation of railways. The 1909 German law on motor vehicles imposed liability on the 'custodian' of a vehicle unless it resulted from 'inevitable accident'. This was a kind of legislative analogy in which the earlier law was used as a benchmark for the fairness of an adaptation to suit the needs of roads. The Road Traffic Law was not a carbon copy of the existing law governing railway engines, but the latter was a benchmark. In France, after many years of hesitation and diverging views in other systems applying the same civil Code, such as Belgium and Luxembourg, the Cour de cassation in 1896 decided that art. 1384, para. 1 (liability of a keeper for things in his/her custody) constituted an independent ground of liability compared with fault under arts. 1382 and 1383. Decided in relation to steam boilers (which also powered trains), it initially created a strong presumption of fault. Initially, the courts applied the analogy of animals and were only prepared to find the driver liable in case of fault proved by the victim (Ibbetson and Bell 2012: 118). But the law was changed in 1924, when the analogy of trains was preferred. Finally, in 1930, at the end of a line of cases it was decided how to treat motor vehicle accidents. In essence, the law had to decide whether to treat the accident as an act of a person (the driver), in which case fault applied, or as the act of a thing, the vehicle. Having shifted the paradigm in this way, the judges then decided on no-fault liability for all the cases, rather than a presumption of fault. So we have here analogy, a benchmark in the treatment of steam-powered boats and trains, and then a judicial decision that the analogy lay here, rather than with animals ridden by men or women. In English law, liability for railway accidents had been decided by negligence. After some hesitation, this was applied to the motor car, especially when the legislator refused to impose a stricter form of liability.

Two points follow. First, that analogy is typically an intra-systemic argument. If the analogue is within one's own system, that shows a strong degree of commitment to the rightness of that solution. Consistency with other legal systems is a weaker argument, because it may be more arguable (certainly from the point of view of authority reasons) whether the previous solution in the other system is actually correct. This helps to explain why there may be different solutions to similar problems between different legal systems. One analogy may work well within one particular legal system, yet fail miserably in another. Second, the argument from analogy is not confined to the judge. The arguments in the German legislature on the 1909 Motor Vehicle Law appealed to the legislation already in place for railways in much the same way that the French and English used the case-law analogies. Analogy is a way of coping with new problems. Rather than invent a completely new rule, the law-maker proceeds incrementally, with the knowledge that the steps are more reversible.

Parable

In classical Greek rhetoric, parable is similar to analogy, but its force is less immediate. Whereas an analogy acts as a form of proof (by way of an example, rather than a rule), a parable is merely suggestive of a solution (Schittko 2003: 35). There is often a poetic quality to the style of parable, whereas analogy is typically focused on real-life examples or hypothetical situations (Schittko 2003: 36). The Jewish use of parable is broader and covers a number of rhetorical devices such as allegory and simile (Jeremias 1972: 20). Explained in this way, there is a connection between analogy and parable. Both analogy and parable use illustrative examples to highlight what is normatively required, but without closing off the scope of the norm by stating a rule or providing a definition. Both are avowedly incomplete normative statements. Analogy provides a reason for doing the same as in a focal case. Parable is more suggestive. Jesus's instruction, 'Go and do likewise', to the addressee of the Good Samaritan parable in Luke 10:37 is not a call to do the same thing as the Samaritan – that is, specifically to help the victims of robbery or of criminal acts – but to treat no one as being beyond the range of loving service (Jeremias 1972: 205). Rather than state a confining rule or definition of 'neighbour', as the scribe requests, Jesus provides a startling example and leaves the scribe to work out what that means for his own life.

In what way is parable part of the repertoire of the lawyer? If parable is essentially prophetic, where the importance lies in the lesson and not in the details, but in the sense of direction to which it points the hearer, then how far does it belong to a judicial process in which the lawyer is trying to persuade a court to reach a decision in a concrete case? If the strength of analogy lies in an appeal to existing commitments, then it is strongest when it relies on actual decided cases, because in such cases commitments have been made. By contrast, a parable is a simile from a hypothetical case. Judicial use of hypothetical cases tends to be about points of detail. Take Bankes LJ in *Hambrook* v. *Stokes* [1925] 1 KB 141 at 151. The case was about a mother who suffered nervous shock in seeing a lorry swerving erratically around a bend where her daughter and friends were walking on their way to school. Previous judicial authorities established that a driver of a vehicle would be liable for nervous shock caused to a person who feared for her own life. In *Hambrook*, Bankes LJ tells the story of two mothers, each holding a small child by the hand as a lorry comes thundering down the road. The courageous mother is terrified, but is devoted to her child and thinks only of its welfare. The timid mother is also terrified. But she lacks motherly instinct and only thinks of damage to herself. The health of both mothers is seriously affected by the mental shock caused by this fright. 'Will the law,' asks Bankes LJ, 'recognise a cause of action in the case of the less deserving mother, and none in the case of the more deserving one?' Bankes provides his own answer 'I think not', but he could have left it hanging. The purpose of the parable is to encourage a rethink. The parable moves the argument forward, but does not prescribe a solution. It helps the lawyer to move beyond what was thought possible. The next stage is for the lawyer hearing the parable to work out what would be a satisfactory rule for deciding such cases. We may no longer believe that the rule about the victims of nervous shock who can claim tort compensation should be confined to those who fear for their own life, but the parable does not lead us to a specific delimitation of those people who may recover when their fear is for the lives of others.

Like the prophet Nathan, Bankes LJ provokes a rethink. But located within a judgement, he cannot leave the ending hanging for the audience to answer, and must find an answer for himself. While this parable serves as a thought experiment, it does not work in exactly the same way as the prophet Nathan. Nathan and Jesus in his parables are often able to get the hearer to provide the punchline, which is far more persuasive than Bankes LJ. It also allows the hearer to provide the solution. But the judge is not a prophet, he or she is a decision-maker. The institutional position of the prophet allows him to call attention to a situation, but not necessarily provide the answer. The parable can serve a purely hortatory function (Jeremias 1972: 43). The prophet is essentially a troublemaker. The judge has to make a decision, and so the parable is then followed up by other reasons why a specific rule deals with the case in hand. The parable is an important, but incomplete, step in the argument about what is the right answer to the immediate case.

Conclusion

Precedent, analogy and parable are three distinct forms of legal justification. A precedent sets out a rule or principle that is to be applied to the immediate case. The legal debate will either be about whether it is indeed an authoritative precedent, or about whether its scope applies to the immediate case. An analogy takes a decided commitment (often an actual decision in a previous case) and seeks to reach a similar outcome in a case which lies outside the rule applied in the previous case. It does not state a complete rule under which both the previous and the present case fall. It is not restating the rule in the precedent case in order to extend its scope. Rather it identifies a relevant similarity that is sufficient to prove a good connection between the previous and immediate cases that the principle 'like cases should be decided alike' justifies a similar outcome in the two cases. A parable is a story within which a hypothetical case is used to challenge the formulation of a rule and to suggest a direction in which the solution to an immediate case may be found within the law. While a precedent provides a fully articulated justification, analogy and parable do not.

Bańkowski's anxiety in *Living Lawfully* was how to hold together attention to the particular and commitment to rules (see Bańkowski 2001: 159–74). He sees in the stories used in analogy and parable ways of going beyond what we know through existing rules and commitments. This chapter has tried to take that insight. Whereas Bańkowski was not sure that analogy would provide a justification of going beyond the existing rules, I have endeavoured to show that it does offer a valid practice of justification in taking the law forward. Bańkowski is right, that analogy is limited and thus conservative.

Parable and analogy provide partial justifications for decisions by making it reasonable to move from one particular to another without necessarily using the intermediary of a generalization, a general rule or principle. In some cases, lawyers dealing with a new situation will feel able to enunciate a general rule. More commonly, they proceed incrementally, by analogy, and see if they like the result. This was seen in relation to motor cars, where a number of analogies were tried before a convincing one seemed to offer a good solution, and then later a principle was formulated. In this way, attention to the particular can be retained as the law is developed. Parable and analogy rely for their force on the insight they offer to patterns within the law, which the experienced legal professional will recognize. Incrementalism is an appropriate way of developing the law. In such a context, analogy offers an adequate justification for the decision in the immediate case, even if it fails to articulate the full picture of the law. Parable, by contrast, provides a partial justification. It offers a critique of potential lines of legal argument and identifies a direction of travel on the legal journey, but does not identify a particular outcome. The injunction 'go and do likewise' requires the hearer to translate the insight into a reason for action in the immediate case.

Bibliography

Bańkowski, Z. 2001. *Living Lawfully*. Dordrecht: Kluwer.

Bell, J. 1983. *Policy Arguments in Judicial Decisions*. Oxford: Oxford University Press.

Brewer, S. 1996. 'Exemplary Reasoning: Semantics, Pragmatics, and the Rational Force of Legal Argument by Analogy'. *Harvard Law Review*, 109: 923–1028.

Dworkin, R.M. 1986. *Law's Empire*. London: Fontana.

Ibbetson, D. and Bell, J. 2012. *European Legal Development: The Case of Tort*. Cambridge: Cambridge University Press.

Jeremias, J. 1972. *The Parables of Jesus* 3rd revd edn. London: SCM Press.

MacCormick, N. 2005. *Rhetoric and the Rule of Law*. Oxford: Oxford University Press.

Peczenik, A. 1989. *On Law and Reason*. Dordrecht: Kluwer.

Portalis, J.-E.-M. 1989. 'Discours préliminaire sur le projet de Code civil'. In F. Ewald (ed.), *Naissance du Code civil*. Paris: Flammarion, 1–62.

Posner, R.A. 2008. *How Judges Think*. Cambridge, MA: Harvard University Press.

Raz, J. 1979. *The Authority of Law*. Oxford: Oxford University Press.

Ritter, R.M. 2005. *The New Hart's Rules: The Handbook of Style for Writers and Editors*. Oxford: Oxford University Press.

Schauer, F. 2009. *Thinking Like a Lawyer*. Cambridge, MA: Harvard University Press.

Schittko, M.P. 2003. *Analogien als Argumentationstyp. Vom Paradeigma zur Similitudo*. Göttingen: Vandenhoeck & Ruprecht.
Sunstein, C. 1993. 'On Analogical Reasoning'. *Harvard Law Review*, 106: 724–91.
Sunstein, C. and Ullmann-Margalit, E. 1999. 'Second-Order Decisions'. *Ethics*, 110: 5–31.
Tracey, D. 1981. *The Analogical Imagination*. New York: Crossroad.
Waldron, J. 2010. 'Treating Like Cases Alike in the World: The Theoretical Bias of the Demand for Legal Unity'. In S. Muller and S. Richards (eds), *Highest Courts and Globalisation*. The Hague: Hague Academic Press.
Weinreb, L.L. 2005. *Legal Reason: The Use of Analogy in Legal Argument*. New York: Cambridge University Press.
Wittgenstein, L., 1953. *Philosophical Investigations*, trans. G.E.M Anscombe. Oxford: Basil Blackwell.

Chapter 14

'Holding the Middle', or 'Dancing on the Edge ...'?

James MacLean

> Well did Aristotle say that virtues in contrast to vices are judicious means between contrary extremes. But the principle holds much more generally than even Aristotle saw ... [B]eauty and all aesthetic value ... 'lies between the fatal extremes of mechanism and chaos'.
>
> Charles Hartshorne (1987: 1)

> Then mark me now; for you stand on a razor's edge.
>
> Sophocles (1974: 152)

Introduction

In the vast literature that surrounds Sophocles' *Antigone*,[1] much has been made of the presence and significance of opposing principles, and how these are embedded and embodied in the clash of personalities that engages the play's two principal characters. Ari Hirvonen, for example, remarks on how the play insists repeatedly on posing the oppositions between Creon and Antigone not simply as differences between male and female but as fundamental oppositions between public and private, state and family, rules and principles, enactment and tradition, reason and emotion, rationality and irrationality, kings' rights and divine rights, and so on, embodied in and between these personalities:

> On the basis of this reading of *Antigone*, I can now construct a system of binary oppositions, where one term is superior and the other inferior. These terms also

1 *Antigone* begins at the point where *Oedipus at Colonus* ends. Following the death of their father, Oedipus, Antigone and her sister Ismene return to Thebes in an effort to prevent the fulfilment of the prophecy predicting that their two brothers, Eteocles and Polyneices, will kill each other in battle. However, on arriving in Thebes, Antigone learns that both her brothers are already dead and, while Eteocles has been given a proper burial, her uncle, Creon, now King of Thebes, has issued a royal edict banning the burial of Polyneices, whom he considers to have been a traitor. In defiance, Antigone buries Polyneices, but is caught. Sentenced by Creon to be walled up inside a cave for ever, she takes her own life. Not realizing that Antigone has killed herself, Haemon, son of Creon and Antigone's fiancé, pleads for her release. Creon relents, but too late and, when Antigone is found hanged in her jail cell, Haemon, filled with despair, kills himself. Eurydice, Creon's wife, takes her own life and Creon is left alone to reflect on his sorrow and loss.

> seem to have a life of their own. They exclude each other reciprocally. The one is nothing more than a negation of the other. One can see the … dichotomy which goes through *Antigone* (and perhaps through Antigone). (Hirvonen 1997: 245)

However, Zenon Bańkowski (2001: 27), on his reading of the play, argues that the central importance of *Antigone* lies not so much in its presentation of incommensurable values, but in the different ways that the main protagonists have 'structured their world [to] avoid tragedy'. This is the real tragedy of *Antigone*, witnessed in the face of a juxtaposition of extremes that appear to exclude each other: 'Creon sets the laws of the state and acts in thrall to them. Antigone … applies, as rigidly, the law of the gods … [T]heir autonomy is merely the heteronomous thrall to their obsession' (ibid.: 33). Each 'draw[s] a line, one round the city and [the other] round the family' (ibid.: 31) and, in so doing, both 'run away from the tension and anxiety of the middle' (2000: 36). While the play has often been read as a clash of opposites in precisely the way that Hirvonen suggests, none the less, for Bańkowski (2001: 34), the more important question is how we deal with this:

> It is not a matter of choosing one against the other but rather what weight to give to them in any particular circumstance … These principles are to be viewed as being held in tension rather than as something we have to choose between. My point is not only that we are not forced to choose one or the other. I want to claim that both are necessary.

What emerges from this contrast, according to Bańkowski, is a distinction between two different ways of reading *Antigone*; from one perspective, 'a dichotomous mode of thinking based on the polarization of seemingly opposite principles'; from the other, 'a recognition of the interdependence and mutually constitutive existence of … opposing terms [that] goes on to explore a new construction of the space within and between' (2000: 34). For Bańkowski, the significance of *Antigone*, in terms of decision-making, lies in what it teaches us about learning how to inhabit this necessary 'space in which two terms co-exist with paradox but without logical contradiction' (2000: 35). Instead of trying to theorize it away through false dichotomies between the universal and the particular, we need to embrace 'a difficult and messy choice … because the distinctions run across each other and we have to hold them in a necessary and inevitable tension' (2001: 41).

In what follows I want to pick up on several strands of thought that Bańkowski uses in his discussion of this play and discuss them, as he does, in terms of their theoretical and practical significance for the context of law. I shall focus, in particular, on his rejection of a dichotomous mode of thinking, and his subsequent identification of 'the middle' as the true space in which authentic deliberation for decision-making takes place. Explicating this notion of the middle in terms of the meaning structure of 'process' thought, I shall demonstrate how Bańkowski's argument returns strong echoes from a number of philosophers within this tradition – notably Alfred North Whitehead, Henri Bergson, Gilles Deleuze and Michael

Polanyi – and that recourse to this tradition helps to provide significant theoretical underpinning for Bańkowski's characterization of the middle as a place where creativity and novelty are always present, infused into every decision-making moment.[2]

Theorizing the Middle: Understanding Process

> What really exists is not things made but things in the making. Once made, they are dead, and an infinite number of alternative conceptual decompositions can be used in defining them. But put yourself in the making by a stroke of intuitive sympathy with the thing and, the whole range of possible decompositions coming into your possession, you are no longer troubled with the question which of them is the more absolutely true. Reality falls in passing into conceptual analysis; it mounts in living its own undivided life – it buds and burgeons, changes and creates. (James 2007: 263–4)

Process thought is founded on a general theory of relatedness. With its roots in the tales of the pre-Socratic Greek philosopher Heraclitus, it stands in contrast to the Parmeneidean-inspired teachings of Democritus, which contend that the ultimate building blocks of reality are essentially atomic entities whose relative motions and relationships to each other are regulated and can be apprehended though the use of general predictable laws. On a process account, what is present derives its existence from the historicity of past events, from what is embedded inescapably within them; therefore we are concerned primarily with questions of emergence (becoming), and only secondarily with questions of substance (being). Perhaps the most succinct formulation of Whitehead's process philosophy is captured in his assertion that '[t] he creative advance of the world is the becoming, the perishing, and the objective immortalities of those things which jointly constitute stubborn fact' (1978: xiv). Reality is this process of creative advance whereby many past events are integrated in the events of the present and, in turn, are taken up by future events.[3]

The central concept of Whitehead's philosophy is that *all things change*. The only things that are real are momentary units of becoming, actual occasions of experience (wafer-thin slices of time), not bits of material substance. Each actual occasion consists of three phases: the first phase, which takes place at an actual occasion's physical pole, consists in the passive reception of data from its antecedent past, from its immediately prior moment of experience; the second phase, which takes place at the mental pole, consists in the entertainment of novel possibilities; and the third phase involves the reconciliation of the other two phases, where the

2 Situating Bańkowski's argument within a process-theoretical framework and reading it from this perspective also provides a means through which to address and reconcile the differences between our two positions, noted in MacLean (2011).

3 For a summary of the Whiteheadian position, see MacLean (2011: 49–63).

desire to conform to and thus perpetuate the past is reconciled with the desire to achieve new possibilities. Here, the occasion assumes a definite form: each actual occasion must choose, in each instant of becoming, what it will become. Collectively, Whitehead terms these three phases the process of *concrescence* of an actual occasion of experience. The tension between the mental and physical poles in the phases of concrescence of an actual occasion of experience is really a tension between conformity to the past and openness to or creativity in the future, a tension between order and chaos; thus the reconciliation of these in the third phase is a reconciliation between the order represented by conformation of the present occasion of experience to its prior occasions and the chaos involved in taking a leap towards an unknown possibility different from, and not given in, the order of prior occasions. The reconciliation of these is a reconciliation of contrasting feelings, between the known and the unknown, between order and discord. Each actual occasion of experience must reconcile these, resolve the discord and contrast and make a decision *for itself* about what *it* will become.

Understood thus, process thought can be seen to emphasize the developmental nature of reality, becoming rather than merely being. Being is the outcome of each process of becoming, the result of the perishing of each actual occasion of experience as it passes from subjectivity into objectivity and the next stage of becoming begins. Each actual occasion of experience is thus both the actual outcome of a particular process of becoming and a potential datum for new processes of becoming with novel and creative outcomes. As Whitehead puts it: 'This is the doctrine of the creative advance whereby it belongs to the essence of the universe, that it passes into a future' (1938: 206–7).

Like Whitehead, Bergson also contends that reality is not made up of distinct things or substances but of thoughts, feelings and impressions arrested from primary process.[4] However, while both testify to the fact that life is continuous and evolving, for ever changing, creating and recreating, Bergson argues that the act of arresting actual occasions from the ceaseless flow and flux of reality, whereby we try to make sense of real life, is a counterfeit motion and one that can only at best approximate life's real experiences. He identifies two ways of thinking, according to which we apprehend concrete reality; that is, two types of knowledge (epistemological and ontological). The first he denotes as 'intellect' methods

4 Whitehead associates the discovery of some of his most famous 'fallacies' with ideas derived from Bergsonian 'spatialization'; in particular, the 'fallacy of simple location', which is a version of the 'fallacy of misplaced concreteness'. Common to all forms of the fallacy of misplaced concreteness is the 'error of mistaking the abstract for the concrete' (Whitehead 1943: 64); that is, of assuming that an abstraction from concrete reality is in fact its totality. In relation to our present discussion, this appears as the assumption that the true nature of reality is apprehended in terms of its composition as material substance. For matter to be 'simply located' would require that we could properly state it to be precisely *here* and *now*, spatially and temporally, in such a way that necessitated no essential reference of its relation to any other region of space or duration of time (ibid.: 62).

whereby we capture the world in substantial terms but do not fully engage with its reality as a continuous flow. The second, 'intuition', denotes a method by which we actually place ourselves directly within the current of something real and live within its flow, identifying with it. Here, in contrast to the static conceptual abstractions and formulations associated with traditional logic, reality is understood to be essentially fluid and changing. Even so, neither view is sufficient by itself: life is grasped and understood not simply in one or the another way but through the act of infusing the intellect with intuition so that each permeates but is not reduced to the other. Bergson (1983: 302) is extremely critical of those intellectual moves by which we attempt to grasp and represent our experience of, for example, time in spatial terms, confusing immobility and real movement, and mistaking one for the other. Time is not merely a conceptual abstraction but the condition of authentic experience. Our notions of time whereby we envisage it as a movement from position A through position B to position C, and so on, only confuse 'clock time' with 'real time' in an effort to provide expression for our general sense of the world as concrete. Such methods of 'simple location' must instead give way to an understanding of the true nature of reality as a continuous flux, so that we begin to understand mobility, not immobility, as being the actual and true nature of reality (1983: 237).

Deleuze, too, understands the movement of becoming as a continuous process, a dynamic, internal, immanent force that pulls in both past and future directions simultaneously, thus generating sensation and intensity. With Félix Guattari (1987), he offers a description of this movement of becoming as 'rhizomatic', drawing attention to the nature of its combinations as 'interkingdoms, unnatural participations'. In other words, they are 'neither genetic nor structural' (ibid.: 267), but are 'multiplicities', 'agglomerations', 'assemblages' of heterogeneous singularities in dynamic compositions. From this basis, Deleuze and Guattari argue that becoming is always in the 'middle', an 'in-between' (1987: 323). Becoming is not about beginnings, progressions and ends, but about lines and intensities: 'we are not interested in characteristics; what interests us are modes of expansion, propagation, occupation, contagion, peopling' (ibid.: 264). Its 'points, places and functions, positions and differential thresholds' (Deleuze 1994: 258), exist as an 'internal qualitative impression endowed with a certain weight' (ibid.: 91), a 'vertiginous movement endowed with a force ... which selects ... expels as well as creates, destroys as well as produces' (ibid.: 12).

What best describes this immanent force is its autonomy: it is entirely self-sufficient. Movement, change and relationality all take place internally, establishing immediately *differences* and *becomings*. Being is the being of becoming, the repetition of difference, the differentiation of difference, the processing of difference in itself. Yet difference is not a difference from something else, and repetition is not the recurrence of the same but rather recurrence of pure difference in itself, without the need to posit an origin. Freed, in this way, from any sense of mere recurrence of the same, repetition is understood as a transforming, creative and productive activity.

To summarize, according to process thinkers such as Whitehead and Bergson, our sensual perception of reality, our direct experience of it, is an undivided whole that cannot be broken up or segmented into different constituent parts without some form of interaction between our physical feelings and our mental valuations. For Deleuze, too, experience is divisible but undivided. It is rendered meaningful not through the act of grounding empirical particulars in abstract universals but through an encounter in which something given to us in experience compels us to think and to carve out novel concepts to make sense of our singular experiences and to verify that sense.

Between Extremes of Order and Chaos: Unity-in-Diversity

> From the falsity of the two extremes … it does not follow that there is no truth lying between them. (Hartshorne 1987: 5)

> Beauty is the mutual adaptation of the several factors in an occasion of experience.(Whitehead 1933: 324)

Let us consider for a moment, the question of what it is that makes an experience valuable in and of itself. According to Whitehead, 'the perfection of Beauty is the perfection of Harmony' (1933: 325) but harmony, while necessary, is not a sufficient condition for beauty: there must also be intensity of experience. An example may help to clarify this. Luskentyre Bay, situated on the wild Atlantic coast of the island of Harris in the Western Isles of Scotland, is a beautiful place. Several miles of pure white sand curve gently into a bay before sweeping out round a grassy headland. It is a place where the sights and sounds of wind and wave, the colour and movement of grass, sand and sea, the taste and touch of pure, salt sea air combine to produce an unrivalled sensual experience: ear and eye, nose, mouth and face are all stimulated together. Out on the water, the sun's reflections are carried effortlessly from one wave into the next as each, in endless succession, is pulled in towards the shore before crashing on the sand. And in the midst of this continuous movement, to and fro, of the forces of creation, something mysterious happens: a calm, a perfect stillness. Between these two extremes of order and chaos silence emerges and a space is constructed that expands and grows. Patterns emerge, of waves and silences all together, producing new and different contrasts. Every silence seems to indicate a break, yet there are no breaks: no beginnings and no ends; just one continuous process in the midst of which is a silence, long and pronounced.

Intensity depends on contrast, the extent to which *diversity* is integrated into experience: 'Beauty in the emphatic sense is a *balance* of unity and variety' (Hartshorne 1970: 304). It is this notion of preserving the contrast between unity and plurality, and avoiding extremes, that underpins our inquiry here. Yet how do we begin, and where ought we to begin, in relating this to our present discussion?

From a process perspective, much depends on the two widely divergent ways of thinking that Bergson notes in relation to time. Conceived spatio-temporally, time fragments reality into separate parts so that what we experience is a mass of discrete, bounded and distinct but connectable, elements. This is the perspective we engage when, as it were, we step outside of the flow of experience and re-direct our attention back to it. Understood alternatively, in terms of pure duration, time is experienced as 'a succession of qualitative changes, which melt into and permeate one another ... without any tendency to externalize themselves in relation to one another' (Bergson 2005: 104). Here, there is no possibility of stepping outside of time and reflecting back on it, but the meaningful experience is a living one: 'Intelligence ordinarily starts from the immobile, and reconstructs movement as best it can with immobilities in juxtaposition. Intuition starts from movement, posits it, or rather perceives it as reality itself, and sees in immobility only an abstract moment, a snapshot taken by our mind, of a mobility' (Bergson 1992: 34).

The implication of these two types of thinking is that there are two ways of producing knowledge, each of which maps on to the distinctions identified earlier in terms of the reading of *Antigone*: the first is premised on the idea that our attention to the particularities of lived experience takes place objectively and retrospectively (Hirvonen); the second suggests that we engage intuitively through a kind of intellectual sympathy whereby we place ourselves within the stream of experience and apprehend its living reality as a continually changing process (Bańkowski). We can also see how they are related. Our experience of reality and our awareness of 'things' as apprehended and individuated through intelligence is based on an originary continuum but, as soon as structure is imposed on it, this ceaselessly flowing reality is halted and captured immediately within a series of 'snapshots' whose relative motions in relation to each other can be calculated and controlled. The point that Bergson makes is that it does not matter how many of these 'snapshots' we make, or how well we set them alongside each other, we can never fully reconstruct the reality of lived experience: 'reality appears as a ceaseless up springing of something new, which has no sooner arisen to make the present than it has already fallen back into the past; at this exact moment it falls under the glance of the intellect' (1983: 47).

This difference, between our experience of things grasped intellectually and living experience grasped intuitively, is also a distinction that we can map as the difference between concrete and real knowledge.[5] Paradoxically, real knowledge must be apprehended under the terms and appearances of concrete knowledge, to be known and experienced as actual, but concrete knowledge can never be real since it is only ever a perspective on reality, an apprehending of real knowledge in terms of its concrete appearance. Thus there is always more in the real than can be apprehended through concrete appearance, however well that is reconstructed

5 The former is defined spatio-temporally in terms of order, sequence, discontinuity, external relatedness; the latter as pure duration, in terms of interrelatedness, continuity, fusion, heterogeneity.

and represented. Deleuze (1991: 42–3) goes even further and suggests that we understand the real only through the movement of its realization; that is, as inseparable from it. It is only in our own attempts to know that we find ourselves in the real. We cannot know it apart from the way it is realized; therefore, to experience movement qualitatively we must place ourselves within the continuity of its unfolding. Understood in this way, knowledge should not be conceived as a co-ordinated movement between different points along a spatial trajectory: 'A becoming is neither one nor two, nor the relation of the two; it is the in-between … [I]t constitutes a zone of proximity and indiscernability … a non-localizable relation sweeping up the two distant or contiguous points, carrying one into the proximity of the other' (Deleuze and Guattari 1987: 323–4).

Deleuze and Guattari employ the notion of 'creative involution' to point to the possibilities they recognize here for what they term transversal or rhizomatic connections across boundaries. Involution describes a creative process whose field of production does not depend on differentiation but involves dissolution of form: a rich field of creative heterogeneous activity that generates differentiation by cutting across supposed boundaries. Such aggregations or assemblages can be conceived as 'rhizomic' webs (ibid.: 27–8):

> A rhizome has no beginning or end; it is always in the middle, between things, interbeing, *intermezzo* … The middle is by no means an average; on the contrary, it is where things pick up speed. *Between* things does not designate a localizable relation going from one thing to the other and back again, but a perpendicular direction, a transversal movement that sweeps one *and* the other away, a stream without beginning or end that undermines its banks and picks up speed in the middle.

What I want to suggest, then, is that all of this philosophical underpinning provides a solid conceptual and practical basis for widening and deepening our understanding of Bańkowski's depiction of the middle as the genuine locus for authentic deliberation in law. Whitehead's thoughts on the true nature of reality as continuous process and the link between this idea of process and the Bergsonian understanding of time, Bergson's own distinction between intellect and intuition and the relations between these in terms of apprehending reality, and Deleuze's philosophical explorations of the creative space of the middle, the in-between, explored in terms of the rhizomic metaphor, all help to provide further assistance for understanding precisely what Bańkowski has in mind when he talks of legal decision-making as 'holding the middle'. All of this might also be seen legitimately to underpin his suggestion that judges must 'pay attention' to the story, by stepping into it and identifying themselves with it. Understood thus, the middle emerges as a place that harbours significant potential for the sort of jumbling up, mixing and scrambling of otherwise taken-for-granted genealogical linkages to which Bańkowski may be seen to allude, delivering instead possibilities for heterogeneous assemblages that will not only confound but also negate, contradict and deny law's closed thresholds, cutting across and beneath its assignable relations and opening a way for the emergence of the creatively new.

Explicating the Middle

> The agony of authorship is to remain with anxiety of beginning and equivocation of the ethical ... Because the middle cannot be mended, because no politics or knowledge may be available or employable, it does not mean that no comprehension or representation is possible, or that it is in any case avoidable. (Gillian Rose 1992: 296)

To clarify his argument in relation to judicial decision-making, Bańkowski draws on the work of Gillian Rose (1992); in particular, on her understanding of the 'broken middle'. It is here that, for Rose, all philosophy must begin. In the middle we encounter not just similarities and differences, correspondences and contradictions, but also the tensions that always already exist in advance of these. For this reason, Rose describes the middle as 'systematically flawed' (1993: 45), a 'perpetual carnival market' (ibid.: 47). It is a parade of contradictions and tensions continually open to challenge and dispute. There is not, and cannot be, any final resolution or false reconciliation of the middle. Struggle is its permanent condition.

In the legal institutional context, precisely because we are always involved in its balances of violence and power in this way, the middle is a difficult place to maintain: it is always an *involved* middle; a broken middle. But our response to this cannot simply be to refuse to make decisions or judgments; rather, we have to acknowledge the risk and the violence of our decisions and stake ourselves, to maintain a position for one thing against another while all the time knowing that that other must none the less also be thought and understood. In this sense, we cannot get away from the anxiety of the middle: we cannot originate, or make new what already exists. The ambiguous, tension-laden space where we find ourselves located is always only 'the middle'.

In an early comment on Rose's work, Rowan Williams (1995: 11–12) portrays it in this way:

> It is this constraining 'already' of such determination, the whole of what Rose conceives as 'law', that in fact denies what power we really possess; the failure to acknowledge this imprisons us. But this liberating awareness of an imperative actuality prior to, and powerful in respect of, our specific desire is also a 'beginning of anxiety', the moral and conceptual source of how we understand what it is to *fail*. When a culture effectively loses this sense of what it is to fail ... the ethical is broken; that is, the agent is left poised unhappily between an external order which, because it has forgotten what failure is, ceases to be a source of power, and an internal critical self-perception, an anxious

> self-perception, that likewise has no access to power, no resolution of its own impotence. What Kierkegaard called the suspension of the ethical has its place in this context.

Indeed, for Rose, Kierkegaard is a thinker par excellence of the 'broken middle', explaining in detail what it means to stake oneself in the standpoint of the middle with an awareness and involvement that always already implicates law and love and violence. And it is this 'always already' aspect, characteristic of the middle, of being willing to stake oneself in spite of that knowledge and awareness, that keeps one from acting with arbitrary violence or in a capricious manner but, instead, allows an acknowledgement of the symbolic violence of law as a necessary fact of the given situation. It is within the given situation that we struggle to the command of love: 'To posit that the ethical is suspended is to acknowledge that it is always already presupposed' (Rose 1992: 148). It is precisely because there is always a strong inclination to conceal or disguise the middle by positing certain concepts as absolute, so that they then assume a transcendent character impervious to further investigation, that Rose explicates the middle as a space filled with tension and seemingly impossible to hold. It is the polarization of opposites that leads to an incommensurability that gives rise to the compulsion to theorize it away.

As Bańkowski and Davies (2000: 37) notes, we can see how Creon and Antigone, in their own different ways, attempt to deal with this:

> [W]hat they do is deny that there is any conflict. For Creon there is no conflict between the demands of piety and love and the demands of justice for the city. Everything … must refer back and be seen under the optic of the good of the city. For Antigone everything is seen … not out of love but rather the *philia* of the family. So, again, there is no conflict; rather, everything is seen as referring back to, and through the optic of, family duties … [T]he particularity of love (Antigone's) collapses into a universalism of laws of which she is the sole interpreter, just as Creon turns the universalism of the city's laws into the particularity of his anger and lust for power.

But this tendency is always assumed in error, argues Bańkowski. What Rose demonstrates so ably is that we can never really escape this anxiety of the middle: law is always imperfect, its institutions, doctrines and practices always to some extent violent and harmful. We need to realize (Bańkowski and Davies 2000: 38):

> that our life is never clear-cut and clean and is always something of a mess. But we must get hold of it as it is. We have to confront ourselves as we are and live our lives from the middle. That place is always anxious and creates the conditions of anxiety … and we must use that anxiety creatively.

So, while others might seek refuge at one extreme or the other of the antithesis, Rose enlists Kierkegaard (and Freud) in an attempt to carve out the middle as a third space, one in which what she calls 'the singular – as a singularity without its contraries of universal and particular' (1992: xiii) will emerge. It is its complete and utter givenness that makes this space such an anxious place, and which compels Rose to snatch back this sense of anxiety from the urge to retreat into sanctified beginnings or utopian ends and to restore it to its rightful place, rediscovering and reallocating it to the middle. As Zygmunt Bauman (1995: 74–5) explains:

> [t]he 'brokenness' of the Middle is lived as uncertainty; an uncertainty from which each act is an attempt to escape ... but which each act only succeeds in deepening ... No recipes of repairing the fissure are to be trusted; the more radical they are, the more they need to be suspected ... Residing in the broken Middle is our common fate. We can live at no other place; there is no other place, nor could there be.

And that is why, for Bańkowski, as for Rose and Kierkegaard, '[t]he way ... forward is by "suspending the ethical" ... refraining from seeing something as an incarnation of the universal' (Bańkowski and Davies 2000: 37). But how exactly do we avoid the inevitable collapse into one extreme or the other?[6] Against what criteria can a balance be achieved between opposing reasons for making a decision?

'We can take this argument further,' suggests Bańkowski (2000: 40), if 'we think of the middle in terms of what Michael Detmold calls the "particularity void" ... the space that exists between the rule and its application'. Detmold (1989: 455–7) cites the confrontation between Pierre and Davoût in Tolstoy's *War and Peace* as an illustration of this: Davoût, under orders to shoot Pierre as a Russian spy, aims and hesitates but does not fire. For Tolstoy, the moment goes 'beyond the circumstances of war and the court-room, and establishe[s] human relations between the two men' (Tolstoy 1978: 1141) and for Detmold (1989: 454–7) this is hugely significant: 'I, the judge, and Davoût, at the moment of practicality entered into the unanswering void of particularity, the realm of love, about which only mystical, poetic things can be said ... or nothing.' In other words, to occupy

6 Consider, for example, the case of *Ealing London Borough Council* v. *Race Relations Board* ([1972] AC 342). Neil MacCormick (1978: 78) argues that the disputed question in that case – whether or not discrimination 'on the grounds of colour, race, or ethnic or national origin' includes legal nationality – is 'not a question about a particular act of discrimination' but 'a logically universal question'. 'But notice what happens,' says Bańkowski (2006: 28): 'The judges talk [about] classes of people who might or might not represent him'; however, in asking about classes of persons, they are now no longer talking about this particular person, 'Zesko, the Polish national and ex-RAF pilot'. In the attempt to simply locate him under a general type, Zesko, the person discriminated against disappears. He has been 'taken out of the picture'; he is 'no longer there'. Moreover, this is only half of the problem, because 'the judge [too] lose[s] particularity in this effort to universalize ... The judge ... acting in the form of law is subsumed into the universal law and becomes invisible ... [T]he judge ... loses particularity and becomes an agent of the Law, and in so doing does not act autonomously but heteronomously, as a means.'

the middle requires 'courage to take responsibility for judgment and action that might go wrong'. The problem is one 'of recognition and discernment' and a 'held tension between particular and universal' (Bańkowski and Davies 2000: 41–2). The particular is not subsumed simply and unproblematically under law but neither is law abandoned (ibid.: 43–4):

> The encounter depends on the individual's ability to recognise the particular instance as both consistent with and different from previous instances ... But one cannot completely abolish the ethical ... There is no final judgement; I can always be wrong ... We have to work from where we are ... We have to engage and take responsibility.

In other words, '[t]he contrast universal–particular must not be suppressed'. No matter how difficult, relating particulars and universals must entail preserving contrast and avoiding extremes; indeed, precisely because '[p]articular entities have universal aspects ... [then] both sides ... must be illustrated in every case' (Hartshorne 1987: 7– 8).

Here, then, we find an example of just the sort of encounter situation that provides a context for Rose's emergent singularity, and Bańkowski is correct to maintain that a reading of Rose helps to disclose a clue to understanding how to engage with this so-called 'particularity void': it is only from our locus *within* the actual situation of encounter that we shall be able also to step, as it were, momentarily *outside* and so become aware of the need to decide – whether to apply the rule or not – and to take responsibility for our decisions (Bańkowski and Davies 2000: 44–5). It is the encounter that is all-important: 'the "particularity void" is not mystical, but rather a statement of the fact that we have to start from the particular situation and not let [our obsession with] the rule make us forget it'. Bernard Jackson (1988) makes essentially the same point, when he argues that it is attention to the detail of the stories of cases rather than the rules under which they are decided that yields a proper understanding of their result. We can only understand the nature of a difference in decision between two ostensibly identical encounters if we pay attention to the details of the story. In other words, it is our 'getting immersed in the practical details and cross-currents of the story [that] drives the judgment on' (Bańkowski and Davies 2000: 49).

Here, in this place that Rose calls the middle, we 'learn to inhabit the tension' between particular and universal and how to do this. That is why the middle is such 'an anxious place'. It is anxious 'because it refuses to [allow us to] abandon either side of the equation ... trying to hold things together that pull us in both ways' (Bańkowski 2001: 77–8). We can see, says Bańkowski, why the position of the judges in the context of decision-making is such a privileged position: they are 'standing in the ground where law meets the particular' (2000: 49). It is in the encounter with particularity, 'with the case itself', that we shall find whether a principle is to be applied or the law suspended. It is in this way that 'one is living in and out of the law but denying neither' (2000: 49). In this way, the law is 'continually being made and remade ... [And] all this is done in the context of the law itself' (2000: 51).

Decision-Making in the Middle

Bob Dylan begins 'All Along the Watchtower' with a statement that catapults us immediately into the middle of a conversation – between 'joker' and 'thief' (Dylan 1974, Bowie 2012). All at once, we inhabit a tension. We recognize it immediately in the sense of urgency and desperation that accompanies joker's appeal to thief for some form of escape. Drawn inexorably into a cauldron of confusion and contingency, we listen as the thief counsels against false positives and any easy way out. Then, all of a sudden, context appears and Dylan populates the scene with princes and women and barefoot servants. Now, time and place come to bear – but only now. Employing carefully the archetypes of 'joker' and 'thief', Dylan transcends with ease the temporal and spatial boundaries that might otherwise imprison both characters in some particular historical epoch. What we hear, instead, is a parable relevant across time and place. Of course, we can still choose to read the ensuing exchange between 'joker' and 'thief' as a simple juxtaposition of different values: first, the two outsiders, united in their exclusion from ordered society; second, the 'princes', representatives of society's order guarding and maintaining its structures of power. We can read it throughout in a detached, objective sense, as some Sophoclesian catalogue of binary oppositions and simple correspondences that creates a 'confusion' from which there appears no 'relief'. Or, we can enter into the story, listening to it, hearing its sense of urgency that draws us relentlessly into the continuity of its unfolding and to unexpected connections. To hear it this way is to enter into its flow, to understand its character as a parable, its rhizomic character as an *intermezzo* that picks up speed in the middle. Just the same way as when looking at *Antigone*, we can view the story as a simple statement of opposites or we can recognize it as something that harbours potential to jumble up, mix, scramble and challenge otherwise ordered schemes of things. We can negotiate its dichotomies, bringing together opposing principles in dialectical transformation or reconciliation, or not; or, we can engage the tension that holds together these opposites and sees beyond, a different way of thinking that cuts across and beneath carefully-guarded dualisms and dichotomies. Dylan concludes the song with a suggestion of an impending storm that strengthens as the two riders approach the castle. Others may be drinking their wine, digging their earth, benefiting from their labours without concern, but the thief counsels the joker to see things differently: while others might go to and fro in interminable confusion, they must hold things together in balance. However, if a new way of looking at things and a new set of values is really to be established, this middle must be held firm. For them, there can be no escape into easy hierarchical universalizing, or particularity. For this new way of thinking to emerge, the held tension of the middle must be embraced, held by these two unconventional rogues dancing on the fringes of society. Whitehead (1978: 339) says: 'Life refuses to be embalmed alive.'. On the contrary,

> [t]he art of progress is to preserve order amid change, and to preserve change amid order … What is required … is order entering upon novelty; so that the massiveness of order does not degenerate into mere repetition; and so that novelty is always reflected upon a background of system … In either alternative of excess … the present is enfeebled.

David Hall (2004: 91–2) makes a similar point:

> [T]he act of understanding is really two acts – not easily combined. To understand is to grasp meaning, which is to grasp patterns as types of order. A pattern is comprised both of particulars and of the manner of their relatedness … Foregrounding relations requires the gathering of details under an assigned pattern … It involves the use of a principle or principles as an antecedent pattern in terms of which to articulate instances or applications … In the second instance, to understand means to discover novel patterns that elicit interest in novel details. These novel patterns are themselves entertained as particulars, as are the constituents of the patterns.

Clearly, 'no legal judgment could give effect to all of the principles held in opposition': every judgment 'accepts certain ideals in its final satisfaction; it rejects, whether consciously or unconsciously, many thousands more' (Tidmarsh 1998: 84–5). But what we find in law, as in life, is that there is freedom to choose and the potential to choose badly and, as such, '[e]rror is the price we pay for progress' (Whitehead 1978: 187). We can always get it wrong, but what is important is this sense of judgment arising from involved participation within the story: the theories that inform our decisions must be 'constructed from the standpoint of the individual actor [not] the observer of action' (Dibben 2004: 14).

This returns us once again to Jackson's (1988: 104) claim about the roles that narrative construction and the comparison of underlying narrative patterns play in decision-making: 'narratives come laden with tacit social evaluation'. He compares, for example, the decision in *Lewis* v. *Avery* ([1971] 3 All ER 907), where a rogue posing as Richard Greene, the actor who played the title role in the television series *Robin Hood*, bought a car with a stolen cheque, against the decision in *Ingram* v. *Little* ([1961] 1 QB 31), where the sellers, two sisters, were defrauded into parting with their car by a rogue who presented himself in person as P.G.M. Hutchinson of a certain address. 'The overall impression given by the narratives [in these two cases] is … different', argues Jackson (1988: 105–6):

> The two sisters may have been defrauded, but Lewis was actually fooled … [T]he contest is no longer one between two equally innocent parties: it is

> between a fool and an innocent, and the fool is at least partly the victim of his own stupidity … [D]ecision-making reflects the social evaluation of the case, which [in *Lewis*] is typified by laughter rather than sympathy.

Mark Dibben (2004: 13) underlines exactly what is at play here when he recalls Bergson's (1913: 8–9) famous account of the nature of the comic:

> Bergson's description of a man running along a street who suddenly stumbles and falls, and of a man whose daily rituals are bespoiled by a mischievous individual who, to the audience's prior knowledge, has filled the man's ink bottle with mud … reveals the importance of individual theorising in our daily lives. The comedy that lies within the pictures we create from these two descriptions comes about, as Bergson's explorations reveal, through the absolute contradiction of the expected in the former, and the absolute extension of the expected in the latter … Expectation arises from the simplification and resolution of multiple possibilities in an effort to reduce the complexity of the world through which we navigate.

But how, in practical terms, does this navigation of complexity occur?

This is something that Michael Polanyi has written widely about. Following very much in line with the tradition of thought that we have traced through Whitehead, Bergson and Deleuze, Polanyi (1962: 17) argues that '[t]he act of knowing includes an appraisal, and this personal coefficient, which shapes all factual knowledge, bridges in doing so the disjunction between subjectivity and objectivity'. Alongside Whitehead, one of the strengths of Polanyi's thought is his strong rejection of dualistic tendencies, such as between practical and theoretical knowledge. For him, all knowledge is personal knowledge, 'participation through indwelling' (Polanyi and Prosch 1975: 44) and all knowledge involves the active participation of the knower. The act of knowing is skilful action.[7]

What Polanyi suggests returns strong echoes in Bańkowski's work. When we talk about certain laws predicting certain outcomes, what we really mean is that *we* can predict outcomes using these laws as *tools*; that is, as tools they are not self-applying but require an action on our part to apply them. He argues that '*we feel our way* to success … without specifiably knowing how we do it' (Polanyi 1962: 62) and what this entails is a recognition that in performing a particular act we are always aware of some things that are not the main focus of our attention: 'we *attend from* something for attending *to* something else' (Polanyi 1966: 4). Polanyi explains what he means by reference to the way that blind people feel their way by tapping with a stick, or the way that we might use a probe to explore a dark cavern (ibid.: 13):

7 For a more detailed account, see MacLean (2011: 100–9).

> Anyone using a probe for the first time will feel its impact against his fingers and palm. But as we learn to use a probe, or to use a stick for feeling our way, our awareness of its impact on our hand is transformed into a sense of its point touching the objects we are exploring … [A]n interpretative effort transposes meaningless feelings into meaningful ones, and places these at some distance from the original feeling. We become aware of the feelings in our hand in terms of their meaning located at the tip of the probe or stick to which we are attending.

But the point is that, in order to take on more specialized tasks, we find that we must first have internalized new knowledge (Polanyi 1962: 101). It is by 'indwelling' in the tools we use that we are able to use them as extensions of ourselves and press outwards to further extend the boundaries at which we make contact with the world around us (ibid.: 59). This involves more than simply paying close attention. What we must develop is an *un*-awareness of the methods and tools we use, something 'achieved by a repeated mental effort aiming at the instrumentalization of certain things and actions in the service of some purpose'. Bańkowski (2006: 37–8) makes essentially the same point when he suggests that how we learn to 'pay attention' is similar to the way that we 'learn a skill like music': we learn by practising, repeating the same act 'until we internalize it in such a way that we can go beyond'. But there is a danger here, too:

> The danger is that we get stuck in the old categories … Because we have seen it so many times we think it is the same again. The paradox is that 'seeing it all before' is also the condition for our being able to move beyond … What we need then is a creative and loving anxiety, caring and anxious attention. We must let the story speak for itself and not be too quick to apply closure by imposing a principle or pattern on it.

What allows us to move beyond in this way, to see things differently and *not* apply a rule when, to all intents and purposes, the conditions of its application are otherwise met? What allows us to act in this tentative, defeasible way?

For Bańkowski (2001: 180–81), the answer is simple and echoes the earlier points of Whitehead and Hall: our creativity emerges from structure: 'we cannot be creative unless we live our lives in a structured way … We know when to act on the impulses we get from the outside because we live in the structured inside … respond[ing] to the impulses when and if they come'. It is a 'common mistake,' he argues, 'to jump to a conclusion before the story has a chance to reveal itself' but '[t]he trick is to explore the story until you know that it is appropriate to stop'; the 'skill is to recognise when to move beyond; when not to apply a pattern'. Understood thus (Bańkowski 2003: 29), law becomes an 'articulation of two systems, the doctrinal and universalizing system which has its own internal world and the more arbitrary and contingent application system which is sensitive to the outside'. Not 'two systems loosely connected' but 'one system instantiated in the articulation of the two'. And what this argument about law's inherent 'open[ness] to the "outside"' points towards is precisely the sort of activity that Deleuze and Guattari suggest when they talk of philosophy as a form of rational experimentation, a critical practical reason in which the creation of novel concepts and understandings produce new means of acting upon the present without controverting what those concepts express. Their value is measured not in terms of truth content but in terms of novelty, their ability to invigorate and imbue with interest our understanding of the present. In this sense, these rhizomic assemblages of new concepts function to bridge the gap between inside and outside, allowing the outside in without contradiction, negation or denial of what is otherwise essentially inside.

We can see how this functions in the legal institutional context if we look at, for example, Bańkowski's (2001: 182–3) characterization of the jury as a form of 'straddling or bridging institution', through which 'the outside filters into the law'. What he means by this is that the jury 'sensitise[s] the court to other impulses that come ... from "beyond"', prompting the court to 'reconsider its own system'; for example, the case of *R* v. *Ponting* ([1985] Crim LR 318), which led to a rethinking of the Official Secrets Act. Charged with a breach of the Official Secrets Act for leaking details regarding the sinking of the Argentinian ship, the Belgrano, during the Falklands War, the defendant was none the less acquitted by the jury, in spite of his admission of the material facts of the case and a strong direction from the judge to convict. Indeed, for Bańkowski, systems of *lay* justice generally seem to have 'a foot in both camps': on the one hand, endowed with a capacity to influence outcomes by injecting fresh insight from a distinctly 'outside' lay perspective; and on the other, actually helping to preserve the 'inside' as being distinctly *legal*. Or one might equally point to the decision in *Mabo* v. *The State of Queensland (No. 2)* ((1992) 175 CLR 1), in which the Australian High Court defined 'native title' as straddling the boundaries between systems of common law and indigenous law in such a way as to emphasize the curious, indeterminate nature of this concept as a hybrid concept recognized by the common law but not actually an institution of it. In this sense, the recognition of the concept of native title operates to open up the space between these two systems as an irreducible difference, generated in and belonging to the held tension of this middle, creating the conditions for the emergence of a novel interpretation that is nothing less than the de-territorializing becoming of law, the becoming-indigenous of the common law and the becoming-common law of indigenous law (Patton 2000: 129). Here, there is neither affirmation of one over the other, nor any reduction of one to the other, but a reconfiguration of the middle as a field of creative heterogeneous activity, which carves out this novel concept as singular; in Rose's terms, 'a singularity without its contraries of universal and particular' (1992: xiii).

Thus there is no dichotomy implied or expressed in applying this 'inside–outside' distinction. The institutional machine that operates to infuse the system with new concepts, ideas and values, has no built-in end-point or identifiable conclusion but is more akin to a Deleuzean heterogenous assemblage, where its processes can always be continued and new concepts fashioned and elaborated. On the one hand, it possesses its own internal skeleton of principles and formal constraints, while, on the other, it is always subject to modification, extension and renewal within the shifting horizons of these constraints. In this sense, the legal world is not a world in which everything is set in stone and predetermined, but rather a world in which the possibilities for creative differentiation from the past are always present, infused into every decision-making moment. Law exists more in terms of a working hypothesis than a prescriptive code. Bańkowski's 'straddling or bridging institutions' provide one way of recognizing and understanding how law functions here as a rhizomic web of concepts, an open-ended, de-territorializing and self-transforming process of becoming.

Conclusion: The Middle as 'Process'

In contradistinction to a system of law based on the oppositional forms of universal and particular, whereby we habitually conceive of the purpose of decision-making as a crossing or bridging of the gap that opens up between them, this chapter has explored the more radical understanding of decision-making that emphasizes its latent relationships through investment in 'the broken middle'. The purpose of seeking to open up our understanding of decision-making in this way is to begin to appreciate how the wider aspects of lived experience, otherwise excluded from consideration or rendered inadmissible for rational discussion in law through law's inherent closure, contribute to its creative outcome. Underpinning this alternative understanding is the work of process philosophers such as Whitehead, Bergson and Deleuze, with their insistence on a reversal of the usual ontological and epistemological priorities of substance over event and order over change. Emphasizing event and change allows Deleuze and others to move beyond the static categories of being. Replacing these closed categories of being with an emphasis on a more open, processual understanding of becoming acknowledges the creative advance of a world that is never already made but always in the making. Understood thus, we can begin to open ourselves up to entertaining possibilities for the unexpected and the novel in decision-making: 'diverse perceptions, diverse feelings, diverse purposes, and other diverse activities' (Whitehead 1927: 9) come together and fuse into one to ensure something creatively new will always emerge. Consistent with this, Bańkowski, following Rose, demonstrates how understanding the true locus of authentic deliberation in terms of the dynamic and broken 'middle' necessitates a relaxing of our frames of reference, a blurring of the boundaries of inside and outside. It is here that decision-makers must position themselves. Similarly, Polanyi, drawing attention to the tacit dimension of thinking and knowing, buttresses this view of decision-making as a skilful act, as active and involved participation.

Emerging almost out of nowhere, like an echo from some unobserved exchange in the interplay between the aged blind prophet, Teiresias, and the two main protagonists of *Antigone*, Creon and Antigone, comes this simple central truth from Bańkowski (2000: 47):

> We have to risk the journey, guided but in the dark.

Bibliography

Bańkowski, Z. 2001. *Living Lawfully*. Dordrecht: Kluwer.

Bańkowski, Z. 2003. 'Legal Reasoning from the Inside Out'. In T. Biernat, K. Palecki, A. Peczenik, C. Wong and M. Zirk-Sadowski (eds), *Stressing Legal Decisions*. Krakow: Polpress, 22–40.

Bańkowski, Z. 2006. 'In the Judgement Space: The Anxiety of the Encounter'. In Z. Bańkowski and J. MacLean (eds), *The Universal and the Particular in Legal Reasoning*. Aldershot: Ashgate, 25–40.

Bańkowski, Z. and Davies, C. 2000. 'Living In and Out of the Law'. In P. Oliver, S.D. Scott and V. Tadros (eds), *Faith in Law*. Oxford: Hart Publishing, 33–51.

Bauman, Z. 1995. *Life in Fragments*. Oxford: Basil Blackwell.

Bergson, H. 1913. *An Introduction to Metaphysics*. Trans. T.E. Hulme. London: Macmillan.

Bergson, H. 1983. *Creative Evolution*. London: Macmillan.

Bergson, H. 1992. *The Creative Mind*. New York: Citadel Press.

Bergson, H. 2005. *Time and Free Will*. London: Elibron Classics.

Bowie, H. 2012. *Reason to Rock: Rock Music as Art Form* [Online]. Available at: http://www.reasontorock.com/tracks/watchtower.html; accessed 10 April 2012.

Deleuze, G. 1991. *Bergsonism*. New York: Zone Books.

Deleuze, G. 1994. *Difference and Repetition*. London: Athlone Press.

Deleuze, G. and Guattari, F. 1987. *A Thousand Plateaus: Capitalism and Schizophrenia*. Trans. B. Massumi. London: Athlone Press.

Detmold, M.J. 1989. 'Law as Practical Reason'. *Cambridge Law Journal*, 48: 436–61.

Dibben, M.R. 2004. 'Process, Enterprise and Demonstrable Applicability: Towards the Liberation of Managed Human Life'. *Concrescence*, 5: 7–17. Available at: http://concrescence.org/index.php/ajpt/article/view/99/61; accessed 10 April 2012.

Dylan, B. 1974. 'All Along the Watchtower'. In *Bob Dylan: Writings and Drawings*. London: Panther.

Hall, D. 2004. 'Whitehead, Rorty and the Return of the Exiled Poets'. In J.A. Polanowski and D.W. Sherbourne (eds), *Whitehead's Philosophy: Points of Connection*. Albany, NY: SUNY Press, 83–102.

Hartshorne, C. 1970. *Creative Synthesis and Philosophic Method*. La Salle: Open Court.

Hartshorne, C. 1987. *Wisdom as Moderation*. Albany, NY: SUNY Press.

Hirvonen, A. 1997. 'Antigone: The Love of the Goddess of Justice'. In Z. Bańkowski, K. Tuori and J. Uusitalo (eds), *Law and Power: Critical and Socio-Legal Essays*. Liverpool: Deborah Charles.
Jackson, B. 1988. *Law, Fact and Narrative Coherence*. Liverpool: Deborah Charles Publications.
James, W. 2007. *A Pluralistic Universe*. Gloucester: Dodo Press.
MacCormick, D.N. 1978. *Legal Reasoning and Legal Theory*. Oxford: Oxford University Press.
MacLean, J. 2011. *Rethinking Law as Process: Creativity, Novelty, Change*. Abingdon: Routledge.
Patton, P. 2000. *Deleuze and the Political*. Abingdon: Routledge.
Polanyi, M. 1962. *Personal Knowledge*. Chicago, IL: University of Chicago Press.
Polanyi, M. 1966. *The Tacit Dimension*. London: Routledge & Kegan Paul.
Polanyi, M. and Prosch, H. 1975. *Meaning*. Chicago, IL: University of Chicago Press.
Rose, G. 1992. *The Broken Middle*. Oxford: Blackwell.
Rose, G. 1993. *Judaism and Modernity*. Oxford: Basil Blackwell.
Sophocles 1974. 'Antigone'. In *The Theban Plays*. Trans. E.F. Watling. London: Penguin.
Tidmarsh, J. 1998. 'Whitehead's Metaphysics and the Law: A Dialogue'. *Albany Law Review*, 62: 1–90.
Tolstoy, L. 1978. *War and Peace*, trans. R. Edmonds. Harmondsworth: Penguin.
Whitehead, A.N. 1927. *Symbolism*. New York: Fordham University Press.
Whitehead, A.N. 1933. *Adventures of Ideas*. New York: Macmillan.
Whitehead, A.N. 1938. *Modes of Thought*. New York: Macmillan.
Whitehead, A.N. 1943. *Science and the Modern World*. Cambridge: Cambridge University Press.
Whitehead, A.N. 1978. *Process and Reality: An Essay in Cosmology*, Corrected edn, edited by D.R. Griffin and D.W. Sherburne. New York: Free Press.
Williams, R.D. 1995. 'Between Politics and Metaphysics: Reflections in the Wake of Gillian Rose'. *Modern Theology*, 11: 3–22.

Chapter 15
A Logical Journey: The Anxiety of the Leśniewski Quantifiers

Burkhard Schafer*

Of Contexts: The Edinburgh School of Legal Theory

It is not easy to say succinctly what the Edinburgh School of legal theory, epitomized by the work of the late Neil MacCormick and Zenon Bańkowski, represents. It is not a specific theoretical position, nor is it a uniform commitment to a specific methodology such as 'ordinary language philosophy' or 'analytical jurisprudence'. From the outside at least, it may look like a rather eclectic mix of, among other things, formal and informal analysis of legal language, constitutional theory or catholic theology; a place where virtue ethics can meet legal formalism and discuss their differences in a friendly way. Its members are as likely to be inspired by catholic social doctrine as by Karl Marx, Adam Smith, Hannah Arendt, Niklas Luhmann or H.L.A. Hart. In seminars or in the common room, one could find oneself as likely to be discussing the implications of the *Factortame* decision as astrophysics, and Gödel's theorem is as often evoked as *Donoghue* v. *Stevenson.* And yet, those who had the privilege to study or work with MacCormick and Bańkowski will none the less insist that there is a very specific flavour, a 'thinking style', that weaves through all these different strands and combines them to become something that is ultimately more than the mere sum of its parts, not a postmodern arbitrariness but rather a unity in diversity that pays attention to the particular voice that different schools of thought and thinkers within these schools can contribute to our understanding of law, while maintaining the ability to link these back to the tradition of 'grand theorizing' and universal accounts of what it means to live a life in the presence of laws and being subject to them. This intellectual attempt to unify prima facie disparate traditions of thought finds its correspondence in their analysis of one important substantive part of their work – the analysis of the legal system of the European Union.

Connecting abstract, conceptual analysis in the tradition of Hart and Austin with specific, substantial issues of law and legal order is another distinguishing

* Work on this paper profited greatly from discussions with Alan Bundy and Andrew Priddle-Higson, whose 2010 MPhil Thesis 'Computational models of Ontology Evolution in Legal Reasoning' develops in particular the technical aspects of multi-context logics discussed in this paper further. All mistakes in this article are, of course, mine alone.

feature of the Edinburgh School. There too, they strived to develop a model that on the one hand preserves the various traditions of legal thinking in the European member states in their distinctiveness, and yet allows for a conceptualization of the EU that goes beyond a mere fleeting alignment of interests of sovereign states. The resulting model thrives on the dynamic tension between the universal and the particular, a recurrent theme, especially in Bańkowski's thinking, and permits one to think of the EU as a unity that requires diversity, and hence is always and essentially conceptually contested. Of the two, McCormick developed the more explicit account of a theory of legal reasoning (see, for example, MacCormick 1978). Here, he developed a middle ground between the theories of Dworkin and Hart, looking in the process more closely at the logical form of legal arguments and their implication for our notion of justice than either of these. *Resolving* a tension by providing a more abstract, meta-level of inquiry was very much a hallmark of MacCormick's method. What might appear to be conflicting at first glance, when seen from the inside, is resolved as complementary rather than contradictory when seen from the outside. We find the same approach in his political philosophy, where he develops a middle ground between an EU conceptualized as a new, monolithic nation state, and an EU that is merely a loose contractual connection between sovereign states (see, in particular, MacCormick 1993). The middle ground is a system of overlapping normative orders, which we move into and out of as we live our lives. These normative orders are no longer hierarchically organized as in Kelsen's approach, and yet their peaceful co-existence is ultimately achieved through a set of rational meta-rules that tell us how to resolve conflicts between them. Part of the rationality of these rules is in turn their logical structure, and the universal constraints on rational practical reasoning MacCormick identified. For this purpose, classical logic is not just adequate, it reflects in its structure the normative concerns of MacCormick. Classical logic is unforgiving of contradictions. It is governed by the 'principle of Pseudo-Scotus', which states that everything can be derived from a contradiction.[1] For the logical analysis of natural language, including legal reasoning, this means typically that the analyst has to resort to 'soft' meta rules of disambiguation that allow him or her to avoid any direct contradictions between sentences. 'Indexicalization' is a typical method that can be employed, rendering, for example, the prima facie contradictory sentences: 'It is raining' and 'It is not raining' consistent by including indices for time and space ('It is raining at 3.00 pm in Edinburgh, but not at 4.00 pm in Berlin'). Commitment to classical logic therefore also means that it becomes a necessity that all conflicts can ultimately be resolved, the meta-rules of disambiguation that prepare the ground for a formal analysis mirroring in many ways the meta-rules of statutory interpretation that resolve apparent contradictions between norms.

1 Interest in the writing of the Pseudo-Scotus was, of course, revived by the Polish Dominican theologian and logician, Józef Maria Bocheński – who had been stationed in Scotland during the Second World War. See, for example, Mates (1965).

While we can see, therefore, a correspondence between MacCormick's choice of logic in his theory of legal argumentation, and his choice of political model in his theory of European integration, the situation for Bańkowski is much less clear. Bańkowski builds on MacCormick's notion of overlapping regulatory circles, but where, in MacCormick, these are largely static, stable and ultimately (made to be) consistent, Bańkowski's model is much more precarious, constantly on the edge and what it has in terms of stability it gains through the permanent 'change-in-interaction' – just like Bańkowski, the person, one could say it has to keep running to remain stable. In the process of engagement and when forming a relationship, individual people, as well as legal systems, change. Individual legal systems do not merely contribute their concepts, histories and modes of problem-solving to a patterned European identity. They change in the process by incorporating parts of the other states' identities into their own – and change those of others in turn, in a constant process of rearrangement. Inconsistencies in this model are not a temporary bug that needs to be resolved, they are a feature that keeps the process going – it is this anxiety that forces us to constantly re-evaluate ourselves in the light of others, who in turn are changed by us, that gives the union its (always contested, always fragile) identity.

What logic is appropriate for legal reasoning in this type of precarious legal system? While Bańkowski wrote about issues of legal reasoning and legal logic – mainly in connection with the computer metaphor of legal formalism (Bańkowski and Schafer 2007) – unlike MacCormick he does not express a clear preference for any specific formal framework of logical analysis. The aim of this chapter is to identify a number of suitable candidates for a logic that could be used as the underpinning for legal reasoning in the type of constantly evolving entity that Bańkowski describes. No definite answer will be given – instead, I shall through a few examples discuss the general features such logic would have to have. As an illustration – and for a sense of location – I shall use the case of *Buchanan* v. *Babco*, a dispute that involves alcohol – Scottish whisky, to be precise, though in logical parlance, the result is isomorphic relative to the type of alcohol, and Polish vodka would serve just as well. It should be seen as another homage to those aspects of Bańkowski's thought that are influenced by the common law tradition and the '*mentalité*' of his country of upbringing, which has remained throughout his life in a creative tension with those aspects that owe more to the continental tradition of his country of birth and that of his ancestry, respectively. I shall show how the reasoning of the judges poses some challenges for logical analysis, which are also typical of the type of legal order Bańkowski describes. Part of the answer will, for obvious reasons, involve Poland and the Polish tradition of logic. We shall look at paraconsistent logics as a first step towards a formal analysis that is more accommodating to paradoxes, to represent the idea of (European Union) law as an essentially contested project. We shall then look at various forms of formal descriptions of ontology evolution. Third, we shall look at a formal logic that owes much to the Polish logician, Stanisław Leśniewski. Its two types of quantifiers allow us to represent shifts in perspective between outside and inside points of view. This will align with Bańkowski's notion of 'bringing the outside in'. Finally, we shall step back and try to derive some general conclusions about the 'design requirements' for a legal logic in a dynamic, multi-jurisdiction environment.

Buchanan v. *Babco*

I shall use one specific case in this chapter: *James Buchanan & Co. Ltd* v. *Babco Forwarding & Shipping (UK) Ltd*,[2] to illustrate some of the pertinent ideas of Bańkowski's conceptualization of a supranational legal order. Starting with a particular case resonates with Bańkowski's emphasis on the role of the particular in legal reasoning (see, for example, Bańkowski 1998). It is not a case of European Union law, but the international law of carriage of goods – none the less, the lessons we can learn from it apply just as much to legal reasoning within the European Union.

Babco Forwarding & Shipping entered into a contract with James Buchanan and Co. for the carriage of 1,000 cases of whisky from Glasgow to Iran. They collected the whisky from a bonded warehouse in Glasgow, loaded it on to a trailer and sent it on its way from Glasgow to Felixstowe, Suffolk, for shipment. On its way from Glasgow to that port it was taken to a lorry park in North Woolwich, London, where it was left for the weekend. When the lorry driver came to collect the whisky after the weekend, he found it had been stolen.

Whisky intended for export is exempt from excise duty, and therefore no duty had been paid on it. However, after it was stolen, James Buchanan became liable to pay excise duty amounting to £30,000 on it – the presumption now being that the thieves would sell it in the UK. The relevant legislation is Section 85 of the Customs and Excise Act 1952. It was stated explicitly in the contract of carriage that it should be subject to the terms and conditions stated in the 'Convention on the Contract for the International Carriage of Goods by Road'. Now, a potential ambiguity arises when the value of the goods is calculated. Article 23 of the Act, so far as it is material, reads as follows:

1. When, under the provisions of this Convention, a carrier is liable for compensation in respect of total or partial loss of goods, such compensation shall be calculated by reference to the value of the goods at the place and time at which they were accepted for carriage.
2. The value of the goods shall be fixed according to the commodity exchange price or, if there is no such price, according to the current market price or, if there is no commodity exchange price or current market price, by reference to the normal value of goods of the same kind and quality …
3. In addition, the carriage charges, customs duties and other charges incurred in respect of the carriage of the goods shall be refunded in full in case of

2 [1978] A.C. 141, 152.

> total loss and in proportion to the loss sustained in case of partial loss, but no further damages shall be payable.

But what was the value of the whisky at the place and time it was accepted for carriage – at the warehouse in Glasgow? It is agreed that there was no commodity exchange price. Was there a current market price? If so, was it £37,000 (including the taxes) or £7,000, excluding them?

What sets this case apart from a rather humdrum example of statutory interpretation in commercial law is the bilingual nature of the governing regulations, as international treatises are published in authoritative versions in both English and French. Initially, Master Jacob, who assessed the damages, formed the opinion that the value of the whisky when it was taken out of the warehouse included the hypothetical excise duty that could have been levied on it. Any other construction would mean, he said, that there were two artificial values existing side by side, one with and one without excise duty. This is in itself an interesting (onto)logical argument that will have to be considered later.

Lord Denning, when the case reached the Court of Appeal, argued that the English version of the treaty was ambiguous and left a gap to be filled. In his opinion, looking at the French version was a legitimate way of resolving this ambiguity. In addition, he argued that not only was the French version of the text helpful for settling the ambiguity, but also that case law decided under the French version of the case was persuasive for doing so. However, French courts, as well the Dutch case that he cited,[3] have a somewhat different approach to legal interpretation. Denning is aware of this difference, and therefore makes the method of interpretation a part of his argument, citing Judge Kutscher's (1976) 'Methods of interpretation as seen by a judge at the Court of Justice, Luxembourg', to show how the principles of construction differ from those applied in the UK, and why a continental approach is preferable.

In the subsequent, second appeal to the House of Lords, the lawyers for the pursuer argued that:

> If there be an ambiguity, even in a case such as this where the English and French texts are equally authoritative, the court can take advantage of the French text. There is no such ambiguity here, and therefore no need to have regard to the French text. We have no expert evidence in this case. Schoolboy French is all very well, but one is here dealing with very subtle shades of meaning. It is no great compliment to the official translators of texts to say that the English is not an accurate reflection of the French. It is not necessary here, to look at the French text. 'Indemnite' is not necessarily used in French in the technical sense in which it is sometimes used in English, of an indemnity against all loss.

---

3 *British American Tobacco Co.* (*Nederland*) *B.V.* v. *Van Swieten B.V.* (Amsterdam Court) (Unreported), Mar. 30, 1977

> Compare article 23, paragraph 4: '... but no further damages shall be payable'. 'Compensation' could be total, but could mean something less.

We face at least three possibilities:

1. That there is a gap in the Convention which can be filled by judicial decision following a 'continental method' of interpretation applied to the French version of the treatise (Lord Denning M.R.) As a subcategory, this may involve citing cases from foreign jurisdictions decided under that law.
2. That the relevant words can be expanded in scope by looking at the French text of the Convention, but interpreting them using common law (UK) methodology (Roskill L.J. and Lawton L.J.).
3. That the relevant words – in English – are, in the context of an international convention, wide enough to include the duty (Master Jacob).

Both the Appeal Court decision and the House of Lords' decision offer interesting arguments on two different levels: first, the discussion if at all, and if so how, the French text of the convention can be used to disambiguate the English text. Second, we find examples of the judges on an object level actually creating bilingual legal arguments. In the speech by Lord Salmon, we find, for example, the statement:

> For my part, however, I consider that the French version 'frais encourus à l'occasion du transport' is no more or less precise than the English version and therefore affords no real help in solving the question which confronts us.

Lawton L.J. argues that the word 'compensation' used in article 23, paragraph 1 had no exact meaning in English Law.[4] He considered that what he described as its 'latent ambiguity' was at once resolved by the French text, which made it plain, 'that the intention of article 23 is to provide an indemnity subject to limits', and he added:

> Since the object of article 23 is to give an indemnity subject to limits, the principal limits being a financial ceiling and the exclusion of consequential damage, it seems to me that paragraph 4 of article 23 should be construed broadly.

He then examined the French text of paragraph 4, and concluded:

> The French phrase 'encourus à l'occasion' conveys the concept of 'arising from', 'occasioned by' or 'resulting from'. The French text has convinced me that the words in the English version of paragraph 4 of article 23 should be construed as meaning 'any other expenses which the owner of the goods has to pay as a result of the carriage of the goods'. The payment by the plaintiffs of excise duty was just such an expense.

4 At 223.

If we want to analyse the reasoning in this decision formally, we need to establish first a criterion for a successful formalization. An adequate formal representation of the case should ideally show:

a. How the judges use foreign legal material to interpret the statute.
b. The procedural arguments on how and when this is to be done.
c. Remain as true as possible to the syntactic surface structure of the arguments – in particular, we should be able to represent that the judges are citing directly words in French in their reasoning.

Paraconsistency and the European Union as an Essentially Contested Project

Using material from other jurisdictions to interpret statutes is an increasingly frequent occurrence in a global economy. Different legal systems have different rules governing the acceptability of such arguments. These rules in turn can become subject to legal argument about the applicability and interpretation, as in *Buchanan* v. *Babco*.

Bańkowski's analysis of the emergence of a European legal order, using ideas from system theory (see, for example, Schafer and Bańkowski 2003) are directly applicable to the scenario we find also in *Buchanan*. The objective of the analysis is to allow a way of thinking about legal systems such as the EU. It tries to avoid on the one hand thinking of them in terms of simple 'superstates', federal entities that replicate the model of the USA. On the other hand, it tries to give them more substance than mere coalitions between sovereign states that are bound to each other temporarily through contracts in international law. It should account for the continuous existence of local, national legal systems in their diversity, while at the same time allow for a process of convergence. The way to achieve this dual goal is to think of the process of European legal integration as a continuous process of becoming, something where conflicts and resolutions between legal systems is not a temporary phenomenon, a mere stepping stone to a classical, coherent legal system, but rather, it is an *essentially* contested project (Christodoulidis and Bańkowski 1998), one that does not ultimately resolve incoherence between the different local legal systems, but exists in the process of achieving only temporarily stable alignments between states. In this process model of European legal integration, EU law provides the framework within which national legal systems 'change through exchange'. A constant process of borrowing or transplanting legal ideas from other EU jurisdictions, mediated by the European courts, is the driving force behind this process. However, the receiving system does not integrate the legal transplant in exactly the same form it had in its original context. Rather, they are 'creatively misunderstood' by the recipient system – echoing the insight from system theory that systems are cognitively open but normatively closed. '*Grenzstellen*', or border stations (Fögen and Teubner

2005), manage this process of transplantation – a typical example being a national court applying the transplantation rules of international private law. Alan Watson's comparative legal concept of 'legal transplant', the adaptation and integration of a foreign legal concept (Watson 1974), is in this approach recast and refined as a 'legal irritant' (Teubner 1998) – legal concepts from foreign law trigger, so to speak, an immune reaction in the receiving body, whose 'antibodies' ensure that the transplant is either rejected completely, or suitably modified and insulated to 'fit' into the recipient system. Developing this biological analogy further, we can think of the European Court of Justice as an immunosuppressant – it decides if the modifications carried out by a national jurisdiction when implementing a directive (which is also a vehicle for transplanting foreign legal ideas) went too far and changed the concept beyond recognition. Developing the medical metaphor, it is akin to taking a cell sample from a person, growing it in a recipient organism (which will change its genetic makeup) and then re-implanting it. A constant flux, a constantly 'inflamed' system that draws its dynamic from the need to incorporate persistent irritants, is the result. Crucially, though, for Bańkowski this is not a mere stepping stone towards a more traditional legal system with its emphasis on systemic coherence. Nor is it simply a federated system where local laws may still be mutually inconsistent, but the borders between them are strictly defined, interaction is limited and we can always determine in principle which judicial sphere is relevant for us at any given point in time. Rather, it is the very process, the constant renegotiation of the local legal identities which inform the collective identity, that is constitutive for the system. It is *essential*, rather than *instrumental* contestation. To the extent that Europe is heading towards 'closer and closer union', this 'union' is at the very least asymptotic, a constant move towards harmonization without, in principle, the possibility of ever reaching it. It is also a moving target – as states and their legal systems change in the process of coming together and absorbing external influences, the meaning of what it is to have a union of *these* states changes constantly.

We can see such a process at work in *Buchannan* v. *Babco*. Of the judges, Master Jacob is the most traditional. The vision of a legal system that models his reasoning is essentially Dworkinian – the path-dependency of English law must not be derailed by external influences, and the chain model can and should be continued using UK law alone. Master Jacob's system is both normatively and cognitively closed, and no exchange takes place, but consistency is maintained. Denning and Roskill, by contrast, are cognitively open to the influence of foreign law. However, Roskill's approach stays normatively closed – the potential irritant is to be interpreted using common law methodology only and thus made compatible with the receiving body of law. That the import may in the process change its originally intended meaning substantially is not just inevitable, it is also desirable. Denning's approach, by contrast, also remains normatively open – to a degree at least, as he too interprets the law inevitably from the '*mentalité*' of a UK trained lawyer. Let us now continue the story hypothetically. Assume that a French court hears a similar case, and in doing so develops French law further by looking at the

UK courts' interpretation of the English text. At least in Denning's case, this would be influenced by his attempt to interpret it in the light of what he thinks a French approach to the French version would have been. We can easily see how French law now might change through an irritant that originally started its journey within the French legal system, not outside it.

One should also note that this process is self-reflective in a crucial way. It is not simply the case that in *Buchanan* v. *Babco*, a small piece of French substantive law was introduced into UK jurisprudence. Rather, by giving reasons for their decision and deliberating explicitly on the method of interpretation that should be used, the case also changes the criteria of what counts as a valid legal argument in UK law. Meta-level and subject-level reasoning are crucially intertwined, and it is this connection that shows why it is not hyperbole to say that, in cases such like this, the very nature of a legal system, its self-understanding, has been changed through an irritant.

Developing a formal account of this type of process is for many reasons a considerable challenge. The most important one I have alluded to already at the start of the chapter: classical logic is unforgiving towards inconsistencies. The reason for this is known as the principle of explosion – from an inconsistent set of premises, every conclusion can be reached. This is the ultimate justification behind Master Jacobs' argument that it is simply not acceptable to have two contradictory prices for the same product at the same time. We can understand informally how the principle works by looking again at our case. Because of disagreement between the judges, we have, at least temporarily, the following two sentences as part of our legal system: 'Babco owes £37,000 and not £7,000' and 'Babco owes £7,000 and not £37,000.' Let us now chose an arbitrary sentence, say 'Britain is a republic'. (It does not matter if the sentence is factually true or false, any sentence will do.)

Let us begin with '*Babco owes £37,000 and not £7,000*' as one of our two premises. From this, we can infer through disjunction introduction that also '*Babco owes £37,000 and not £7,000*' or 'Britain is a republic' must be true. The reason for this is that a disjunction is a weaker statement than asserting each component individually: if I already know that A is true, I also know that the weaker 'A or B' must also be true. This is, of course, the magician's trick, for now we can infer: If 'Babco owes £37,000 and not £7,000' or 'Britain is a republic' is true, and we also know (again, as a premise) that 'Babco owes £7,000 and not £37,000', it must be the case that 'Britain is a republic' is true. This is the straightforward application of the disjunctive syllogism: if I know that 'A or B' is true, and I also can show that A is false, then B must be true. Obviously, we can now also prove that Britain is not a republic, using exactly the same inference, and indeed every sentence we wish – even the proposition: 'Zenon Bańkowski is a happy-go-lucky hedonist with no worries in the world', which would defy the very theme of this book and through a Gödelian paradox of self-reflexicity cause harm to the autopoetic system that is the reader – as Zenon precisely did *not* argue in Bańkowski (1994).

Since this is obviously unacceptable, classical logic had to find ways to deal with the ubiquitous inconsistencies found in most legal systems. One family of logics has been developed with the specific aim of preventing logical explosion, and is therefore a good first candidate for a logic that could underpin legal reasoning in the type of multi-layered system Bańkowski had envisaged. Paraconsistency, a term coined by Miró Quesada in (Quesada et al. 1976), enables a more discriminating approach to inconsistencies. There are by now quite a number of competing formalisms that try to achieve the same aim, details of which can be found in Brown(2002) or Priest (2002). I shall only give a first impression of the field here, and focus on some aspects that are of particularly philosophical perspective. While the term 'paraconsistency' comes from the 1970s, when the interest in theories with this feature was booming, formal logics that today we would call 'paraconsistent' are older. The first formal account of a system that blocks logical explosion was developed by (of course) a Polish logician, Stanisław Jaśkowski, in 1948 (Perzanowski 1999). Jaśkowski's main idea was the logic of discourse: in a debate, a participant proposes positions or beliefs that (if they are honest) are true according to the participant. They will, as a bare minimum, be self-consistent, yet will often be inconsistent with those of the opponent. To model the discourse from the sum of its constituent parts, Jaśkowski formalized this in the form of a discursive logic, with a possible world semantics. If I assert a sentence A in a discourse, then from the perspective of the discourse, this is interpreted as the much weaker 'it is possible that A' ($\Diamond A$). This allows for the translation of sentences of the new discursive logic into the language of model logic, typically *S5*. A then holds in a discourse already if A is true in some possible world of the set of all possible worlds M over which S5 is interpreted. And since A may hold in one world but be false in another, both A and $\neg A$ may hold in one and the same discourse.

There is something intuitively appealing about this approach in legal contexts. Legal adjudication is a dialogical process. Not only that, when it comes to high-level, precedent-setting adjudication in appeal cases, it is almost inevitably the case that both sides will be able to make good arguments for their respective positions – if one side was obviously untenable, the case would have been terminated long before. If, then, the very best judges disagree among themselves in their respective speeches too, it seems inevitable to conclude that the various interpretations are at the very least all possible, though eventually one may turn out to be more plausible than the others. So while 'from the inside', every party's monologue argues that their interpretation A is *true*, from the outside, the perspective of the dialogue, what they are really arguing is just that their interpretation is *possible* – and they may even realize that this holds true for the other side as well, though they would not admit to that explicitly. It is precisely on this transition from the inside perspective of the discussants to the outside perspective of the dialogue, or legal system, that Jaśkowski's logic is based.

The idea that 'world views' or belief systems will typically be internally coherent, but mutually inconsistent, so that every formal representation that models talking about several such systems needs to be able to handle inconsistencies, has been developed; for example, by Batens (1998). However, this also shows the limitations of a paraconsistent analysis, both formally and from a philosophical perspective. While it allows us on the object level of the formal language to tolerate inconsistencies and to represent them, on the meta-level they disappear and become indices to possible worlds. So, while we can represent the statements 'Babco owes £37,000 and not £7,000' and 'Babco owes £7,000 and not £37,000', their meaning, seen from a meta-language perspective, simply becomes 'there is a world where Babco owes £37,000 and a different world where he owes only £7,000'.

There are possible worlds (possible legal systems) where Babco owes £37,000 and not £7,000, and then there are (other) possible worlds were the reverse is true. The contradiction disappears. But, of course, we could have achieved the same in the object language and stayed within the formal framework of classical logic, by talking explicitly about jurisdictions or interpretations. The statements: 'Interpreted within the French system, Babco owes £37,000 and not £7,000' and 'Interpreted within the common law system, Babco owes £7,000 and not £37,000' are, of course, consistent. This, one could argue, is similar to another observation Bańkowski made about modal deontic logics in general (see, for example, Bańkowski and Schafer 2007): they ultimately destroy the idea of normativity by translating it into descriptive terms; that is, the deontically demanded becomes what is actually the case in some possible world. Here, the normative tension is destroyed by separating the contradicting propositions and assigning them separate worlds. They now exists peacefully side by side, but are precisely no longer 'essentially contested' – the contest disappeared in the analysis. So we may need something more, something that represents the dynamic aspect of the creation of order through the contest of conflicting ideas.

Ontology Repair and Europe as a 'Journey'

In 'The Journey of the European Ideal' (Bańkowski 2009), the idea of the process character of a constant becoming and reshaping of the legal order in Europe was made explicit. Above, I have given a short account of the underlying process by which the contractual framework of the EU provides a setting where normative systems can exchange component parts. It may therefore be a good starting point to give a formal account of these component parts (for example, the concept of contract), and with that, look at the development of a formal ontology rather than take a theory of legal reasoning as a starting point. The standard definition of an ontology for computer science was given by Tom Gruber (1993) as 'An explicit specification of a conceptualisation', where a conceptualization is 'an abstract simplified view of the world that we want to represent for some purpose'. For lawyers, especially continental lawyers, the 'ontology' of a law is what is described in the general part of a Code – the part where the domain of the law is specified, what it is 'about'. So we could translate the role of the general part of a Code as saying that 'private law is about persons, things and objects (top level categories), the first is divided into natural and judicial persons (specification of the top level concepts)'. These component parts, legal concepts, act as an irritant in the recipient system, which then has to transform both itself and the irritant to reach a brief moment of stability – only to export this newly achieved concept to it originators. Eventually it receives the recycled version back again, and the cycle repeats itself. Similar processes are tackled by system engineers in artificial intelligence research. A computer system may receive an input that is inconsistent with its knowledge base. Rather than having a logical explosion, the system tries to repair itself, making the necessary modifications autonomously. For this, it needs to reason also about the very process of repairing itself, making notions such as 'context' explicit. It would require a formal ontology representation of the two putative objects, the French and the English 'market price' (one with taxes as a necessary part, and the other without), valid in their respective contexts, and then formalize the meta-reasoning that compares, matches and ultimately combines (repairs) the two.

Context logics (Serafini and Giunchiglia 2002) are one such approach that has very similar aims. The term 'multi-context logics' (MC logics) refers to a family of logics for the representation of contextual reasoning based on the principles of locality and compatibility.

Principle of Locality

Reasoning uses only part of what is potentially available; as an English lawyer, I will not normally use French precedents to argue my case, even though I know that there is such a thing as 'the French legal system' and that I can, if necessary, draw on this resource. The part that is used while reasoning is called the context (of an argument). Note that while this is similar to a possible world, the notion is much more fluid and task-specific.

Principle of Compatibility

There is compatibility among the reasoning performed in different contexts. I mention this principle just so that I can (partly) violate it. One of the potential problems of the paraconsistent approach outlined above is that it preserves the inconsistencies but prevents conflict between them. This could be seen as an almost postmodern 'anything goes', especially in those forms of paraconsistent logic such as Graham Priest's 'dialetheism', where sentences can indeed be both true and false at the same time (Priest 1998). I noted above the method pluralism that is characteristic of the Edinburgh School. It would, however, be a mistake to identify this eclecticism with arbitrariness. Openness to ways of thinking was always tempered by the tradition of the Scottish enlightenment and its firm commitment to rational discourse. This also involves a 'reality principle' – there is just one reality, of which we can get a better and better understanding. Without a commitment to a destination, even if it is only an aspiration or 'regulatory ideal', the very concept of journey becomes meaningless. While we can realize through a meta induction that the process will never end, and that the journey ultimately is the goal, this can only be the result of an inductive inference, and not our starting point. Only if we have an incentive to go beyond the inconsistencies are they able to play their transformative role and push us forward.

In multi-context logics, therefore, we have as a fundamental assumption that repair is possible; that – at least temporarily – consistency and stability can be achieved. To do this, these logics view context as a set of interacting formal theories, each with its own language, semantics and axiomatic system. Relations between contexts are represented as interaction between theories. The fact that these theories have their own language makes them particularly suitable for issues such as *Buchanan* v. *Babco* – something that traditional logic that takes place in the 'heaven of propositions', independent of any specific natural language, cannot replicate. In a classical logical approach to modelling, the logician would rely on the legal expert to give *the* logical structure of the relevant piece of international law – this has to precede any attempt to model the reasoning by the court. From a classical logic point of view, if does not even make sense to speak of the French and the English representation of this law; the very issue that is at the heart of the legal debate would already have to be resolved in the process of translating the natural language into code. By contrast, multi-context logics can talk about 'the Act in its French law context' and 'the Act in its English law context', where a bridge rule between the contexts ensures that we speak about the same Act, but an Act with different logical form in each context.

The notion of context as an individual's partial and approximate theory of the world plays an essential role here. The crucial shift from modal logic to contextual logic is that the first encodes an 'objective' perspective on problems – based on the concept of a possible world, whereas the second encodes a 'subjective' perspective – based on the concept of context. John McCarthy (1993) advocated the use of context to cope with exceptional cases to general rules. We can create rules that apply in general contexts, and overrule them in specific situations – something that 'fits' Bańkowski's emphasis on the dialectic between the universal and the particular. The basis of McCarthy's contextual logic is an *ist(c;p)* predicate, which asserts that proposition *p is true in* context *c*; and linking axioms, which assert a relationship between *ist* predicates for different contexts.

McCarthy further developed the idea by introducing an 'outer context': all propositions are asserted with respect to a context, with the outer context as the containing framework for all contextual assertions – a first step perhaps for an analysis of Bańkowski's notion of 'bringing the outside in' as yet another way to describe the process of changing oneself (or one's legal system) through a 'Gestalt switch' between inside and outside contexts.

The Giunchiglia (or 'Trento') model of context is based on the idea of a multi-context (MC) system. These systems are based on similar intuitions to the McCarthy model of context, but rather than introducing an *ist* predicate, MC systems have context as part of the meta-logic and introduce 'bridge rules' to enable inter-context reasoning. This difference also means that contexts and bridge rules are not language objects in a MC system, so we cannot reason about them explicitly. This is why I shall later combine this approach with McCarthy's. A context consists of a logical language (for example, first order logic), a set of axioms in this language (for example, the rules of English law) and a set of inference rules. The notation *c*:*F* is used to express that formula *F* is true in context *c*. Reasoning between contexts is done by using bridge rules – rules whose premises and conclusion belong to different contexts.

In the examples of contextual propositions I give, I use the Trento notation *c*:*p* to indicate that proposition *p* is true in context *c*. However, I use the McCarthy approach to contexts, so they can be treated as first-class objects within the logic, crucial to making explicit the reasoning of the judges. The notation *c*:*p* should be considered as a shorthand version of the assertion *ist*(*c*;*p*).

A legal-system context would define the rules that govern the reasoning and procedures within a given legal system. These rules place constraints on how lawyers can behave in a legal case, within that legal system. For example, there might be the following rule in the English legal system:

> English law: For all *X*;*Y*: similar (*X*;*Y*) & There is a *V*;*V′*:verdict (*X*;*V*) & verdict (*Y*;*V′*) –> *V* = *V′*

which states that, in the context of English law, if two cases are similar then their verdicts should be the same.

This rule (partially) expresses the principle of binding precedent in English law, and for a formal analysis can have a twofold purpose: it is an element of the context within which the decision takes place, and at the same time can form part of the argument the parties are making – 'We are in the context of English law, and hence interpretation *X* should hold' versus 'We are in the context of English law, and should change this context so that *Y* holds'. Self-reflexivity is one driver behind the ability of a system to repair itself, and to grow through the importing of new elements which can also be 'context changing'.

Bringing the Outside In: Leśniewski Quantifiers

We have seen above two crucial requirements for any suitable formalism to represent legal reasoning in the type of legal system Bańkowski envisaged. It requires an ability to represent multiple contexts – not contexts that remain in splendid isolation, but that interact with one another and share component parts. For this, we also need the ability to reason explicitly about contexts – the one we find ourselves in, and the one we perceive from the outside. Where the formalism allows for different languages for different contexts, reasoning in multi-language contexts such as the EU becomes possible. In the multi-context logics that we have seen above, the same statement can be interpreted differently, depending on whether an 'outside' or 'inside' perspective is taken. Change happens in the system in particular if we 'bring the outside in' – a key concept in Bańkowski's jurisprudence.

The disadvantage of these approaches, however, is that they stray far from the syntactic surface structure of the legal arguments. Once we have translated Denning's speech into a formal representation using the language of MCL, it is no longer an easy task to reconstruct the original natural language version. In making radical changes to the syntactic structure of the original in this way, these approaches betray their origin in automated theorem proving and computer science. They are needed if we want to leave the reasoning process to a machine, but they are less suitable for a formal analysis of legal reasoning that tries to gain jurisprudential insights from the process.

Inside–outside ambiguities are studied in philosophical logic, in particular in the formal analysis of belief statements and other 'intentional' contexts: Ponce de León searched for the fountain of youth. The fountain of youth does not exist. Does this mean Ponce de León searched for something that does not exist? That answer depends on what perspective we take. From the perspective (the context) of an outside observer, the statement is certainly true, and the substitution legitimate. From the inside perspective, it is more problematic. Had we asked León: 'Are you searching for something that does not exist?', his answer would have been a clear 'No, of course not, that would be silly.' Here, the substitution should fail.

In law, this issue frequently arises in the context of criminal intent. Assume that Peter met Paul a long time ago during a holiday trip. Paul started an affair with Peter's wife. Peter, enraged, vowed to kill Paul and followed him to his country to do so. Unknown to Peter, however, Paul is the president of this country. If Peter now attempts to kill Paul, we may not be entitled to replace 'Paul' by 'the serving president', at least not if we want to give a true account of Peter's beliefs from the inside perspective. The legal implications are obvious: depending on the legitimacy of the substitution, we may be able to charge Peter for both attempted murder and terrorism offences, or only for attempted murder. He intended to kill Paul, but he did not intend to kill the president (in one reading), which may be the required *mens rea* for a charge under laws that protect the president *ex officio*. Modal terms such as 'believes that', 'intends to' or 'promises to' introduce referential opacity into language, and mere co-extensionality is not enough to guarantee that the truth value of a statement remains the same after substitution of co-referential terms. Since the 1950s and the work by Saul Kripke and Jaako Hintikka, intentional contexts like this are normally analysed within the framework of a 'possible worlds' semantic (see, for example, Kripke 1965; Hintikka 1962). From Kripke (2005), we also get an influential bilingual example, which draws us even closer to the issue in *Buchanan* v. *Babco*: imagine a French citizen, Pierre. Pierre, proudly French and monolingual, believes, on the basis of some films he saw, that: 'Londres est joli' ('London is beautiful'). Much later, Pierre moves to London without realizing that London = Londres. In England, he immerses himself in British culture and learns English the way a native speaker would learn it, without translating from French. Pierre lives at this time in a very unattractive part of London, which he now associates with the word 'London', so he comes to believe that London is not beautiful. According to Kripke, Pierre now believes both (a) that 'Londres est joli' and (b) that London is not beautiful. But what does he believe of London – is it pretty or ugly? One natural way to render this into a language that philosophers find helpful is to say that Pierre believes *of London* (*de re*, the actual object) under the description (*de dicto*) 'London' that it is ugly, and he believes of London under the description 'Londres' that it is beautiful. In this case, we use the quotation mark to preserve the exact form of his belief expressed in the foreign language. We have seen above that this tool is also used by the judges in *Buchanan*. In Lawton's speech, we find, for example: The French phrase 'encourus à l'occasion' conveys the concept of 'arising from', 'occasioned by' or 'resulting from'. If we want to preserve this type of reasoning, we need to enrich our logical language with a quotation function "" that takes states of affairs *X* as their argument, and turns them into language-specific linguistic objects. This allows us to represent the same legal rule in different linguistic contexts. This alone is sufficient to prevent logical explosion, as the resulting objects are no longer sentences that can be true or false, and hence contradict each other, but, ontologically speaking, objects (think of the actual ink molecules that make up a written word – the sign – and ignore everything it signifies – its meaning). In this sense, 'Babco must pay £37,000' and 'Babco need not pay £37,000' do not contradict each other, any more than 'House' and 'Fish' do. They are all objects we can *talk about* – '"Babco must pay £37000" is a sentence with five words' is, for example, a true sentence, as is '"Fish" has four letters' – but as objects, 'Babco must pay £37,000' or 'Fish', they are not of the right category to be true or false.

However, with this solution we would again lose too much – we insulate ourselves from contradictions, but can no longer 'see' the underlying relation between these objects that interested us in the first place. Therefore, we need to find a way to 'talk about' or 'quantify over' the objects *within* the brackets. We want to say things like this: 'Causation *de re*, as actual object under the French legal description "*encourus à* l'occasion" conveys the idea of "*arising from*"'. This is we want to establish, that two expressions in different languages can, after all, be about the same objects. The technical solution for this was developed by two other Polish logicians, Stanisław Leśniewski (1929) and Kazimierz Ajdukiewicz (1934).

Leśniewski's determined nominalism resulted in a rejection of the referential interpretation of quantifiers. While *words* such as 'whisky' undoubtedly exist, we should not, in our logical analysis, commit ourselves to the existence of anything more than that, and in particular not a ('*de re*') entity out there in the world – whisky – named by the term 'whisky'. Ajdukiewicz saw the potential of this approach for the analysis of intentional contexts and refined Leśniewski's ontology to take the distinction between real and intentional objects into account (Dolling 1995). The solution here follows the spirit, if not the technical detail, of his analysis. A full technical exposition can be found in Schafer (1998), based on an earlier idea by Blau (2008). In this approach, alethic, deontic and epistemic expressions are interpreted as predicates, not as operators. Modal predicates take special kinds of structured objects, sentences, as their arguments. Each predicate carries a *type* '•' or '∘', indicating whether its argument position is interpreted referentially, about the world (•) or substitutionally (∘), about the linguistic expressions. Intuitively, we could say that a Leśnieswski quantifier 'grasps' an expression or word from the big bag that is our universe, a classical quantifier grasps an object named by a word and substitutes it where the variable is.

Correspondingly, I distinguish *de re* and *de dicto* variables $x^{\bullet}$ and x°. *De dicto* variables correspond more closely to Leśniewski's uniform variables. Consequently, a sentence of the form $\Box x^{\circ} P^{\circ} x^{\circ}$ is true if a name can be found which, when substituted for the bound variable yields a true sentence. The predicate P could stand, for example, for the property of being mystical. If the name 'Santa Claus' is in our universe of discourse, the sentence is true.

The working of this formalism is best understood if we look at some examples. Above, we had the situation that a person, Peter, wants to kill another person, Paul, whom he suspects of being a rival. He kills Paul with a knife. Since it is only possible to kill existing people, and if Paul was (also) the president, he therefore also killed the president. This fact is therefore formalized with *de re* predicates, as

$$M^{\bullet\bullet}(a, b). \qquad (1)$$

Here, the *de re* types guarantee that both argument positions are interpreted referentially; they refer to the same object, however you describe it.

Peter, however, has also formed beliefs about the situation: he believes certain sentences to be true. As indicated above, sentences are treated as complex objects that can occur at *de dicto* argument positions. Not surprisingly, the belief predicate has in its second position a *de dicto* type:

$$B^{\bullet\circ}\,(a,\text{“}M^{\bullet\bullet}(2)\,(a, b)\text{”})$$

where B = believes; M = murders; a = Peter; b = Paul.

This expresses the idea that Peter believes 'I murdered Paul', but since 'Paul' is within the scope of a quotation mark, it is now no longer possible to substitute 'Paul' by 'the president'.

However, we can also 'bring the outside in' and express, from the outside perspective, the idea that Peter believes of Paul, under the (inside perspective) description 'Paul', that he killed him, and under the description 'the president', that he did not kill him:

$$\exists x^{\circ}\, y^{\circ}\, (x^{\circ} = b \;\&\; y^{\circ} = c\; B^{\bullet\circ}\text{“}(a,M^{\bullet\bullet}(a, x^{\circ})\text{”} \;\&\; -\, B^{\bullet\circ}\text{”}(a,M^{\bullet\bullet}(a, y^{\circ})\text{”}))$$

where b = Paul and c = the president.

The same structure allows us to preserve the syntactic composition of the relevant bilingual arguments made by the judges. Lord Denning, for example, argues that the market-price *de re*, under the description '*encourus à l'occasion*' has the property of being £37,000, but under the description 'resulting price' only the value of £7,000. The logical structure is the same: *c* is now 'resulting price'; and *b* is '*encourus à l'occasion*'.

Conclusion

Both MacCormick and Bańkowski thought of the European Union as an entity different from both a traditional nation state and a mere contractual arrangement that co-ordinates the efforts between such states but leaves their identities unchanged. The resulting model is one of multiple, mutually inconsistent spheres of regulation that none the less coexist. However, MacCormick's approach remains ultimately beholden to Kelsen: the tensions are acknowledged but isolated and rendered harmless through meta-rules that tell us in which context we are for any given situation. This is particularly true for his later work, such as MacCormick (1999), where the more radical pluralism of his earlier writing found in 'Beyond the Sovereign State' (1993) finds its resolution in 'pluralism under international law'. For the type of legal system that emerges from such a model, classical logic remains appropriate to model legal reasoning within the system. By contrast, Bańkowski's approach is more radical; dynamic but also precarious. It gains whatever temporal stability it has only by being constantly in flux, like a spinning top requiring constant momentum. Anxiety, in this sense, does indeed become a creative force – the constant need to redefine oneself in the face of the 'irritants' one incorporates from the outside. To model reasoning in this type of system, logical tools different from classical logic are needed, tools that are capable not just of handling contradiction, but also allowing contradictions and tensions to challenge us and thus become creative forces. I discussed very briefly three different families of approaches that can provide such a logic, or at least explicate aspects of Bańkowski's theorizing. Two of them were heavily influenced by the Polish school of logic, and the second of these I developed while working in Edinburgh with Bańkowski. It is not claimed that any one of them can give a full account of the richness of his thought. Nor is it fruitful to decide which of them is better suited to the task. Rather, they should be seen as a first approach to a contribution to a 'universal logic' in the sense that Jean-Yves Béziau (2007) uses this term, as a study that attempts to give an account of which features will be common to all suitable logical structures that could express a certain conception of legal reasoning and legal system. While the term 'universal logic' is recent, it too has its roots in the Polish logical tradition, in particular the works of Alfred Tarski (Beziau 2007). The account remains deliberately sketchy. It is, as always, a journey. I was truly privileged to travel a short time on it together with Zenon Bańkowski.

Bibliography

Ajdukiewicz, K. 1934. 'The World-Picture and the Conceptual Apparatus'. In K. Giedymin (ed.), *Ajdukiewicz, The Scientific World-Perspective and other Essays*. Dordrecht: Kluwer, 67–90.

Arruda I., Miró Quesada, F., Da Costa, N. and Chuaqui, R. 1976. 'Meeting of the Association for Symbolic Logic: Campinas, Brazil 1976', *Journal of Symbolic Logic*, 43: 352–64.

Bańkowski, Z. 1994. 'How does it feel to be on your own? The person in the sight of autopoiesis'. *Ratio Juris*, 7(2): 254–66.

Bańkowski, Z. 2009. 'The Journey of the European Ideal'. In K. Reid et al. (eds) *Towards an EU Directive on Protected Funds*. Dordrecht: Kluwer, 149–72.

Bańkowski, Z. 1998. 'Parable and Analogy: The Universal and Particular in Common Law'. *European Company and Financial Law Review*: 138–63.

Bańkowski, Z. and Schafer, B. 2007. '*Double-Click Justice: Legalism in the Computer Age*'. *Legisprudence,* 1: 31–49.

Batens, D. 1998. Paraconsistency and Its Relation to *Worldviews. Foundations of Science*, 3: 259–83.

Béziau, J.-Y. 2007. 'From Consequence Operator to Universal Logic: A Survey of General Abstract Logic'. In J.-Y. Béziau (ed.), *Logica Universalis: Towards a General Theory of Logic*. Berlin: Springer 3–18.

Blau, U. 2008. *Die Logik der Unbestimmtheiten und Paradoxien*. Heidelberg: Synchron.

Brown, B. 2002. 'On Paraconsistency'. In D. Jacquette (ed.), *A Companion to Philosophical Logic*. Oxford: Oxford University Press, 628–50.

Christodoulidis, E.A. and Bańkowski, Z. 1998. 'The European Union as an Essentially Contested Project'. *European Law Journal*, 4(4): 341–54.

Dolling, E. 1995. 'Real Objects and Existence'. In V.F. Sinisi and J. Woleński (eds), *The Heritage of Kazimierz Ajdukiewicz*. Amsterdam: Rodolpi, 83–100.

Fögen, M.T. and Teubner, G. 2005.' Rechtstransfer'. *Rechtsgeschichte*, 7, 38–45.

Gruber, T.R. 1993. A Translation Approach to Portable Ontology Specifications. *Knowledge Acquisition*, 5: 199–220.

Hintikka, J. 1962. *Knowledge and Belief – An Introduction to the Logic of the Two Notions*. Ithaca, NY: Cornell University Press.

Kripke, S. 1965. 'Semantical Analysis of Modal Logic II: Non-Normal Modal Propositional Calculi'. In J.W. Addison, L. Henkin and A. Tarski (eds), *The Theory of Models*. Amsterdam: North-Holland, 206–20.

Kripke, S. 2005. 'A Puzzle about Belief'. In A. Margalit (ed.), *Meaning and Use*. Berlin: Springer, 239–83.

Kutscher, H. 1976. *Methods of Interpretation as Seen by a Judge at the Court of Justice: Judicial and Academic Conference*. Luxembourg: Court of Justice of the European Communities.

Leśniewski, S. 1929. 'Grundzüge eines neuen Systems der Grundlagen der Mathematik'. *Fundamenta Mathematica*, 14: 1–18.

MacCormick, N. 1978. *Legal Reasoning and Legal Theory.* Oxford: Oxford University Press.

MacCormick, N. 1993. 'Beyond the Sovereign State'. *Modern Law Review*, 56: 1–18.

MacCormick, N. 1999. *Questioning Sovereignty: Law, State, and Nation in the European Commonwealth.* Oxford: Oxford University Press.

Mates, B. 1965. 'Pseudo-Scotus on the Soundness of Consequentiae'. In A.T. Tymieniecka (ed.), *Contributions to Logic and Methodology in Honour of J. M. Bochenski.* Amsterdam: North-Holland, 321–41.

McCarthy, J. 1993. 'Notes on Formalizing Context'. *Proceedings of the Thirteenth International Joint Conference on Artificial Intelligence*, 1: 555–60.

Perzanowski, J. 1999. 'Fifty Years of Parainconsistent Logics'. *Logic and Logical Philosophy*, 7: 21–4.

Priest, G. 1998. 'What Is So Bad About Contradictions?', *Journal of Philosophy*, 95: 410–26.

Priest, G. 2002. 'Paraconsistent Logic'. In D. Gabbay and F. Guenthner (eds), *Handbook of Philosophical Logic, Vol. 6.* Dordrecht: Kluwer, 287–393.

Schafer, B. 1998. 'Leśniewski Quantifiers and Modal Arguments in Legal Discourse'. *Logic and Logical Philosophy*, 6: 133–55.

Schafer, B. and Bańkowski, Z. 2003. 'Emerging Legal Orders. Formalism and the Theory of Legal Integration'. *Ratio Juris*, 16: 486–505.

Serafini, L. and Giunchiglia, F. 2002. 'ML Systems: A Proof Theory For Contexts'. *Journal of Logic, Language and Information*, 11: 471–518.

Teubner, G. 1998. 'Legal Irritants: Good Faith in British Law or How Unifying Law Ends Up in New Differences'. *Modern Law Review*, 61: 11–32.

Watson, A. 1974. *Legal Transplants: An Approach to Comparative Law.* Edinburgh: Edinburgh University Press.

PART 5
Looking Back/Looking Forward

Chapter 16
The Long Goodbye: A … Life In and Out of the Law

Zenon Bańkowski

Uczyniwszy na wieki wybór
W każdej chwili wybierać muszę

Having made my choice for eternity
Every moment presents that choice anew

Introduction

What follows is the valedictory lecture given at the Law School three months before the seminar on which this book is based. It finishes with acknowledgments, which are important for me to keep there. So I would like to start by thanking all the contributors to this book and to the seminar both for the beauty of their work and for the kindness that they showed me in taking the time and patience to produce such careful and insightful analyses. I am honoured.

Please Don't Let Me Be Misunderstood

Po ichniemu nie rozumiem on po ludzku też
Lecz jest wódka więc jest tłumacz przy niej mów co chcesz

He can't understand – his foreign makes no sense to me
But there's vodka, our translator – she lets us say what we please

I once wrote an article on systems theory and it began with a parody of Teubner's book on the subject written in the style of Raymond Chandler, with myself as Philip Marlowe, as follows:[1]

> I knew what disorder was when I reached the city. It was awash with noise. Order from noise, they called it, but I wasn't so sure. I'd have to check on that, but I was finding it difficult to communicate outside. I was working on the Paradox Case. The smartest investigators in legal science had been in on

1 Bańkowski (1994).

this one. But they hadn't been able to get to the bottom of it. It was one of the biggest heists of all time. Everyone knew that the Teubner mob was behind it but they just couldn't make anything stick. They always came out clean. Every rule was matched by a counter rule. The cops had thrown everything at the case and it had got them nowhere. A lot of men on the ground wouldn't solve this case. It needed more than firepower. So, they had come to me. I'd been hired to deconstruct the case – break it down and make its ugly antinomies clear. Help start the big clean up. It needed it. You couldn't go there any more without getting lost in a maze of self-reference.

This was more than just a job for me. It was personal. I had lived here as a kid. I wanted to recreate the world I had known then, before the paradox boys had moved in and taken over. An honest place where things had clear meanings and rationality was the name of the game. It wasn't like that any more. Nothing had a clear meaning now. You couldn't put your finger on truth or reality. Everything solid melted into air. I was going to crack it, even if it meant using a thousand references.

I had heard that Blind Legal Evolution was in town, still playing the same old clubs we used to go to as kids. Maybe he could help. He had always lived there and knew his way around the maze of interlocking meaning that was the city. Surely he could help me get it clear. Help me break out of the fog of self-constructed meaning and get to the reality that I knew was there. I caught up with him in the Enlightenment club. The air was thick with the sweet smell of the materiality continuum. Episodic couples flitted by, lost in the never-ending dance of regulation. I saw him in the corner but he was no help. He was a sad case, lost in the hot air of his own reality construct. He had been here too long and it showed. He could only mumble the old blues numbers I remembered so well. But they all seemed to have different meanings now. I could only make out the odd words, variation, selection. They told me nothing.

The noise was getting louder. More and more communicative events were being spawned. I knew I had to leave before I got lost in some strange hypercycle. The answer wasn't here anyway. But where was it? The references told me nothing. I realized they were a trap. Follow them and I'd be lost in a cycle of self-reference. The key was control. How did they run the place? It just didn't seem possible. Nothing was predictable here. Nothing seemed to depend on anything else. Everything was contingent and random. This was the biggest paradox of all. They had made this place the chaos it was. Placed it outside of reason and order. Beholden to nothing but the rules it chose. Yet they understood its self description and self production so well that they could get what they wanted from it. Behind it all was Teubner. He had understood the city and made it his own. What was his secret? How did he do it? I was getting nowhere fast. The place was getting to me. I had to get out.

Seeing Blind Legal had scared me. He had no idea where he was going. He was lost in his own world. His life unfolded according to its strange laws.

> Nothing outside that protective wall could reach or move him. He didn't have to worry about the world outside; as far as he was concerned it didn't exist and he was happy like that. I didn't want to believe that. There had to be a truth that you could get to if only you dug hard enough. I had to believe that – I couldn't carry on if I didn't. And yet the Paradox Case was making me doubt this. The paradoxes were piling up faster than I could see through them. The cops had thought it would be easy. But I had known different from the start: the causalities were more subtle than they had thought.
>
> It was not a matter of linear progression. You couldn't go directly to the answer; you could only approach it in a roundabout way. My first thought was to jump out of this mire that I was sinking into but I knew that was wrong. To crack the case I had to throw myself into a maze of meanings that made up the city and hope that I could pull myself out when the time came. There was no point in asking and looking for help. You had to forget the outside and be sensitive to the city's noise. Use the interference of the city's own structures to jump from one area to the next. You had to construct your own meanings and let them take you deep into the circularities. I let the seductive pull of the regulatory trilemma take hold of me. Things were beginning to make sense. I could feel the distant clap of a choc exogène and I could feel a strong perturbation. Things were getting clearer, I could see the answer. Suddenly a loud noise filled the continuum. I realised it was God laughing. Everything was clear.

The Windmills of Your Mind

In that passage, I tried to imagine a fictional world where systems theory was true, and what the experience of living in such a world might feel like. At the end of my career in the university system, I might be forgiven for thinking that I do not need fiction any more, and the academy is a microcosm of that world where 'individuals have not only lost control but in relation to which they might also absolve themselves of responsibility for autonomous action' (Cotterrell 1992). In thinking we are free from delusion, we fall into another illusion. We think we reach out to others but all we do is to touch ourselves in the mirror we have created and called 'the outside'. We delude ourselves that we care for others when we only care for ourselves. We do not adjust to others – we adjust to ourselves. And our incommensurable discourses adjust to that mirror image and not to the outside. The world breaks down into self-absorbed circles, secure and confident in their righteousness. Everything is lost in the reflection of self. We lack the love to shatter the mirror and if we do not find it we will destroy ourselves and the world.

But here in Edinburgh we have managed so far to keep the barbarians at the gate! And in particular in the Law School we have managed to keep our *ethos* as we adapt to change. Certain things, I do regret, however. In conforming to the *diktat* on the 'efficient use of space' of the University's *soi disant* space management group, we had to convert the shrine of Our Lady of the Photocopy into an academic office.[2]

Life Re-Imagined

At times in our lives we are faced with decisions we have made and things we have done that cause us to re-understand and re-evaluate our lives as something we did not think of before. But this is not a matter of the re-evaluation of some of the decisions and actions we have done in the past. Rather, it is a matter of seeing our history differently. We can see this when we judge people. In liminal cases

---

2 The religious house of Our Lady of the Photocopier is to be found in a leafy corner of Cambridge. It is secluded but very near to St Edmund's College, which is fertile soil for its apostolate. I first came across this order when I was at mass at St Edmunds. After mass the celebrant offered to go and photocopy some articles for me. I went with him, thinking we were going to a shop which had photocopying facilities. However, when we got there I was surprised to find myself in the mother house of the Little Sisters of Our Lady of the Photocopier. I met and conversed with the Mother Engineer (as the Mother Superior is called), Sister Mary Xerox. She told me the history of the order.

It originated with the miracle of Our Lady of the Photocopy. One day a professor found his secretary temporarily absent. Having urgent photocopying to do, he went to the photocopying room to do it himself. Halfway through this work, the 'No toner' sign came on followed by an immense flashing of lights. Then everything went dark and a huge jam ensued that, even with his best efforts, he could not clear. In despair, he said a decade of the rosary, as he was wont to do at times of crisis. He set about his task again but still to no avail. As he was about to leave, his work not done, a tall, beautiful secretary dressed in blue came into the room, as though from nowhere. She cleared the jam, pressed the button and, smiling, disappeared. His work clattered out and he took it from the machine. Only then did he realise that the machine had operated with no toner and no paper and was still jammed. The machine clattered again and a new photocopy came out with a perfect, though mysterious, image of Christ.

The professor showed this modern day Turin Shroud to some of the secretaries, but none could offer an explanation. Gradually the idea took hold among them that the photocopying room should become a Chapel and that they should dedicate themselves to trying to replicate the miracle to prove its truth. Of course, this never happened and over the years they realised that their apostolate would be to help processors of the Word everywhere. They would found an order that would be dedicated to help those who felt loneliness and terror when faced with the vagaries of the photocopying machine. Here in an atmosphere of prayer and meditation (each photocopying begins and ends with a photocopy of the Holy Rosary) the machines would always work.

Just as Our Lady had helped the harassed professor so, in the best traditions of monastic hospitality, they would help others in similar distress. In such a way eternal recurrence would be achieved and the Word would be proclaimed through its photocopying. The order was founded and made secure through the generous sponsorship of the Xerox corporation and now has houses in many university towns. It does not stand still and is ever-expanding and entering new fields. At the moment it is deeply involved in the World Emailaprayer Year. It is at the cutting edge of prayer copying and transmission technology.

we do not just judge the act, but the act causes us wholly to re-orient our view of that person's biography. Nick Clegg, the UK deputy prime minister, might be a contemporary example. We might not just castigate his actions; they also cause us to re-orient our view of him. We no longer see him as a selfless 'new politician' but rather understand his actions through the optic of political self-interest and lust for power. We create a new story for him. And also with ourselves – decisions I take may make me re-evaluate my actions and my history. I see myself as a different sort of person with a different story, and this might be not only for ill but also for good.

The above touches on the idea of a coherent narrative of one's life, of being able to tell a story about the sort of person you are and what that entails for your actions. This begins to have connections with virtue ethics. One can also see affinities to Dworkin and the metaphor of the 'chain novel' or, as I prefer to call it, 'soap opera'. But there are disanalogies. Dworkin is, after all, *Law's Empire*. And that metaphor is appropriate, law is everything and it swallows everything back into itself. There is no outside; there can be no external scepticism. It is rather like systems theory, where the outside is only a construct of the inside and we are trapped in the maze of its circularities. So here the decision is, as it were, re-evaluated into our life, but our life is not re-evaluated by it.

What I want to concentrate on here is how something from the outside impels us to see our lives and our autobiography as something radically different – our life is re-evaluated by the outside. But we do not build it on a completely new truth that destroys everything that went before. George Orwell in *1984* (Orwell 2013) caricatures this way of looking at it. In the society of that book, as indeed in many actual societies, history is rewritten and what was known before no longer exists. But we cannot do that, because we cannot expunge what we thought of ourselves and build a completely new truth. An adult life cannot be understood in terms of childhood, but it is, as McCabe (1968) says, part of the maturity of adulthood to be able to understand and accept one's childhood. Putting away 'childish things' does not mean that I deny that I ever was a child! A conversion experience does not entail denying my past; rather, it entails re-evaluating and understanding my actions in a different light, and seeing myself as someone who then believed, and thus acted, differently.

We do not have to understand ourselves as being a new person but as one who had within him or her what he or she now sees as a false understanding of him/herself and an appreciation of how that impacted and impacts on the person as he/she now sees him/herself. What are the implications of this?

First, there are things we cannot wipe away. We cannot just wipe the slate clean and start again. A new view of our history does not mean that we start anew and 'move on'. We are always the prisoners of what we were and did, however wrong that view was. We can see this in Steiner's (1996) story *Return No More* – a story that Rowan Williams (2000) uses when he illustrates this fantasy. He shows how, in situations of reconciliation and transition, we sometimes think that, by accepting guilt and being sorry, we can purify ourselves without having to take into account of how the world and we have been changed through the consequences of past decisions. We think, therefore, that the self can stand outside of time. For example, take the second Gulf War and the situation in Iraq – to say that we recognize that it was wrong and a dreadful mistake and we should pull out immediately is to think that our recognition of the mistake is enough to let us start afresh and absolve us from having to deal with the chaos of the consequences of that initial decision.[3]

Second, we have to accept that there is part of the way in which we construct ourselves, part of our selves that is outside our control, located in a history of sometimes difficult relations with others, over parts of the actions and consequences of which we have no control. Our selves are in part irrevocably at the mercy of others and the idea of the self-contained, autonomous, enlightenment self is a fantasy – the sort of fantasy that plays itself out in Richard Dawkins and A.C. Grayling, among others.[4] There are things we cannot understand because we are not, and cannot be, totally in control, and it is hubris to think otherwise. Later, I want to stress how the way that we connect is through the mutual experiences of our vulnerability rather than the pride in the power of reason to bring good and enlightenment to the world.

The Long Goodbye

This brings me back again to the 'Long Goodbye'. When one evaluates and re-interprets one's life, it is in a sense (with all the provisos I have sketched out above) goodbye to one's previous life. The times when one does that are at moments of crisis, when one is forced to make decisions that might change the view you have of yourself. But the time for this sort of reflection does not only occur at these moments. There are critical moments in our lives, *rites de passage*, when we are in effect invited to do this – to look back and see what we make of our lives. Marriage, the death of a parent or the birth of a child are all such moments, and we have rituals that embrace those times. Lent within the Christian religion also serves as a time to do so. And, of course, the time of one's retirement also invites one to reflect in such a way.

It is a '*Long* Goodbye', for though there are fixed points where we have institutional space to do this re-evaluation, it is something that is ongoing through the lives we lead. At any time the decisions we have to make might overturn our lives and force us to think of ourselves anew. And the time and place of this is something (see above) over which we have no control. We are not proud ahistorical selves but selves that operate in a contingent history.

Moreover, we say goodbye in a radical way, for when I lose the identity I held to before and now see myself, or am forced to see myself, in a different way, in a sense I 'die to myself'. It is that fear of being different, of departing from our stable security that makes us fear and try to avoid this (we saw how amnesia or the denial that we have ever changed is one way of avoiding this).

---

3 The situation in Afghanistan is similar.

4 See Eagleton (2009).

So as I retire I seek to re-evaluate my life. I have been very luck in my scientific life, since much of what I write has been connected with some of the issues raised above and how that impacts on the way one lives in the world in and through law. In that way one can say that much of what I have written has been in some way about myself. An amazingly narcissistic job, exploring oneself! So this 'Long Goodbye' will seek to look back over my life both in and out of the law, personal and scientific, and see where I go from there.

A Life in Three Parts

Roughly, one might divide it into three periods. Though these periods are not so clear cut and there are long transition periods, they could be articulated through three of my projects that I think have defined my work. In what follows, I shall look at these periods, trying not to make the mistakes of over-inclusion or over-exclusion as detailed above. There will be continuity within the context of radical change. The last period is not something that is finished but is evolving. It is where I am now and where I hope to continue in my retirement – hence again the 'Long Goodbye'.

So, roughly, the three periods are: (i) *Images of Law* (1976) – which might be seen as being out of the law; (ii) *Living Lawfully* (2001) – where that vision was ameliorated and in effect was looking at a way of being in the law; and (iii) 'Beyond Text in Legal Education' (current) and *The Ethical Life of Legal Institutions* – where one might say that the whole space of law and non-law becomes problematized – feeling through an idea that perhaps in or out are the wrong descriptions.

Images of Law

This was written with passion from the soul. It said law was an 'imperial' code (thus anticipating *Law's Empire*!). It claimed to be a 'dispassionate look at law from a Marxist standpoint', but it was anything but that. It was in part wild and anarchist; it was about making people free. This 'freedom' was expressed politically, albeit in a vague and opaque way. But it was also ethical and personal in that it was about how I, or law teachers and academics such as my group were, could be free and at the same time help in building such a society. It was then about the authenticity, honesty and *bona fides* of my reference group. And, more, it was about *my* authenticity and *my* personal honesty (I recall a handwritten draft of something called, 'How can I be free: thoughts of a law teacher'). And, of course, its vision for political action, touched by its almost existentialist concern for authenticity, meant that not much could be achieved through law. Law was the enemy, it destroyed people and therefore we should abolish it and replace it with a correct [*sic*] politics – for reliance on it would hamper the task of setting people free.

In that I took an anarchist stance seriously. Authoritarianism and domination, personal and political, was the enemy. I had stopped going to Mass and remember arguing with a (still) Catholic friend why disbelief was not a cognitive thing for me but rather the impossibility of *believing* in a Being who told you what to do. And law was like God – it prevented you from being free. So I could not be in the law because I thought of it as in some way stopping me from living a true life.

How that translated was into a political practice, and the only political practice that was acceptable and available was an anti-authoritarian political stance which put oneself right outside the law. One can see that in the book. I wrote it with Geoff Mungham and he translated much of that, 'Law destroys you' scream into accounts of how it did that in sociological practice (duty solicitor schemes, trials, legal aid). Geoff was the calming influence who prevented it from being a really wild book – in earlier versions it read like 'a scrapbook from the underground'.[5] But its political message remained and in that it was a child of its time and became an attack on legal activism to enable us to stay outside the law.

With that I fell into a legal and authoritarian trap[6] and refused to step outside of a particular way of doing things. But it was also about identity – I was in thrall to a particular image of myself. When I wrote *Images of Law*, I thought I was doing something risky by putting myself beyond the respectable political pale. But perhaps I was in reality eschewing risk and staying in the comfort and security of my radical position. Anarchists are sometimes psychologically enslaved to rules, because they think of law as something completely categorical, as something that one obeys or not. If that is their view there seems to be nothing in between – the only way they can cope with the cognitive dissonance of bad and corrupt rules is to abolish them entirely. There is no way one might 'bend the rules' or live in the precarious balance between them and love. That is seen as being altogether too risky. To anticipate somewhat, that risk is one I now want to take. At that time, falling into one or the other side was the safe option – and I fell outside the law.

In a colloquium on 25 years of *Images of Law*, Peter Goodrich (2002) talks of that book through his own optic. Much of what he says is true, if sometimes cruel. The book presciently showed the failure of certain movements, but it replicated and performed this failure in its own writing – the failure of the book was the image of the failure of that form of radicalism in law. Ultimately, for me, the politics and its failure was not the point. What I was still obsessed about was what law did to human beings, and I had to understand that[7] in something more than the institutionalization of it in concrete reality and a political practice that would oppose it. I was trying to get at something metaphysical that I could see only dimly. But I did not leave *Images* behind and write in analytic philosophy, forgetting it, neither eschewing it nor affirming but leaving it as a trace, a blast from the past. I did write about political practice and the religious imageries that

5 As one publisher's reader said!

6 See Bańkowski (2001), ch. 2.

7 I remember a friend and colleague at the time, Geoff Pearson (1975), whose book, *The Deviant Imagination,* brillliant though it was, disappointed me because it was about sociological theorists of deviance and not the deviant imagination that I wanted to live!

Goodrich notes (as well as the embodiment and the erotic!). I have never denied my past, but gradually I began to see what was right and wrong with that God I hated at that time.

Living Lawfully

I now come to the second period living in the law and *Living Lawfully*. What was that about? Again, contrary to Goodrich, *Images of Law* is not erased from view. It is mentioned in this book and indeed I attempt to rework its themes (in a less wild way!). I do not deny my past.[8] Here I try to see to see how an ethical life and a society under law might fit together. Part of my aim then, was to rethink and reconstruct the anarchism of *Images of Law* – to claim that the nebulous and vague freedom espoused there could be made more concrete and be found in a different view of anarchism, one that need not reject law *tout court*.

Legality

I concentrated first on what I thought was right in what was said about law in *Images*. I started from Judith Shklar (1986), who characterized it as legalism and saw it as an ideology that suffused Western legal systems and those who staffed them but also seeped through to societies as a whole. The concentration on rules above all else makes them lose their sense of contingency; we see them as insulated from politics, values and preferences, and the effect is to make them appear objective and unchangeable. They appear to have a life of their own, islands of stability in a sea of chaos and they control us rather than we control them.[9] Shklar's book brilliantly shows the deficiencies of legalism. Shklar, a serious and respectable political theorist, compared to a wild anarchist 'lawyer', was seen as something of an anarchist by lawyers even though she shows in her book, albeit in a rather opaque way, how there was space for law; something different from legalism. Ironically, I also agreed with those lawyers, but it was a good thing! I confused her description of legalism with all there was to law.

In *Living Lawfully* I started breaking out of that straitjacket. There I characterized it as a move from legalism to legality. Three letters, I said, could make all the difference. That play on words was important, because I did not want to discard legalism completely – I wanted to keep the legal. The metaphor here was of the robot. Law in a large part made one act unthinkingly – 'not thinking about it' but proceeding on its channelled and pre-determined pathways and making people, in a way, slaves of the law. That was important and something that was the gift of Western modernity. Weberian formal rationality meant we obeyed the law because it *was* the law, and the more we behaved like that the better. In that sense, law was,

8 New Testament, John 13:38.

9 See the affinities with systems theory exemplified by the novel *Chronicle of a Death Foretold* (Garcia Marquez 2008).

as Raz (1975) argues, an exclusionary reason – it excludes us from thinking about the substantive reasons for that action and the more that theory becomes a reality, the better. But the mistake was to think that that was all there was to law. Christ condemns the Pharissee who thanks God that he is not like the sinners he sees before him, not because he is a bad man but because he thinks that following the law is all you have to do, is all there is to the ethical life.[10]

The Cincinatti Kid

But following the rules does not exhaust the law. One also has to be able to 'do the wrong thing at the right time'. This means re-conceptualizing anarchism as breaking the law creatively. But this then means one has to look at creativity and the aesthetic. There are two things that can be said here.

First, creativity does not come *ex nihilo* – you have to have a thorough grounding in an activity before you can break through to something new. It is the understanding of the skill and its protocols that enables you to move beyond. Creativity stems from structure, otherwise it is merely nihilistic. One can draw an analogy with art. Here it has been argued by some that non-figurative painting can best be done by those who have been classically trained. True creativity, it might be said, is derived from discipline. It is only then that your creativity allows you to start changing the rules of the discipline. Non-figurative art is not a matter of just slapping paint on to a canvas. The analogy of grammar and writing reinforces this point. It is only those who have mastered the rules of grammar who can then go on to write well and with style. It is only those who have got to this point that are able to play with the rules of grammar. Neither is writing merely slapping words on to paper.

Second, the combination of this knowledge and the moving beyond enhances the activity as a whole. A game of football played by two competent teams is extremely boring, because there is no brilliance. But a game played between teams of extremely skilful players is also unsatisfying, since it stops being a game of football and becomes merely an exhibition of individual skill. What one needs is a high level of competence enlivened by flashes of brilliance. For that is what makes it a game of football, the highly competent play suddenly and unpredictably erupting into brilliance – the two elements enhancing each other and making a better whole. It might also explain why top-level basketball is curiously unsatisfactory. The players are all too brilliant, which makes the game, paradoxically, routine and boring – there is nothing that stands out.

So, in terms of this analogy we need the unthinking routine of the law and the flashes of genius and innovation that come out of it to enhance both. Think of marriage and Luhmann's (1985) somewhat pessimistic systems theoretic view of it. In this, marriage is in reality two oscillating cycles. We have grand passion where everything is done for its sake, and the whole universe is thematized by the love

10 New Testament, Luke: 18, 10–14.

between the parties. This is too much and it soon collapses into marriage, where everything is routinized and stable and we just go on through the pre-determined channels of the relationship. We are doomed, Luhmann says, to oscillate from one to the other, never finding a resting place. In terms of my *Living Lawfully* image, however, the one enhances the other to make a more aesthetically pleasing union.

Fulfilling the Law

Here I sought to redress the balance between concentrating on the *thanatos* of law; of law as the restraining, civilizing force that is necessary to hold in check the *eros* of love, the love central to our contingent, passionate natures. Not however, as before, to cast the law aside, for love is dangerous and we can only approach it with caution – embracing it wholeheartedly can kill us. So while 'law' and 'love' were central, they were not seen as opposed to one another. I argued that the ethical life should be seen as not one or the other of law and love, but as the interlinking and tension between the two. So it was not law or love, rather the precarious intertwining between the two that I sought. Law and going beyond it are inseparable and I tried to show how, in breaking the law, you are fulfilling the law. Truly to follow the law implies being able to break it and recreate it anew – in breaking the law you are following it. But, and this is important, neither does it imply doing away with the law.

> Think not that I have come to abolish the law and the prophets; I have come not to abolish but to fulfil them. For truly, I say to you, till heaven and earth pass away, not an iota, not a dot, will pass from the law until all is accomplished. (New Testament, Matthew 5: 17–18)

All of this meant that I now stepped back into the law. For the emphasis is on a continual recreating of the law, of stepping outside of its boundaries but then drawing it close around you again. The image is one of being inside and dragging the outside in. I used the image borrowed from Gillian Rose (1992) of 'living in the middle', a position of tension where decisions are made and imbued with precarious anxiety. However, much of the way I instantiated this had a somewhat different imagery. Thus, in talking of exclusionary reasons, I likened that exclusion as being akin to a thick curtain drawn across the stage, and in supporting Schauer's (1991) idea that you could take a brief look at the substantive reasons, I likened that to raising the curtain briefly and to see what was outside. This carried over to the idea of 'suspending the ethical', [11]where in certain situations one suspends the universal only to bring it back again perhaps recreated by that suspension. The image all the time was of being placed firmly behind the curtain and on the stage – not in the middle even though another central image I used, Detmold's

11 See Rose (1992).

(1989) 'particularity void', implied being in the space between knowledge and application of the law. All the images of 'middle' drifted to positions 'inside'.

Beyond Text and the Ethical Life of Legal Institutions

Living Lawfully was also concerned with political questions, and much of this book, again *pace* Goodrich, is concerned with working out politics and political practice. When I looked back over *Living Lawfully*, I was surprised about how much this was concerned with political theory and political questions, and how little I now attend to these more specific questions of political theory. The cognitive task of what to do and how to build societies is all very well and important:

> Words of the middle region, such as right, democracy, person, are valid in their own region, which is that of ordinary institutions … Minds capable of solving problems of this kind can be formed in a law school. (Weil 1990: 286)

But I think that what I became interested in was something more. The existential question: *why?* This is summed up by Simone Weil, who says that behind all the talk of law and rights is a cry for justice, and we have to learn to respond to that: 'For the sustaining inspiration of which all institutions are, as it were, the projection, a different language is needed. (Weil 1990: 286) This led me to take the space of the middle seriously and to try to work with such spaces and increasing thinking 'beyond text' to art and movement and other modes of cognition to explore the ethical life of (legal) institutions. What I am interested in here is not so much what it is morally right or wrong to do, but what is the 'directing idea' behind an institution and how that structures the ethical life we lead. So, if someone is a lawyer we ask not what are the rules for moral conduct in that institution (what are the codes of legal ethics, for example) but what sort of life is that of a lawyer, compared to a teacher, a social worker or a soldier. And that will depend on how the governing ideas of that institution can connect to the human good. And if that, as I imply in *Living Lawfully* and more specifically beyond, is the way we order our lives in general, then this implies a normative question about the institution of our daily life as well as more specifically about the institution of law.

Institutions of Love

I want, then to argue, for a particular vision of the institution of law and of institutions as something geared to realizing our common good and not a regrettable necessity, there to enable us to live our lives the way we want. This implies institutions based on a deep connection. The connection happens through exchange, which can be seen as a sort of 'give and take' that opens us to creative transformation, and our ethical lives and those of our societies become dynamic and can grow. What does this imply? The theologian and social philosopher, John Milbank (1995), gives us a clue. He sees the self as being in flux through what he perceives as a universalized practice of giving. This should be seen not as something beyond exchange, but rather as part of the practice of asymmetric exchange. We do not expect an equivalent in return – rather, we have to be open to whatever we receive, because that is what changes us. It is because of this continual giving and receiving that the self is always in flux and never fixed. We find ourselves through the continuous process of exchange; that is, giving ourselves to others and being open to receive quite often unexpected (and perhaps unwelcome) gifts in return. These we work on and they are the agents of our transformation. This happens at all levels, from individuals to different levels of community. Community is thus constituted by exchange, both internally and externally, at all levels. It is in this way that we do not hold on to an unchanging identity. This implies a practice of being open to the stranger, to a practice of treating, as Milbank says, 'all aliens as neighbours'. At the group level this implies being open to the outside – always being ready to go beyond the limit despite that limit being what at the time defines our existence. Not doing this means a closed and totalizing community.

We can see some of the implications of this if we look (appropriately) at education. We can think of teaching as a journey where, in a sense of wonder, teacher and student journey with and towards each other, rather than being in a monological institution where a teacher imparts knowledge to a student:

> Gifts are possible when teaching is particularly inclined to surprise the person who is getting the gift and to make the giver wonder about the other's responses. I intend to give a gift just as the planned lesson but the lesson cannot be completely controlled. The way it has been received might give some appreciation or disappointment but what the student has done with the gift can only be imagined by the teacher. (Galea 2006)

To anticipate a theme I take up below: when teaching in an institution where the language of instruction was English but that was not the first language of the majority of the students, I found it useful to use metaphors and analogies, the images made it easier to understand at the point I was making, but more than that it gave them space to explore in and around the concepts. But this had another effect, which was also important in situations where everyone had the same language. What it meant was that I was no longer able to control so tightly what I was teaching and often had strange and unexpected things back that also helped my work! I had to learn to accept the return, however unexpected.

The Crisis of Faith

But we still have to answer the existential question that *Living Lawfully* led me to. Why bother to have such institutions of love? Why bother to work for them? What can make us do that? Because that constant exchange, of self and community continually being changed and recreating themselves in perhaps completely different and unexpected ways, can be terrifying. The process can be likened to dying and being recreated as something different, and, of course, we resist that sort of death and take steps to avoid it.[12] How, then, do we come to be able to *see* others and connect with them, and thus share our mutual vulnerability?

I realize that question had always been at the core of my soul and was brought into focus again by what I can only describe as a crisis of faith. I thought that faith had gone and I had long sloughed off my Catholicism. I was a left-wing academic with some success in Marxist- and anarchist-inclined writings. But I still had, as I now see, my existential *angst*. The first Gulf War began and the bombs started and it was all brought to a head. Here I am, I thought, spending my life teaching political and moral philosophy, looking at the ways in which we can live together, love each other and make the best possible world for ourselves. But what does it all mean? I was not sure that it meant anything to me apart from the trajectory that my scientific work was on. As for the rest of the world, it clearly meant nothing – I taught all this and did the world care? No – it just carried on. So the second phase of my scientific life began in bombs and pain and the real crisis of faith.

Living Lawfully looked into the abyss and started to move towards resolution. But perhaps it was still too much in thrall to the power of enlightenment rationality, and perhaps Goodrich was right, that after *Images* I was too much in the analytic and general jurisprudence mode. But as I moved away from the political theory and the technical legal reasoning to concentrate more on the ethical, and the universal and particular, I started moving away from the Kantian God. More was needed than that sort of rationality. We needed to learn to *see*.

What was seeing in this sense? Raimond Gaita (2000) offers a striking image of this. He talks of a nun he encountered while working as a student in a psychiatric hospital. There, as was common in those days, the inmates were treated like animals by the majority of the staff. Gaita and some of the staff tried to treat them, as he hoped, like human beings. But the nun, by the quality of her interaction with the inmates, put them all to shame. She *saw* them. What was that *seeing* and how is it the 'sustaining inspiration' of the institutions I sought?

Seeing

To *see*, you need to cultivate what Simone Weil (1951) calls 'attention':

> Attention consists of suspending our thought, leaving it detached, empty, and ready to be penetrated by the object; it means holding our minds within reach of this thought.
>
> This is both active and passive. It demands active concentration and intelligence. One needs to be unselfconscious not grasping but alertly and

12 For example: the fear of immigration 'destroying our way of life' can be seen as a fear of dying.

> intelligently waiting. The key is openness and it is in these moments that one is open to illumination. Weil applies this to education. Students should 'pay attention' and listen, not expecting a result or outcome straightaway but waiting and trusting that it will come to them. Otherwise, in trying to grasp the meaning impatiently, they will lose it. It is not just a sort of active contemplation. It also has other connotations of paying attention to, caring for. One can apply this to the judge – do not apprehend the particular situation immediately with the rule lest you lose its message. Wait and let it speak to you in the first instance at least.

For Weil, attention is also something that is the ability to hear and receive what people are saying when they are *in extremis*. For her, the spiritual and the political come together, because it is, as she says in her essay on education, a way of coming to the love of God but also to the love of one's neighbour. It is the way we can be moved by and enabled to help those in radical need, those she calls the afflicted.

This is very far-reaching. With attention, the unafflicted helps the neighbour, the one who is afflicted. Attention is difficult. Self-regarding motives are not enough even if it is from a wish to help the poor. That patronizes them and sees them as a type, the poor, and not as individuals who are in pain. We have to be able to pierce through to that cry of pain and not mask it or hide by, for example, rights talk. It is related to a respect for persons but it is not Kantian. It is not to reduce everything to a rationalistic objective standpoint. That is not engaging with the person; rather it is thinking of oneself as superior, trying to bring the other person to where your superior knowledge and self already are. There should be no objective distance between myself and the afflicted. No wonder, for Weil, the parable of the Good Samaritan was central. That parable can be viewed as performative, in that it enjoins one to 'Love thy neighbour', not by giving a wider definition of neighbour, but by telling you to make the one in need your neighbour by acting like one to them. The Samaritan *sees* the one 'fallen among thieves' and by his act transforms him and makes him come alive.

Let us now go back to Gaita's nun, because it is she who exemplifies what is going on here. The point is that she does not feel different or distant from the inmates with whom she interacts. She embraces them as they are and becomes like them. And this, it seems to me, is the problem sometimes with the disability approaches of, among others, Nussbaum. They do not embrace the disabled; rather, they want to make the disabled like themselves – they have a cool rationality, albeit full of compassion; their religion is Kant. They are not mutual partners in vulnerability and suffering but they are there to help from their superior position. In doing it this way, however, they cannot see. They 'feel the other's pain' but have none of their own.

Beyond Text and the Dance of Life

So, where do we go from here? In looking at these questions, both to understand '*seeing*' and to provide a space for it, the 'Beyond Text in Legal Education' project was born.

What was that about? When people view art objects in galleries, too often they rely on textual explanation, looking for the text in the catalogue to explain it and not letting the object explain itself. Some curators try to get people to engage the art object without text, to use their imagination to let the object speak to them and not be subsumed by the text. Lawyers face an analogous situation when they encounter events that need a decision; too often, they look to the text and do not experience the particularity of the situation by letting it speak for itself. Beyond Text in Legal Education[13] experimented with ways of doing just that. The project was an exercise in 'multi-sensory jurisprudence' in the sense that it wanted to look to the possibilities of exploring the law and legal education through and on the body rather than just focusing on cognition through and by text. The centrepiece of the project was an experiential workshop that brought together three artists (one visual-based, one movement-based, and a curator) with legal professionals, legal scholars and legal education (both tertiary and professional) policy-makers from the UK and the USA. The artists were all experienced in working with people who have had little or no exposure to the production and/or appreciation of visual and movement-based art. The artists led a two-day integrated workshop, focusing on both the production and appreciation of visual and movement-based artworks. So we aimed at exploring 'the space to see', wherein the skills that will enable lawyers to develop the ethical imagination could be nurtured Where they could learn to experience the vulnerability of the situation – allowing it to speak to them, to transform and breathe life into it.

How do we reason there? In *Living Lawfully*, I explored what I called parabolic reasoning, and here the metaphor of movement, of letting the story and the parable take you to unexplored and unexpected places was the focus. But in 'Beyond Text in Legal Education', apart from visual artistic activities, I took that metaphor more seriously in what might be called the dance of life, ethics and law. Learning to 'see' not through text but rather as a function of the way that our bodies pick up cues and adjust themselves to situations and in this way learn to fit into patterns. We learn as much through our bodies as through text. Think of a technique common in dance classes. The participants walk ever faster in the room all the time trying not to get in each other's way. What they are learning to do, sometimes at a subconscious level, is to negotiate their space with someone else's space. But one can also see this as a way of learning some form of liberalism; how I can accommodate my desires and values to those of others. Only here, I do not learn it through my mind, so to speak, but through my body.

Let us take an analogy. What makes a good footballer is not just the skills that he or she has but also the ability to locate him/herself in time and space. What this means is that if you were to stop a game and blindfold the player, he or she would be able to tell you where he/she was in relation to the rest of the players. And this is not only at that particular time, but also where the

13 Visit www.law.ed.ac.uk/beyondtext. See the film of the project at www.youtube.com/watch?v=WOXqYAqlUDI&list=FLyxlrbbnogflCJo19E33xMQ&index=5.

positions were before he/she was stopped, and where the positions might be at some time in the future. What he or she is able to do is to see the game as an ever-changing diachronic matrix, and everyone's respective place in it. One might also see morality as something like this, about seeing connections in the never-ending dance of life, but not just synchronically but also diachronically, as did the footballer.

We can see how law can typically be said to work in this way. Thus *Donoghue* v. *Stevenson*, the case that founded the Law of Negligence in the UK, arises from a connection that was never seen before. Someone became ill from drinking ginger beer contaminated by a slug. The obvious connection is between that person and the vendor, who are contractually connected. But another connection is seen between the drinker and the manufacturer, who is held to be liable in negligence. But this does not necessarily have to be conservative in the sense of seeing what is already there – for we might think of it also as seeing the possibility of connection and thus both seeing and creating it. In that case, also significantly, the parable of the Good Samaritan was a central feature.

Conclusion

Borderlands

In *Living Lawfully*, though 'living in the middle' and the space of the 'particularity void' featured, the abiding metaphor was of a border, a zone where one reached out and could be transformed from the stable base. But perhaps in looking at this mutual exchange and self-giving it is time to use that metaphor more seriously and to think of it as the place we occupy all the time, a place that is itself a border zone. And perhaps these transitional zones are where we live all the time? Rowan Williams (2008) in his lecture on Sharia Law characterizes the Rule of Law as that transitional space wherein identities are generated and exchanged. For him, it is a mistake to think of the Rule of Law as some overarching identity of citizenship, which then allows other identities to exist. Rather, it is something that creates the space where irremediably pluralistic societies manage their overlapping identities. In that sense, then, one could see this as the in-between space, where identities are created and renewed. What we see here is not something that manages different identities and cuts them back if they conflict with the lowest common denominator of universalism, but rather it is where, through the medium of that universalism, different identities accommodate each other, all of which involves the dangerous and risky process of offering oneself out for negotiation and renewal, and not knowing where one might end up. What is important here is not to find what different groups have in common; what, as Rawls, says 'reasonable people can reasonably agree on', but rather how we can live together and deeply disagree, and that is the experience of living in the borderlands, of thinking of the border-space as an opportunity for such continual exchange. Krzysztof Czyżewski, the

Founding Director of the Borderland Foundation,[14] an organization based in the small town of Sejny on the Polish–Ukrainian border that encourages and facilitates cross-border dialogues, says 'within these regions an authentic community, born in the struggle of dissimilarities, is the most likely to appear'. The borderland is a 'chance to reinvent agora – that meeting place that gave rise to democracy itself'.

Keep On Running

Goodrich (2002) said that *Images* was about destroying the 'God of my Fathers' for emptiness. In *Living Lawfully* I replaced Him, but with someone perhaps too Kantian. I now begin to feel my way to something different. Where and what is that God? That is where I am now. One thing I am sure of is that I find Him in that never-ending and transformative space of mutual, self-giving and re-creation. There stability is not secured from a firm base inside with forays outside, but paradoxically in the instability of continuous transformation. An example might be in looking at running and walking. Running, though it appears more insecure, is actually more stable because one is in equilibrium so long as one keeps going. Walking is more unstable, because it is more like controlled falling. One is always trying to bring both feet to the ground – but running is like flying.

Goodrich says, after *Images* I left that life behind, forgetting it and taking to running. I did run, both literally and metaphorically. But not to forget, rather, to *see*. When I did my final exams in Dundee in 1969 there was one question in the general philosophy paper that struck me, 'How can I search in a drawer for a button that is not there?' I did not answer that question – I thought it might be about religion and in any case I did not know for what I was searching. This chapter has been an attempt to answer that question. And the answer is that there is no answer, and the search is the thing – and perhaps one can tie it to theology and the 'pilgrim church'. Be that as it may, 'Beyond Text in Legal Education' will continue for me as an exploration of what living in the parable, searching in those spaces for that God means. I will keep on running.

Bibliography

Bańkowski, Z. 1994. 'How Does It Feel to Be On Your Own? The Person in the Sight of Autopoiesis'. *Ratio Juris*, 7(2): 254–66.

Bańkowski, Z. 2001. *Living Lawfully*. Dordrecht: Kluwer.

Bańkowski, Z. and Mungham, G. 1976. *Images of Law*. London: Routledge & Kegan Paul.

Cotterrell, R. 1992. 'Viewing Legal Discourses Sociologically'. In G. Skąpska, J. Czapska, K. Daniel, J. Górski, K. Pałecki (eds), *Prawo w zmieniającym się społeczeństwie*. Kraków: Uniwersytet Jagiellonski, 55–70.

14 Visit www.pogranicze.sejny.pl for more information.

Detmold, M. 1989. 'Law as Practical Reason'. *Cambridge Law Journal*, 48: 436–71.
Eagleton, T. 2009. *Reason, Faith and Revolution*. New Haven, CT: Yale University Press.
Garcia Marquez, G. 2008. *Chronicle of a Death Foretold.* London: Penguin.
Gaita, R. 2000. *A Common Humanity.* London: Routledge.
Galea, S. 2006. 'Iris Marion Young's Imaginations of Gift Giving: Some Implications for the Teacher and the Student'. *Educational Philosophy and Theory,* 38(1): 83–92.
Garcia Marquez, G. 2008. *Chronicle of a Death Foretold.* London: Penguin.
Goodrich, P. 2002. 'Zenotypes: On the Modes of Reproduction of Critical Lawyers'. *Social & Legal Studies,* 11: 425–43.
Luhmann N. 1985. *A Sociological Theory of Law*. Trans. E. King and M. Albrow; ed. M Albrow. London: Routledge & Kegan Paul.
McCabe , H. 1968. *Law, Love and Language.* London: Sheed & Ward.
Milbank, J. 1995.' Can the Gift Be Given?' In G. Jones and S.E. Fowl (eds), *Rethinking Metaphysics.* Oxford, Basil Blackwell, 119–54.
Milbank, J. 1996. 'Socialism of the Gift, Socialism by Grace'. *New Blackfriars*, 77: 532–48.
Orwell, G. 2013. *1984*. Penguin Books: London.
Pearson, G. 1975. *The Deviant Imagination: Psychiatry, Social Work and Social Change.* London: Macmillan.
Raz, J. 1975. *Practical Reason and Norms.* London: Hutchinson University Press.
Rose, G. 1992. *The Broken Middle.* Oxford: Basil Blackwell.
Schauer, R. 1991. *Playing by the Rules?* Oxford: Clarendon Press.
Shklar, J. 1986. *Legalism*. Cambridge, MA: Harvard University Press.
Steiner, G. 1996. 'Return No More'. In *The Depths of the Sea and Other Fiction.* London: Faber & Faber, 1–17.
Weil, S. 1951. 'Reflections on the Right Use of School Studies With a View to the Love of God'. In *Waiting for God.* New York: Harper, 105–16.
Weil, S. 1990. 'On Human Personality'. In D. McLellan (ed.), *Utopian Pessimist: The Life and Thought of Simone Weil.* New York: Poseidon Press, 273–88.
Williams, R. 2000. *Lost Icons*. Edinburgh: T & T Clark.
Williams, R. 2008. 'Civil and Religious Law in England: A Religious Perspective', Foundation Lecture delivered at the Royal Courts of Justice, 7 February.

Podziękowania

When I was a sixth-former at grammar school, my Latin teacher, Brian Quinn, told me something I have never forgotten. He said that the hard part of teaching in a grammar school like ours was that often the pupils were much cleverer than the teachers, and the challenge was to accept, live and work with that. That thought has never left me. I have been lucky in my life and in my job. I teach in one of the best law schools in the UK and it is ranked among the best world-wide. Here, inevitably, we have students who are far cleverer than their teachers. I have here at Edinburgh, where I have spent virtually all my working life, tried to be open and act on what my teacher told me. I hope I have in part at least succeeded in this exercise in practical humility, for it brings the joy of a never-ending challenge and of pushing one's science into new and unsought, and unthought, places. If you do not close yourself off in the carapace of a protected identity, you will flourish – though inevitably you will be something different from when you entered but your journey will be enhanced.

There are, then, many here who will recognize the Bańkowski of the different periods I have described, both in what I wrote and what I was. Some will be pleased and some surprised at where I am now. I want here to thank those students who accompanied me during the various stages and from whom I learnt so much. For *Images* there are Stuart Midgely and Emilios Christodoulidis. For *Living Lawfully*, Claire Henderson Davis, Fernando Atria and Claudio Michelon. For 'Beyond Text in Legal Education' and *The Ethical Life of Legal Institutions*, Maks Del Mar, whose enthusiasm and generosity of spirit has revitalized me for work beyond retirement. Lastly, there have been two people who have accompanied me most of the time. In science, my teacher, colleague and friend, Neil MacCormick – who died, sadly and too early, and at whose memorial service, and at his request, I read the parable of the Good Samaritan. Finally, there has been my sister, Urszula Bańkowski who has not hesitated to point out when I have strayed from that path of practical humility and who at the same time has been my strongest defender. I thank her for everything – for our conversations and above all for her care and love.

I finally come to an end and I do so with a reflection on identity. During the Second World War, there was a Polish Medical School at the University. But the Law Faculty also ran a Postgraduate Diploma in Law for Polish students during those years. As a son of these students, it has been important for me to carry on that Polish presence. In those days there were not many Poles in Edinburgh, and to hear Polish spoken on the street was something exotic and strange. With the collapse of communism and Poland's entry into the EU, things have changed and Polish has become normal – one can hear it on the street and not be surprised. I speak more Polish now than I had ever done before! Indeed, Maks Del Mar, whom I thanked above and with whom I will continue to collaborate, is Polish, and it has given me great pleasure to be able to conduct our work in the two languages of English and Polish. But that experience and Neil MacCormick's work on identity has led me to think again about mine. The song playing as the audience came into the lecture was Boże Coś Polskę (God Save Poland). We used to sing this a lot on public occasions in the Polish community. We sang it with the final line as, 'God grant that we can return to a free homeland.' I have always considered myself a Pole and so I am. Now, however, I no longer search for that mythical homeland. I have changed and my home is now here in Scotland – I no longer have to return. In that spirit, I finish with Rilke:

> Wer du auch seist: am Abend tritt hinaus
> aus deiner Stube, drin du alles weißt;
> als letztes vor der Ferne liegt dein Haus:
> wer du auch seist.
>
> Whoever you are: step out of doors tonight,
> Out of the room that lets you feel secure.
> Infinity is open to your sight.
> Whoever you are.

Chapter 17
Afterword

Neil Walker

I recall very well all three (and counting!) Acts of Zenon Bańkowski's intellectual life. Each has left a deep and quite different impression on me, but each has also contributed to the integrated picture I hold of my friend.

I read *Images of Law* in 1978 as a callow and impressionable youth just embarked on the second year of his undergraduate law studies at the University of Strathclyde in Glasgow. I was introduced to the book by Pete Robson, my jurisprudence course lecturer and Bańkowski's erstwhile student classmate at the University of Dundee. Thinking back, I consider it a tribute to Pete Robson as well as to Bańkowski that such a radical text could find its way on to the top page of a Reading List for a general undergraduate course. I am not even sure that it ever attained such exalted status at Edinburgh – the author's own intellectual home then, as now – though if it did not then it certainly should have done.

In any case, this impressionable youth was duly impressed – and that was before I read a word of it. The fact that it was a Routledge Direct Edition – the first in the UK market to be printed direct from the typescript – gave it that distinctive *samizdat* feel. The sense of its having come out of left field was reinforced by the author's exotic moniker. How could a book written by someone called Zenon Bańkowski – not a name found on many mailboxes in the West of Scotland – fail to have a radical game-changing message?

And once I began to read I was not disappointed. This was a book that took seriously the question of whether and on what terms a life lived in pursuit of the law, in whatever office, could ever be justified. But it was also a very practically engaging book, one that looked at legal process in the raw. Then, as now, Bańkowski wrote in a remarkably fresh manner, as if this latest piece was the first or most important thing he had ever committed to paper. I had not met him, and would not do so for a number of years to come, but I could already hear his voice (though I did not reckon on the Nottingham accent!). I admired, as I always would, his ability to inhabit his own argument so fully – an aptitude that too many academics never possess or are rapidly trained out of. I also admired his ability to combine the macro- and the micro-context. I well remember Pete Robson telling me that, his theoretical interests and philosophical sensibility notwithstanding, Bańkowski had also been a good enough and sufficiently curious doctrinal lawyer to win the Scots Law undergraduate prize at Dundee. I am not sure if he continued to keep Rettie by his bedside, so to speak, but his interest in the detail of legal events certainly shine through in *Images*, as indeed it has in all of his subsequent work.

As Claudio and Maks reminded us in their Introduction, Bańkowski is indeed more than a philosopher. He is a jurist.

Fast forward 21 years. I am on holiday in a cottage in Wexford, Ireland with my family. I am by now Bańkowski's friend. We were Edinburgh colleagues for ten years. I have since moved on to pastures new at the University of Aberdeen, but we still meet and talk about work on a regular basis. I have promised to read his recently completed manuscript of *Living Lawfully*. I have been eagerly awaiting that pleasure, though I also harbour minor feelings of resentment. After all, it is *my* holiday – precious novel-reading time (not to mention family re-bonding). Don't get me wrong – I really, really do want to read the manuscript, and soon, but perhaps not this very fortnight. But if I don't do it now I will simply fail to find the time.

I devise a plan. A chapter a night will easily get me through the text. It will also work as a reading method. In Bańkowski's work, especially the mature work of *Living Lawfully*, the whole is certainly greater than the sum of the parts, but the parts can nevertheless be digested and appreciated in splendid isolation. The parables reinforce each other, the metaphors build, the images accumulate, and the flow is lateral and complementary rather than progressive and sequential. The plot thickens in all directions rather than unfolding in one.

All of this means that I can return each evening to my rustic kitchen table with renewed appetite for the Zenon*fest*. And soon the residual irritation leaves me. I thoroughly enjoy my nightly readings of the manuscript. I look forward to them. I 'get' his message about legality's occupation of the anxious middle between legalism and unencumbered agency in a deep way. I see more clearly than before what he means and think it a profound contribution, more complex but just as personally engaged as the message of *Images* – to our understanding of how the jurist thinks and should think about the law.

The book has lived strongly with me ever since. It is Bańkowski's best work. I will not call it is his crowning achievement, since sovereignty is a treacherous metaphor and in any case I continue to think there may well be more to come. But it is an important book, and one that can and should be read across doctrinal sub-disciplines and legal-philosophical traditions. I do not exaggerate when I say that I have recommended it to more doctoral students, colleagues and other serious thinkers about the law than any other book I have read. That is partly because of the significance of its dual message about the ethical inescapability of living by rules and the irreducibility of an ethical life to rule-following. But it is also about the irreducibility of the book to anything other than itself. I have always prided myself on a certain ability to paraphrase, to synthesize, to 'reduce'. But *Living Lawfully* defeated me. I would often end my Bańkowski-pitching conversations with 'you simply have to read it for yourself'.

A tad lame, perhaps, but well-intended advice, and advice I continue to hand out freely today. It is also the reason, I would venture, why Bańkowski's influence has been more intensive rather than extensive. He cannot easily be packaged and pigeon-holed, which means that his ideas, however influential they have been among those who are properly acquainted with them, have often not been as widely disseminated as they deserve to be. But, of course, dissemination is a double-edged sword, and I am not sure Bańkowski would have preferred to be a widely scattered, half-understood footnote rather than someone whose work actually meant something to a significant number of fellow travellers.

And finally to the age of 'Beyond Text in Legal Education' – a project to which I was not properly introduced until my return to Edinburgh from Florence in 2008 and my happily renewed collegiality with Bańkowski. Here my memories are less specific, my impressions more diffuse. That is partly because it is a more recent body of work, something he is still working through. It is also about a deeper ambivalence on my part. I have been to a couple of seminars, and read some of the co-authored papers Bańkowski has written with Maks Del Mar. But the text, of course, is precisely not the thing. Rather, it is the non-textual performance and experience, including the short film, *Beyond Text in Law*, in which the medium is self-consciously tailored to the message.

I have watched the film a number of times. Rather like my experience with eating black olives, I, quite literally, cannot get enough of it. I am not sure how much I like it, but feel compelled to try again and again to find out. I confess to feeling both frustrated and intrigued. Frustrated, because I am such a dyed-in-the-wool textualist and, when confronted with embodied knowledge or, indeed, any knowledge irreducible to textual form, I nevertheless want to be convinced and enlightened in my own inevitably textually textured terms. Intrigued, because as such a dyed-in-the-wool textualist, I know that I *cannot* be convinced and enlightened unless I am open to going beyond these terms.

But in many ways this latest body of work makes perfect sense, both as a development of Bańkowski's earlier writings and as a reminder and reiteration of its distinctive resonance. As he explains in his valedictory essay, 'The Long Goodbye', perhaps by the conclusion of *Living Lawfully* its author had taken the methods of enlightenment rationality as far as he was able or minded to do in his exploration of the anxious middle of *A Life* (both) *In and Out of the Law*. And certainly, Bańkowski's latest work retains its familiarly ineffable quality, its trademark interiority, its bespoke sense of a search in which there is an internal connection between self-understanding and understanding the world. The anxious jurist is also the jurist of anxiety. He appreciates that faithful stewardship of an ideal of law as well as remorseless criticism of its practice depends in part upon the contribution of the jurist whose concerns both reflect and reflect upon the concerns of the law itself.

* * * *

I have chosen to write this short note of tribute in lightly biographical mode not from a mood of self-indulgence, but because it instructs me, and I hope also others, in something else that is significant about the contribution of Zenon Bańkowski. The reference to the *Life In and Out of the Law* is not just about the precarious and unsettled relationship between rule-following and the ethical life. It is also about how, for Bańkowski, the life of the mind has been no nine-to-five activity, but, quite simply, a way of being inextricable from all else that he does. To the extent that he thinks about such things, therefore, he would not wish for his life to be 'audited' in separate academic and non-academic segments. He would instead want his 'impact narrative' to be holistically conceived and written. One modest way of respecting that wish is to present Zenon as he has appeared to me serially and cumulatively over a career and a life – to show the overall impression he has made on one respectful and admiring friend.

One final point. Just as the life of the mind knows no 40-hour week, it also knows no 40-year career – no condition of superannuation. Over to you again, Mr Bańkowski. I eagerly await Act Four.

Bibliography of the Works of Zenon Bańkowski

Books

Bańkowski, Z. and Mungham, G. 1976. *Images of Law*. London: Routledge & Kegan Paul.

Bańkowski, Z., MacManus, J.J. and Hutton, N. 1987. *Lay Justice?* Edinburgh: T&T Clark.

Bańkowski, Z. 2001. *Living Lawfully*. Dordrecht: Kluwer.

Bańkowski, Z. 2008. *Vivendo Plenamente a Lei*. Rio de Janeiro: Elsevier. Trans. L.D. Bortolozzo, A. Maria, C. Michelon, F. Neta and L.R.R. Rieffel.

Edited Books

Bańkowski, Z., Brown, P., Bloomfield, T. and Asquith, S. 1979. *Legality and Community*. Aberdeen: Aberdeen University Press.

Bańkowski, Z. and Mungham, G. 1980. *Essays in Law and Society*. London: Routledge & Kegan Paul.

Bańkowski, Z. and MacCormick, D.N. 1989. *Enlightenment, Rights and Revolution: Essays in Legal and Social Philosophy*. Aberdeen: Aberdeen University Press.

Bańkowski, Z. 1991. *Revolutions in Law and Legal Thought*. Aberdeen: Aberdeen University Press.

Bańkowski, Z., White, I. and Hahn, U. 1995. *Informatics and the Foundations of Legal Reasoning*. Dordrecht: Kluwer.

Bańkowski, Z., Tuori, K. and Uusitalo, J. 1997. *Law and Power: Critical and Socio-Legal Essays*. Liverpool: Deborah Charles Publications.

Bańkowski, Z., Morton, A. (ed.), Blount, G., Barron, S. and Hughes, J. 1998. *Beyond Fear: Vision, Hope and Generosity*. Edinburgh: Saint Andrew Press.

Bańkowski, Z. and Scott, A. 1999. *The European Union and Its Order: The Legal Theory of European Integration*. London: Blackwell.

Bańkowski, Z. 2005. *Epistemology and Ontology: IVR Symposium 2003*. Lund, Sweden: Franz Steiner Verlag.

Bańkowski, Z. and MacLean, J. 2006. The *Universal and the Particular in Legal Reasoning*. Farnham: Ashgate.

Bańkowski, Z. and Del Mar, M. 2009. *Law as Institutional Normative Order*. Farnham: Ashgate.

Bańkowski, Z. and Del Mar, M. 2013. *The Moral Imagination and the Legal Life: Beyond Text in Legal Education*. Farnham: Ashgate.

Bańkowski, Z., Del Mar, M. and Maharg, P. 2013. *The Arts and the Legal Academy: Beyond Text in Legal Education*. Farnham: Ashgate.

Research Reports

Bańkowski, Z. and J. MacManus. 1983. *Lay Justice in Scotland*. Scottish Government Health Directorates.

Articles/Chapters

Bańkowski, Z. 1973. 'Pornocracy'. *Cambrian Law Review*: 22–9.

Bańkowski, Z. and Mungham, G. 1974. 'Warwick University Ltd (Continued)'. *British Journal of Law and Society*, 1(2): 179–84.

Bańkowski, Z. and Mungham, G. 1976. 'The Jury in the Legal System'. In P. Carlen (ed.), *The Sociology of Law* (Sociological Review Monograph, 23). Keele: Keele University, 202–25.

Bańkowski, Z. 1977. 'Anarchy Rules OK?', *Archiv für Rechts und Sozialphilosophie*, Bd.4 LXIII(3): 327–37.

Bańkowski, Z. 1977. 'Beyond Legal Activism'. *Law and State*, 3: 4–9.

Bańkowski, Z., Mungham, G. and Young, P. 1977. 'Radical Criminology or Radical Criminologist?', *Contemporary Crises*, 1: 37–50.

Bańkowski, Z. and Mungham, G. 1977. 'Distorted Images'. *City of London Law Review*, Autumn: 53–61.

Bańkowski, Z. and Mungham, G. 1977. 'Professional Socialisation', reprinted in *Schooling and Society* (Supplementary materials). Milton Keynes: Open University Press.

Bańkowski, Z. and Mungham, G. 1978. 'Law and Lay Participation'. *European Yearbook for Sociology of Law*: 17–31.

Bańkowski, Z. and Mungham, G. 1978. 'A Political Economy of Legal Education'. *New Universities Quarterly*, 4: 448–63.

Bańkowski, Z. 1979. 'The Social Context of Juvenile Justice in Scotland'. In Z. Bańkowski, P. Brown, T. Bloomfield and S. Asquith (eds), *Legality and Community: Politics of Juvenile Justice in Scotland*. Aberdeen: Aberdeen University Press, 87–98.

Bańkowski, Z. 1980. 'Political Trials in Contemporary Wales'. In Z. Bańkowski and G. Mungham (eds), *Essays in Law and Society*. London: Routledge & Kegan Paul, 53–71.

Bańkowski, Z. and MacManus, J. 1980. 'Lay Justice: Some Preliminary Considerations'. *SCOLAG Legal Journal*: 80–83.

Bańkowski, Z. and Mungham, G. 1980. 'Introduction'. In Z. Bańkowski and G. Mungham (eds), *Essays in Law and Society*. London: Routledge & Kegan Paul, 1–7.

Bańkowski, Z. and Nelken, D. 1980. 'Discretion as a Social Problem'. In S. Asquith and M. Adler (eds), *Discretion and Welfare*. London: Heinemann Educational, 247–69.

Bańkowski, Z. and Maher, G. 1981. 'Ordinary Language and Judicial Discretion'. *Rechtstheorie*, 12: 1–8.

Bańkowski, Z. 1981. 'Commissioning Legal Services'. *Scots Law Times*, February: 37–42.

Bańkowski, Z. 1981. 'The Value of Truth'. *Legal Studies*, 1: 257–68.

Bańkowski, Z. and Mungham, G. 1981. 'Lay People and Law People in the Administration of the Lower Courts'. *International Journal of Law and Sociology*: 85–100.

Bańkowski, Z. 1983. 'Anarchism, Marxism and the Critique of Law'. In D. Sugarman (ed.), *Legality, Ideology and the State*. London: Academic Press, 267–91.

Bańkowski, Z. and Mungham, G. 1983. 'Political Trials in Contemporary Wales' (reprint). In J. Lundskær-Nielsen and O. Vadmand (eds), *Contemporary British Society*, Vol. 2. Copenhagen: Akademiske Forlag: 153–6.

Bańkowski, Z. 1984. 'Law Left Right Behind'. *University of New South Wales Law Review*: 362–76.

Bańkowski, Z. 1986. 'Speech Acts, Legal Institutions and Real Laws'. In D.N. MacCormick and P. Birks (eds), *The Legal Mind: Essays for Tony Honore*. London: Oxford University Press, 121–35.

Bańkowski, Z. and D.N. MacCormick. 1986. 'La Théorie des actes de langage et la théorie des actes juridiques'. In P. Amselek (ed.), *Théorie des actes de langage, ethique et droit*. Paris: Presses Universitaires de France, 196–204.

Bańkowski, Z. 1987. 'Law and the Welfare State'. *European Yearbook for Sociology of Law*: 301–9.

Bańkowski, Z. 1988. 'The Jury and Rationality'. In P. Duff and M. Findlay (eds), *The Jury Under Attack*. Sydney: Butterworths, 8–26.

Bańkowski, Z. 1988. 'Anarchiste – vision du droit in Dictionnaire encyclopédique de théorie et sociologie du droit'. In A.J. Arnaud, *Dictionnaire encyclopédique de théorie et de sociologie du droit*. Paris: Librairie générale de jurisprudence et de droit, 14–16.

Bańkowski, Z. 1989. 'Institutional Legal Positivism'. *Rechtstheorie*, 3: 289–302.

Bańkowski, Z. 1989. 'La science de la legislation en Angleterre'. In P. Amselek (ed.), *La science de la legislation*. Paris: Presses Universitaires de France.

Bańkowski, Z. 1989. 'The Rule of Law and Participatory Models of the Legal Process'. In H. Jung (ed.), *Alternativen zur Strafjustiz und die Garantie individueller Rechte der Betroffenen*. Godesberg, Germany: Forum Verlag, 61–76.

Bańkowski, Z. 1989. 'The Jury and Reality'. In P. Nerhot (ed.), *Law, Interpretation and Reality*. Dordrecht: Kluwer, 226–50.

Bańkowski, Z. and MacCormick, D.N. 1989. 'Some Principles of Statutory Interpretation'. In J. van Dunné (ed.), *Legal Reasoning and Statutory Interpretation*. Arnhem: Youda Quint, 41–53.

Bańkowski, Z. and MacCormick, D.N. 1990. 'La teoria degli atti linguistici e la teoria degli atti giuridici'. In T. Giapelli (ed.), *Teoria degli Atti Linguistici; Etica e Diritto a cura di A Filipioni*, 196–204 (translation of Bańkowski and MacCormick 1986 (P. Amselek (ed.)), 227–245).

Bańkowski, Z. 1990. 'Institutional Legal Positivism' (reprint). In Korean Association IVR (ed.), *Philosophy of Law and Social Philosophy: East and West*. Seoul: Pŏmmunsa, 287–303.

Bańkowski, Z. 1991. 'The Institution of Law'. *Ratio Juris*, March: 79–85.

Bańkowski, Z. 1991. 'Analogical Reasoning and Legal Institutions'. In P. Nerhot (ed.), *Legal Knowledge and Analogy*. Dordrecht: Kluwer, 198–216.

Bańkowski, Z. 1991. 'Ambiguities of the Rule of Law'. In H. Jung (ed.), *Issues of Law and Morality*. Merching, Germany: Forum Verlag, 101–12.

Bańkowski, Z. 1991. 'La Teoria de los Actos de Habla y la Teoria de los Actos Juridicos'. In *Annuario de Filosofia del Derecho*, 8, 219–38. (Translation of Bańkowski and MacCormick 1986 (P. Amselek (ed.)), 227–45.

Bańkowski, Z. and MacCormick, D.N. 1991. 'Statutory interpretation in the UK'. In D.N. MacCormick and R.S. Summers (eds), *Interpreting Statutes: A Comparative Study*. Aldershot: Dartmouth Press, 359–406.

Bańkowski, Z., MacCormick, D.N., Summers, R.S. and Wróblewski, J. 1991. 'On Method and Methodology'. In D.N. MacCormick and R.S. Summers (eds), *Interpreting Statutes: A Comparative Study*. Aldershot: Dartmouth Press, 9–28.

Bańkowski, Z. 1992. 'Reasoning by Analogy and Legal Institutions' (translation of 'Analogical Reasoning and Legal Institutions'). In G. Skapsk (ed.), Prawo w Zmieniącym Sie Społeczeństwie. Kraków: Adam Marszałek, 205–20.

Bańkowski, Z. 1992. 'Review of *Law, Ideology and Punishment* (Alan Norrie)'. *Modern Law Review*, November, 876–81.

Bańkowski, Z. 1993. 'Social Justice and Democracy'. In R. Bellamy (ed.) *Theories and Concepts of Politics*. Manchester: Manchester University Press, 77–97.

Bańkowski, Z. 1993. 'Don't Think About It. Legalism and Legality'. *Rechtstheorie Beiheft*, 15: 45–58.

Bańkowski, Z. 1994. 'Common Market?'. In S. Bulmer and A. Scott (eds), *Economic and Political Integration in Europe: Internal Dynamics and Global Context*. London: Basil Blackwell, 161–8.

Bańkowski, Z. 1994. 'How Does It Feel to Be On Your Own? The Person in the Sight of Autopoiesis'. *Ratio Juris*, March: 254–66.

Bańkowski, Z. 1996. 'Law, Love and Computers'. *Edinburgh Law Journal*, 1(1): 25–42.

Bańkowski, Z. 1996. 'Analogical Reasoning and Legal Institutions' (reprint). In Z. Bańkowski, I. White and U. Hahn (eds), *Informatics and the Foundations of Legal Reasoning*. Dordrecht: Kluwer, 177–90.

Bańkowski, Z. 1996. 'How Does It Feel to Be Out On Your Own? The Person in the Sight of Autopoiesis' (reprint). In D. Nelken (ed.), *Law and Communication*. Aldershot: Dartmouth, 63–80.

Bańkowski, Z. 1996. 'Positivismo juridico institucional' (translation of 'Institutional Legal Positivism'). *Cuardenos Informativos de Dercho Historico Publico, Procesal y de la Navegacion*, December, 5253–74.

Bańkowski, Z. 1996. 'Law, Love and Computers' (reprint). In F. Fleerackers, E. van Leeuwen and G. van Roermund (eds), *Law, Life and Images of Man: Modes of Thought in Modern Legal Theory: Festschrift for Jan M. Broekman*. Berlin: Dunker and Humblot, 26–40.

Bańkowski, Z. and Scott, A. 1996. 'The European Union?' In R. Bellamy (ed.), *Constitutionalism, Democracy and Sovereignty: American and European Perspectives*. Aldershot: Avebury Press, 77–95.

Bańkowski, Z., White, I. and Hahn, U. 1996. 'Introduction'. In Z. Bańkowski, I. White and U. Hahn (eds), *Informatics and the Foundations of Legal Reasoning*. Dordrecht: Kluwer, 1–61.

Bańkowski, Z. 1997. 'Power and the Institution of Law'. In Z. Bańkowski, K. Tuori and J. Uusitalo (eds), *Law and Power: Critical and Socio-Legal Essays*. Liverpool: Deborah Charles Publications, 159–73.

Bańkowski, Z. 1997. 'Subsidiarity, Sovereignty and Self'. In K. Norr and T. Oppermann (eds), *Subsidarität: Idee und Wirtlichkeit. Zur Reichweite eines Prinzips in Deutschland und Europa*. Tübingen: J.C.B. Mohr, 23–39.

Bańkowski, Z. 1997. 'Nie pozwalam'. In A. Aarnio, R. Alexy and G. Bergholtz (eds), *Justice, Morality and Society: A Tribute to Aleksander Peczenik on the Occasion of his 60th Birthday*. Lund, Sweden: Jurisforlaget i Lund, 53–68.

Bańkowski, Z., MacCormick, D.N. and Marshall, G. 1997. 'Precedent in the UK'. In D.N. MacCormick and R. Summers (eds). *Interpreting Precedents: A Comparative Study*. Aldershot: Dartmouth, 315–55.

Bańkowski, Z., MacCormick, D.N., Morawski, L. and Ruiz Miguel, A. 1997. 'Rationales for Precedent'. In D.N. MacCormick and R. Summers (eds), *Interpreting Precedents: A Comparative Study*. Aldershot: Dartmouth, 481–503.

Bańkowski, Z. 1998. 'Parable and Analogy: The Universal and Particular in Common Law'. *European Company and Financial Law Review*: 138–63.

Bańkowski, Z. and Christodoulidis, E. 1998. 'The European Union as an Essentially Contested Concept'. *European Law Journal*, 4: 341–54.

Bańkowski, Z. 1999. 'The Journey of the European Ideal'. In A. Morton and J. Francis (eds), *A Europe of Neighbours? Religious Social Thought and the Reshaping of a Pluralist Europe*. Edinburgh: Centre for Theology and Public Issues, University of Edinburgh, 149–72.

Bańkowski, Z. 1999. 'Transparency and the Particular'. *Cultural Values*, 3: 427–44.

Bańkowski, Z. and Christodoulidis, E. 1999. 'Citizenship Bound and Citizenship Unbound'. In K. Hutchings and R. Dannreuther (eds), *Cosmopolitan Citizenship*. Basingstoke: Macmillan, 83–104.

Bańkowski, Z. 2000. 'It's Good to Talk: Comment on Webber'. *Australian Journal of Legal Philosophy*, 25: 167–74.

Bańkowski, Z. and Schäfer, B. 2000. 'Mistaken Identities: The Integrative Force of Private Law'. In M. van Hoecke and F. Ost (eds), *The Harmonisation of European Private Law*. Oxford: Hart Publishing, 21–46.

Bańkowski, Z. and Davis, C. 2000.' Living In and Out of the Law'. In P. Oliver, S. Douglas-Scott, and V. Tadros (eds), *Faith in Law: Essays in Legal Theory*. Oxford: Hart Publishing, 33–52.

Bańkowski, Z. and MacCormick, D.N. 2000. 'Legality without legalism'. In W. Krawietz, R. Summers, O. Weinberger and G. von Wright (eds), *The Reasonable as Rational?*. Berlin: Duncker and Humblot, 181–97.

Bańkowski, Z. 2001. 'Europe and Beyond'. In B. Lewandowska-Tomaszczyk and I. Czwenar (eds), *A New Curriculum for English Studies*. Piotrków Trybunalski, Poland: Piotrków College Press.

Bańkowski, Z. 2001. 'Law, Love and Legality'. *International Journal for the Semiotics of Law*, 14: 199–213.

Bańkowski, Z. 2002. 'Images of Images of Law'. *Social and Legal Studies*, 11(3): 445–53.

Bańkowski, Z. 2003. 'Legal Reasoning from the Inside Out'. In T. Biernat (ed.), *Stressing Legal Decisions*. Kraków: Polonia Press, 27–46.

Bańkowski, Z. 2003. 'Europe In and Out'. In K. Nuotio (ed.), *Europe in Search of Meaning and Purpose*. Helsinki: Forum Juris/University of Helsinki Publications, 21–50.

Bańkowski, Z. and Schäfer, B. 2003. 'Emerging Legal Orders. Formalism and the Theory of Legal Integration'. *Ratio Juris*, 16: 486–505.

Bańkowski, Z. 2006. 'In the Judgement Place'. In Z. Bańkowski and J. MacLean (eds), *The Universal and the Particular in Legal Reasoning*. Farnham: Ashgate, 23–39.

Bańkowski, Z. 2007. 'The Risk of Reconciliation'. In S. Veitch (ed.), *Law and the Politics of Reconciliation*. Farnham: Ashgate, 49–68.

Bańkowski, Z. 2007. 'Bringing the Outside In: The Ethical Life of Legal Institutions'. In T. Gizbert-Studnicki and J. Stelmach (eds), *Law and Legal Cultures in the 21st Century: Unity and Diversity*. Warsaw: Wolters Kluwer Polska, 193–217.

Bańkowski, Z. and Schäfer, B. 2007. 'Double-Click Justice: Legalism in the Computer Age'. *Legisprudence*, 1: 31–49.

Bańkowski, Z. and Del Mar, M. 2008. 'Na Progu'. *No Foundations: Journal of Extreme Legal Positivism*, 5, 142–4.

Bańkowski, Z. 2009. 'W przestrzeni sądzenia. Sędzia i niepokój spotkania'. In P. Kaczmarek (ed.), *Z zagadnień teorii i filozofii prawa. Lokalny a uniwersalny charakter interpretacji prawniczej, Wydawnictwo Uniwersytetu Wrocławskiego*. Wrocław: Wrocław University Press, 167–86.

Bańkowski, Z. 2010. 'Il giudice e la vita etica del diritto'. *Ragion Practica*, 34: 73–90.

Bańkowski, Z. 2011. 'Espaco do julgamento: A ansiedade do confronto'. In R.P. Macedo, Jr and C.H.C. Barbieri (eds), *Direito e Interpretacao: racionalidades e instituições*. São Paulo: Diretto GV/Saraiva.

Bańkowski, Z. and Del Mar, M. 2011. 'The Torch of Art and the Sword of Law: Between Particularity and Universality'. In Oren Ben-Dor (ed.), *Law and Art: Ethics, Aesthetics and Justice*. London: Routledge, 163–74.

Bańkowski, Z. 2012. Neil MacCormick (translated into Ukrainian by Dr Vyacheslav Bihun), *Philosophy of Law and General Theory of Law*, 1: 286–300.

Bańkowski, Z. 2012. 'Neil MacCormick: An Epilogue'. In N. Walker (ed.), *MacCormick's Scotland*. Edinburgh: Edinburgh University Press, 231–40.

Bańkowski, Z. 2012. 'Law, Integration and Process'. In D. Augenstein (ed.), *Integration through Law Revisited: The Making of the European Polity*. Farnham: Ashgate, 113–18.

Bańkowski, Z. 2013. 'The Space to See'. In Z. Bańkowski and M. Del Mar (eds), *The Moral Imagination and the Legal Life: Beyond Text in Legal Education*. Farnham: Ashgate, 11–32.

Translation and Editorial Work

General editor (with D.N. MacCormick) of the *Law, Enlightenment and Revolution Series*. Seven vols from the World Congress in Legal Philosophy held in Edinburgh, 1989.

'Philosophie du droit et théorie des actes de langage' by P. Amselek in *Théorie des actes de langage, ethique et droit* (P. Amselek, ed.), Paris: PUF, 1986, translated as 'Philosophy of Law and the Theory of "Speech Acts"'. *Ratio Juris*, December 1988, 187–233, (A. Bańkowska as co-translator).

Sądowe Stosowania Prawa by J. Wróblewski, translated as *Judicial Application of Law*, Dordrecht: Kluwer 1992, (J. Wróblewski as co-translator; ed. with D.N. MacCormick).

Rechts als autopoiesches System by G. Teubner, translated as *Autopoiesis in the Legal System*. Oxford: Blackwell, 1993 (editor of translation).

Law and Language: The Italian Analytic School. 1996 (ed. M. Jori and A. Pintore). Liverpool: Deborah Charles (translator, with Simona Stirling).

Index

acclamation, 106–8
Ackerman, Bruce, 106, 108–10, 112
Adams v. *New Jersey Steamboat Co.* (1896), 245
Amnesty Committee, 76
analogy, 314
  connectedness and, 246–8
  as imperfect justification, 246–8
  as a justification for legal decisions, 248–9
  justificatory force of, 244, 249–52
  reasoning by, 241–2, 248–9
  as a 'second-order' strategy for reaching decisions, 247–8
Analytic Imaginary, The (2002), 46
Anns v. *Merton* (1978), 242
Antigone, 7, 141–2, 149–52, 257–8, 263, 269
  Bańkowski's point, 146–7
  fidelity, 150–52
anxiety, notion of, 2–3
applied legal statement, 102
'archetypes' of the legal, idea of, 22
Arendt, Hannah, 46, 71, 114, 277
Aristotelian pedagogy of virtue, 89
attention, concept of, 234–5, 312–13
autonomy, 38, 48, 87–8, 104, 128, 142, 146, 157, 161, 163–8, 177–8, 183, 189–90, 195, 202–3, 210, 229, 258, 261

Badiou, Alain, 7, 150–51
'banality of evil', 71
Barry, Norman, 28
Bates v. *Batey & Co* (1913), 242
Bauman, Zygmunt, 30, 70, 267
Bay, Luskentyre, 262
'Beyond Text in Legal Education' project (2013), 4, 305, 313–15
Big Society, idea of, 34, 39
Booth, William, 174–6, 178, 180–82, 191
bridging institutions, 49, 59–60, 273, 274
  Zenon's work on, 59
British welfare state, 215–16

capabilities approach
  applied to contract, 197–200
  conception of equality of opportunity, 206
  to development, 209
  as a practical realization, 210–14
  welfare economics, 200–209
capacitas argument
  capabilities to convert wealth to advantage, 201–9
  of contract law, 197–200
  of economic actors' choices, 211
  market operations, neoclassical conception of, 199–200
  Sen's views of market freedom, 201
Caparo v. *Dickman* (1990), 243, 249
capitalism, 28–30, 33, 60, 144–5, 188
  categories of, 40
  communist criticisms of, 214
  ethical varieties of, 188–9
  kinds of, 190
  Marxist accounts of, 29
  moral economy and, 37
  political economy and, 36
  as a 'tightly coupled' system, 38
  welfare state, 35
Castoriadis, Cornelius, 168–9
Catholicism, 124, 312
Centre for Law and Society, 2
Chandler, Raymond, 299
Chile, 101
  introduction of a bill, 102–3
  Land Reform (agrarian reform) in, 127
  people's will, 102
Christian theology, 114–15, 120, 134
Citizenship and Social Class (Marshall), 30
class society, theory of, 30, 37, 71, 73

commodity fetishism, 200, 214, 218
competitive markets, 207
Constitution, imposed by dictatorship, 101
  people's will and, 102
consumption, in market economies, 182–4
contract, capabilities approach to, 197–200
contractual exchange, 176, 178–81, 202
co-operation, 104, 119, 177, 179–81, 188, 190
coordinated market economies (CMEs), 188–9
corporate capitalism, 28, 33
corporate organization in CMEs, 189
cost–benefit analysis, 204–5, 212
creative involution, notion of, 264
criminal law and criminal procedure, limitations of, 74
'critical' historiography, 69
'critical legal studies' (CLS) movement, 29, 143
Customs and Excise Act (1952), 280

David, King, 243–4
Dawkins, Richard, 113, 121–2, 304
Deakin, Simon, 195, 210–11, 213, 218–19
Decent Society, A (1996), 71
decision-making, 9, 33, 39, 84, 88–90, 92–8, 109, 146, 148, 208, 212, 233–6, 248, 258–9, 264–5, 269–70, 274
democracy, 73, 103, 119, 134, 213, 310, 316
  civil society and, 71
  Dewey's analysis of, 32
  e-democracy, 107, 109
  idea of the public as the foundation for, 40
  institutions of representative, 107–8
  liberal, 15, 21
  participatory, 128
  political principle of, 107
  radical, 168–9
  social, 28, 123
democratic forms of popular participation, 107
democratization of governance, 52
denial of alienation, liberal–conservative debate, 117–20
Dennet, Daniel, 121–2
Derrida, Jacques, 149
'destructive splitting' syndrome, 72
Detmold, Michael, 267–8, 309
development
  Amartya Sen's critique, 227–8
  economic-growth-oriented approach, 227–8
  GDP approach to, 226–7
  human rights approach, 227–9
  importance of participation in, 233
  notions of, 226–9
  poverty and, 226
  reflect approach, 234–5
  rights-based approaches, 227–8
Dewey, John, 5, 34–5
  concept of the social self, 30
  idea of the public, 27, 30–33, 39
Dibben, Mark, 271
disembeddedness, concept of, 173–4, 191
division of labour, 74, 90, 205, 207
Donoghue v. *Stevenson* (1932), 242, 277, 315
duty-constituted goods, 181
Dworkinian ideal of Hercules, 246–9
Dworkin, Ronald, 197, 245, 247
  idea of a systematic integration of values, 17
  views on jurist's role, 15–17
Dylan, Bob, 269

e-democracy, 107, 109
Edinburgh School of Legal Theory, 277–9
embeddedness, concept of, 47, 173–5
epistemological uncertainty in Bańkowski's theory, 168
equality before law, 21
'ethics without morality,' 71
European Union
  consumer law, 210
  jurisdictions, 283–4
  legal order, 283–4
exchange, institution of, 181
exchange-values, 182–3
ex nihilo creation of God, 113–14, 308

faith/atheism antithesis, 122
faith in law, 143–5
fidelity, notion of, 7, 142, 147, 150–52

Fine, Sidney, 28
Finnis, John, 22
  'focal meaning' of law, idea of, 22
Fordist' system of economic governance, 33
formalism in Bańkowski's theory, 155, 158–60, 163
Frankfurt School theory, of critical legal studies, 29
Fuller, Lon, 22, 147

Gaita, Raimond, story of nun, 230–31, 312
Gauck Commission, 75
Gauck, Joachim, 75
'general' welfare state, idea of, 28
general will, idea of, 131, 159–60, 165–7, 169
George v. *Skivington* (1869), 242
German Democratic Republic (DDR), 75
global ethics, 73
God hypothesis, 112–15, 134
  apophatic idea of, 135
Great Transformation, The (Polanyi), 173–4, 177, 191
Greene, Richard, 270
Guattari, Félix, 261, 264, 273
guilt-silencing, process of, 72

Habermas, Jürgen, 30, 174
Hall, David, 270
Hambrook v. *Stokes* (1925), 253
Hart's Rules (Ritter), 250
Haunted Lands, The (1995), 70
Hayek, Friedrich, 7, 177, 190–91, 216, 219
heteronomous societies, 168
heteronomy, 87–8, 101, 104, 134, 146, 157, 159, 164–5
higher education, 27
Hobbesian state of disorder, 19
human rights, approach to development, 227–8
  Baxi's critique, 228–9
Human Rights Violations Committee, 76

iconoclasm, 142
idea of law, doctrine of, 13–15
  central values of, 19
  in its cultural setting, 21–3
  juristic focus on, 19–20
  objectives set for, 21
  Radbruch, Gustav, 19, 22
  by socio-historical conditions, 21
images in legal theory
  hypothesis related to the role of, 44
  legal theorist, imagery of, 48–64
    acrobatics and pyrotechnics, 57–8
    attack of the machines, 52–3
    bridges and acid, 58–60
    curtains, borderlands and doorsteps, 62–4
    Finnish on the loudspeaker, 60–62
    hungry tigers, 53–4
    masks and robbers, 50–52
    Robo-Judges or Robo-Citizens, 54–6
    tuning in, 56–7
  levels of embeddedness, 47
  of thought, 44–8
  use of, 43
Images of Law (1976), 48, 49, 141–5, 161, 305–6
  early iconoclasm of, 142–3
  law's vision, 149
  Wittgenstein's image, 143–4
Imperial Liability Act (1871), 252
incapacity doctrine, 198
incremental innovation, 188
infantile communist, 118–19, 122–3, 125
Ingram v. *Little* (1961), 270
Institute for Change, Memory and Reconciliation, 76
Institute for National Memory, 75
institutional concept of the people, 103–6, 137
institutional forms, 75, 102–3, 108–9, 125–6, 128, 136–7
institutional space, 233, 304
intelligibility, notion of, 105, 136
interpersonal morality, virtues of, 46

James Buchanan & Co. Ltd v. *Babco Forwarding & Shipping (UK) Ltd*, 280–87
  case background, 280
  European legal order and, 283–7
  legal reasoning in, 281–3

'outside' or 'inside' perspective, 290–94
Johnson, R.W., 78
jurisdiction, 38, 149–50, 282, 283, 287
sociology's, 27, 30–34, 40
juristic craft, idea of, 22
juristic style, 17–19
juristic wisdom, idea of, 22
jurists
idea of law, 13–15
meaning of, 1–2
moral responsibility, 16
role of, 15–17

Kaldor–Hicks transfers, 204
Kay, John, 186
Krygier, Martin, 71

La Caze, Marguerite, 43
Analytic Imaginary, The (2002), 46
concept of images in philosophy, 46–8
Langridge v. *Levy* (1837), 242
law, 307
Bańkowski's conception of, 155–69
breaking the, 159
Creon's confident statement of, 149–50
distinction with love, 147
non-negotiable idea of, 20
as rule-following, 145
seizing of, 144
structural inability of, 144
tax, 164
universality and particularity, 147–8
'Law Left Right Behind' (1984), 50
law's values
evolution of, 16
triangle of, 21
Le Doeuff, Michèle, 43–8, 53, 57, 59, 64
Philosophical Imaginary, The (1989), 44
legal certainty, 20–21
legal concept, 84, 97, 104–6, 136–7, 284, 288
legal decision-making
concept of, 89
pedagogical concept, rule-following, 86–90
peripheral conceptual perception, construction of, 90–94
practical wisdom and, 97
rule of law and, 94–8
virtues and the theory of, 84–6, 96
legal issues, in time and place, 16
legality, concept of, 6
legal journalists, 14
legal reasoning, 279
concept of, 89, 95
de dicto argument positions, 293
Leśniewski's ontology, 290–94
locality and compatibility, principles of, 288–90
'outside' or 'inside' perspective, 290–94
use of context, 289
legal strategies, for dealing with the past, 73–5
Leviathan (Hobbes), 130–31
Lewis v. *Avery* (1971), 270
liberal individualism, 33
liberal market economies (LMEs), 188–9
Lippmann, Walter, 33, 34
Living Lawfully (Zenon Bańkowski), 3, 84, 86, 87, 141, 145, 307, 314
ethical aspect of 'living lawfully,' 157–8
institutions for, 165–9
Jesus, interpretation of, 165
lack of law's political aspect in, 161–2
legal (and moral) reasoning, 158
morality and moral judgements, 162–3
notion of legality, 155, 156–7
problem and the solution live together in, 161
Locke, John, 5, 43, 47, 70, 175
Longmeid v. *Holliday* (1851), 242
Louden, Robert, 85–6
love, ethic of, 229–33, 310–11
degree of rationality, 232
grounding of rights in, 231
principle of welfare and, 229–30
relationship between law and, 232–3
Weil's analogy of, 230–31

Mabo v. *The State of Queensland* (1992), 273
MacCormick, N., 44, 87, 244–5, 247, 277–9, 294, 318

MacIntyre, Alasdair, 86, 87, 174, 185–7, 189
Margalit, Avishai, 71, 73
market economies
  Aristotle's standpoint, 176
  Booth's views, 175–6
  capitalist and non-capitalist, 188
  condition of disembeddedness, 173–4
  consumption, aim of, 182–4
  defence mechanism of, 177
  economic production, conduct of, 184–8
  good of exchanges and, 179–81
  MacIntyrean practices in, 186–7, 189
  modern, 179
  as 'moral' but not 'ethical,' 175–9
  moral economies and, 173–5
  normative character of, 173, 175
  political choice or decision in, 189–92
  principle of neutrality, 177
market institution of contractual exchange, 178
market liberalism, 34
market operations, neoclassical conception of, 199
Marlowe, Philip, 299
Marshall, T.H., 30, 215
  concept of citizenship, 27, 28, 30, 34–6
Marx, Karl, 29, 126–7, 277
McCabe, Herbert, 162–3, 165, 303
McCarthy, John, 289–90
Mead, George Herbert, idea of the social self, 27
middle position, 309
  decision-making of, 269–74
  standpoint of, 265–9
mode of signifying, 111, 119, 129
modern society, idea of, 33, 37, 74, 177
'monumental' historiography, 69
'moral economy' of inequality, 36
morality
  of duty, 22
  public and private, 72–3
moral obligation, of public truth-telling, 70–73
Motor Vehicle Law (1909), 252
Mourning Becomes the Law (Rose), 166
Mullin v. *Barr* (1929), 242
multi-context (MC) system, 288–90

Nazism, 19–20, 108, 135
negative theology, 110
  creation of world, 112–15
  political, 115–20
neutralization of people, 107–8
Nietzsche, Friedrich, 69–70, 73
non-alienated life, idea of, 116, 119–20, 126, 134
North, Douglass, 179–80
  chief function of institutions, 179
  conception of institutions, 179–80
  contractual exchange, 180
Nussbaum, Martha, 146, 149, 156, 184, 228, 313

obligations of exchange, 191–2
'Occupy' movement, 39
'On the Uses and Disadvantages of History for Life' (1874), 69
order and chaos, extremes of, 260, 262–5
Osiel, Mark, 74

parable, reasoning by, 243–6, 253–4
  Jewish use of, 253
paraconsistency, 283, 286
Pareto optimal equilibrium, 199
people
  democratic concept of, 137
  institutional concept of, 103–6
  as a negative concept, 134–6
  neutralization of, 107–8
  post-institutional concept of, 136–7
  pre-institutional concept of, 106–10
  pre-political feature of, 106
people's will
  Chilean case, 102
  as a double metaphor, 129–34
  in form of acclamation, 106–7
  institutional concept and a pre-institutional concept of people, 103–10
  law, significance of, 104
Pérez, Carlos
  alienation, 115–20
  concept of revolution, 127
  dichotomy 'reform-revolution', 125
  Marxism, 124, 125
Perrow, Charles, 37

Philosophical Imaginary, The (1989), 44
phronesis, concept of, 84–5, 90–92, 158
Pigouvian welfare economics, 205
Podgórecki, Adam, 73
Polanyi, Karl, 7, 29, 38, 173, 174
Polanyi, Michael, 271
police powers, of search and seizure, 76
political economy, theory of, 28, 36–7, 127
political morality, 17
political representation, 110, 164, 166, 169
political theology
  identified by Juan Luis Segundo, 111–12
  negative, 115–20
  Protestant principle, 123–5
  secular theorists' views, 110
Portalian principle, 136
Posner, R.A., 219, 241, 244–5, 249, 251
poverty and development, 226
pragmatism, 245, 249, 251
pre-legal concept, 104–5
pre-political feature of people, 106
'problems of the files,' 75
process, understanding of, 259–62
  continuous process, 261
  differences and becomings, 261–2
  Whitehead's philosophy *all things change,* 259–60
production in a market economy, 184–8
Proposición de un Marxismo Hegeliano (Carlos Pérez), 115
Protestant principle, 123–5, 135
Proudhon, Pierre-Joseph, 126–8
public and private morality, difference between, 72–3
public, Dewey's idea of, 27, 31–3, 39
public truth-telling, 76
  moral obligation of, 70–73
  necessity of, 72
  and reconciliation, 74

Radbruch, Gustav
  argument about Nazi law, 20
  and his critics, 17–19
  idea of law, 19, 22
  recantation, notion of, 19
  views on jurist's role, 15–17
Rawlsian economics, 200, 205–6, 207
Rawlsian primary goods, 200, 220
Raz, Joseph, 181, 245, 308
reasonable foreseeability, 243
reasoning
  by analogy, 241–2, 248–9
  by parable, 243–6, 253–4
recantation, notion of, 18–19
Rechtsstaat constitution, 107
reconciliation, 17, 21, 73–7, 118, 120, 234, 260, 265, 269, 303
reform-revolution dichotomy, 125–9
Reparation and Rehabilitation Committee, 76
revenge and stigmatization, 74
reverse Machiavellianism, 72
revolutionary action, 126–7
Road Traffic Law, 252
Rose, Gillian, 141–2, 146, 157, 166–7, 265–8, 273–4, 309
Rosenberg, Tina, 70
rule of ascription, 102
  article 5, 103
  article 7, 103–4
  secondary, 103
Russell, Daniel, 86
R v. *Ponting* (1985), 273

sacramental understanding of politics, 120–23, 125, 133, 135
Satz, Debra, 182
Schmitt, C., 107–11, 124
School of Law in Edinburgh, 2
Schwan, Gesine, 72–3
scissors movement, 35
secondary rules of ascription, 102–3
self-confidence, 72
self-esteem, 72
self-organizing community, 39
self-ownership, 129–30
Sen, Amartya, 195–6, 200–203
  criticism of commodity fetishism, 204
  views of market freedom, 201–7
Shklar, Judith, 70, 147, 232, 307
Simmonds, Nigel, 22, 147–8
situation, concept of, 150
social anxiety, 2
social citizenship, Marshall's concept of, 27, 28, 30, 34–6, 215

social class
  citizenship and, 28–9
  decline of, 36–40
Social Contract, The (Rousseau), 131
social inequalities, 5, 27, 29, 30
  ideas of, 36
  'moral economy' of, 36
social interdependence, notion of, 28
social knowledge, 30
social reform, 28, 30–31, 38, 40, 127
social relationships, 30
  based on civility, 71
  contractualization of, 60
  kinds of, 190
social rights
  of citizenship, 27–8, 35
  growth of, 27
social scientific knowledge, 33, 35
social self, Mead's idea of, 5, 27, 30–31, 34, 37, 40
sociological theory, 'legislatory' tendency of, 30
sociology
  jurisdiction, 30–34
    normalized version of, 35
  professional ethos for, 34–5
  and the welfare state, 34–5
sovereignty, 14, 28, 101–3, 320
Spheres of Justice (Walzer), 191
Stigler, George, 208
Stone, Julius, 13
substantive value of consumption, 183
Sunstein, C., 246–50
Supiot, Alain, 195

tax avoidance, 155, 160, 164
testament, function of, 4, 104–5, 133
theory of alienation, 115–18
  denial of alienation, liberal–conservative debate, 117–20
  notion of sacrament and of sacramental practices, 120–23
Theory of the Constitution (Schmitt), 110
Thompson, E.P., 36
totalitarianism, notion of, 117–18
tout court, 90
Truth and Reconciliation Commission (TRC), South Africa, 75
  committees of, 76
  facing the past as constitutional process, 76–8
  power of, 76
truth-telling, 73
  criminal law and, 74
  moral obligation of, 70–73
  reconciliation through, 76

United Nations (UN) Declaration on the Right to Development, 227
unity-in-diversity, 262–5
universal human brotherhood, 112
utilitarian economics, 204
'utopian' ideas of reform, 33

Veitch, Scott, 147–8
virtue ethics, 85–6, 89, 277, 303

Waldron, Jeremy, 110, 113, 230, 250
War and Peace (Tolstoy), 267
Weil, Simone, 55–6, 111, 230–32, 234, 310, 312–13
Weinreb, L.L., 245, 247–50
welfare, Barry's critique of, 28
welfare economics, 196
  capabilities approach, 200–209
  correlation between opulence and well-being, 200–202
  George Stigler's criticism, 208
  Sen's views of market freedom, 201
welfare reforms, 38
welfare state, 28, 214–17, 232
  British, 215–16
  capability approach and, 214–17
  capitalism, 35
  growth of, 27
  limits of, 29
  national, 38
  nature of, 232
  sociology and, 34–5
Western legal systems, 87, 307
Whitehead, A.N., philosophy of, 259–60
Williams, Rowan, 112, 124, 266, 303, 315
Wittgenstein, L., 5, 43, 113–14, 120, 143–4, 250–51
Wolf, Erik, 16